PRAISE FOR *THE LIVING TEMPLE*

"A well-written, inspired, and in-depth course on witchcraft and associated magical traditions; this comprehensive guidebook is a priceless treasure for the true seeker focused on the balanced and integrated development of the self as a spiritual, magical, and ethical being."

—**Orion Foxwood, author of** *The Faery Teachings* **and** *The Tree of Enchantments*

"A thought-provoking guide and valuable tool for personal transformation. This book will be an invaluable resource to teachers, Priests, and Priestesses of the Craft."

—**Ellen Dugan, author of** *Natural Witchery* **and** *Garden Witchery*

"Christopher is, in my opinion, the finest of the new generation of Wiccan educators and authors. Few books have ever been written capable of guiding a solitary practitioner into the inner mysteries. He takes the student through the initiatory concepts and practices of the seven archetypes, which will bring the reader into the joys of spiritual wisdom."

—**Rev. Paul Beyerl, founder of The Rowan Tree Church and author of**
The Master Book of Herbalism

THE LIVING TEMPLE OF WITCHCRAFT

VOLUME ONE

ABOUT THE AUTHOR

Christopher Penczak is an award-winning author, teacher, and healing practitioner. Beginning his spiritual journey in the tradition of modern witchcraft and Earth-based religions, he has studied extensively with witches, mystics, shamans, and healers in a variety of traditions from across the globe to synthesize his own practice of magick and healing. He is an ordained minister, herbalist, flower essence consultant, and certified Reiki Master (Teacher) in the Usui-Tibetan and Shamballa traditions. Christopher has been involved with the Gifts of Grace Foundation and is a faculty member of the North Eastern Institute of Whole Health, both in New Hampshire. He is the author of many books, including *Ascension Magick*, *Magick of Reiki*, *Spirit Allies*, *The Mystic Foundation*, *Instant Magick*, and *The Inner Temple of Witchcraft*. For more information, visit www.christopherpenczak.com.

THE LIVING TEMPLE of WITCHCRAFT

MYSTERY, MINISTRY, AND THE MAGICKAL LIFE

VOLUME ONE:
THE DESCENT OF THE GODDESS

CHRISTOPHER PENCZAK

Llewellyn Publications
Woodbury, Minnesota

First Edition
Fifth Printing, 2018

Book design and format by Donna Burch
Cover background and moon image © Photodisc
Cover design by Lisa Novak
Interior illustrations by Llewellyn Art Department, with the following exceptions. Woodcuts on page 179 are from Francesco Maria Guazzo's *Compendium Maleficarum: The Montague Summers Edition* from Dover Publications. Art on page 296 is from Éliphas Lévi's *Dogme et Rituel de la Haute Magie*.
Quotation on page 192 excerpted from *Angels, Demons & Gods of the New Millennium* © 1997 by Lon Milo DuQuette with permission of Red Wheel/Weiser, www.redwheelweiser.com, 1-800-423-7087.

Llewellyn is a registered trademark of Llewellyn Worldwide Ltd.

Library of Congress Cataloging-in-Publication Data
Penczak, Christopher.
  The living temple of witchcraft, volume one : the descent of the Goddess / Christopher Penczak.—1st ed.
    p. cm.
  Includes bibliographical references and index.
  ISBN 978-0-7387-1425-7
  1. Witchcraft. I. Title.
  BF1566.P445 2008
  133.4'3—dc22
                                                                                    2008028682

Llewellyn Publications
A Division of Llewellyn Worldwide Ltd.
2143 Wooddale Drive
Woodbury, MN 55125-2989
www.llewellyn.com

Printed in the United States of America

Other Releases by Christopher Penczak

City Magick: Urban Spells, Rituals and Shamanism

Spirit Allies: Meet Your Team from the Other Side

The Inner Temple of Witchcraft: Magick, Meditation and Psychic Development

The Inner Temple of Witchcraft Meditation CD Companion

Gay Witchcraft: Empowering the Tribe

The Outer Temple of Witchcraft: Circles, Spells and Rituals

The Outer Temple of Witchcraft Meditation CD Companion

The Witch's Shield

Magick of Reiki

Sons of the Goddess

The Temple of Shamanic Witchcraft: Shadows, Spirits and the Healing Journey

The Temple of Shamanic Witchcraft Meditation CD Companion

Instant Magick

The Mystic Foundation

Ascension Magick

The Temple of High Witchcraft: Ceremonies, Spheres and the Witches' Qabalah

The Temple of High Witchcraft Meditation CD Companion

The Living Temple of Witchcraft, Volume One, Meditation CD Companion

The Living Temple of Witchcraft, Volume Two: The Journey of the God

The Living Temple of Witchcraft, Volume Two, Meditation CD Companion

The Witch's Coin

The Witch's Heart

Acknowledgments

To the Five Wise Women who have changed my life, each a priestess, healer, and teacher on her own path:

To Laurie Cabot—for the path of the witch, as priestess, artist, and scientist;

To Joanna Pinney Buell—for the path of the healer, as spiritualist and business person;

To Stephanie Rutt—for the path of the warrior, as minister and bridge maker;

To Wendy Snow Fogg—for the path of the green wise woman, as steward and medicine maker;

And most especially to Rosaria Maria—for the path of the Great Mother in all ways.

To all my friends, and my coven, clients, teachers, and students for encouraging me to put my energy where my mouth was and truly start my ministry and life path. Special thanks to Steve Kenson, Ronald Penczak, Adam Sartwell, Laura Davis, Christina Colangelo, David Boyle, Jessica Arsenault, John Walker, Leandra Walker, Bonnie Kraft, Alixaendreia, Bonnie Boulanger, Spirita Dulce, Timothy Bedell, Chris Giroux, Ginella Cann, Scott Cann, Derek O'Sullivan, Ed Newton, Amanda Crowell, Sandi Liss, Kevin Moscrip, Matthew Sawicki, Joe Hughs and Doug Kaylor at Otherworld Apothecary (www.otherworld-apothecary.com), S. Rune Emerson, Michael Lloyd, Ea, Jeremy Bredeson, Hyperion, Mark Gracy, Charles Gracy, Laehar, Ali Harris, Carolyn Kepes, Mark Bilokur, Thom Baker, Rosina, Azure, Dennie, Colleen, Jerusha, Christian Medaglia, Nancy, Olga, Ania, Claire, Varti, Kim, Lee Ann, Jean, Mary, Moondragon, Jocelyn Van Bokkelen, Francie Koll, Jan Brink, Wren Walker, and Fritz Jung.

A thank-you to all my friends in the writing and teaching world. Your conversations, lectures, books, and e-mails have profoundly influenced me and show up everywhere in this book. Thank you for your inspiration and ideas, and for challenging my own ways of thinking and doing. Thank you Kala Trobe, Dorothy Morrison, Raven Grimassi, Stephanie Taylor, Orion Foxwood, T. Thorn Coyle, Ellen Dugan, Judika Illes, Donald Michael Kraig, Jason Augustus Newcomb, Lon Milo DuQuette, Michelle Belanger, Patricia Monaghan, Edain McCoy, Trish Telesco, R. J. Stewart, Phyllis Curott, Janet Farrar, Gavin Bone, Sharynne NicMhacha, Oberon Zell-Ravenheart, LaSara FireFox, and Maxine Sanders.

Thank you to all my magickal communities, in particular the Between the Worlds brotherhood, and the folks at the Unicorn Books, Lap of the Goddess, Circles of Wisdom, and Misty Meadows communities.

Thank you to those whose words of wisdom and observations made it into the book by name, and to those who remain nameless or were part of a poetic amalgam figure to better illustrate a point and not get bogged down in the particulars, as well as retain your anonymity.

Thanks to everybody at Llewellyn, past and present, who have supported the vision of the Temple of Witchcraft book and CD series, including Andrea Neff; Donna Burch; Lisa Novak; Natalie Harter; Beth Scudder; Alison Aten; Jennifer Spees; Steven Pomije; Michelle Palazzolo; Elysia Gallo; Nancy Mostad; Tom Bilstad; Karl Anderson; Jerry Rogers; and Carl, Sandra, and Gabe Weschcke.

A magickal, heartfelt, and very special thanks to Lisa Braun Dubbels for all her hard work, love, support, advice, and friendship over the years.

To all the readers, reviewers, and retailers of the series, and most importantly the students of the Temple of Witchcraft tradition, may you all be blessed with the love of the Goddess, God, and Great Spirit. Thank you.

For there are
three great mysteries
in the life of man—
love, death, and resurrection—
and
magick
controls
them
all.

—The Descent of the Goddess

CONTENTS

LESSON SIX

Temple of the Brow: Vision and Knowing . . . 215

LESSON SEVEN

Temple of the Crown: Union with Spirit . . . 253

EXERCISES

FIGURES

Introduction

Mystery, Ministry, and the Magickal Life

We've all heard of the "three Rs" in basic education, a saying to emphasize the fundamentals of reading, (w)riting, and (a)rithmetic. Though we know that a well-rounded education consists of far more than simply reading, writing, and math, these disciplines provide the fundamental and necessary tools to be successful at any level of education. These skills help us pursue history, philosophy, science, literature, and the creative arts. Though they seem like only basic skills, they are skills used over and over again, and they further develop and become more complex as you use them. As you explore the language, you learn the meanings, spellings, and pronunciations of more words to add to your vocabulary. You are better able to express yourself in writing and understand the writings of others. As you learn more math, you apply the same calculation skills to more specific areas of mathematics to measure and explore the world.

In witchcraft, we also have fundamentals. Many people looking for "advanced" topics in magick and witchcraft can find a lot of interesting and esoteric techniques, but when they lack the fundamentals, they lose sight of the purpose of the techniques and how to integrate them healthily into everyday life. The most "advanced" witchcraft books are deceptive. They are the books that take you back to fundamentals but give you a new insight and understanding of them—an understanding that can only come from having a wide range of experiences. Only then can you really put your education together. You realize that the fundamentals of witchcraft, like reading, writing, and arithmetic, must serve you your whole life, and they must develop and mature as you develop and mature.

I see the fundamentals of witchcraft expressed in the "three Ms" of mystery, ministry, and magick, or more specifically, what I think of as magickal living. Each expresses a very important facet of our lives as witches. Each "M" develops certain skills within us, allowing us to live fully as a witch in all things. Being a witch is not as easy as it sounds. Although anybody can self-dedicate, or feel that they have always been a witch, the true test is how you live your life. Many claim the word *witch*, but do not live as witches. Many do not have any understanding of these fundamental building blocks that are a part of a witch's life. Some don't because they haven't had the opportunity to learn. Few books talk openly about the three Ms as both a philosophy, and a set of practical instructions open to those who seek the experience.

Mystery is the fundamental aspect of witchcraft as a mystic religion, as a spiritual tradition. We are a mystery tradition. We are a school for the soul. The mysteries of life and the Otherworld are all things that can be intellectually discussed by the theologian, but we are an experiential religion, and we must experience the mysteries firsthand. We have gnosis, direct knowledge of the mysteries, for the true essence of the mystery cannot be put into words. The mysteries of birth, life, sex, death, magick, spirit, and reincarnation are our realms. Talking about something is not the same as experiencing it. Intellectual discussion is no substitute for communing with these divine powers, just as reading about reproduction is no substitute for actually having sex. Two initiates of the mysteries understand each other, on a deep and fundamental level, without words, even if on a personal level they may disagree or dislike each other. The mysteries are not personal. The mysteries are beyond the personal. They are universal. The experience of them moves us beyond the personal, expanding us to a cosmic consciousness, even for a brief moment, and our role as initiates of the mysteries is to remember and then live from that expanded state of awareness.

There are many ways to frame the mysteries when we seek to teach them, to give students enough information and background to prepare them for the experience. Without preparation and purification, physically and spiritually, the inner alignment that opens the gates to the mysteries will not occur. In this Temple of Witchcraft series, I have sought to teach the mysteries in a cycle of five branches, corresponding with the five elements of the pentagram.

The first level was fire, through *The Inner Temple of Witchcraft*. It dealt with the psychic mysteries, what may be called the oracular mysteries, for in days of old, one would visit the oracle, a priestess or priest who would divine the future, often through inner sight. With this stage of fire we set the inner flame, and with it, we can "see" psychically through the veil of space and time and, most importantly, see into ourselves. Whether our skills are literally the psychic sight, or simple psychic impression, we work on the gifts of insight, intuition, and psychic development, to trust the inner flame to guide us in the mysteries. With this light we are forced to purify, to clear out the shadows by illuminating them, and throw the unwanted artifacts of our past into the fire as a sacrifice. It is only through our healthy inner life that we can walk the path of the witch. In the ancient mystery traditions, the initiates were led into the depths of the temple or cave by torchlight. This is our inner torch.

On the second level of training, we explored what most consider witchcraft to solely be, the fertility mysteries, through *The Outer Temple of Witchcraft*. Through the element of earth we learned how to partner with our material world and the spirits of the material world. We learned how to commune with the four elements. We learned to know the gods in all of nature, as all things are manifestations of the divine. We learned to manifest our needs and dreams through the art of magick, flow with the tides of the Moon, Sun, and stars. We learned the creative fertility within us, within the union of priestess and priest, and within the union of Goddess and God. Fertility is the creative power, the life force, and it can be guided into many things, from the crops and harvest, to the comfort of our lives, to deeper spiritual meaning. But if one cannot take care of needs of the material world, there will be little time for thought, energy, ward the higher pursuits.

level of training embodied the ecstatic mysteries. Though many would ecstasy for sexual pleasure and think it would be an extension of the fertility rites, this is the true meaning of ecstasy, the shaman's ecstasy—to become loose from the flesh and traffic with spirits of nature and the Otherworld. Though the journeying skill is encouraged in the previous levels, here we build upon it to a much greater extent through *The Temple of Shamanic Witchcraft*. More importantly, we face the mysteries of the shadow, the dark self in the Underworld. We learn through the element of water to love the shadow as we love ourselves. We learn not to deny its power, but integrate it healthfully into our overall being. We learn the ways of medicine, of spirit power and partnership, to prepare ourselves for this shadow trial.

The fourth level of training is through the air element, through knowledge and study or arcane and often confusing magickal knowledge. It is the intellectual branch, where the seekers of knowledge might grow the fruit of wisdom if tending to the branch properly. We learn the magick of the Qabalah, the Tree of Life that has overshadowed the Western traditions for centuries. In *The Temple of High Witchcraft*, we learn its connection to our pagan past, and how to integrate the best aspects of it in our future. We also learn how to think better, to process information and the direct experience we have of the divine. We are challenged to map out our beliefs, ideas, and experiences to better communicate them to ourselves and to others. One might think of this level of knowledge as the gnostic mystery, for the original meaning of the word referred to direct knowledge of the divine. Here the witch is challenged to learn tradition, but to go beyond the authority of tradition and synthesize something new.

When one looks at the pattern of these four elemental mysteries, the initiation cycle of the Temple of Witchcraft tradition follows the reverse of what we have called the alchemical alignment. With earth in the north, fire in the east, air in the south, and water in the west, rather than switching the elements of east and south, we create a dynamic tension between polarities. By following the elemental associations of the five levels of teaching, we have a pattern of moving widdershins from the east, north, west, and south, as we spiral inward to the center. This unwinding motion actually refines us, clears us, and heals us, moving us closer to the quintessence, the fifth mysterious element that separates and binds the other four, as symbolized by both the center and the edge of the circle. These are the four branches of the mysteries as I see them. The central link to them all, the trunk of the tree, in the center, in spirit, is the mystery of service.

Ministry is the call to service. You cannot be a witch just for yourself. It really goes against the nature, the calling of a witch. And to be a witch is a calling. It is a fundamental call from your soul. Though some would choose it, thinking it's "cool" or trendy to be a witch, it's not something you can really choose, just as you can't really choose to be homosexual, African, or left-handed. You can identify with it and embrace it if it's a part of you, or try your best to reject it and not act upon it, but it's a fundamental part of you. In Eastern traditions, the performance of selfless service as a spiritual path is known as karmic yoga, the yoga of action. We too, as witches, are called to action.

In days of old, witches performed service. Today they still do; we are called to service. As a religion of clergy, we are all priestesses and priests. We are all the servants of the Goddess and God. We all have a role to play in the unfolding of this world. Many of us believe that we are called to this world, in this time and place, because the old ways need to be remembered, and the Mother and Father need us here and now in a time of spiritual, moral, and environmental crisis. As priestesses and priests, we are here to facilitate energies moving from one world to the next. We are stewards of deep teachings and a loving relationship with the planet. We are here to help turn the Wheel of the Year and aid the balance of humanity with nature. We are an interface between the physical world and the spirits. At least these are our traditional roles in a society where magick is a part of that society. We have gifts to share. We first learn how to master those gifts better for ourselves and our own needs, and then we are able to offer our talents to the world. Our abilities, our talents to move energy, are a lot like water flowing through a pipe. We are the pipe. We are the channel for something greater. A pipe that is never turned on, never opened to let the water flow, eventually stagnates and rusts. It cannot be used.

Witches can perform many types of services. Some take the step to become public clergy. Public clergy can offer services to the community in a variety of ways. We are the mentors, ceremonial leaders, and counselors of the community. Many acts of service, of clergy, are not as overt. Service is public education, political activism, environmental activism, and building interfaith relationships. Some witches direct their magick to the overall healing of the planet, and target specific places of crisis or disaster.

The most important service isn't necessarily found on a business card or when someone puts up a shingle over his or her door, metaphorically or literally, as "community witch," but when that person lives the life of a witch and models a healthy, happy, balanced life. Everything you do contributes to the overall well-being and collective consciousness of the planet. In an age where people struggle to find harmony, happiness, and health, modeling such a lifestyle to show people that it is possible can be the greatest act of service ever committed. No words, formal teachings, or proselytizing are needed. If someone inquires how you are living your life, you can share with that individual the tradition, ideas, and tools that got you where you are today. But simply contributing such a life to the collective consciousness, carving out a path in the psychic roads for others to travel, is a great service. By living a seemingly ordinary, but magickal, life, you are providing a much needed service to the world.

The magickal life can be the most elusive of the three Ms. We start by learning the science of magick, the ideas behind how and why it works, and how best to construct our spells. Then we learn to do magick. We practice the art of magick, how to actually apply it to our own individual needs. But something happens in the process. The magickal and mundane blend and weave together on the most fundamental level, and we become the magick. Everything we do is magick. *Everything we do.* We wake up to the fact that every thought we think, every word we say, and every action we take is magickal, contributing not only to our own reality, but all of reality. We realize that as priestesses and priests, every action is a ritual, and it is done in service to the gods, from the loftiest Sabbat to taking out the trash. Everything becomes spiritual, and we truly know the spiritual in everything, just in different shades. Brushing your teeth can be as important as lighting a candle if you are aware of the magick. We awaken to the fact that we are magickal creatures, and we always have been. The only thing different now is that we are conscious of it, and conscious of the joy and responsibilities that go along with being magickal creatures.

Some people in the Craft don't ever learn to live a magickal life. Just as there are "Sunday Christians" who only apply their teachings by going to church on Sunday but don't live in true communion with their god every moment of every day, there are Sabbat pagans. Sabbat pagans are those who attend the main holidays, either as a chance to party or, though they feel they are doing genuine work, to experience "feel good" rituals that never challenge them to grow, expand, or become more fully conscious.

Many people are okay with this, and are clear that at this point in their lives, that is as much as they can commit to their spirituality, and it sustains them. Others have this Sabbat-only attitude, but claim to be priestesses and priests of the Old Religion and desire to be recognized as community leaders and elders, even though they haven't done the work involved. They never do much ritual or magick beyond these special occasions. They don't have a regular spiritual practice. They don't meditate. They don't journal. They don't work their craft in the art of herbs, stones, or symbols. They don't live magickal lives, seeing the magick in every moment. They often don't speak the truth to themselves and to others, and even though they are not intentionally lying, there is a disconnect between what they think and what is reality. They often speak in ways that don't reflect their goals, desires, and dreams, never thinking to neutralize these unwanted patterns. They are usually in job or home situations in which they are terribly unhappy, yet they feel stuck, either because they do not have the magickal skills to change their reality, or because they have talked themselves into thinking that such magick for "personal gain" would be immoral in some way, and this is their karma that they must experience. That's just an excuse, and it is not worthy of the Craft they claim to embody. They don't realize that everything they are thinking, saying, and doing is contributing to their reality. They have not realized that they are magickal creatures, forces of nature in harmony with nature. They have not discovered and implemented their will, and they certainly are not living magickal lives.

For one to truly and effectively live a magickal life, one needs to awaken to the spiritual component in everything. We do that through the mysteries. The mysteries bring us awakening upon awakening, initiatory experiences that release us from the confines of the ego and of the personal self, and give us a glimpse of something greater, and of the potential of how great we can be, individually and as a people.

We learn to refine those awakenings, building magickal skills. At first our magickal lives and our mundane lives are very separate. We don ritual robes. We assume circle names. We keep very formalized and disciplined practices. When we are in circle, we assume one stance. When we are in "normal" life, we have another. This separation keeps us from going crazy when we are getting our grounding in the magickal world, so that we can function properly in the ordinary world. It helps us ground one foot in the physical and mundane, while the other is in the spiritual. We learn to stand between the worlds and anchor ourselves in whichever world we need. We know we can reach through the veil across space and time to do our magick, and we can become quite effective in assuming and releasing our state of magickal consciousness.

Soon the shift happens, where our core doesn't hop from one side of the veil to the next, jumping the "hedge," so to speak, as we anchor in the physical or spiritual world. We start to truly exist between the worlds simultaneously, yet can function in each quite effectively. We become something greater than what we could be by living in just one world. We become a bridge, an interface between the worlds. The magickal becomes ordinary and the ordinary becomes magickal. The two weave seamlessly together. In that process, we discover our True Will, our mission and purpose. We become clearer on what we are here to do and how we are to share our gifts with the world. We integrate the mysteries and the magick with our ministry, and we begin living a magickal life in every moment, beyond what most people comprehend. It is in that moment that we really embody the role of the high priestess or high priest.

The final step of the Temple of Witchcraft training, of the degree of spirit and the mystery of service, is the call to be high priest/ess. Many people learn a lot about magick and the Craft, but never learn how to experience and apply the mysteries, ministry, and integrated magickal life to take the next step. This is a book for those who don't have physical teachers but feel the call for service, or want to supplement what physical teachers and mentors have taught them.

No book can make you a high priestess or high priest. Not too long ago, people would have said that no book can guide you through the skill of self-dedication and initiation to walk the path of the witch, yet that is how many of us come to the path, because there were no other choices, or no other choices that were right for us. I do agree with the critics of book training. No book can *make* you a high priestess or high priest. But neither can any person. A teacher can proclaim you a rank, perform an initiation ritual, and recognize you by giving you any of the appropriate documentation for that tradition, but the alchemy of becoming a high priestess or high priest is internal. All those outward acts can only hope to catalyze the internal process. If you don't do the work yourself, it doesn't matter who proclaims you a high priestess or high priest, for it will not be true. And if you do the work and have the direct experience of the divine calling you to service and you answer that call fully, training yourself to the best of your ability with the resources available, then the alchemy will occur within you, and it doesn't matter who disagrees or denounces you, for you will know the truth. Others will know the truth by your work, by your heart, by the way you carry yourself in the world, and by your life. I know many people who have the formal rank of a high priest or high priestess but, in my opinion, really aren't acting that way based upon their actions and life. But who am I to tell them? There could be whole other sides of them that I'm not privy to, yet I can't help but think that some people are looking more for the title than the training. And I know many witches with no formal rank who, in my opinion, through their words and deeds, are high priestesses or high priests.

This book is a teaching tool to help you master the divine inner alchemy between you and the gods, to reach this new level of being through the mysteries, the ministry, and the magickal life. Though a book cannot confer an official title or rank in a lineage tradition, those who do this work and have these experiences are considered high priestesses and high priests in the Temple of Witchcraft tradition by the Hidden Company that guides these teachings. As more people work through the teachings of this five-level modern tradition, and make inner-plane contacts, more energy is added to the spiritual current of the tradition, the *egregore*. Though nobody is conferring a current through physical initiation like a British Traditional lineage, doing the work itself connects you to the current and helps awaken you.

The structure of this book is a bit different from the previous ones. There are not the familiar four introductory chapters—just one. Volume Two follows this same structure. We skip any long sections filled with preliminary information and basic exercises, for the previous four books and levels of training are all the introduction to the tradition you need, and we enter the lessons immediately. Based upon the apprenticeship I teach to my students, which lasts over a year, the book format has been extended to a nineteen-month course, echoing the nineteen-year Meton cycle of the Sun and Moon, the period of time it supposedly took to complete full druidic training.

This course is not for everybody. Most who start my Witchcraft I: Building the Inner Temple course do not make it to Witchcraft V. This is for those who aspire to self-mastery, who want magickal training to challenge their beliefs and prejudices, who want to personally experience the mysteries and ultimately serve the greater good. We must each serve our self and our truth, serve the gods, serve our community, witchdom, and the planet herself. The fifth level of training is the trunk of the tree, and it must dig deeper and reach higher than any of the others. Before students can register for this course, I make them take a questionnaire. Though it seems easy at first glance, these are questions you should ponder and really think about before you take the class. I make prospective students complete the questions and return their answers to me. Some write short statements and others write whole essays. Whatever is needed to search your thoughts, feelings, and motivations, it will prepare you for this work. I've provided these questions in appendix I. Before you start Lesson One, answer them in your Book of Shadows or journal.

Though I encourage eclecticism and personal experience, many seek an eclectic path to avoid thorough training, to pick and choose what is easy and comfortable. They seek a personal tradition that is wide, but not very deep. It's funny, but until I started teaching extensively, I didn't realize this. I always identified with eclectic witchcraft. It was so much easier than saying I was a Shamanic-Hermetic-Thelemic-Theosophical-Green-Faery-Folk Witch. I spoke to a good friend, a high priest of a lineage-based tradition, and his impression of eclectic witches wasn't very good, and he felt that they usually didn't know what they were doing or talking about. I always thought the opposite, as a good eclectic witch has to be well informed not only about one tradition, but about many.

The Temple of Witchcraft series in general and this book specifically is crafted to be both wide and deep, giving you the foundation to take your magick and spiritual practice in any direction you choose, with a broad worldview, strong practice, clear understanding, and direct experience. This course is designed to look at all the nooks and crannies, to make sure nothing is avoided. Tough training is necessary for one to be a high priest/ess. The first part of this course is designed to take you through seven temples, seven lessons based on the seven basic archetypes of the chakras, planets, alchemical operations, and gates of the Underworld. The concepts are very similar to the Orphic and Eleusinian mysteries, the descent to the deep and the death and rebirth that occurs when we face the chthonic powers of the Underworld. It is the tale of Inanna, the Descent of the Goddess. This sevenfold pattern is being reclaimed by many modern witchcraft teachers, including Janet Farrar and Gavin Bone. These first seven lessons serve as the bulk of the mysteries and the hardest part of the course. It is the intensive part I teach when I'm dealing with students in the flesh, taught over seven very powerful weeks together. Then the seven gates are followed up in Volume Two of this work, with a cycle of the zodiac, the twelve stellar stations, moving through the patterns of the elements, seasons, and personal archetypes, like the Mithraic mystery schools. Following the pattern of the Sun moving through the twelve signs, the initiate moves through the full cycle of experience. The twelve zodiac lessons are a chance to broaden your experience, revisit some lessons in the past, and grow in your confidence and abilities as a high priest/ess, taking what you learned in the first seven temples and applying it to the cycle of your life. The entire coursework culminates with a self-initiation ritual.

Though this book is complete in itself as a series of lessons, it is really meant to be used in conjunction with Volume Two. *The Living Temple of Witchcraft* does build upon the lessons of the previous books in the series. One should have a strong background in witchcraft, magick, meditation, shamanism, and ceremonial magick before embarking on this course, if not completing the courses contained in the previous four books. Any information contained in the previous books will be notated with the following abbreviations, with a chapter or exercise number. *The Inner Temple of Witchcraft* is marked with *ITOW*. *The Outer Temple of Witchcraft* is marked with *OTOW*. *The Temple of Shamanic Witchcraft* is *TOSW*. *The Temple of High Witchcraft* is *TOHW*. (*The Living Temple of Witchcraft* will be *LTOW*, vol. 1 and vol. 2.)

As a part of this nineteen-lesson training, I suggest you work with a magickal cord, also known as the cingulum. Cords have always been associated with the traditions of witchcraft and with initiation. Scholars look to Stone Age cave painting of a figure with a cord around the leg. The ritual garter is seen as a witch tool and found in some burial sites. The cord is aligned with the noose, as a symbol of sacrifice, of offering yourself to the gods. Modern witches use cords to "take the measure" of initiates, either with the ritual cords, or with measured strings to ensure initiation oaths are kept. In ritual, the cords are used as a prayer rope, with knots like a rosary or mala-bead string. They are bound together in circle dance. They are used to control the flow of blood to open the psychic gates. They can be used to measure out and draw the circle, or mark the boundary of the circle. Cords can also be used to bind in magick, and to bind and transfer energy to tools such as a staff or stang.

For this course you will be working with two cords. For the final initiation you will add a fifth strand to your ritual robe cord, adding a black, white, or purple cord for spirit to your previous four cords of red, green, blue, and yellow. During the course-work, I suggest you measure out another three cords, of your three favorite colors, your three power colors. These may represent the "rays" of your soul from a Theo-sophical perspective. For now just pick the three colors that you are drawn to use. Measure them out for the height of your body. Ritually braid them in circle. At the completion of each of the nineteen lessons, in ritual space, make a single knot in the cord. In the end, you will have a cord of nineteen knots, used for magick, affirma-tions, focus, and binding. Your braided end can be taped together, to prevent the braid from coming undone, and you will not need to put in a final knot until the end of the course. This will become a form of witch's ladder, infused with the mysteries, minis-try, and magick you have learned over this period.

Most importantly, the cord is a tool binding you to the gods. You offer yourself, like the ritual noose, to the gods, and are not only bound to them, but also merged with them. The cord becomes a connection, like the umbilical cord, but flowing two ways. The cord signifies a relationship between you and the divine powers. I think of the cord like the ball of string given to Theseus by Ariadne as he entered the maze. The maze was not just the home and trap of the Minotaur, but the labyrinth into the mysteries. A cord, a connection, can be the deciding factor between success and failure when we face the gods in the center of the labyrinth. Ariadne is like the weaver god-dess, showing us how to work with the strands of magick, to keep connected to her, even in the depths. With the strand, we stay linked to the outer world and linked to the inner world; we are creatures between the worlds, learning to live in the space beyond space, the time beyond time. We learn to live in that place of Perfect Love and Perfect Trust, and we bring that magick out of the labyrinth and into all the worlds we touch.

I wish you many blessings as you enter the labyrinth and face the mysteries. May they lead you to your purpose, to your ministry, and to living a magickal life in every moment of every day.

Blessed be,
Christopher Penczak

The Seven Gates of the Goddess

The Mystery of the Seven Gates takes our practice to a deep place, the place of self-knowledge, experience, and transformation. This mystery gives us the true skills to embrace the role of the high priestess or high priest, as our old self "dies" to be reborn in a new form. Before you enter the mystery and seek this transformation, you should really consider what it means to be a high priest/ess.

Like asking the question "What is a Witch?" back in the *ITOW* course, if you ask "What is a high priest/ess?" you will also get a multitude of answers. Witchcraft is a religion of clergy. We are all priests and priestesses. Some claim that role before any training. Other traditions confer that role upon completion of the first or second degree of training. It means one can effectively move energy by performing ritual, opening gates between the worlds, doing magick in a sacred space, and, most importantly, releasing the ritual and closing all gates. A high priest/ess must do all that and more.

The role of the high priest/ess manifests in the role of the minister. Although we are all clergy, witches still recognize, honor, and put to work those of us in the community who are called to minister both to other witches and to the world in general. Ministry in any religion is a calling, a vocation, yet everybody drawn to witchcraft is really called to be a minister on some level. Being a high priest/ess is simply accepting the highest level of responsibility to that calling.

High priest/esses act as teachers, taking on students, organizing groups and covens, and passing on the knowledge and experience they have learned to other generations. Like gardeners, they plant seeds and encourage growth, but each plant eventually has to grow in its own unique way, and a good teacher recognizes that truth. These ministers play the roles of counselors, mentors, and cheerleaders to their students. Many go beyond the witches in their charge, and offer their services to the greater pagan community, and/or the greater community at large. Formally or informally, they are sought out for advice, wisdom, divination skills, healing, and rituals, and to mark life passages. Many seek out supplemental skills or at least training recognized by the mainstream world, to help them offer their wisdom to the world and be recognized by society. Some get training in social work, psychology, medicine, or alternative healing. You'd be surprised how many pagan ministers are in very healing roles, and are often very "matter of fact" about their religion. It's not like they show up in pointed hats and black robes. They simply do their job, but they approach it from the perspective of a witch. If religion isn't mentioned in the situation, they won't necessarily bring it up either, but if it is, many will proudly state their tradition and use it to open a dialogue if one is wanted or needed. Ideally, they become role models in the pagan world, and examples of healthy, happy, and holy pagans to the rest of the world. In a time when so many of our examples of witchcraft are seen on teen television shows, it's important to show the realness, the groundedness of witches in the modern world.

A high priest/ess is a mediator of energy, a bridge to facilitate the movement of energy between the worlds, gently guiding the wheels of life toward creation and destruction in an attempt to keep balance, harmony, and peace between the human world and all others. High priestesses and high priests are ambassadors to the other realms as well as leaders in the physical world. We represent the human world to our nonhuman spiritual allies in nature and in the otherworlds. Many of our rituals and public services are really to help connect our community, individually and as a group, to the spiritual world.

Ultimately, high priest/esses are those who are living magickal lives, who are integrating all aspects of their training into their daily lives. In many ways, witchcraft is a form of alchemy, and in fact it is perhaps the first and truest form of alchemy. We may think of alchemy as the work of the laboratory magician, making elixirs of immortality and transforming lead into gold, but if we peel back the stereotype and know that it is a magickal art for enlightenment, we understand that the key theme and central tenet of the alchemist is transformation. The lead of density, karma, and difficulties is transformed into the gold of enlightenment—beautiful, untarnished, and radiant.

Though the stereotype of witchcraft is simply casting spells and curses, witchcraft is really an alchemical art, the art of transformation. As a mystery teaching, it aims to educate us in the mysteries through direct experience, and it is that direct experience that transforms us and changes us, as well as our relationship with the cosmos. This changes how we relate to ourselves, others, and the world in every moment of every day. We learn that everything is magickal and always has been. Everybody is doing magick. Every thought you think, every word you say, and every action you take is putting your will into action and manifesting your reality. Everything is magick. As we identify with the magick, we in many ways stop "doing" magick, for we realize that we are the magick. We also realize that everything we do is a theurgic offering to the divine to unite our personal will with divine will and manifest our divine will in the world.

Though some very lucky people know they are magickal from the beginning, and act that way, they are lucky. Most of us come from a society that does not encourage or understand magick, let alone encourage us to "be" magick. When we begin our training, we learn that most traditional methods make a conscious barrier between the magickal and mundane. Those who are naturally in-tune often find it silly. Why wear special clothes, take special names, or use exotic and special tools? Everything is special. They are right, but this separation between the magickal and mundane will provide some very important skills for the aspiring magician or witch.

We create a magickal persona, a boundary between our self in the circle, in vision, who experiences a non-ordinary reality, and the sense of the self who is outside of the circle, who goes to work every day, pays bills, deals with family, and experiences the consensus reality that everybody shares. Many witches will tell you there is a fine line between magickal and crazy. A large percentage of people who are classified with debilitating mental illnesses are often very magickally talented people. The problem is, they don't know how to shut off their abilities, or tune them down, so they can function in ordinary reality. When you experience visions, spirit contact, psychic awakening, and magickal power, it is easy to lose touch with the ordinary reality of everyone else, and it becomes difficult to put your abilities to good use. Without firm grounding, without true education in the magickal arts, it is easy to go on a personal power trip, getting caught up in delusions of grandeur, or to completely overload yourself and short-circuit your energy system. Some simply scare themselves so much that they shut down those abilities as a safety mechanism and can't reawaken them.

By creating a separation between the two states, the novice witch knows the feeling of each, and how to shift from one side of the veil to the other and back again. Rituals, clothing, jewelry, and magickal names can help make the shift that occurs in consciousness. Many aspire to their highest selves and ideals in the magickal realm, to lessen the ego and work from a place of higher will. If you've been involved in the pagan community for any length of time, you know that while that is the ideal, it doesn't always work out that way.

Once the initiate can easily shift between these states, and there is no personal dysfunction, then a more subtle alchemy occurs. Rather than just have an on-and-off switch for magick, the various shades of awareness open up—states of awareness between full-on magickal reality and full-on consensus reality. Instead of being at one end of the spectrum or the other, you move along the spectrum of possibility, like moving from note to note on a musical scale, or color to color on the rainbow. These wider shades of magickal experience will have been occurring for some time before this level of training, and each is a challenge to remain grounded yet open. You might "see" the aura when talking to somebody in daily life, get a flash of insight, hear a message from a guide, or sense the land spirits or anything else magickal in a wide range of possibilities. In most situations, we must be aware of the experience, yet not let it dangerously distract us from what is at hand—speaking to someone, driving, walking, etc. Those who are very gifted but lack this initial training of separation are the archetypal "flakes" of the metaphysical movement. You can't really deny their talent, but you have to wonder if it's really serving them. They can't apply it or control it, and it creates many difficult social situations, because they aren't grounded enough in the consensus reality to relate to those without this psychic ability. Many witches go through this archetypal stage. That's fine, as long as it's a stage. Witches who aspire to be high priest/esses are many things, but flaky, ungrounded, and nonfunctioning should not be among their traits. We have to have one foot firmly planted in the material and one foot firmly planted in the spiritual. The emphasis is on the firmness.

For the aspiring high priest/ess, the shades in between continue to open to the beauty and magick of the worlds around us, physical and nonphysical. In the context of our religion, we truly break the conditioning of "normal" society and see everything as the divine manifest, and find the beauty and spirit in everyone, every thing, and every moment. Suddenly every act we do takes on a spiritual aspect. Though it might not always feel like it, we realize that everything we do is connected to everything else, and if we approach our whole lives like a series of rituals or spells, everything we do is a ritual of offering to the divine. Everything we think, everything we say, every interaction we have with someone, and every action we take is an opportunity to devote ourselves and our energies to the divine, Goddess and God, and to the manifestation of our higher will.

With that change in consciousness, over time, we no longer have our barrier between the magickal and nonmagickal. And we no longer have the subtle shades of magickal color between the two extremes. We suddenly find ourselves "rooted" in the entire spectrum of magickal experience. We are aware of the spaces in between, fully functioning and grounded in the material world, conscious of the forces and energies around us in the spiritual worlds, and at one with all the possibilities in between. Our focus can shift from one area to another through the use of all the skills we have gathered in creating the boundary, learning ritual, and working with psychic development, but we find ourselves becoming something new, a creature of this between space. We become the crossroads.

The crossroads is intimately linked with witchcraft, magick, and the occult. It has been seen in some ages and traditions as the joining of three roads in a *Y*, or the crossing of two roads in an *X*, reaching out in four directions, but in either case, it is a place in between. Witches worship at the crossroads, for its energies are like the magick circle itself, between the worlds. Many of our rites are at in-between times (midnight, dawn, noon, and twilight) and places (beaches where the sky, sea, and land meet; hill-tops where the land and sky meet; rivers, ponds, bogs, and clearings in the forest). Crossroads and liminal, or between, places and times are nexus points between the material and spiritual worlds. Strange things happen there, and many of our superstitions tell the uninitiated to avoid them because they are bad luck. Yet the witches are encouraged to visit, for we know and respect their power. Like the seven gates, the crossroads is a place of initiation. To become like the crossroads or the underworlds, you must immerse yourself in them.

The more we attune to these between-the-worlds energies, the more we embody the archetypal power of the crossroads. We become, quite literally, a swirling vortex of energy, a nexus point of forces. That is what it means to be a high priest/ess. We become a nexus point, but to truly serve as that connection, as that mediating opening, we must be fully trained and grounded in the use of our abilities. As a nexus point for these forces, we bring change to all with whom we come in contact. We become the "place" meta-phorically, between the worlds where all things are possible. As in sacred space, often what is said or thought around us occurs unconsciously, and we often act as a mirror to whatever people bring to us, just as the Goddess of the crossroads holds up that mirror by her very nature. One of our modern pagan sayings about the Goddess is, "She changes everything she touches…and everything she touches changes." We become her agents of change simply by being at this level of crossroads consciousness.

Change and mirroring are not always welcomed by the general population, for they are both hard to bear. As those who bring change by our very nature, it is one of the reasons why witches, even in classical pagan times, have been thought of less than kindly, or even fully reviled. We have neopagan fantasies of the ancient world's witch—much loved, respected, and celebrated by society, and while there have been times and places where that was or is true, one need only look at classic Greek writings, pagan writings, to see the fear concerning witches. Yes, those sources only tell the scholars' points of view, and we really don't know what the people thought of those considered witches, but they don't paint a portrait of universal appeal. Witches have always been feared on some level. From our modern perspective, we can say that archetypally witches force people to see the dark, to see the shadow, and witches show people that it is up to them to take responsibility for their own darkness, because no one else will do it. Yet few see it that way, and they blame the messenger—thus the persecutions of the witches.

We have also had ourselves to blame in the process, as many forget the holy nature of their Craft, and let ego cloud it. Least anyone read this and think I'm calling for all witches to go out and take all matters into their own hands personally, it's important to know how impersonal and detached this process can be. We don't need to personally determine who needs to change and who needs to confront their shadow self. By doing this work for ourselves, we move the world toward it. As we enter this state of crossroads consciousness, between the worlds, we are really entering a place of Perfect Love and Perfect Trust. Those who get personal, who feel they need to be the personal hand of justice, of karma, of curses, often miss the point and are not quite where they think they are spiritually. The people who need to change, to face the dark, will be attracted to the crossroads vortex that we become. If we are continually praying that our every action be in accord with divine will, that we offer every action up to the divine, then the interactions we have with everybody will be what they need to be, whether we realize it or not. You can have a completely mundane conversation with others and not realize that you changed their lives, and not consciously realize that they have changed yours, yet both occurred.

Becoming the crossroads is the conscious realization and acceptance that we are magickal entities. The process of witchcraft as a mystery tradition is awakening to the fact that we are magickal entities, creatures of nature and supernature, of humanity and the spirits, for there is really little difference between them. They are the same. Make no mistake, we are totally human. We feel our emotions as intensely as anyone else, if not more so, yet we are totally divine. We consciously accept that we are more than human, we are the crossroads, the nexus point where we are devoted to service to the divine. We live in sacred space, now carrying the magick circle, the crossroads between the worlds with us always.

Ultimately, this philosophy must force us to ask what witchcraft truly is. Modern witchcraft is a revolution—transforming one person at a time into something fully human and fully spirit, a guardian between the worlds, living in a state of constant change yet eternal awareness. An even more important question is *why*. Why are there witches in the first place? Some eastern European traditions tell tales about magickal eggs that are made every year, filled with charms that bind evil forces that seek to escape and destroy the world. As long as those charmed eggs are made, we are protected. If someone doesn't do it, somewhere in the world, then we are finished.

Witches are like the egg makers. We are guardians, caretakers, and balancers, performing our duties and rituals on a multitude of levels, not necessarily to bind evil, but to keep the flow of energies between all worlds in balance. As long as someone, somewhere, is mediating the flow of energies at the holidays and communing with the spirits of the land, the dead, the elements, angels, and gods, then we will survive. Perhaps the world is in the state it is in because so few people do this work, as many indigenous and pagan cultures have been wiped out. Many of us have been "called" by the Earth Mother and the Hidden Company of witches from the past to return, to redress this imbalance. The ministers of our traditions, the high priests and high priestesses, hold this duty of caretaking, guardianship, and balance above those who are simply following a pagan path, for we are hearing the call to service and consciously dedicating our lives to this path.

WITCHCRAFT AS A MYSTERY SCHOOL

A mystery is something unknown, and implied in the term are those who seek out the unknown, who want to know and immerse themselves in the mystery and ultimately "solve" it. However, the ancient mysteries are not necessarily puzzles to be solved, because they do not have one single answer for everybody. The mysteries are spiritual wisdoms that must be experienced firsthand to truly "solve" them, yet the nature of the mystery is that there is no solution. One simply becomes a keeper of the mystery by embodying its wisdom and applying it to life. It becomes a part of you, a part of the process of becoming magick, of becoming the mystery.

The mystery schools of the ancient world are really traditions of initiation, for the direct experience of the divine, the initiator experience, begins the process of embodying the mysteries. Subsequent initiations are often referred to, particularly in Wicca, as "elevations" because once you have been initiated, once you have "begun," you cannot begin again, but you simply further the mystery. Each subsequent initiation is like bringing you as the student further into the temple, into the next chamber you did not even know existed. Teachers and traditions can only give you the keys to the doorway of mystery. They can't make you experience it. They can give you the keys, train you in how they work, and make sure that, in their eyes, you are ready, but they cannot turn the keys for you. Many do experience the rituals without experiencing the mysteries, and many experience the mysteries without having any ritual.

We find formal mystery schools detailed in the ancient world, particularly in Greece and Rome. We have the Orphic mysteries, based upon the figure Orpheus, who descends into Hades after the shade of his deceased wife, Eurydice. He faces King Hades and Queen Persephone and successfully makes a bargain, yet he ultimately loses his bride. Near and dear to witches are the Eleusinian mysteries, popularly reconstructed in the modern age through a variety of formats, though we have no real knowledge of what they actually did, only educated guesses. Gerald Gardner devotes a whole section in *Witchcraft Today* to the Greek mysteries. Although aspects of the Mithraic cults of Rome were adopted into Christianity, the basic tenet of the resurrected god enacted through mystery play while in subterranean temples is very similar to the other Mediterranean mystery systems. When we look at the priesthoods of other ancient cultures, such as the Sumerians and Egyptians, it is easy to see the same tenets in their mythologies, such as those of Inanna, Isis, and Osiris, and imagine similar mystery school trainings in those cultures.

In our modern society, it's easy to believe that the practices of mystery schools have completely disappeared. Some witches and magicians claim lineage from traditions that have kept the mysteries going, but irrefutable proof is not forthcoming. Many who believe that they hold such lineages don't feel the need to justify them to others. Modern traditions have sought to reclaim the essence of the mystery-school tradition. The Golden Dawn and its offshoots are probably the most well known and influential. Lineage-based Wicca, including Gardnerian and Alexandrian traditions, as well as their descendent traditions, is also a form of mystery school training.

Mystery schools, ancient and modern, have many points in common, regardless of the religious tradition that surrounds them. In the end, the mysteries are the mysteries, and initiates of the mysteries recognize each other across traditions. I have Christian mystic friends with whom I have more in common spiritually than some Wiccans I know who have not delved beyond the surface teaching of Wicca. My Christian friends and I are able to share, empathize, and understand each other on a deep level, and not argue about "doing things right" or the aesthetics of ritual practice. There are many mystery paths that get you to the top of the mountain, or the heart of the Underworld, but they all hold several points in common.

The experience of it is the most important. I remember speaking to a student regarding healing and past lives. She just didn't get it at all and argued intellectually about it for the whole class. Once she experienced it directly, she got it and found it a very helpful "mystery" of the healing arts. But until we both had a common vocabulary, it was very difficult to communicate about something so personal.

Greater and Lesser Mysteries

The teachings can be divided into two categories, of greater and lesser importance, though where that dividing line occurs is different for different traditions. Generally, the lesser mysteries are the preparations, work, daily skills, and little revelations that lead to the greater mysteries of life, death, love, will, and empowerment. We can think of our initial training, our meditation, and our first rituals as the lesser mysteries. They are powerful and life changing, but they really lead to the large transpersonal experiences of greater mysteries. Those who experience the greater mysteries are often brought into a system of training to help them pass the experience on to the next generation. Some divide the greater and lesser mysteries into the outer court for the lesser and public teachings, and the inner court for the greater and private oath-bound teachings. In essence, the lesser mysteries are the secrets you must not reveal, or at least that was the case in ages past. They are techniques. They can endanger when not used properly, and they can be misunderstood out of the context of mystery training. The greater mysteries are those that cannot be revealed, not because of oaths, but because they are ineffable. You simply cannot express them to those who have not experienced them, and if they have been experienced, there is no need for discussion.

Purification

Initiates on the path are prepared for the mysteries through a variety of purification rituals. They are purified in body, mind, and emotions to get a clearer view of the self. Without purification of the consciousness, of the energy field, profound and visionary experiences can become muddled and confused. Traditions such as ritual baths, fasting, and particular clothing are used to alter the initiate, but also periods of silence and introspection. In our modern day, journaling and forms of therapy are also used to clear away the familial, societal, and self-created programs, to get closer to the true nature of the initiate without these other influences.

Unlocking the Hidden Powers

Mystery training helps the initiate unlock the ability to alter consciousness and experience things with new senses and perceptions. Some training grants lifelong skills, such as meditation, pathworking, or shamanic training. Others use specific rituals to unlock these abilities for the initiation rite itself, but the individual might have difficulty accessing them again under other circumstances. In either case, the initiate is opened to his or her own hidden powers of the psyche.

True Nature of Reality

However it is experienced or later described, this is the true mystery. The initiate experiences the "true" nature of reality. Through ritual and training, consciousness is expanded to such a point that the initiate has a direct experience of the divine. Often this direct experience is framed in the context of the ritual and religion presenting it, yet the feelings, thoughts, and direct experience it evokes are eternal and cut across all cultures and time. Later such experiences might be described as "God/dess," "Spirit," "oneness," "love," "light," "the void," or "the web," among many others, yet none really convey the mystery. Though keeping rituals secret can be helpful to those who are about to experience them for the psychological and energetic effects they can have when unknown, the true mysteries will always remain a mystery, for no amount of knowledge can truly impart them to those who have not directly experienced them.

True Will

Much of the mysteries focus on this fusion with divinity, but when one returns from this experience to be grounded in the "normal" world, a sense of purpose or mission, what a magician would call True Will, becomes clearer. Motivations become less personal. In fact, through the training of the mysteries, be it Wicca or any other magickal tradition, there is often a trifold process. The bulk of the initial work, particularly the purification, is personal. It focuses on the individual's relationship with the self. Then the interplay between others in the school, often the coven, who act as mirrors while working on our interpersonal skills, the relationships between people, serves us on the spiritual path. The final stage is developing a transpersonal view, a global or cosmic view of our place and purpose, which, like the mysteries themselves, is both humbling and empowering. Our sense of True Will, our purpose and mission in the world, really comes from this transpersonal viewpoint. Sometimes the initiatory experience only gives the next step to fulfilling the True Will, but the sense of divine purpose is strengthened.

Initiation

Initiation is the culmination of all the previous points, integrating them together. After being sufficiently purified, consciousness is expanded through a ritualized experience. Often an energy, known as a current, is transferred from initiator to initiate, or from the group to the initiate, and this current alters consciousness, shows the true nature of reality framed in that tradition's worldview, and gives knowledge of the initiate's True Will. Initiation is useless if the initiate does not then act upon it, integrating and using the newfound awareness. Like a college degree hanging on a wall, it has no use if you don't apply the knowledge and experience of your education in the world.

Extended Family

The bonds of initiation in a particular tradition confer a sense of sisterhood/brotherhood amongst the initiates. A good modern analogy is college fraternities and sororities—going through ordeals that share some similarities with mystery school initiates, minus the spiritual tones and revelations, members of the group have a bond. Only those who have gone through that tradition have that bond, and they will often aid each other throughout life. General witchcraft initiations confer a bond, the witch bond, among all others who are witches, regardless of tradition. We are all children of the Goddess and God, and sisters and brothers in the Craft of the Wise. Those in specific lineages have a further bond. They are directly connected energetically to all those before them. They have a connection to the past, to those who have experienced and then taught the mysteries before. As an extended family, this comes with both its share of blessings and difficulties. Like families, traditions often squabble and have fights, yet like family, they are bonded and can't really get rid of each other. No one can truly be "un-initiated," although they can choose not to associate with members of their order. Members of a tradition can bring you many teachings, blessings, and a sense of belonging, just like a family.

The paths of enlightenment that confer the mysteries are said to come in three major routes. The first is the path through devotion. Many follow a path of prayer and faith, devoted to the divine, with whatever traditional imagery they have of the divine, and the intense devotion focused solely on the divine brings them through the purification, meditation, true knowledge, and True Will. Those dedicated to a particular image of the divine find brotherhood/sisterhood in those who are also devoted to that image of the divine. Though devotion usually occurs in the context of a religious faith, the mainstream religions' institutions usually do not sponsor a formal mystery school, but they simply provide an avenue to enlightenment by educating people on the faith. On the path of devotion we have many of the traditional religions. Many seekers have found their path through devotion to Christ, Mother Mary, or a saint. Those dedicated to a particular god, through practices ranging from paganism to dedication to a Hindu godform or Eastern bodhisattvas, can find a path through devotion. Those who focus on the monotheistic father image of the Book—the Old Testament, New Testament, and Qur'an—can also follow a path of devotion, though each of these traditions has its emissaries. In the Old Testament and Qur'an, figures are often met by angelic messengers delivering the word of God, but they rarely have a direct personal relationship with God. For Christians, the figure of Jesus Christ is the personal intermediary between God and mortals.

The second major path is the path of study. It is an intellectual path, studying the world, which is either seen as the divine, from an immanent-divinity perspective, or the creation of the divine, from a transcendent perspective. Either way, the study of the world, of nature, has been a classic path of the enlightened philosopher. Through studying both physical phenomena in science and nature, as well as the philosophy, texts, and traditions of those learned people who have come before, who have studied the world, the divine can be experienced. We see this path of enlightenment in those mystics who are close to nature, who find the God in everything. We see it in the saints who found their enlightenment through nature and the animals, such as St. Francis. We see it in the alchemists of the East and West, who study the world to know the nature of God and their own souls. We also see it starting in the modern scientific community, through the work of quantum physicists.

The last major path is the path of doing. Some would call it the path of yoga, performing actions to "yoke" themselves to the divine or find "union" with the divine, as *yoga* is often translated as "yoke" or "union." Others see it as the path of ritual and movement. You must perform ritual and movement. It is not silent devotion and prayer. It is not observation and study. It is interaction with the forces of the universe and the forces of the self. It is the path of magick.

When you look at the three paths, they are not separate roads of the crossroads, heading out in divergent directions, but an interwoven braid. One can be devoted, intellectual, and a magician all at the same time. The best initiates combine all three paths, but often one of the paths will call them to explore the mysteries. I was called by the study path, not necessarily the direct observation of nature, but a desire to understand how this could possibly work. A friend and mentor of mine found her path through an inherent deep devotion to the creator, which she then studied, and she learned rituals to better attune to the divine. Some are simply called by the path of magick and know how to work their will in the world, and in that working, they become closer to the mysteries.

The paths of the mysteries for a practicing pagan can be divided into other, more specific categories. A look at these paths can help you understand where you have been and where you are going.

The Path of Ecstasy

The first path most associated with witchcraft across the ages is the path of ecstasy. In his work *The Birth of Tragedy*, Nietzsche used the term *Dionysian* to describe this principle, in balance with the Apollonian principle as the two driving forces in Greek culture. Named after the Greek god Dionysus, this principle is embodied by drunkenness, madness, pleasure, enthusiasm, and ecstasy. In such states, an individual gives up his or her individuality to become part of a greater whole. Music and freeform dance are indicative of this path of ecstasy, for they overcome the rational and individual mind. It is very shamanic in the sense of the shaman's ecstasy—becoming loose from the flesh. The image of witchcraft covens experiencing a wild rite of sexual passion, wine, dance, and song, in the ancient pagan world, and the images of the medieval witch Sabbat having union with the horned god figure, are very Dionysian. The path of ecstasy can be seen in the Fool card of the tarot, a figure so in tune with divine nature that there are few rational thoughts and worries, just trust on the path, as well as the Strength card, which when depicted as Lust, is the spiritual ecstasy of union with the divine. One can also see the submersion of identity in the Hanged Man card, suspended between life and death, standing between the worlds.

The Path of Clarity

The path of intellectual analysis explores individuality, structure, reason, and distinction. Nietzsche calls this force Apollonian, after the Greek god of the Sun, light, poetry, and medicine. The mysteries of the light, of understanding how things work, of clarity and how the individual relates to structure and form, are Apollonian. Visual art with pattern or design, as opposed to freeform art, is Apollonian—sculpture in particular, since the sculpture as an individual entity must be freed and separated from the stone. Form is the way the art of sculpture is expressed. Nietzsche saw Greek tragedy as the tension between the Apollonian and Dionysian path. The Apollonian path appears to be the path of the witch as priestess or priest in the temple. These are the public rites of sanctioned institutional religions. Those who climb the hierarchies of structured rituals are following an Apollonian path. One can look to the mysteries of the Golden Dawn and see the path of Apollo, the path of light and analysis. The Apollonian mysteries can be seen in the Sun card in the tarot.

The Path of the Ascetic

The path of the ascetic is a mystery tradition of renouncing the world and all forms of worldly pleasure. Many renounce possession and any vanity regarding the body. The seeker lives simply, though some move beyond this to severe fasting, denial of the body, and physical mortification through scourging, piercing, tattooing, and other pain-inducing rites. Many Eastern paths of discipline are not as harsh, yet they would still be considered ascetic paths. The path of the ascetic, of renouncement, is embodied by the Hermit card in the tarot, shutting out the world to find the light of the inner star.

The Path of Seership

The seer is one who is chosen by the spirits and finds enlightenment through contact with the otherworlds, and with nonphysical beings. Understanding of the universe, of magick and the true nature of reality, is through a kinship with the otherworlds. Those on a path of seership will often receive the call through an extended illness or bout of depression, which puts them in isolation and eventual communion with the spirits. The Chariot card, which truly represents the spiritual voyage as well as a potential physical voyage, is the embodiment of the seer's path. The Priestess card, depicting the one who holds open the gates between worlds, is also an archetype of this path.

The Path of Life

The path of life is almost the exact opposite of the ascetic path. One embraces life in all its forms and, through this embracement, finds that the mysteries of the universe shine through all aspects of the cycle of life. Many would see witchcraft as an agricultural mystery, a mystery path of life. This is our tradition as the fertility cult. We are stoking the life force and working with it in the land. Those who practice Green witchcraft, herbcraft, gardening, and farming, and those who commune closely with nature are on the path of life. I think of Henry David Thoreau as a fairly well-known modern initiate on the path of life. Though not a witch, he embodied the understanding of the mysteries of this path. As he wrote in his book *Walden*, "I went to the woods because I wished to live deliberately, to front only the essential facts of life, and see if I could not learn what it had to teach, and not, when I came to die, discover that I had not lived … I wanted to live deep and suck out all the marrow of life …" The Empress card, as embodied by the fertile earth, is the image of the path of life.

The Path of Death

Matching our path of life, yet not quite renouncing the world like the ascetic, is the path of death. While some will find the mysteries in the germinating and growing principle, others find the mysteries best through death and spiritual rebirth. They are two sides of the same coin. We can look to the mysteries of Eleusis and the cults of Osiris as both death cults and agriculture cults. The Egyptians in particular had a focus on death. Although many people think their view was on death exclusively, they enjoyed and focused on life as well, but they did not fear the mysteries of death. The Orphic mysteries are certainly about the land of the dead, and the human journey there. The path of the goddess Inanna, although a goddess of the earth and heavens, embodies a myth with parallels to agricultural and stellar cycles, in which she is confronting the goddess of death, her sister, and is reborn. Agricultural mysteries, as they work with the making of spirits, the fermentation mysteries, are all about death and rebirth, an alchemical process. Sacramental meals, the eating of bread and wine, be it for the grain and grape gods, or for the modern savior, are filled with the death mysteries. We are consuming their flesh and blood, so we may live. The Death card of the tarot obviously embodies the death mysteries, but we may also look to the Temperance/Art card, sometimes known as Alchemy, to follow it.

The Path of Gender

The path of gender, unlike the fertility mysteries of life, can focus on one or the other gender exclusively. Here we have the male mysteries and the female mysteries, both valid paths to the divine. The female mysteries focus on the Goddess and how she manifests through things exclusively feminine, as well as characteristics and powers associated with the feminine. Mysteries of the Moon, moontime, childbirth, home, nurturing, intuition, and creativity are explored. Male mysteries have focused upon the hunt, the way of the warrior, and the cycles of the Sun. It's important to realize that in other societies, what we consider "male" and "female" can be cultural and differ greatly. One needs only to look at the image of the Amazon warrior to know that the image of the warrior is not exclusively male. Though modern witches often focus on the balance of the male and female, many find the divine through focus on just one aspect. To a certain extent, the path of gender can also include the path of gender identity for those who do not neatly fall into either side, as well as the path of sexual identity through orientation. Straight, gay, lesbian, transgendered, and intersexed people all have their mysteries. The Lovers card, as well as the Empress/Emperor and Priestess/Magician, embody the ways of gender.

The Path of the Hearth Flame

This is a service path devoted to the mysteries of the home, the family, food, children, and mate. Though these matters seem mundane to most of us, they are a source of rich wisdom and deep spiritual learning that should not be ignored. Our family informs us about ourselves, our own "enlightenment" and lack thereof, in both peaceful and traumatic times. The acts of service that involve caring for a family are embodied by the Greek goddess Hestia and her Roman counterpart Vesta, and are seen in the image of the Empress of the tarot, though most often lacking the fire imagery.

The Path of Service

The path of service is a part of the devotional way, but rather than focusing that devotion on a divine image or tradition, it is focused on humanity or on the planet through service. One is so devoted to the world—and the people, animals, and plants in it—that the divine is found through this service and devotion. In the East, such a path might be called karmic yoga, the yoga of action. The Hierophant is the closest tarot image we have for the path of service.

The Path of the Eclectic

People who stumble into the mysteries, or explore bits and pieces of each path, are still on a mystery path. The path of the wanderer, the seeker, is just as valid. I had a student who was very attached to the path of the seeker, and in one of her initiations, she made a spontaneous announcement that she vowed to always be a seeker. In her mind, she meant that she would be open to all things and never stop learning. Though I agree with the sentiment, I've found many who are attached to being a seeker, never becoming a "finder." You need to find and practice something, to anchor yourself to later continue the search. I've seen many a festival attendant dabble in a variety of rituals and have a mystery experience, an initiatory vision that awakens them. The difficult part of this path is that, as a wandering path, there is no clear way in or clear way out, nor anyone with the responsibility to guide and aid you. You are on your own, and you can easily become confused, deluded, or stuck. For this reason, many traditionalists are against the "eclectic mysteries." This path does work, but it works when you put all the work into it. The Fool is the archetype of the eclectic, for we all begin by wandering and falling into whatever is before us.

Each of these paths represents one way into the mysteries. Just like the three main ways of devotion, observation, and action, they do not represent exclusive ways, where an initiate must choose one of these paths to the exclusion of others; they are gateways. Most of us on the path now can recognize that we walked through at least one of these gates. Most of these mystical paths fall under the main way of doing, for as individuals on magical paths, we must take action! You can also look to see how most can be divided into the two main categories of Dionysian and Apollonian. The paths of ascetics, life, and service have a more Apollonian flair, while seership and death have more in common with Dionysus. Eclectic mysteries and those of gender have a mix of both, depending on the focus of the mystery. As you grow, you realize your path can embody many of these wisdom teachings simultaneously, though their outlooks and philosophies might differ.

Modern witchcraft is a synthesis of all these paths as they come together and separate again, making the whole greater than the sum of the parts. I look at the mysteries in a simplified manner, seeing five levels of the mystery, of training, working in synthesis: the visionary or seership mysteries of the fire and the first level, the fertility mysteries of earth and the second level, the shamanic or ecstatic mysteries of water and the third level, the Gnostic mysteries of air and the fourth level, and finally the mysteries of service for spirit and the fifth level. These are the aspects of modern witchcraft that have worked best together for me.

Like the traditions of Voodou, witchcraft absorbs to survive. We practice a scavenger religion that lets other wisdom rot in order to fertilize and feed our tree. Witchcraft reconciles the mysteries of the male and the female, the God and the Goddess, showing that both are needed to form creation. Witchcraft reconciles the path of the linear and nonlinear mysteries. The ancient city-state traditions of Egypt, Sumer, Greece, and Rome have a much clearer line to them, as these mysteries are written. The traditions of the Celts are much more shamanic, otherworldly, and nonlinear, yet witchcraft brings them together. It reconciles the traditions of the temples, of the formal mystery traditions founded by priests and priestesses, with those of the wild ones—the hedge witches, the cunning ones without structure, authority, or buildings. Witchcraft reconciles all of these mysteries together in the form of the greatest mystery of all—paradox! How can all of these things be true, simultaneously? The experience of the mysteries is the resolution of paradox within the soul of the initiate.

Some will look at the eclecticism of modern witchcraft and feel that a reconciliation of all the mysteries leaves them with one bland soup that contains nothing of value or distinction. My friend Azure thinks that modern witchcraft has a lot of problems because so many people say that everything is equally valid and it doesn't matter what technique you use. He tried to explain it with a basketball analogy. If you want to be an NBA (National Basketball Association) star, or really any kind of athlete, you study with someone who has already done it, who has a successful plan. With this plan, this pattern that is proven to work, you too will get there. There is a path. It's hard, but it's faster and better than wandering. You learn what you need to be the NBA star, and you go and do it.

Though I understand his analogy, and his criticism, I don't agree. And I don't agree with his original premise. Everything is not equally valid in modern witchcraft. Techniques that work are valid. If they don't work for you, you have to find the techniques that do. The traditions are somewhat like operating software for a computer. You need to find the software that works best for your hardware. There are lots of techniques and traditions that hold no value for me, though I don't feel the need to tear them apart if they work for someone else. What works for one successful NBA star might not work for another, yet they are all there, in the NBA. Azure later told me that in terms of spirituality, it's okay to value everything, but in terms of magick, a specific path must be followed, because magick is a skill and talent that is honed with practice, just like the NBA star's athletic skill. It was then I realized that we were speaking two different languages, because for me, there is no separation between my spirituality and my magick. Once you have entered into that crossroads consciousness, you can't separate magick from spirituality, for everything you do is magick and everything you do is spiritual.

There are many paths, even within witchcraft. Rather than watering down the individual paths, they can be woven together under the umbrella of witchcraft, and as each path crosses, it teaches something new to the other. A braided rope is stronger, collectively, than a single strand.

The Places of Initiation Are Within

Initiation is such a controversial word. Like *witch* and *high priest/ess*, it means different things to different people. Many look to the initiatory rituals of Wicca and related traditions as the only valid initiation into witchcraft, and into the mysteries. Yet, when one thinks about the art of witchcraft, those following a familial or hereditary line will tell you that there were few initiation rituals. You were quite literally born into it, though the family may recognize those with talents and "adopt" them. Ritual initiations stem from the idea of making family out of non-blood relatives, like those traditions found in Native American cultures. Such a process was applied in the temple tradition, making sisters and brothers in wisdom.

The modern witchcraft initiations of three levels are definitively Masonic, though you can argue who influences whom—did secret cults of cunning men influence the European Masons, or did cunning men who were Masons bring the practice into traditional Craft? Or far more likely to most historians, was it absent in witchcraft until the modern Renaissances of magick and witchcraft? Many of the founders of modern Wicca, like the members of the Golden Dawn, were already Masons. Did they introduce the three-degree practice relatively recently?

There are non-Gardnerian lines of witchcraft that do initiator rituals. Maxine Sanders, an elder in what is known as the Alexandrian tradition, after her late ex-husband Alex Sanders, reported in a lecture in Georgia in 2006 that her three levels of initiation and elevation where characterized by initiation, penetration, and celebration, and while Alex did have experience in Gardnerian witchcraft, the tradition they were practicing developed along a separate line from Gardner and his New Forest coven. Other hereditary traditions of witchcraft describe a more shamanic-style initiation than Masonic degrees, putting initiates through ordeals and demonstrations of skill.

When I think of initiation, I think of the process of initiation, regardless of the ceremony that surrounds it. To me, initiatory experiences are those that awaken you, expand your consciousness, connect you to something greater than your individual self, or simply show you that you have always been connected and leave you forever changed. This is the essence and aim of every mystery school's teaching. If it occurs through a formal tradition and lineage, or through sincere and thorough self-training, self-education, and self-initiation, it matters not.

Robert Cochrane, also known as Roy Bowers, a vocal opponent to Gardner and Gardnerian witchcraft, is credited with the teaching, "A Witch is born, and not made; or if one is to be made, then tears must be spilt before the moon can be drawn. For the Lady chooses whom she wills to be Her Lover, and those She loves the most, She rends apart before making them Wise." I have many friends who agree. You either are a witch or are not a witch, like being gay or from a specific ethnic background. If you have a strong and sincere interest in the Craft, then that is probably your strongest indicator that you are a witch, and training and rituals will help awaken that within you. If you are insincere in your call to the Craft, then no ritual will truly make you a witch, for you are not called by the Lady.

Doreen Valiente, the high priestess of Gerald Gardner, is responsible for much of the beautiful Wiccan poetry that has become standard in our tradition. She later worked with Cochrane for a short time, and she is well known for the question, "Who initiated the first witch?" She has a point. Where did it start? Someone must have made a direct connection to be able to pass on that lineage. Though initiatory lineage traditions have something that most self-initiations do not, a current of energy, a bank of power built up by that tradition, it must have started somewhere. It must have been passed on from inner-plane sources, the Hidden Company of inner-plane priests and priestesses of witchcraft. Ideally, in the best physical initiation rituals, the priests and priestesses on the other side, the ancestor witches, as well as the fey, the gods, and spirits, reach through the initiator's body and hands to lay blessings upon the individual and transfer the current.

If that link can be forged once directly, it can be forged again, and a different current can be brought through. One of the main aims of the Temple of Witchcraft tradition is to create a teaching that has a "current," a thoughtform built by those who have been practicing it and forging a personal link to the inner planes. This is to create a method where people can tap into it through their sincere actions and not be dependent upon a physical teacher if a reputable one is not available. Some teachers in the physical world use initiation as a carrot to dangle before their prospective students, and they use it to build their cults of personality, using the lure of secret knowledge that can't be found in a book—though many more deny initiation because they feel the students have not met the requirements or level of training. For those who want to work directly with the inner-plane teachers, this is a potential method. They will accurately determine what is best for you, without any personal politics. If the source of the current comes from the inner planes, then the places of initiation are really within. Initiation occurs beyond space and time, for it really occurs on the inner planes.

THE SEVEN CHAKRAS AS SEVEN TEMPLES OF INITIATION

The best model I have found for the initiation and elevation process of the mysteries while teaching in the context of modern witchcraft is the sevenfold process. We see our initiation mysteries in many of the sevenfold symbols of modern occultism.

For the witch, the seven steps are embodied in the tale of the Descent of the Goddess. This tale is told or reenacted in initiation rites at the second or third degree, depending on the tradition. Though there are many versions of the tale, including a modern Wiccan recitation, the origin most likely lies with Inanna, Queen of Heaven and Earth. While the modern Wiccan tale is abridged, and sometimes confusing to the seeker, the tale of Inanna, while still a mystery, does not omit the seven important gateways to the Underworld.

LEGEND OF THE DESCENT OF THE GODDESS

Now our Lady the Goddess has never loved, but she would solve all the mysteries, even the mystery of Death. And so she journeyed to the Underworld.

The Guardian of the Portals challenged her: "Strip off thy garments, lay aside thy jewels, for naught mayest thou bring with thee into this land." So she laid down her garments and her jewels, and was bound as are all who enter the Realms of Death, the Mighty One.

Such was her beauty that Death himself knelt and kissed her feet, saying, "Blessed be thy feet, that have brought thee in these ways. Abide with me, but let me place my cold hand on thy heart."

She replied, "I love thee not. Why dost thou cause all things that I love and take delight in to fade and die?"

"Lady," replied Death, "'tis age and fate, against which I am helpless. Age causes all things to wither, but when men die at the end of time, I give them rest and peace, and strength so that they may return. But thou! Thou art lovely. Return not; abide with me!"

But she answered, "I love thee not."

Then Death said, "An' thou receivest not my hand on thy heart, thou must receive Death's scourge."

"It is fate—better so," she said. And she knelt and Death scourgest her tenderly. And she cried, "I feel the pangs of love."

And Death said, "Blessed be!" and gave her the Fivefold Kiss, saying, "Thus only mayest thou attain to joy and knowledge," and he taught her all the mysteries, and they loved and were one, and he gave her all the Magicks.

For there are three great events in the life of man: Love, Death, and Resurrection in the new body; and Magick controls them all. For to fulfill love you must return again at the same time and place as the loved one, and you must remember and love them again. But to be reborn you must die and be ready for a new body, and to die you must be born; and without Love you may not be born; and that is all the Magicks.

Figure 1: Legend of the Descent of the Goddess

Inanna descends to the Underworld, to the domain of her sister, Erishkigal, who is painfully pregnant. In each level of the Underworld, seven in all, she is asked to remove one of her garments, one of her vestments of power, as payment to pass through the gate. One notices an interesting pattern as the items are removed from the top of the head downward, until she is naked before her terrible sister in the lowest level of the Underworld. She is killed, and through her own ingenuity and aid from the divine powers, she is resurrected, stronger than before. She is reborn in the world after attaining the mysteries of death. Inanna's story is one of initiation. We see all descending goddesses as initiatiates. Persephone goes through a similar experience in Greek mythology. Astarte, and her seven veils, are similar to the image of the seven levels of the Underworld.

My favorite telling of the descent of Inanna is found in the beautiful translations of the Sumerian cuneiform in *Inanna: Queen of Heaven and Earth* by Diane Wolkstein and Samuel Noah Kramer. It both accurately and artistically tells the tale of Inanna in a way that makes the seven gates of initiation apparent.

The seven gateways and the seven payments are reminiscent of the Hindu chakra system, much adopted by modern pagans and magicians to describe the energy centers found in the human body. As Inanna descends and gives up each article, they almost exactly correlate with the chakras, starting with the crown. Each step down is a step deeper into the seven gates of the energy system, from the most sublime and spiritual to the densest root. When she finally gives up her robe, her only outer covering, at the seventh gate, she is brought before her sister naked and helpless, corresponding to the newborn child, and the first energy center at the base of the spine, where the struggle is for survival itself, for life over death. And there, through the seventh gate, she experiences the mystery of death and rebirth. When you observe the seven chakras, descending or ascending, you see a set of teachings that represent the ways of learning, of both life and the mysteries of magick and the initiate. By studying the sevenfold model, by looking at the chakras as the temple of initiation within yourself, you can experience the mysteries common to all of us and become elevated through those mysteries into self-mastery, which will fully prepare you for the role of the high priest/ess.

Sevens repeat themselves time and again in our lore and mythology. We have the obvious days of the week with their sevenfold planetary associations. The ancients looked at seven, not ten, planets in astrology. The Sun and Moon, along with Mercury, Venus,

Figure 2: Labyrinth

Mars, Jupiter, and Saturn, were the wandering stars, as the outer planets couldn't be easily detected. These seven planets correspond to the "seven heavens" of the cosmos, a good corollary to the seven "hells" of the Underworld, though an initiate knows "As above, so below," and the concepts of up and down, heaven and hell, are just reflections of each other.

In the Cretan maze, the labyrinth image of the ancient civilization, we find a seven-fold turning pattern (figure 2). Modern labyrinth enthusiasts believe that walking this particular mandala actually balances the seven chakras. Similar images are found in Cornwall and Glastonbury. The Tor of Glastonbury (figure 3), when walked in a spiraling motion, has a seven-step process. Many people report profound experiences and awakenings simply by walking the path that spirals up and down the Tor, the hilltop, and meditating at the top near St. Michael's Tower, a powerful site where ley lines are said to converge in a vortex of tellurian power. Many believe the Tor was once surrounded by water, and it may have contributed to the myth of Avalon. The top of

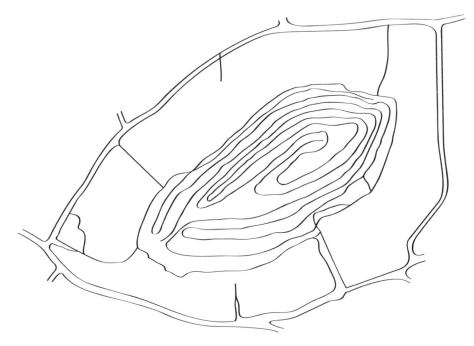

Figure 3: Glastonbury Tor

the Tor was an island, the sacred land of the priestesses of the old religion. While the pagans left no permanent structure on the Tor, Christians in the later era built a tower to St. Michael there. The ley lines that converge there are described as the Michael and Mary lines (which strikes me as Christian terminology for God and Goddess) and the earth's Pingala and Ida channels, intersecting at a chakra point on or in the Tor. Today Glastonbury serves as a holy site for pagans, Christians, and those involved in the New Age, though skeptics say that the Tor's path is a tiered farming remnant, not a spiritual labyrinth. In our modern day of paradox, it can now be both.

Though not specifically a spiraling labyrinth, modern metaphysicians, such as author Barbara Hand Clow, look at the Egyptian temples along the winding Nile River as initiation temples for an extended chakra system. Each temple specialized in the teachings of the chakras, similar to the stages the goddess Inanna experienced through her descent through the seven gates. Metaphysical Egyptologist Ahmed Fayed has also done a lot of work corresponding the Egyptian temples with the Nile, and he influenced my own modern understanding of the temple system. Traditional Egyptologists would squarely argue that the Egyptian Nile temples have nothing to do with the Hindu chakras, but for the Khemetic-inclined witch, such a system, even if it's wholly a modern correspondence, can be quite helpful in pathworking and rituals.

The Celtic Otherworld is divided into three basic realms, much like the shamanic World Tree, but instead of a vertical axis, they are described as concentric rings. The central realm is the Underworld realm of Annwn (figure 4). In the legends of King Arthur, the realm of Annwn itself is divided into seven rings. Each realm has a castle, or *caer*, which one must pass through on the search for the Holy Grail in the center, Caer Sidi. Caers were traditionally thought of as defensive earth mounds, or even the prehistoric burial mounds associated with the faery folk, but later, particularly in the poem "The Spoils of Annwn," they were associated with otherworldly castles. The realms, the concentric rings, are separated by rings of water, which is why one needs entrance to the gate, with its drawbridge, to pass the moat. The seven castles are known as Caer Ochren, Caer Fandy-Manddwy, Caer Goludd, Caer Rigor, Caer Fredwyd, Caer Pedryfan, and Caer Sidi. Though this is the order of castles used by many witches today, no clear-cut "chakra-like" order is given in their original texts. We speculate the original source material was garbled in translation, or purposely coded and mixed up. This is the order of the caers I was first introduced to, and it works best in a comparison with the seven gates. The aforementioned Tor of Glastonbury has been associated with Annwn, through the god known as Gwynn ap Nudd, who guards the gate between the worlds. For many Celtic legends, the concept of Otherworld and Underworld is the same, providing an excellent corollary between Annwn and the realm of Inanna's sister, Erishkigal. The rings of Annwn, the Descent of the Goddess, the seven planes of reality, and the Cretan labyrinth are all models to describe the Otherworld and the places of initiation we find through communing with these energies. Annwn is not just a map of the Otherworld, but related specifically to the Underworld, to the cauldron of the Underworld that shapes creation. Just as Inanna goes through seven Underworld hells, the Celtic heroes descend into these seven rings of Annwn. This parallels similar ideas in Aztec mythology of thirteen heavens and nine hells symbolically, if not literally. Though it's enticing to think that the ancient Celts, Sumerians, and Aztecs used the energy system of the chakras in the way that we do today, via the esoteric teaching

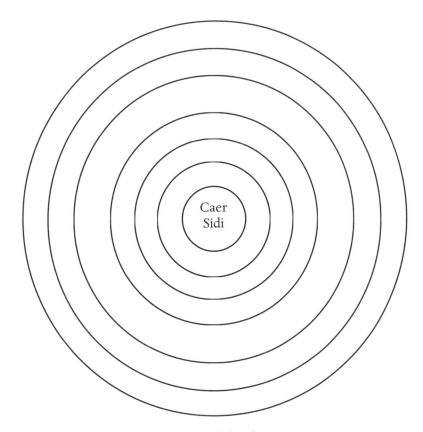

Caer
Sidi

Figure 4: Seven Circles of Annwn

of India, we have no proof. Yet they provide interesting models for the modern pagan practitioner.

Theosophical lore and the mysticism of modern ascension spirituality teach the concept of seven rays, colored much like the rainbow. The color associations are similar to the chakras, but they are not quite an exact corollary. Each ray has an archetypal quality to it, and a variety of spirits, ascended masters, and angels are associated with guiding and mediating each ray's energy in the world. The three primary rays are based on the primary colors—red, blue, and yellow. From the third, or yellow ray, emanates their combinations of green, orange, indigo, and violet. The ray associations are described as follows:

First Ray	Red	Will and Power
Second Ray	Blue	Love and Compassion
Third Ray	Yellow	Active Intelligence
Fourth Ray	Green	Harmony through Conflict, Nature, Art
Fifth Ray	Orange	Concrete Science
Sixth Ray	Indigo	Religion and Devotion
Seventh Ray	Violet	Ceremonial Order, Magick, Ritual

Witches are obviously most concerned about the seventh ray, as in this system, it is the ray that guides our tradition, along with a mix of the green ray. Kevin Saunders, in his book *Advanced Wiccan Spirituality*, makes a comparison of the seven rays with the Celtic teachings of the Stag of Seven Tines. It's as if the creative force embodied by the horned god radiates out each of these seven archetypal energies from the seven tines of his horns. Though many would think these teachings have no place in serious magick, the magicians from the turn of the century, the notables who have influenced Wicca from the Golden Dawn such as Dion Fortune, spoke of the science of the rays to describe the soul and the soul's mission.

In alchemy, we have the seven major operations of the alchemical process. The generalized three-stage process of separation, purification, and cohabitation—where a substance, or initiate, is taken apart, purified, and put back together stronger than before—can be expanded into the sevenfold process of calcination, dissolution, separation, conjunction, fermentation, distillation, and coagulation. These seven stages are related to the seven planets and the seven alchemical metals. Modern alchemists link them to the chakras and tarot cards. Some alchemical lore speaks of a tower, a meditative construct similar to our inner temple teachings. It is also known as the Interior Castle or the Keep. This tower often has seven levels, where the operations are performed in the inner realm, as the initiate climbs the tower to the highest realm. The alchemist's tower uses the same symbolism as the gates of the Underworld and the descent of Inanna, though the path ascends rather than descends. Some fear working with these energies directly in the body, and they use images outside of the body, such as this tower, to safely activate and align the forces that produce a change within us. The alchemist's fire is the same as the yogi's kundalini. It's the witch's inner fire or inner power as well. Alchemy developed out of the herb practices and smithcraft so intimately associated with the witch and magician. Nature is the greatest alchemist ever, transforming all things, and we know that nature, as the Goddess and God manifest, is the greatest teacher and initiator. We are a religion that ultimately venerates nature, the divine manifest, as the major way we experience the divine. Alchemy is simply another exploration of divinity through nature.

The mystery of the cakes and ale/wine in Wicca is overlooked by many modern witches. The original mystery of the tradition includes the planting, cultivation, growth, and then transformation of the raw materials—the grains, yeast, and fruits—through baking and fermentation, to the finished products of food and drink, the stuff of life. Reflection upon each step, and in fact, making your own breads and spirits, can be a rich, active form of ritual and meditation for understanding the transformational process the initiate undergoes, much like the laboratory process of alchemy. In the Sumerian version of the Descent of the Goddess, Inanna is restored to life by her faithful servants through the Food of Life and the Waters of Life, miraculous substances that resurrect her. Only substances that have "died" and have been reborn can confer that power to another. Many modern witches shy away from such sacraments as they consider them to be too Christian. I know I originally felt the same, but these traditions have deep pagan history to them. Though I have not been fortunate enough to have the land to cultivate wheat or grapes from seed and make my own cakes and wine, I've raised many plants from seeds to eventually harvest and transform into medicines, potions, and charms. The process of cultivation added deeply to my understanding of the life force within the green world, and within myself.

Author Nigel Pennick, in his book *Secrets of East Anglian Magic,* briefly touches upon a six-grade system of rank and initiation, based upon the "Miracle of Bread" in the lore of East Anglian magick and the Horseman's Guild. The six levels he shares with his readers are the Plough, Seed, Green Corn, Yellow Corn, Stones, and Resurrection. If we allow the addition of a seventh, the consumption of the bread, we have a pattern that fits quite nicely into our sevenfold teachings of this text. As Pennick is a member of a non-Gardnerian tradition known as the Way of the Eight Winds, one can wonder how the Miracle of Bread fits with older, less popularized forms of witchcraft. By looking into this often-forgotten wisdom, we can find other keys to deepen our own experiences. Since little is written on these Horseman ranks, the information in each lesson regarding the Miracle of Bread is really based upon my own musing of the titles and my experiences in plant cultivation and baking.

Even the Left Hand Path traditions have a system of initiation. Rather than explore ritualistic initiations, Don Webb, author and priest of the Temple of Set, in his book *Uncle Setnakt's Essential Guide to the Left Hand Path*, outlines a model of life initiations for the Left Hand Path magician. This too is in seven stages with virtues and vices, much like our study of the sephiroth of the Qabalah. Though many witches will not seek out any wisdom that is labeled Left Hand Path, I think these stages are worth a deeper look by any initiate, and we will be examining them in detail as we progress. Many witches could learn a lot by understanding this process of life initiation and the pitfalls one can encounter.

	Stage	*Vice*	*Virtue*
1	Wandering	Narcissism	Magickal Curiosity
2	Shock	Hubris	Quantifiable Pride
3	Daydreaming	Forgetfulness of Past Orthodoxies	Sense of Humor
4	Shock	Despair	Openness
5	School	Attachment to the Thoughts of Another	Moderation
6	Shock	Obsession with Magick	Synthesis
7	Work	Emotional Servitude	Cunning

All of these sevenfold patterns can be found in the symbol of the septagram, or Faery Star (figure 5). Initiates of traditions using the seven-pointed star have symbolism and teachings on the star's inner meanings that basically follow the previous teachings—that the points are the seven gates to "hell" or the seven rays emanating from the divine.

Ultimately, initiation, in whatever form, is like planting a seed. The initiation must take root. Some initiations fail. Some are never nurtured. Some grow wildly and then wither, never bearing fruit. Some describe initiation as lighting a flame. Once the flame is lit, by the gods or by a lineage teacher, it is up to the student to nurture it, feed it, and make it grow into a roaring fire. The fire then becomes the secret flame that purifies and transforms, shining out from you. Many initiates let the light go out and the

Figure 5: Seven-Pointed Star

initiation does not "take" into a transforming experience. The initiation experience or ritual is really just the beginning of the process. If you have a stronger understanding of the inner mechanism of your own consciousness expansion, then you will be better equipped to nurture all your initiatory and elevation experiences and grow into an adept, leader, and high priest/ess.

EXERCISE 1

Inner Temple as a Mystery School Meditation

1. Get into a comfortable position. Take a few deep breaths and relax your body, starting at the head, and bring your awareness and relaxation down through the body to the tips of your toes. As you breathe, release the tension. Relax your mind. Release any unwanted thoughts and worries as you exhale. Relax your heart and open it to the love of the Goddess and God. Relax your soul and follow your inner light, guidance, and protection.

2. Visualize a giant screen before you, like a blackboard or movie screen. This is the screen of your mind, or what is called your mind's eye. On the screen of your mind, visualize a series of numbers, counting down from twelve to one. With each number, you get into a deeper meditative state. You are at your ritual consciousness. Everything done at this level is for your highest good, harming none.

3. You are now counting down to a deeper, more focused meditative state. Count backward from thirteen to one, but do not visualize the numbers this time. Let the numbers gently take you down. Thirteen, twelve, eleven, ten, nine, eight, seven, six, five, four, three, two, and one. You are now at your deepest meditative state, your magical mindset, in complete control of your magical abilities. Say to yourself:

   I ask the Goddess and God to protect and guide me in this meditation.

4. In your mind's eye, visualize the great World Tree, reaching up to the heavens and deep below the earth, larger than any tree you have ever seen. Simply know the tree is there and it will be.

5. Imagine the screen of your mind's eye is like a window or doorway, a portal you can easily pass through. Step through the screen and stand before the World Tree. Hear the wind through its branches. Smell the earth where its roots dig in. Feel the texture of the bark. Touch the tree and place in it the intention of visiting your inner temple. Look around the base of the giant tree for the passageway to your inner temple. Go now through the tunnel to your inner temple.

6. Look around the familiar inner temple. Take notice of any changes that have manifested since the last time you have visited. The changes reflect changes in your own inner self. Call upon any of your familiar spirit guides, and ask them for any messages you need at this time.

7. Now ask your guides' aid in dedicating this inner temple as your own personal mystery school. Fill the temple space with your intention and bless-

ing. You might feel it take a shape or form that is different. Go with it. The familiar gateways might lead to different places. From the temple we will be working with seven initiatory temples, for the seven chakras. Each will lead to the next. You could find the image of the seven-pointed star, seven concentric rings, or the labyrinth etched into your temple.

8. Once done, return through the World Tree tunnel that brought you to this place, and stand before the World Tree. Thank the World Tree for this journey. Step back through the screen of your mind's eye, and let the World Tree gently fade from view.

9. Return back to normal consciousness, counting from one to thirteen and then from one to twelve. You do not have to visualize the numbers. Wiggle your fingers and toes, and slowly move to bring your awareness back to the physical.

10. Take both hands and raise them up over your head, palms facing your crown. Slowly bring them down over your forehead, face, throat, chest, abdomen, and then groin, and "push out" with your palms facing away from you. This gives you clearance and balance, releasing any harmful or unwanted energies you might pick up during your magickal experiences. Tell yourself:

    I give myself clearance and balance. I am in balance with myself. I am in balance with the universe. I release all that does not serve.

11. Ground yourself as needed.

Homework

- Complete the questionnaire in appendix I.

- Perform exercise 1. Record your experience in your Book of Shadows (BOS) or magickal journal.

- Have your personal working cord of your three power colors braided and consecrated, ready to be used in each lesson when a knot will be tied at the completion of that lesson to signify your completion (see introduction). You can have it braided, and hold it as you perform exercise 1. I chose the colors that aligned best with my own personal sense of soul mission with the colored rays of Theosophy, choosing the ray of will (red), the ray of nature and art (green), and the ray of magick (violet).

TIPS

- Your inner temple might change, or destabilize during this Living Temple of Witchcraft process. This is totally normal. As you change, it changes, as it's a reflection of you. This is a time and course inducing great change. You will never be the same again, and your temple will reflect it. Find a "solidness" in yourself, and in your relationship with your spirit allies, rather than in an attachment to a specific form for your inner temple.

Lesson One
Temple of the Root:
Survival and Origin

Rather than descend as the Goddess did, from the crown to the depths, we begin our journey of self-mastery at the base, at the bottom, embodied by the root chakra. Here we have the powers of survival. It is this energy, red, mixing the powers of both fire and earth, that anchors us in the world and gives us the drive to survive. The procreation principle, for pure survival and pure pleasure, is found through the root. It is the passing on of genetics for the future. It carries the templates of our blood, our ancestors, and the origins of our people.

Prepare for this month's lesson and workings by adding tools to your altar that resonate with the root chakra. Place a single red candle on the altar. Use red stones, such as raw rubies, garnets, or red jasper around the candle. Sexual statuary and tools will be appropriate, such as a phallus and/or yoni image. Use any incense or oils that are associated with Saturn, the primary planet of the root chakra, for its grounding earth aspect, or its secondary planet, Mars, for its fiery red color. Place any tools on the altar that reflect the energies of the root chakra and the first temple you will be exploring.

Before you get into the lesson and hear a teacher's perspective on this lesson, first listen to your body. If all the temples of initiation are within, by feeling them within yourself, you will get many clues as to your own personal work in each temple of initiation, and how well connected you are to its power. This goes beyond any simple chakra scanning and balancing. We don't seek to balance the chakra in relationship to the rest of the energy field. We seek to immerse ourselves in its mysteries and fully integrate them into our consciousness.

Exercise 2

Contemplation on the Temple of the Root

1. Sit quietly in a comfortable position and enter a meditative state. Call upon higher guidance, through your own spirit guides and the Goddess, God, and Great Spirit.

2. Place your hands on the root area. Some imagine the root at the base of the spine, the tailbone, while others see it at the perineum point, between the anus and the sex organs. I suggest gently cupping your hands near the perineum point in the way that is most comfortable to you.

3. Feel the energy of the root chakra. Start with your hands, but let any sensations move through your entire body. You might feel as if your entire energy field is surrounded in red light. Ask the root chakra to reveal its mysteries to you.

4. Observe the thoughts, feelings, visions, and insights you have, as well as messages you receive, while attuning yourself to the Temple of the Root. These will guide you in this lesson to your own personal work.

5. When done, return yourself from the meditative state. Thank the energy of the root chakra as well as your spiritual guidance, and give yourself clearance and balance.

Magickal Teaching: Origin

Force: Gravity

Chakra: Root

Function: Survival

Body: Physical

Tool of the Goddess: Robe

Alternate Tool of the Goddess: Gown

Color: Red

Ray: First—The Ray of Will and Power

Elements: Fire, Earth

Planet: Saturn

Metal: Lead

Signs: Aries, Sagittarius

Emerald Tablet Rubric: Its Father Is the Sun

Alchemical Operation: Calcination

Totem: Crow

Plant: Horsetail

Sephira: Malkuth

Tarot, Lunar: Trump I—Magician

Tarot, Solar: Trump VIII—Justice / Adjustment

Tarot, Stellar: Trump XV—The Devil

Life Stage: Birth / Wiccaning

Hermetic Principle: Mentalism

Musical Note: C

Day of the Week: Saturday

Castle of the Underworld: Caer Ochren—Castle of Dread, Castle of the Shelving Tide, the Castle of Ceridwen, the Enclosed Castle, Castle of Keys, Castle of Trees

Egyptian Temple Site: Elephantine Island, Aswan

Left Hand Initiation: Wandering
Vice of Initiation: Narcissism
Virtue of Initiation: Magical Curiosity
Stage of the Bread Miracle: Plough
Challenge of the Temple: Materialism
Blessing of the Temple: Sensuality

The Temple of the Root teaches us the first lessons of life. It is the foundation of the mysteries, teaching us how to survive in the world and where we come from—at least our physical origins. Mastering our needs in the physical world is a key component to the witch's expansion into deeper levels of consciousness. Much of the first training witches undergo is for spellcraft. Outsiders look at our spell books, seeing charms for money, love, sex, healing, and protection, and wonder if we are a spiritual tradition at all. To the outsider, those things don't seem very spiritual, because our world, at least much of our Western world, has been brainwashed to think that taking care of your physical and emotional needs, your base needs, is not spiritual. We have been brain-washed by the dominant institutions to think that renouncement and denial are the spiritual roads, while indulgence and exploration are not. For a witch, nothing could be further from the truth.

Our first magick is usually for ourselves, involving these base needs, because until we take care of our absolute needs and our longing desires, we won't have the energy or awareness to enter into more expanded states of consciousness and hear the call to serve. We follow a middle path. We don't believe you need riches and luxury to do well, nor do we believe you need to live in poverty. We believe you should be healthy on all levels, having proper food, home, and heat, and healthy emotionally, drawing to you appropriate friends, lovers, and spouses, while warding off and protecting yourself from the people and situations that will drain your energy. Once you have those basic needs met, you will have your foundation for deeper studies, and a true understanding that your thoughts and words create your reality. You will have skills to maintain and improve your daily life as your circumstances change, and will not feel victim to the world, but a partner with it. As you take care of these needs, you will develop relation-ships that will strengthen you. Your current friendships and family relationships could grow deeper, clearer, and more spiritual as you transform and affect them. You might also lose some of your friends as you walk the path, and you might gain new ones who understand and support you. This is your sense of foundation through your family of both blood and spirit. They serve to support you and you support them. As you hear the call of the high priest/ess, you will then serve as the foundation for the next generation.

When we think of the Stone Age witches, the archetype is not of the young hunter or gatherer, physically taking care of the tribe, but the older wise one, or wounded warrior, who has served the community in that capacity but now serves their spiritual needs. The foundation for the tribe is there, taking care of their needs for food and shelter. With those needs met, other aspects of culture begin to develop, from shamanic forms of witchcraft and magick to the arts. If they were individual and alone, with no sense of foundation and family, culture would not have developed, nor magick, and the need for individual survival would have been paramount.

By fostering a sense of where you come from, as well as your circle of support—those who are family and who are like family—you will have the assistance you need to pursue other avenues in life, including spirituality and magick. However, unlike the tribal witches, most of us do not rely on our tribemates directly for our basic daily needs of food and shelter. We belong to an overall society that has structures to provide for these needs so our sense of origin and foundation goes far beyond those individuals we know personally. In this modern age, we have to start looking at the whole world, not just our local communities, as our tribe.

THE MYSTERIES OF THE PHYSICAL BODY

When the Goddess descended to the Underworld, the last of her possessions, given at the seventh gate, was her robe. The robe covers the body, protecting the body from the elements. In reality, the robe is not her last physical possession. Her body is. The body is the first thing we own when we come into this world, and it is the last possession we relinquish when we leave. The robe simply covers the body. As she faced the powers of the Underworld, she did so like a newborn babe, naked. She could hide behind nothing. In many ways, this is the secret teaching behind being skyclad in ritual. It's not simply to prevent the energy from being impeded, as some traditions teach, for we know cloth doesn't impede magickal force if it can easily pass through walls and go around the world.

In *The Charge of the Goddess*, a famous Wiccan ritual poem drawn from *Aradia, or the Gospel of the Witches* and reworked by Doreen Valiente, the Goddess says, "You shall be free from slavery, and as a sign that you be free you shall be naked in your rites. Sing, feast, dance, make music and love, all in My presence, for Mine is the ecstasy of the spirit and Mine also is joy on earth." Being skyclad is being free from slavery, and at the time of *The Charge*'s original writing in the Aradia teachings, it would include the slavery of society, if not actual slavery. Those in the circle would not hold worldly ranks or castes, for all are equal in the circle. The Goddess is also bidding us to enjoy the flesh through dance, music, touch, affection, and sexuality, linking the powers of spirit to those on Earth, to the body. They are all acts that lead to the Goddess. What prevents us from enjoying those things, in taking part in the pleasures of life and the body? The repressive structure of our society, and the "armor" we put on through our clothing, marks our social status. How often have you judged others by what they were wearing? Have you ever been wrong? I know I have.

Being skyclad is more than just taking off your clothing so that we are all the same, without rank or status. It is a concept to be held in your heart. The time when we were purest, and simply enjoyed things based on sensation, was in childhood, like the naked babe who doesn't know she is naked. It takes us back to the lifestage of birth, of the child blessing or Wiccaning. By disrobing, the Goddess teaches us to be innocent in the heart and mind, to be open, regardless of what we are or are not wearing. We are called to be more childlike.

I'm often accused of being naïve or too innocent when it comes to worldly affairs and business. I assume that people are what they say they are, and that they are telling me the truth unless I have reason to believe otherwise. I am pretty open about most of my life and experiences. I've been told by some that I'm too open, yet I think of it as being skyclad. Though I may be "naked," I don't feel cold. I don't feel defenseless. It is in those moments that I feel the Goddess all around me. In the end, there is very little anybody can use against me, because I'm open and sharing with almost everyone. If my assumptions turn out to be wrong, I act accordingly, but I'd rather trust and be wrong than lose the opportunity to make a true connection. I trust my instincts, but I also trust myself and my Goddess, and I know that if I'm anchored in my truth with my will, and acting ethically, there is very little that can bring me harm. I don't need to conceal myself under rigid armor or a façade of any kind as long as I maintain the sacred space in and around me.

The Temple of the Root teaches us many things about the body. Not only is it the temple of taking care of the body, of physically nourishing and protecting it, it is also the temple of enjoying the body, enjoying the things we physically take into the body. We enjoy the senses. We enjoy the tastes, touches, smells, sounds, and sights. Our physical senses are the points on the pentagram, but few witches do anything to actively develop them. We are so desiring to open their psychic equivalents, we don't focus on the sacredness of the world all around us.

How often do we really taste the food we are eating? Americans in particular have a strange sense of taste due to all the preservatives in our food. I'm amazed when speaking to friends from other countries who talk about how bland our food is compared to theirs. I didn't notice until it was pointed out to me, and I started both traveling more and taking notice of where my food comes from and how it was prepared, fresh or packaged. It is an amazing difference.

We rarely actively and consciously smell our food before we eat it, yet that is an important part of the meal. We do not pay very much attention to our sense of smell, yet it is a part of our early warning system. We can smell "fear" and other emotions, just like animals do. Those who have a greater olfactory awareness know that even with impeccable personal hygiene, all people have a personal scent, even without oils, perfumes, and colognes. It often has to do with the foods consumed. You usually don't smell those around you who come from the same ethnic group and consume the same foods, but if you visit others, you can tell the difference in scent, both in the home and in the scent on the skin.

While the second chakra is about emotional intimacy on a sexual level, the root is about pure physical pleasure. We all need to be touched, and touch is an amazing way to make a connection with another, as well as stimulate your immune system and generally improve health. Touch doesn't always have to be sexual. It can be sensual, affectionate, or nurturing. Massage is a great form of healing touch with a wide range of applications.

Sound is another amazing component to full sensory experiences. Most of us listen to sound in a linear way, paying attention to sequences of words and the cadence of melody of a voice or instrument. Yet there is a wide range of "vertical" sound, of layered harmonies and depths of sound. It's most apparent in classical music, yet everything has a depth of sound to it. We learn to block out sounds. When we meditate, we can become hyperaware of all the sounds in the house, and see them as a distraction. But paying attention to sound, to the pitch, rhythm, dynamics, and timbre, can be a deep meditation in itself. Whether you are outside in a forest or in a city somewhere, close your eyes and meditate upon the sounds.

Lastly, sight is the most focused-upon sense, yet our eyesight continues to grow worse and worse. Many of us, as students of the occult, have a great love of books. With the Internet and modern media, we are using our eyes more to the detriment of their skill and the other senses. Yet our vision is not as static as people think. After reading Jacob Liberman's book *Take Off Your Glasses and See*, I began studies in holistic and magickal eye care, and I realized that sight fluctuates with consciousness and can be improved upon with exercises, meditation, and magickal remedies. Though I have not lost my glasses at the time of this writing, over a few years my optometrist has weakened my prescription strength as my vision has improved. Learning to "see" in different ways, rather than merely a short-range, reading focus, has opened my psychic sight as well.

EXERCISE 3

Opening the Senses

1. This is a great exercise to do in a quiet spot outdoors, but it's not necessary to be outdoors to do it. Set out before you a piece of food, a small quantity of oil or incense and something with a noticeable texture.

2. Perform Exercise 1: Inner Temple as a Mystery School Meditation (page 45), steps 1–3, to get into a meditative state.

3. As you breathe, feel the energy flow through your body, moving with your breath.

4. Open your eyes gently, and imagine breathing through your eyes, drawing prana in through the eyes and out through the eyes, revitalizing your sense of sight. Feel your eyes awakening. Look around your environment, gazing at the world in an open focus, not staring too long at any one thing. Do the colors seem different? Do the shapes and outlines seem different? How?

5. When ready, begin the same process, but through your ears. Imagine that you are breathing through your ears and that the prana carries sound in a new way, revitalizing your sense of hearing. Feel your ears awaken. Listen to all the sounds in your environment, wherever you are. Is the sound different? How so?

6. Repeat the process, but with your nose. You are already capable of physically breathing through your nose, but focus on the energy going in and out, revitalizing your sense of smell. Feel your nose awaken. First smell your current environment. Can you smell anything now that you couldn't a few moments ago? Then smell the oil or, if using incense instead, light the incense and smell it. Does it seem different to you?

7. Breathe energy through your skin, but particularly through your hands. Feel the energy going in and out, revitalizing your sense of touch and sensitizing you not only to energy, but to physical matter and to temperature. Awaken your sense of touch. Pick up something and feel its texture. Does it feel different to you?

8. Finally, breathe through your mouth, but also your tongue, your taste buds. Feel the energy going in and out, revitalizing your sense of taste. Feel your mouth awaken. Eat something. Notice how it tastes. Pick up on the full range of flavor, being present with each bite.

9. Breathe energy simultaneously through the eyes, ears, nose, skin, and mouth. Feel all your senses awaken. Affirm that these senses will remain awake.

10. End with exercise 1, steps 9–11.

In the teachings of alchemy, the powers of the first temple are embodied by the process of calcination. To calcinate something, you heat it until it is reduced to white or gray ash. Classically, it is said that you are reducing it to "bone." This process resonates with the planet Saturn, and Saturn is the planet that rules the bones and the healing of the bones. Saturn is also the planet of the taskmaster, the harsh teacher that manifests your karma. It is the discipline necessary to make the spiritual journey. In the alchemical formula of The Emerald Tablet, a key Hermetic document outlining magickal thought and the seven alchemical operations in its poetry, the first operation is cited in the line, "Its father is the Sun." Spiritually, calcination is used to burn away all preexisting structure, to burn away all that doesn't serve. Through an awakening of the inner spark, the secret fire, the safe structures of life are burned away to reveal something deeper and more true. It is the spark of kundalini rising, the inner fire that burns within the crucible of the body. It is the inner light that brings introspection. It is an opportunity to purge the self of false ideas and images, and get a glimpse of the true nature of reality.

The Left Hand initiation system marks the first stage as the precalcination time, where one is wandering in the world, believing that things are as they appear, as society has told them. The potential initiate moves as the wind blows, following the conventions of society, family, or what appears to be fate, with no real direct interaction of True Will. At this point, one might be very self-involved and attached to the image and identity built, yet an initiate will have a magickal curiosity, a desire to know if there is more beyond what he or she has been told.

The Egyptian Temple of the Root is found in the city of Aswan. Aswan is where the country of ancient Egypt was said to begin, and it was considered a major site of trade. It was a garrison town, protecting Egypt, as well as a site of quarries where stone for various temple and statue projects was mined. Aswan's major god was Khnum, the ram-headed god who created people from clay on a potter's wheel. His temple is found on Elephantine Island. The Temple of the Root relates to the birth experience, or creation, as the root is our first chakra, activated most when we are born and developing mass and the physical body the most rapidly. When we are young, our main job is survival, gaining enough size, weight, and food to survive in the world. The temple deals with the transfer of worldly goods, physical protection, and material representations of the divine.

The mysteries of the Plough in the Miracle of Bread relate well to the root chakra lessons. As the mysteries of the root deal with being grounded in the physical world, anchored, in agricultural lore, the land must be opened, so the seed can be planted and take root. In many ways, the most physical action is the ploughing of the land. The plough and land also share sexual symbolism as phallus and yoni.

The first castle of Annwn, Caer Ochren, has been described in several ways in the modern Welsh traditions of witchcraft. Translated as the "Castle of Dread," the "Castle of the Shelving Tide," the "Castle of Ceridwen," and the "Castle of Trees," each gives us some understanding of the nature of this first level. The Castle of Dread evokes the feeling many have about the leaden mysteries and the power of Saturn. The tides fall on the edge, the boundary between the worlds where we must cross to become initiated. Ceridwen is the great initiator of bards and poets, for it is really her cauldron that lies in the center of Annwn. Some translations look at it as the Castle of "Shelving" or "Sloping" Sides, with practitioners believing it to be a reference to the hips or ribs, citing it as an energy center in the body, like a chakra. The Castle of Trees is also a boundary, between the civilized world and the forest, the hedge and bramble that divides the two. Witches of old lived at the edge of the village, literally near the edge, as "betweenness" is common to the role of the witch. We often say we start the spiritual journey lost, unable to tell the forest from the trees. In the depths of the forest, we lack perspective. We cannot really see what is happening in our lives. Trees are also deeply rooted in the land. As the translations have puzzled even scholars, other potential meanings are the "Enclosed Castle" or the "Castle of Keys."

A key teaching of this first temple is that things are not as they appear. As we reduce things to the bone, purifying to the core and stripping away things that are unnecessary, we learn that there is more to reality. When unlocking the true secrets of the body and our needs, we also learn that we are more than our body. This teaching is found in every mystical spiritual tradition, even those such as ours, which holds the body as the divine manifest. It's absolutely true, yet not the whole story. We must learn to embrace, but not overly identify with, the body, for the physical body is simply one of seven bodies we have. Each is like one of the seven robes we don as we pass through the gates to enter the world.

Life and birth themes are found in this gate, like the naked newborn child, but also death themes, for death is simply rebirth into the land of spirits, and birth is like a death to the land of spirits. The gateway swings both ways. Consciousness survives in new forms, in new worlds. Our lower-chakra Scorpionic energy is embodied by sex and death, another way of saying life and death, for the two are intimately tied, and both are associated with the lower body and the root through the reproductive and eliminative systems.

Mystic traditions use death themes and fetishes in their initiation rites, including skulls and bones, crematoriums, funeral pyres, open graves, and graveyards. Each tool is a trigger to remind you of your physical mortality, and to enjoy life while you are here, yet remind you of your spiritual immortality that goes beyond this body, place, and time. This meditation on the skeleton continues that tradition.

EXERCISE 4
Skeleton Meditation

1. Perform Exercise 1: Inner Temple as a Mystery School Meditation (page 45), steps 1–5, to go to your inner temple. Feel your inner temple dedicated to be a mystery school. Feel it permeated with the energies of the Root Temple. You might feel it all around you, or you might be guided to go into another chamber, a separate room that is your Temple of the Root.

2. Search for a mirror, the reflective surface. It could be the same mirror you have worked with before in your first visit to the inner temple (*ITOW*, chapter 14).

3. Look at yourself in the mirror. Take a good, deep look at yourself, as you truly appear in this world, in the world of flesh and blood.

4. As you gaze at your reflection, feel your clothing dissolve away. Look at yourself naked, skyclad. What do you like about your body? What don't you like about your body? Notice your physical attributes. Notice the color of your eyes and hair, the texture of your skin, your build and your birthmarks. What was inherited from your family? What would you change if you could, and what would you keep? Why?

5. As you gaze intently at your naked body's reflection, feel your skin slowly dissolve or peel away. There is no pain. Look at yourself beneath the skin, at the muscles.

6. Peel the muscles away as you look at the organs they protect. See your heart and lungs. See your veins and arteries. See your digestive system, your esophagus, stomach, intestines, liver, and kidneys. See your glands as they secrete hormones.

7. Peel away the organs of your body and look at your nervous system and skeleton. See your eyeballs in your skull. Know your brain is encased within the skull. See the nerves connecting to the spinal cord, detached from the muscles and other organs. See the nerve fibers reaching out of the spine and going through the space where your body once was.

8. Peel away the nervous system, brain, and eyes, leaving just bone. Gaze upon your skeleton, your witch bones, the structure to your power, made from the body of the Earth Mother herself, and your gift here on this Earthwalk.

9. Calcinate your bones. Burn them down to ash. Reduce your skeleton to one simple bone cell. Look into the cell, past the cell membranes into the center, the nucleus. In the nucleus is your DNA, all the physical traits you have are encoded into these twisted chains of molecules, entwined like Hermes' caduceus or the rising snakes of the kundalini through the chakras.

10. Let the cell dissolve into nothingness. Perceive your true self. What do you see, feel, and know?

11. Reform your first cell, with your DNA in the center. Take this time to heal your DNA of any and all problems, any genetic factors that do not serve your highest good any longer. Ask for the blessing of your DNA by the gods. Activate your natural healing powers and sense of health in these genes. You might get flashes of your genetic ancestors, even from generations unknown, stretching back into ancient civilizations. Let their images and messages wash over you. Affirm you will remember them. Bless and thank your DNA and your ancestors.

12. Put yourself together, reversing the process step by step. Let the cell that is you grow and divide rapidly, forming a skeleton. Feel yourself transformed in your witch bones, the core of who and what you are in this life. Bless and thank your skeleton.

13. From the skeleton, form your brain, spinal column, and nervous system. Bless and thank your nervous system.

14. Start filling in your internal organs. See your eyes and tongue, your heart and circulatory system, your respiratory system, your digestive system including stomach, liver, kidneys, and intestines all forming. See your reproductive system. Feel your glands and immune system. All your internal organs go to their proper places. Bless and thank your organs.

15. Cover your body with your muscular system, all healed and in perfect working order. Bless and thank your muscles.

16. Cover your muscles with your skin, and then with your hair and any other features. Bless and thank your skin and hair.

17. Look at yourself in the mirror and know that you are not just your body, yet your body is divine and you are in partnership with it. It is the most perfect vehicle you can have in this lifetime for your specific purpose. Work with your body to bring out your maximum health on all levels.

18. Finish exercise 1, steps 8–11, to return to normal consciousness.

The Mystery of the Spiritual Ages

When we explore the Temple of the Root, we ask ourselves not only where we come from in terms of our body, our physicality, and our tribe, but also where we come from in the larger, spiritual sense. What is our origin? Why are we here? We look to mythologies and creation stories to understand our role in the world, to know where we have been, to better understand where we are going.

Like all mysteries to explore, there are the outer courts and the inner courts. The familiar creation stories we hear in our mythologies are closer to the exoteric teachings of a society, while deeper mystery teachings are kept in secret. There are a number of strange stories presented to the initiate, a secret history and hidden teaching that, like the calcination process, burns away the familiar structure and leaves a spiritual essence, like the purified white ash. Yet these secret teachings are almost unrecognizable to those outside of the mysteries.

Are the secret teachings true? Yes, of course they are. But are they literally true, or true in a mythic sense? That is the question. What can be true for one tradition is simply an allegory for another. Those who assume their truth is *the* truth for all enter dogma and lose the mysteries. The secret teachings simply awaken the initiate to a totally new way of looking at the world, turning things upside down. That is precisely what they are meant to do.

When I first heard these teachings in the context of witchcraft, I thought it was crazy. Here I was, in a practical, down-to-earth, self-empowering tradition, and then I was introduced to all of this nonlinear pseudohistory that people were taking as literal fact, and I thought it was nuts. In fact, I had a teacher who said, "You can see why we don't share this with the general public." She gave the impression of passing on a secret lineage of forbidden knowledge that we were would be entrusted with as the lineage is passed on to us. At the time, I thought that was amazing. Was it just the impression, the atmosphere necessary to pass it on, or was it fact? I still don't know, but I'm open to the mysteries. The craziness of it all actually served as a catalyst, causing me to explore world traditions to find the strands of truth other cultures have, and see what matches up and what is different. I even found it in magickal comics going along with the same mystery theme, in *The Invisibles* and *Promethea*. It pushed me out of the safe little zone of spells and rituals only for the witch, and made me seek the wisdom teachings of the world. Without my comfortable worldview, my neat framework into which everything fit, I had to seek out deeper, truer teachings and verify or modify for myself the ones that I received. I give credit to these teachings for making me a better witch and a seeker of the mysteries.

Though some would suggest that I not reveal these mysteries in a printed medium, they are available widely across the world in print and have been seen in the advent of the Theosophical movement, with their own particular spin on the world's spiritual origin. Their teachings have been adopted and expanded in the modern New Age movement known as ascension spirituality. There is nothing here you cannot find for yourself. As I thought it was all crazy in comparison to witchcraft teachings, I was surprised to find well-respected occultists and witches at the foundation of our modern renaissance of magick taking these teachings seriously. These teachings are still available in print, and they are passed on in various forms in initiatory traditions. I have simply distilled and synthesized the points that were most relevant for me. You are encouraged to study the world myths and find the parts that work best for you.

The essence of these secret teachings on the true nature of the world is that this world we all know is not the first world, nor shall it be the last. We are one step in a longer staircase of worlds. We are one rung on the ladder of spiritual evolution. In essence, the world is not as it appears to be.

The teachings are divided into two branches, one on time, and one on space or location. These other worlds occurred in different ages, and the core of these worlds' civilizations existed in different places, where the land of this planet looked very different from how it does today, populated with very different beings. Though our secret history seems absurd to modern science as a literal truth, it's grounded in age-old wisdom that predates science, wisdom that was the sacred science of its age. When we look at the world, and what the ancients left us, we still marvel at their wonders, neither knowing exactly how or why they built what they did. As modern people, it's easy to think we have all the answers, yet time and again new discoveries are showing us that we have barely scratched the surface of what there is to learn. It's only our arrogance that assumes no other culture on Earth could have learned more, or learned differently, in ages past.

The first fundamental teaching of the secret history deals with time. Time moves in patterns and cycles. As witches, we know this. We watch the cycles of the Moon, Sun, and stars. We learn the pattern of the seasons, of growing and withering. We see the cycles of life and death before us, for they are the true sacred texts of a witch. Yet we can only observe the cycles and seasons of our own lives. What happens when we look at time in a larger perspective? We see larger cycles and patterns. As above, so below. They follow many of the same familiar forms, but manifest in larger ways. They manifest as Great Ages.

As weeks fit into months, and months fit into years, years into decades, and decades into centuries, the larger pattern is what is called an age. Ancient cultures across the world recognized these great cycles of time. How did they learn of them? They couldn't have observed them. Did they notice the patterns, and extrapolate the past and present, or did they, as many legends say, receive the information from an otherworldly source? No one can say for sure, but today, we as modern mystery school students can look at the patterns of past mythologies, and see how our modern brethren have incorporated them into current belief systems.

Mayan and Aztec

The mythos of Central America has caught the attention of many people in the pagan and New Age worlds. It gives one of the most complete pictures, with six worlds to show our ancient lineage. Based upon an ancient sacred calendar, the Mayan timekeepers had methods of accurately predicting planetary orbits and even the solar sunspot cycles, showing that their level of knowledge was far beyond what we ever thought possible. Their mythos and calendar also influenced the Aztecs of the same region.

The Mayans described six worlds. The first world was the world of the jaguar. To the Aztecs, this was the First Sun, the Sun of the earth. Giants ruled the land. In this mythos, the God force is divided much like the Oak and Holly Kings of modern paganism, into Quetzalcoatl and Tezcatlipoca. In the First Sun, the dark god Tezcatlipoca ruled over the earth and the giants. Quetzalcoatl rose up against Tezcatlipoca, and the First Sun was devoured by jaguars. The second world was the world of Wind to the Mayans and Aztecs. In the Second Sun, Quetzalcoatl ruled. He ruled well until the end of the age, when this Sun was destroyed by winds summoned by Tezcatlipoca. The third world was the world of Storm. The Third Sun was ruled by the god Tlaloc, the rain and storm god. Tlaloc upset the balance between Quetzalcoatl and Tezcatlipoca, so Quetzalcoatl brought down a fiery rain to destroy this age. The fourth world was the world of Water, and it was ruled by the goddess of the jade skirt, Chalchiuhtlicue. As a world of water, it would only be natural that this world would be destroyed by floods, and many think this age was the origin of the Great Flood myths, including the story of Noah in the Christian and Jewish Bibles, although there are actually far more ancient pagan tales. The fifth world, or Fifth Sun, is our world. It is the world of Motion or Time. It has not been destroyed yet, though sacred calendars of the Mayans say the end is imminent, specifying the winter solstice of 2012. According to some interpretations of the Aztec calendar, the age was to end in 1987. It will be followed by the sixth world, known as both the world of Earthquake and the world of Incense. It is prophesized to be a golden age of enlightenment, but it will be precipitated by natural or psychic disasters, shocking the world into harmony, or culling out the most diseased parts of civilization.

Hopi

The Hopi of the North American Southwest have an intricate system of worlds that has also gained popularity in the New Age community as native medicine teachings are integrated into the larger whole. The Hopi believe in five worlds, though we currently live in the fourth of the cycle. Their myths detail the nature of each world and how it was destroyed, and relate it symbolically with a part of their sacred ceremonial building, the Kiva.

The first world, or Tokpela, was the time of nature, when humanity was one with the spirits of nature and there was no separation. Fire destroyed the first world. The fire pit of the Kiva correlates with the first world. The second world, or Tokpa, is described as the "fall" from nature, as humanity first separated from the source, creating tribes and villages. Perhaps our Western understanding of this period is more influenced by Christian theology, but it is the classic separation from the divine forces that occurs in creation stories. The hole within the Kiva symbolizes the second world. Ice destroyed this age. The third world, or Kuskurza, was the time of cities, when tribes and villages developed even greater disconnection. The ladder is the Kiva part relating to the third world, which was destroyed by the flood. The fourth world, symbolized by the Kiva entrance, coming up from the ladder of the third world, is not yet destroyed. Known as Tuwaqachi, it is the realm of the present day. It is believed to end soon, and lead us to the fifth age, but the way to the fifth age is not yet clear.

Vedic

The Vedic traditions of India provide some of the best understanding and information of the Great Ages. Their term for one of these ages is the *yuga*, and they describe the yugas in terms of metals. The descending luster and values of the metals show the devolution of spiritual awareness, but also the promise of a new age restoring the ancient wisdom. The names are similar to our scientific terms of Stone Age or Bronze Age, using the material at hand at the time as the age's signature. The yugas are divided into four basic cycles, with some describing a sequence of four descending periods and then four ascending periods, only to repeat the cycle again. They are known as the Satya or Krita Yuga, Treta Yuga, Dvapara Yuga, and Kali Yuga. One teaching says that we descend through these four yugas, each of which lasts for a different time period, and teachings offer conflicting time periods and starting dates, only to start again at the golden age. Another teaching states that we must ascend from another Kali period, climbing our way back to the Satya-Krita Yuga.

The Satya-Krita Yuga is equated with the Golden Age, or the highest aspect of the Atlantean era. In this time period, people experienced the divine directly through meditation. The Treta Yuga is the second period, a Silver Age, where sacrifice is one of the highest mediums of divine communion and metal power is harnessed. We descend further with the Dvapara Yuga, or Copper Age. Worship, as opposed to sacrifice or meditation, is the primary key to divinity. Science flourishes in this time period, an age associated with the death of Krishna. The Kali Yuga is the fourth level, marked by the use of "gifts" and the predominant awareness solely of the physical world and authority figures. We are currently said to be in the Age of Iron, or the Kali Yuga. Though mostly seen as a goddess of destruction and demons, Kali is also embodied in Mother Nature. The Kali Yuga is marked as humanity's collective "dark night of the soul." Some of us have to experience the pain, horror, depression, addiction, and compulsion, while others act as anchors for the timeless wisdom, so that we, in partnership, can move on together to the next cycle. Though teachings on the yugas differ, whether we are heading for another Golden Age or are in the midst of an ascending Kali Yuga, all agree that we are currently in some form of the Kali Yuga.

Greek

Like the Hindus, the classical pagan Greeks divided the ages in terms of metal, descending from gold. The first age was the Age of Chaos, the Age of Creation. From the void was birthed the Great Mother, Gaia, and from her, the sky father, Uranus. Though we think of them in myth as literally Earth and Sky, in their most cosmic "octaves" they are the powers of matter and energy. It was prophesized that Uranus would be deposed by one of his children, and so he kept his children in the womb of the mother, never releasing them. One child, Chronos, used his sickle to castrate his father from inside the womb and then release his siblings, in the process creating the goddess Aphrodite and the triple Furies.

The time of creation yielded to the Golden Age and the Titans, the siblings ruled by Chronos, known as Saturn to the Romans. The world was populated with the golden men. Upon the end of this world, from the uprising of Chronos's children, the golden men ascended to be the heavenly spirits. Zeus, son of Chronos, led his siblings, the Olympians, in a war against the Titans and eventually overthrew his father, instituting the Silver Age. Initially under Zeus, the world was populated by men of silver, whose spirits eventually went to the Underworld beneath the earth. Men were then made of ash, in the Bronze Age, but they, too, perished and made their way to the Underworld. Eventually humans were created, and we entered the Age of Heroes, the time when humans intermingled with all sorts of mythic beasts. The Age of Heroes bridges the gap between the Bronze Age and our current Iron Age.

I was taught by some witches that the Age of Heroes was a literal time, but a time when the veil between worlds was thin, and humans interacted with spirit creatures on a similar vibration, and now that our vibrations have separated, there is no physical evidence of them. I'm not sure if that's true, but it's an interesting explanation, and it puts a lot of our mythic history into a new context if we look at it with this theory in mind. The Iron Age was ushered in when a Titan, Prometheus, an elder god, defied Zeus and gave fire to humanity. Pandora was fashioned by Zeus, and she let out all the ills of the world, as well as hope, utterly transforming humanity into the experience we have today. The Iron Age is said to be the last of the devolving ages, and the next era will be a renewed Golden Age.

Celtic

While Celtic mythology is entwined like a Celtic knot—beautiful, but hard to follow linearly—we can still find hints of the ages and ancient lands in their stories. The various invasions of Ireland have been described not as literal invasions over a short period of time, but as a mythic cycle of creation and destruction with major spiritual forces, eventually bringing the arrival of humanity as the modern Irish people. The "races" of each invasion are like the Theosophical root races, as some are human, while others are godlike or monstrous. One has to keep in mind that although modern pagans and magicians might see this as a degraded mythic cycle, it could involve genuine historic migrations, interwoven in a Christian framework, for all the references to it come from medieval manuscripts written in the Christian era.

The first invasion was before the biblical flood, led by Cessair, the granddaughter of Noah. Though she thought the pure land of Ireland would be a refuge from the flood, she and her followers were wiped out, all except Fintan, who magickally transformed into a salmon and saved the record of his people. Through a series of magickal transformations, he later became an eagle, then a hawk, and then human, becoming advisor for the later settlers known as the Fir Bolgs. The second invasion was by the Scythian named Partholon. He brought the first cattle to Ireland. Strangely, he fought the Fomorians, who did not have an origin in the "invasions" of Ireland, but simply were there. It is thought that they did not settle on the island proper. Some see the Fomorians with the original Irish gods of chaos, or equate them with the Greek Titans as an elder race of gods. They are described as ugly, misshapen giants, often cruel and oppressive. Partholon and his people were all wiped out by a plague, but one survived. Tuan mac Cairill, using magick similar to that of Fintan, transformed and lived to tell the tale, transforming first to a stag, a boar, an eagle, and then a salmon. He was caught and eaten, and then reborn as a human, writing the first tales on the history of Ireland.

The third invasion was by another Scythian named Nemed. He too battled the Fomorians. The Fomorians ruled and oppressed the Nemedians for a time. Although Nemed achieved some measure of success with his people against the Fomorians, the sea rose up and drowned him and his people. The fourth invasion was by the Fir Bolgs, who were the first race to establish kingship and justice in the land. They were also the first to use iron spear points in the land. The Fir Bolgs had no problems with the Fomorians. The fifth invasion was by the Tuatha de Danann, the group of Irish gods familiar to most modern witches. They came from northern or western isles, with great weapons and technology. Accounts vary as to their origin, as they are sometimes seen as otherworldly beings, and sometimes as the descendents of the Nemedians. The Fomorians started as their allies until they settled in Ireland. The Tuatha fought and eventually displaced both the Fir Bolgs and the Fomorians. The Tuatha were displaced by the Milesians, who settled in Ireland and became the dominant race of Ireland we know today. The essence of the Tuatha still survived, as the gods beneath the land, and some see them as the elder faery race. They are immortal, guiding and vexing Irish heroes centuries later and providing a link to the oldest mysteries of the land.

Norse

Norse mythology is a bit different from others, without the neatly defined set worlds, yet its creation and destruction cycle can be seen in a light similar to other classical mythologies. In the beginning was a world of fire and ice, with a gap or chasm between them where nothing could live, similar to our concepts of energy, matter, and the void. Fire and ice eventually touched, forming the hermaphrodite ice giant Ymir and the cow Audumla. The cow created the first god, Buri, while Ymir created the ice giants. Buri begat Borr, who then created three brothers, Odin, Vili, and Ve. The three slew Ymir, who became the Orgalmer, the primal noise of creation, and out of his body, the nine realms were constructed. From the creation emerged the first humans, and the division and war of the gods known as the Aesir and Vanir, or sky and earth gods respectively.

Eventually the two warring tribes reached a truce with the Aesir in prominence, and they "exchanged" prisoners, so the popular Vanir gods Freya and Frey became a part of the Aesir cosmology. Most interesting in the development of the worlds is the prophecy of Ragnarok, the end times and the rebirth of a new world. Generally it is believed that the forces of chaos will overrun the forces of order and goodness. Loki, his monstrous children, the giants, and the dead will rise up after the murder of the solar figure Balder, defeating the gods. It is already prophesized who will fight whom, and who will kill whom. Certain gods will survive. Balder will rise from the depths and claim the heavens and a new order, and a new humanity will grow from the ashes of the old. Scholars wonder if this apocalyptic view is influenced by Christianity, or some pre-Christian theology, possibly related to Zoroastrianism. As in the other mythologies, the death of one age gives birth to a new age.

British

While we tend to think of the preceding stories of worlds and ages ending as apocalypses from ancient or alien cultures we no longer relate to, we find a possible remnant in a tradition that very much relates to our path as modern witches.

THE LIFE OF A YEW, THE LENGTH OF AN AGE

> The lives of three wattles, the life of a hound;
> The lives of three hounds, the life of a steed;
> The lives of three steeds, the life of a man;
> The lives of three men, the life of an eagle;
> The lives of three eagles, the life of a yew;
> The life of a yew, the length of an age;
> Seven ages from Creation to Doom.
> —*Nennius (ninth-century historian), "Seven Ages"*

Author Nigel Pennick, in his book *Practical Magic in the Northern Tradition*, outlines a cycle of Great Ages based on a poem from English folk lore. According to Pennick, the life of a yew is one age, and there are seven ages from the creation of the world to its doom, giving us the cycle of 5,103 years in total. It is interesting to see the parallel with the Norse traditions of the yew, or needle ash, being the World Tree of their mythos. Perhaps every age has its own World Tree?

Three wattles are the life of a hound	9 years
Three hounds are the life of a steed	27 years
Three steeds are the life of a man	81 years
Three men are the life of an eagle	243 years
Three eagles are the life of a yew	729 years

We find a similar animal-age correlation in the Welsh mythology of Mabon. In the Welsh-influenced Arthurian mythos, the tale of Arthur's search for Mabon takes the knights to seek the wisdom of five animals. Each animal is interpreted as the animal totem of a previous age, old enough to know the mysteries. When asked the ritual request, "Tell me if thou knowest aught of Mabon, the son of Modron, who was taken when three nights old from between his mother and the wall," each one fails, directing the knights to the next eldest animal, from the previous age, until they find success with the eldest and wisest of creatures, the Salmon. The youngest of the elder beasts is the Blackbird of Cilgwri, followed by the Stag of Rhedynfre, the Owl of Cawlwyd, the Eagle of Gwernabwy, and then the Salmon of Llyn Llyw.

Theosophy

The Theosophy of Madame Blavatsky gives us one of the most detailed accounts of the Great Ages, and much of her lore has been integrated into the wider New Age movement. Blavatsky details a cycle of incarnation, where the spirits of the world, the elder races, descend from an ethereal and nonhuman state, on the higher planes of existence. In each age, they move closer to the human world and human bodies of this age. The prophecies say they will ascend back up to the higher planes, more evolved for their excursion into the material form.

The first age was the age of the Polarians, who "lived" in Pangea, the mythic first continent. People today think of Pangea as all the continents in one land mass, before continental drift broke them apart, creating the first true motherland. Modern pagans see Pan and Gaia, Father and Mother, in the name of this land. The Polarians were gigantic, androgynous, and completely etheric, spirits of a sort, who guided the development of the planet from their plane.

As the age ended, the Polarians developed a new race, centered on a land known as Hyperborea, found in Greek myths as the land beyond the North Wind where Apollo spent the winters. Legend said those who lived in Hyperborea never aged or died if they chose not to, and the land was full of gold, guarded by griffins, though those descriptions don't seem to fit the Theosophical model. Later writers associated the barbarian age, and stories of the popular fictional character Conan, with Hyperborea, as well as the roots of monstrous races in the H. P. Lovecraft fictional story cycles. Hyperborea has also been associated with the British Isles. According to Blavatsky, the race of Hyperboreans is mysterious, but more physical than the Polarians.

The third world was the land of Lemuria, sometimes known as Mu, though various sources state that Mu and Lemuria were the same, or completely different locations. Lemuria was said to be a continent, or perhaps a vast grouping of islands, in the Pacific Ocean. Here, life in a form we can recognize developed. The Lemurians have been described in a variety of ways, from peaceful, intuitive, androgynous beings, to barbaric monsters with a third eye on the back of their heads and elongated heels so they could walk backwards and forwards. Some modern teachings say that although they were primitive, they were guided, and sometimes "channeled" or possessed, by higher spiritual intelligences to develop civilization. Lemuria sank beneath the waves, in a manner that is usually described as gradual, seeding cultures in the Americas, the Pacific, and Asia.

By the end of the Lemurian Age, the continent of Atlantis was said to have risen in the Atlantic. The Lemurians evolved, eventually dividing the sexes and creating the mythic race of Atlanteans. Described in almost godlike terms, the Atlanteans were said to have created a city-state civilization, temples, magick, technology, and a variety of marvels that would be awed even today. They created another golden age, but they eventually fell from grace and, with their acts of hubris and abuse of technology, they destroyed themselves, triggering the Great Flood that is recorded in so many cultures. The tale of the familiar biblical flood actually has its roots in Sumerian myth, and parallels can be found all over the world. It's important to note that Atlantis is the only one of the previous Theosophical worlds of which we have any historic record in any way. Plato cites the tale of Atlantis, telling us the original story came from the priests of Egypt, whose mystery teachings were said to be descended from an Atlantean priest. Other cultures hint at the presence of Atlantis.

The fall of Atlantis gives us the fifth world, that of modern man. The races were said to split into five—white, black, red, yellow, and brown. Though not politically correct by today's standards, the Theosophical model shows our age to have not one cradle of civilization, but five. Collectively this fifth race is known as the Aryan race, but refers more to linguistics than skin tones, for in this system, the darkest Hindu is considered Aryan. As you can imagine, much misunderstanding and misrepresentation has occurred with this teaching. The sixth age brings the melting pot of those divisions back together. Said to be developing and evolving primarily in America is the Meruvian race, preparing for the next world. The seventh and final epoch of Theosophy will be led by the Paradisians, restoring us to a more etheric nature but retaining the wisdom of our material incarnations.

Thelema

The teaching of Aleister Crowley divided time into three major epochs, based upon the Egyptian gods. The time of the matriarchy, of Stone Age people, of witchcraft and magick, was under the auspices of Isis. In the Age of Isis, the earth-reverent cultures, seeing the feminine in the world, were dominant. As the hunter/gatherers changed their ways to those of an agrarian society, the Age of Osiris began. The hallmark of Osiris's age is sacrificed gods associated with the vegetation, which is sunlight in its perishable form. The worship of Osiris, Dumuzi, Tammuz, Dionysus, and Balder are all indicative of the Age of Osiris. The peak of the Osirian Age was the rise of Christ and Christianity. Yet the rise of Christianity began the disassociation of the gods of the land. Crowley was said to preside over the Equinox of the Gods, when Osiris gave up his "chair," giving the world to his son Horus, and the Age of Horus began in 1904. The prophet of the Aeon of Horus was Crowley, and the individualistic message of Thelema became the key concept of the aeon. Horus represents the undying solar consciousness.

The origin of life started as a mystery, with only the woman's role understood fully in the Age of Isis, and the menstruation cycle echoing the power of the Moon. Then the concept of death and resurrection, the rising and setting Sun of the day and of the year, became dominant as the male mysteries were understood with the role of man in conception. With Horus's aeon, we know the Sun doesn't go out—our planet simply turns on its axis, so we are aspiring to the eternal enlightenment. Others interpret the Age of Horus in a benign view, as the union of Isis and Osiris, the best traits of female and male together. Classically, the images of Horus are the avenger and warrior.

Chaos Magick

Though Chaos magick as a whole does not have a creed or system of beliefs for all practitioners, particularly concerning the mysteries, Peter Carroll, arguably the founder of modern Chaos magick, outlines his own aeons. Each of his main trends can be further subdivided into two sections. Similar to Crowley, he sees the early years of human consciousness as shamanistic, like the Age of Isis, classifying them as animist and spiritist. In the formal religious phase, similar to the Age of Osiris, we have the first formal religions of the pagan priest/ess and then the monotheists. In the Age of the Rationalist, we have the atheist and then the nihilist. In the coming age, his Age of Pandemos, we have the Chaosist evolving into something wholly unknown, because Carroll left the next phase open.

Astrological

The astrological model is the most helpful to the more grounded occultist, because it further subdivides the Great Ages into trends that we can see moving through our more recognizable history. The astrological cycle of ages occurs due to a wobble in the rotation of the Earth's axis. Like a wobbling top, the Earth's pole shifts, pointing from one star to another over a long course of time. The effect of this shift creates a phenomenon called the Procession of the Equinoxes.

Two forms of the zodiac have been recognized. The first is called the sidereal zodiac, and it is based upon the constellations of the stars that we recognize as zodiac signs. This zodiac is used in India's Vedic astrology system. The tropical zodiac divides the sky into twelve thirty-degree segments, starting the cycle with Aries, at the point where the Sun appears on the vernal equinox. At one time, the sidereal and tropical zodiacs were in alignment, but due to the wobble in the axis of the Earth, the sidereal

	One	Two	Three	Four	Five
	Void	Air	Fire	Water	Earth
Mayan	First Jaguar	Second Wind	Third Storm	Fourth Water	Fifth Motion/Time
Aztec	First Sun Earth Tezcatlipoca Devoured by jaguars when Quetzalcoatl and Tezcatlipoca fight	Second Sun Wind Quetzalcoatl Destroyed by wind summoned by Tezcatlipoca	Third Sun Rain/Storm Tlaloc Destroyed by fiery rain from Quetzalcoatl	Fourth Sun Water Chalchiuhtlicue Drowned in floods	Fifth Sun Motion Common history Not destroyed yet
Hopi		First World Tokpela Nature Fire destroyed Fire Pit	Second World Tokpa The Fall Tribes and villages Ice destroyed Hole (Umbilical)	Third World Kuskurza Cities Flood destroyed Ladder (Reed)	Fourth World Tuwaqachi Present Day Not destroyed Kiva Entrance
Vedic Yugas		Krita Yuga Golden Age	Treta Yuga Silver Age	Dvapara Yuga Copper Age	Kali Yuga Iron Age
Greek Ages	Chaos Uranus and Gaia Creation	Golden Age Chronos Golden Men into Holy Spirits	Silver Age Zeus Silver Men into Underworld Spirits	Bronze Age Age of Heroes Ash Men into Underworld Spirits	Iron Age Pandora and Prometheus Men and Women of Flesh
Theosophy	Pangea	Hyperborea	Lemuria	Atlantis	Modern World
Astrology				Leo Ancient Civilizations	Cancer Matriarchy
Thelema					Isis Matriarchy Paganism Mother

Figure 6: Great Ages

				Six
				Spirit
				Sixth Starts in 2012
				Sixth Sun Earthquake/Incense New Age Started in 1987
				Fifth World
				Dvapara Yuga
				New Golden Age
				Age of Light
Gemini Advent of Writing	Taurus Building	Aries Warriors Invasion of Europe	Pisces Sacrifice Christianity	Aquarius New Humanity New Age
		Osiris Sacrificed Gods Organized Religion Father		Horus Synthesis of Both Child

Figure 6: Great Ages

sign at the vernal equinox is different from the tropical sign. It takes the sidereal zodiac about 2,166 years to transition from one sign to the next, moving backwards through our zodiac cycle. Whatever sidereal sign is at that position is said to influence the planetary consciousness for that two-thousand-year period. It is the sign ruling that age.

Currently we are at the cusp of a transition, and this is what people mean when they say we are entering the "New Age." We are transitioning out of Pisces and into Aquarius. Yet the cycle is so large that occultists and psychics have disagreed about when this shift was to occur or when it is going to occur, and they have given a wide range of years, including 1905, 1969, 1972, 1985, 2000, 2005, 2010, 2012, 2020, and 2080. Craft elder "Old" George Pickingill gives us the widest time frame; allegedly he calculated that we are in the sixth sub-age of Pisces, ranging from 1808 to 2116, with the seventh and last subdivision of Pisces from 2115 to 2424. The Golden Dawn's calculations focused on 2010, while the Mayan calendar and modern metaphysician Terrence McKenna each determined the date to be the winter solstice of 2012, a date that most modern metaphysical practitioners favor.

Looking at our history, the rise of the hunter/gatherer tribes occurred in the Age of Cancer. Cancer is the sign of the Great Mother, of the Moon. We have a mythos that gives us a matriarchal image of the ancient world, and a period of Goddess reverence and Moon magick. Prior to the Age of Cancer, if the ancient civilizations such as Atlantis existed, their rise and fall fits well in the Age of Leo, the sign of the lion, of ego development and of potential pride. Many of the myths of Atlantis center on the pride and corruption of the Atlanteans to create their own doom. The Age of Gemini was heralded by a transformation in spoken and written language, as humanity developed more intricate systems of communication and relationship, eventually settling into an agrarian society. We have the rise of Mercurial gods giving the arts and sciences to humanity. The Age of Taurus is the time of the ancient civilizations, of building structure. As the Moon is exalted in Taurus, lunar goddesses were still revered, but we have the rise of the bull cults. In the Age of Aries, the sacrifice of rams became more prevalent, and we have the rise of the empires, the age of the warrior conquering the land—from the Celtic and Teutonic tribes of Europe to the rise of the Roman Empire. The rise of Christianity marks the Age of Pisces, as the warrior god is replaced with the solar, sacrificed god. The institutional hierarchy of the spiritual *over* the material, rather than the spiritual *in* the material, becomes the dominant paradigm, and vertical organization of society grows through institutions such as the church.

The Age of Aquarius is prophesized to be a time of quick and sudden change, and sometimes associated with disasters and trauma, like its opposing sign, Leo. But many believe the disasters will be mitigated to the etheric realms if humanity is of a sufficient level of consciousness and evolution. We need not suffer a physical cataclysm and death, but the death of an outmoded society and harmful structures. The blessings of Aquarius are brotherhood/sisterhood; lateral organization; equality; utopian ideals; social, political, and environmental consciousness; innovation; and individuality. The key to Aquarius's often confusing teachings is that we all must be unique, but all serve the greater good. We can only serve the greater good by being our unique selves. If we conform to someone else's vision, then we are not serving in the highest way possible. The lateral relationships of Aquarius encourage a paradigm in which everybody's religion, race, sexuality, ethnicity, and opinions can be valued.

When you look at these mythologies, they are at times categorized by the elements, starting with the void, where applicable, and moving through the remaining traditional elements, usually as air, fire, water, and earth, and ending with the coming prophesized age of spirit. Each culture correlates the time periods of the ages in different ways. With different calendar methods, there is no one way to correlate all of these teachings in a linear fashion, but figure 6 gives us some understanding of how the mythic teachings are remarkably similar.

When looked at from an archetypal view, you can see some of our scientific truths told in the only way they could be told at the time, through myth and allegory. Couldn't the tales of giants and monstrous beings in the first days of creation be tales of the dinosaurs? How else would they be described? Ancient "archaeologists" gathering together bone fossils found and constructed elaborate skeletons of "giants" with monstrous heads. As the most learned people of their time, they presented the "facts" of giants in the ancient world, so myths of the time of giants are no more far-fetched than our stories of dinosaurs. The ancients didn't have the knowledge to reconstruct the bones in the way we do today, creating the image of the dinosaurs. They created images that fit their worldview. Wouldn't it be interesting to find that in a thousand years we were wrong, and the creatures of the ancient world didn't look anything like our image of dinosaurs? It was just the best we could come up with at the time, but we were missing an important piece of information that would change it. It's only our modern arrogance that assumes that we are always correct and that those in the past were inferior. Some day, our culture will be the people in the past.

Couldn't the disasters of the end of the ages be the historic comet strikes, ice ages, volcanic eruptions, and tectonic upheavals? How else do we describe the vast changes our planet has undergone? Would a comet strike be seen as a rain of fire? Would climate shifts describe the floods and ice? Did the ancient seers see the Earth's past in spirit vision and relate it in story in a way they and their people could understand? I think so. It starts to put this "crazy" information about the world ending many times into a modern perspective. Here science and magick give us two different views on the same topic.

THE MOTHERLANDS

The second great secret teaching of the ages is based upon location, a sense of origin from one vast motherland, from which we, as humans, or we, as witches/magicians/ mystics, specifically descend. It's a hope that if we find such a motherland, we can reconcile the paradoxes of our diverse traditions, and find some "pure" form of our magickal spirituality.

Even if we do find a motherland in the physical realm, such reconciliation will never happen. Everything must grow, evolve, die, and be reborn. We are not the same ancient people, so the systems of an ancient land won't serve us. But myth, prophecy, and a connection to ancestral wisdom give our current knowledge a perspective that serves to ground us and provide a platform from which to build the future. We must be cautious about what is our mythic history and what is our factual history. The two can coincide, but both histories serve very different purposes. Our mythic history's purpose is to inspire and give us, as a people, a story that inspires.

Many would credit the focus on ancestral motherlands to the rise of Theosophy and its influence in the budding occult world of the time. Not until the writings of H. P. Blavatsky did we see a strange synthesis of all this material on the Great Ages, with new information and names that would become commonplace in the New Age and occultist circles. The Theosophical Ages of Madame Blavatsky are anchored around mythic locations—continents that are no longer known but were once the cradles of the world's civilization. They birthed a race that is equally unknown to modern humans, yet they all hold a deep archetypal fascination for us. But the names found in Blavatsky's works are often drawn from our myth and history. They have roots that reach further into the past than the relatively recent Theosophical movement. Theosophy simply synthesized many concepts into a workable, yet sometimes clunky, framework of ages, continents, and races, so students of the eternal wisdom would have a story of the human soul evolving through the ages, as science gave us the story of the human body evolving through the ages.

For the Western occultist, no other mythic motherland fascinates us more than Atlantis. Though many modern occultists shudder at the mere mention of Atlantis, it holds sway in our collective consciousness. Unlike many of the other stories of ancient lands, the tales of Atlantis go back to Plato's *Timaeus* and *Critias*. They are linked to the mystery teachings of the Egyptians, with whom many modern witches and magicians find a spiritual kinship. Was Atlantis a real place to Plato, as one might assume upon first read? Or was Atlantis an allegory and commentary on his current Greek society, intended as a warning for his people, and even for future generations like us, about the price of arrogance? We don't really know for sure. Either way, Atlantis holds something important to show us, since his writings, its mythos, and the energy people have put into it as an otherworldly pattern have grown.

It's interesting to note that out of all the myths of the various ages we have experienced as a planet, most of the sacred teachings agree that the world previous to this one "ended" in flood. The flood myths of many cultures, popularized in the biblical flood of Noah's ark, survive and have been catalogued by modern myth seekers. If it is simply an allegory, why would we all have flood myths? Something water-related obviously happened, either on the physical plane, or in the collective consciousness, to create such a strong impression.

After the sinking of Atlantis, both colonists and escapees were said to populate the rest of the world, seeding their wisdom and bringing both their advanced technology and magick to more primitive parts of the world. Native American myths and prophecies that have been adopted by the New Age speak of the four races meeting at the four corners at the start of the next age. Their colors—red, yellow, black, and white—are like the color associations many have for the four elements and directions.

The Theosophical lore gives us a fifth race, with the color "brown," and I learned from my teachers and inner-plane work that the mystery of this current age is embedded in the union and cooperation of the five races. The secret sign that we must use to keep the mystery and magick working toward the evolution of the next age is the pentacle. That is one of the reasons why we wear it and use it in ritual.

Another "teaching" some witchcraft and mystical traditions receive is that the planet's original orbit was 360 days per year, but a cataclysm altered our orbit, adding five extra days, also relating to the five points of the pentagram and five races. The concept of adding five days to the year is found in Egyptian mythology. Thoth prophesized that the goddess Nuit would give birth to a great king of the gods. Fearful, Ra cursed her, forbidding her to have children on any day of the year. The god Thoth had to win five days of light from the Moon in a contest, to gain five extra days, for the children of Nuit to be born. She gave birth to Osiris, Set, Isis, Nepthys, and Horus the Elder. The calendar was then reorganized into 365 days.

While some lore says the Atlanteans were of the "red" race and settled in the Americas, Western occult lore gives the "white" race precedence in Atlantis. Various accounts tell of an advanced Greek and/or pseudo-Celtic society that ruled over the island nation of Atlantis. In the tales of the Tuatha de Danann, the gods who were the children of Danu came from the west, possibly Atlantis, in what some described as magnificent flying boats, arriving to settle in Ireland. They came from the four corners of the globe, bearing magickal weapons and tools, and they were far more advanced than the Fomorians who were then occupying Ireland. The true Celtic people from Europe subsequently "invaded" Atlantis and viewed the Tuatha de Danann as gods. The Tuatha admired the magick of the Celts and, rather than fighting off a new invasion from a people they admired, descended into the land, retreating from the physical world. They maintained contact with some. Those would most often be identified as witches, or faery seers, and they influenced Celtic myth, magick, and society.

Other accounts focusing on the legends of Arthur and Merlin have evolved into the modern witchcraft mythos. Alexandrian witchcraft, as noted in *The Alex Sanders Lec-*

tures, touches upon the teachings of Atlantis and how they have influenced the Craft. In many tales, the "magical" characters of the Arthurian cycle are said to come from Atlantis, bringing their esoteric wisdom and sometimes mixing it with the native forms of magick in the Celtic territories. Those who foresaw the cataclysmic flood of Atlantis gathered together and encoded their teachings in the ancient world, preserving the wisdom in the myths of Egypt, Greece, and the Americas. Many think the unusual linguistics and genetics associated with the Basques—being markedly different from the Indo-European people and most likely having a different origin—make a strong case for associating them with Atlantis, and the Basque people have had historic links to sorcery and witchcraft. Merlin, also spelled *Merlyn* and *Myrrdin*, and the Lady of the Lake were priest and priestess of the Atlantean religion, coming from the western lands. Some modern witches believe these not to be actual people, but titles, as the high magus and priestess of Albion, of England, and many people have held the titles. There is said to be an entire order of Merlins working on the inner planes. They hold the mysteries of the sacred land, of bloodlines, and of harnessing the tellurian dragon power and balancing the relationship of the people with the land through the king and queen, who also act as a priest and priestess. They keep the mysteries of the sword and grail, and pass on their knowledge to initiates today. The tales we have today of Arthur's court are both a corruption and a romanticization of the true teachings.

While that is a very interesting concept, and I think there is some mythic truth to it, we certainly have no proof of it as literal fact. We really have no definitive proof that there was an Arthur or Camelot, and if there were, they certainly didn't appear the way we see them in the movies and novels, with shiny knights and a large castle.

Atlantean wisdom has been adopted by many traditions claiming secret knowledge and ancient lineage, but we have no absolute proof. Even still, it's a powerful concept to work with in vision, and often we find out our mythic truths and psychic impressions have more validity than the current understanding of science and history allow us to believe. Many well-respected occultists have used the workings of Atlantean mythos to frame their teachings. One need only look to the excellent novels of Dion Fortune, particularly *The Sea Priestess*, to see the Atlantis mythos, and its reincarnated priestess and priest in action in the context of modern magick. Many popular novels link the characters of Arthur's court to Atlantis.

In *Liber LI: The Lost Continent*, Aleister Crowley outlines his own vision of Atlantis. He details a heritage of magicians, seven in any given age, each of whom holds one seventh of the knowledge of Atlantis, and how when the venerable mage K-Z decided to die, he passed this post and knowledge on to Crowley. It's unclear if this benefactor was flesh or spirit, for Crowley says that K-Z departed to join "them" on Venus. In fact, with his commentaries on the essay, it's unclear if Crowley saw this account as literal fact, higher dimensional reality, or simply a poetic allegory. Crowley details a society organized in "houses" with magickal law and a slave race, concerned with the production of a magickal substance known as *zro*, perhaps a substance akin to refined prana. The high house of Atlantis was concerned with the creation of life, using this substance and the ability to bridge the gap between Earth and Venus. Their experiments would seem barbaric and monstrous to us today. He states that the legends of the war between gods, giants, and Titans are the wars of Atlantis. The cataclysm was caused by an experiment to bridge the gap and reach Venus. Unlike other accounts of Atlantis, Crowley's states that they succeeded on some level, moving their civilization to Venus, and in their wake, the space left behind where Atlantis, or Atlas was, filled with water, creating the Great Flood across the world. He also gives us reason why we cannot find remains of Atlantis on the ocean floor.

Atlantis played into the cosmology of occultist Michael Bertiaux, author of *The Voudon Gnostic Workbook*, as well as in the teachings of traditional Craft enigma "Old" George Pickingill, if the written accounts of him are to be believed. Alex Sanders makes mention of Atlantis in *The Alex Sanders Lectures*, and Doreen Valiente had a soft spot for the lost continent in her writings. Keepers of her last version of her Book of Shadows say that much of it was devoted to Atlantean witchcraft connections. Beyond the realm of ceremonial magick and witchcraft, you find advocates of Atlantis in influential psychic Edgar Cayce, Congressman Ignatius Donnelly, unorthodox educator Rudolf Steiner, and Sikh leader Yogi Bhajan, as well as a whole host of modern spiritual teachers and gurus.

I've had amazingly insightful past-life memories in Atlantis, Lemuria, and other mythic lands. I've had students with no real conscious knowledge of these tales come back from trance with memories of such places that would correlate quite well. My own teachers and training included veiled references to Atlantis, the Lady of Lake, and the mysteries of the Merlin, yet it was up to me to dive into my spirit and blood, to seek those mysteries out for myself. Much of the experience has deepened my own understanding of myself and my soul history. I teach the techniques to my students for the same reason, regardless of whether or not any of us can "prove" our past lives or ancient soul lineages. As many have theorized, they could be perfectly true, yet could have occurred in a dimension that was not on this physical plane of existence.

Ideally, knowledge of the secret history and Great Ages puts your life, and your soul's journey in the history of the world into larger context. It gives you the perspective of an initiate, whose journey is timeless, rather than one who is mired in the here and now, in the mundane details of life without seeing any bigger picture or greater purpose. The secret knowledge is initiatory in nature, for it expands your consciousness simply by knowing it. But by making a personal connection to it, finding part of your story in the Great Story, you truly transform. Experience this final initiation in the Temple of the Root, to find your spiritual origin, part of your soul's history.

EXERCISE 5

Exploring Your Spiritual Origin in the Great Ages

1. Perform Exercise 1: Inner Temple as a Mystery School Meditation (page 45), steps 1–5, to go to your inner temple. Feel your inner temple dedicated to be a mystery school. Feel it permeated with the energies of the Root Temple.

2. If you desire to have a spirit guide to aid you and work directly with you, open the gateway of guidance (*ITOW*, chapter 14) and call upon your guides to be with you.

3. Go to the gateway of memory, the gateway you have opened to explore your past lives (*ITOW*, chapter 16, and *TOSW*, chapter 14). Ask to access your first life, your first incarnation on planet Earth, your first root race. Open the gateway.

4. As you open the gate, you see the familiar hallway with many doors on either side. You are not called to the ones near the opening of the gateway. Move deep, going down the tunnel, further and further back in time, to the end of the hallway. You will be guided to a door at the end of the hall, either

the very last door, directly in front of you, or one of the doors to the side, but near the end of the hall.

5. Open the door. Step through the door. You might find yourself "stepping" into your earliest root-race life, or moving down a set of stairs, slowly entering the life. With your spirit guides' help, explore this life. Ask yourself, "Where am I? What am I? What did I look like before I had this face, or any face at all? What age is this? How does this root of my incarnations influence my current life and True Will?" Do not judge. Do not try to make it match any of the mythologies or systems you have learned. Go with your first impressions now and analyze it later.

6. When you have completed your exploration, or at least completed as much as you can in the first session, return back through the doorway of this life and close it. Return to the inner temple, by walking the hallway and coming back through the gateway of memory. Close the gateway. Ground yourself in the inner temple and reflect on the experience. Ask your guides to help you understand or clarify anything you experienced. Try to understand your reason for incarnating, and the place and age where you were. Understanding that can give you great clues to your overall magickal purpose and motives.

7. Finish exercise 1, steps 8–11, to return to normal consciousness.

The red ray, or first ray, of Theosophy is described as the ray of power and will, but it is the guiding force of nations and the root races of culture. It is the impetus of creation. Exploring the power of the red ray and the root chakra helps us understand where we come from and how we've been imprinted over various ages.

Most who are drawn to the witchcraft traditions will find themselves with a long soul history on this planet, as they have developed a great love, a great relationship with the Mother, and they return again and again. However, many spiritually-oriented people today find that their soul origins are fairly recent to this planet, and they have memories of existing in other realms, on other planets, and as other races of beings. If this is the case for you, explore these memories as a part of your Temple of the Root work.

THE NEW AGE

Understanding the Great Ages and motherlands all serves to create a framework and foundation to prepare us for the New Age. Though many think of the New Age as an overused phrase, grown trite with commercialization, I still think of it as a powerful name, evoking the best we have to offer the world. An important thing to realize, as the mysteries are handed down to us, is that they occur outside of space and time, so we are always on the cusp of the New Age, just as we are always heading toward a new dawn. We are also always heading toward the apocalypse, to the end of the world. It's just a matter of perspective. Do you see it as death or rebirth? We are constantly re-birthing our society, and are challenged to offer our best to the world.

The New Age is not a time on a calendar, automatically ordained to happen even if we do nothing. We must become part of the process, though astrology and mathematics can give us insight to this shift. The Mayan calendar's date has become the most popular of the time marks. The calculations of the Mayan calendar perfectly match the "Time Wave Graph" of eccentric visionary and psychonaut Terrence McKenna, who also predicted the end of time as we know it to be the winter solstice of 2012. Other predictions give us a much later time. Zsuzsanna Budapest, in her book *Summoning the Fates*, says that we are only in a sub-age of Aquarius, and it truly begins in 2320. We must remember that it is the end of *a* world, not the end of *the* world. It's simply a transformation of the world and its people.

Why is this information important to the training of the witch, and in particular the high priest/ess, as many traditional witches try to distance themselves from what they see as ungrounded New Age teachings? First, it gives us a perspective and history that we lack as modern witches. We don't have a mythos that is accepted as fact. We don't have the Bible or Qur'an. We don't have the centuries-old Vedas. We borrow from so many myths and sources, and this mythos gives us a solidity that is needed, but with a fluidity so that it can be adapted and personalized for particular groups and individuals.

More importantly, we study it because it is my fervent belief that witches will play a vital role in the birthing of this new aeon, and we must understand where we have been, both historically and mythically, to help craft the course of where we are going.

We are called here and now for a reason. We have stretched across the eons, from our first root race to now, because we are the priestesses and priests of the Mother. We have answered her call, and we are here to restore a vital part of the world's theology, mythology, ecology, and ethics that has been lost and ignored by the human tribe for so long.

If we deem this age the Age of Aquarius, Aquarius is ruled by two very "witchy" planetary figures, traditionally ruled by Saturn and in the modern era ruled by Uranus. Saturn is associated with Chronos, the god of the Greek Golden Age, the god of grain and time, who carries the crescent sickle. He is the lord of death as the grim reaper figure, and later is referred to as an Old Devil and likened to a horned god. Saturn rules Capricorn, the sign of the Goat, and all its associations with Pan, the Great God of Witches. Almost all the horned-god figures have witchcraft associations. In the Qabalah, Saturn is linked with Binah, the dark goddess and the primordial ocean. She is the power from which all things take shape and form, the vast Isis as primal mother. Uranus is the planet of unorthodoxy and sudden change. Though classically seen as the sky father to Mother Earth, he is also related by astrologers to the rebellion force and linked with the Titan Prometheus. Prometheus is the light bearer, bringer of knowledge to those on Earth, equated with Gnostic concepts of Lucifer as the lord of light and brother to Diana.

Aquarius is literally the sign of the water bearer or cup bearer, referring to Ganymede, the cup bearer of Zeus. The homosexual relationship between Zeus and Ganymede shows that homosexuals and the entire queer community, like witches, will have a pivotal role to play in the next age, and we can see that happening with the rise of awareness around gay rights and the GLBT community. The cup imagery relates so strongly to our sacred mysteries of the Great Rite and the Holy Grail. Though overlaid with Christian imagery, it goes back to the Cauldron of the Goddess and the Cup of Immortality, Inspiration, and Healing. Aquarius's teachings are about individuality, yet they include the overall community good. Modern paganism is one of the few traditions that can have both structure and flexibility—it encourages direct experience and yet provides a history, theology, and understanding. The hierarchy of the Piscean Age must be replaced, and the circle is a powerful and universal symbol to replace the ladder of the previous age.

If we place the Wheel of the Year on the cycle of the Great Ages, the Age of Aquarius relates to Imbolc, though the Wheel of the Year would move in reverse to the procession of the zodiac. Imbolc is sacred to the goddess Brid, or Bridget, goddess of poetry, healing, and smithcraft. We are entering the fire goddess's age of light. A faery priest once told me that the "second coming" was going to be in the form of a redheaded woman, because that image was the hallmark of the New Age. I'm not sure where he got his information, but it matches the cosmic Bridget/Imbolc imagery quite well. Imbolc is the time of awakening the Goddess from her slumber, and though I don't think she's been truly slumbering this past age, I think she has been dormant in our consciousness, as humanity has focused on God the Father. Witches are bringing the image of Goddess the Mother to popular consciousness.

According to the Andean shamanic tradition, we are entering the *Taripay Pacha*, the Age of Meeting Ourselves Again. Rather than apocalypse or fantasy world, the three worlds—over, middle, and under—will collapse into one harmonious whole. It will be the traditions that stand between the worlds that will guide the rest of the world into understanding a multidimensional consciousness. Witches are the walkers between the worlds. We must be prepared. We learn these secret histories and mystery teachings to prepare us, so that we in turn may serve the world. The beloved and inspiring Craft elder known as Lady Circe often said, "The witches are here to lead humanity to the light and to bring back the glory of the Goddess." It's time we begin.

HOMEWORK

- Do exercises 2–5 and record your experiences in your journal or BOS.

- When you complete the trials of this chapter, braid and tie your first knot in your cord in a ritualized manner.

- Work with a ritual robe. If you don't have one, obtain or make one, and work with the robe in the meditations and rituals of this book. If you prefer to work skyclad, make the act of robing and disrobing a part of your ritual.

Tips

- If you did not go to the very last door in the gateway of memory, know that at some point in your training, you should return and try to explore the last door.

- You are encouraged to explore your past incarnations in the ancient world. It can be valuable to bring back memories of magick theory, theology, and most importantly technique. These bits of soul wisdom will empower and transform your personal practice of magick. Be open to receiving these keys.

- Learn to build an integrated meditation and ritual practice. As a high priest/ ess, no one is going to tell you step by step what you should be doing or when you should be doing it. You have to determine what skills and exercises you need as you progress. You have to set your own schedule, learning when to push yourself and when to take a break. Look over the previous work from *ITOW*, *OTOW*, *TOSW*, and *TOHW*. Which exercises, rituals, and practices do you need to do regularly for your own benefit? Look at appendix II for suggestions in scheduling a meditation practice.

- Be more aware of your physical senses. Sharpen and use all five whenever possible. Bring them into a harmonious system that gives you information.

Lesson Two
Temple of the Belly:
Purification and Relationship

The second of the seven temples brings more complexity to our training, as does each in turn. Moving from the base needs of the root, of survival and questions of where we come from, the Temple of the Belly deals with how we relate to our surroundings, and in particular, the people in them. Corresponding with the color orange and the belly, it deals with the "gut" consciousness, the primal instinct. Usually connected with the element of water, for the intestines and the womb imagery, the second temple is the temple of feeling. The intestines help our body discern what is good for us and what is not, filtering out waste from nutrients. The second temple's powers are similar, but they extend beyond the physical into all aspects of our lives. They help us distinguish between panaceas and poisons, and between those individuals with energies that bless and strengthen us and those who curse and weaken us, intentionally or otherwise.

Prepare your altar using the correspondences of the belly chakra. Use an orange candle and orange stones. Mother Goddess imagery is appropriate. As you prepare your altar, prepare your body, and enter direct relationship with the belly energy center. This interior star will guide you in whom and what to trust.

EXERCISE 6

Contemplation on the Temple of the Belly

1. Sit quietly in a comfortable position and enter a meditative state. Call upon higher guidance, through your own spirit guides and the Goddess, God, and Great Spirit.

2. Place your hands on the lower belly area, near the navel. A variety of sources list this chakra at the navel, two finger lengths above the navel, two finger lengths below the navel, or just above the pubic triangle. More importantly, where do you feel the energy? You are ultimately the best judge. Place your hands there.

3. Feel the energy of the belly chakra. Start with your hands, but let any sensations move through your entire body. You might feel as if your entire energy field is surrounded in orange light. Ask the belly chakra to reveal its mysteries and guide you.

4. Observe the thoughts, feelings, visions, and insights you have, as well as messages you receive, while attuning yourself to the Temple of the Belly. These will guide you in this lesson to your own personal work.

5. When done, return yourself from the meditative state. Thank the energy of the belly chakra as well as your spiritual guidance, and give yourself clearance and balance.

Magickal Teaching: Instinct
Force: Polarity
Chakra: Belly
Function: Instinct

Body: Etheric

Tool of the Goddess: Lapis Measuring Rod and Line

Alternate Tool of the Goddess: Sandals

Color: Orange

Ray: Fifth, the Ray of Concrete Science and Technology

Element: Water

Planet: Jupiter

Metal: Tin

Sign: Cancer

Emerald Tablet Rubric: Its Mother Is the Moon

Alchemical Operation: Dissolution

Totems: Goose, Frog, Fish

Plant: Lemon Balm

Sephira: Yesod

Tarot, Lunar: Trump II—Priestess

Tarot, Solar: Trump IX—Hermit

Tarot, Stellar: Trump XVI—The Tower

Life Stage: Coming of Age

Hermetic Principle: Polarity

Musical Note: D

Day of the Week: Thursday

Castle of the Underworld: Caer Fandy-Manddwy—Castle on High, Sea Castle

Egyptian Temple Sites: Kom Ombo, Edfu

Left Hand Initiation: Shock

Vice of Initiation: Hubris

Virtue of Initiation: Quantifiable Pride

Stage of the Bread Miracle: Seed

Challenge of the Temple: Fear

Blessing of the Temple: Trust

The mysteries of the Temple of the Belly deal with our primal relationships. The root mysteries deal with our relationship to our primal selves, to what we bring with us, through our blood and spirit. The second mysteries expand to reach beyond our selves, and relate to the larger world around us. Beyond our base needs and desires, a primal yet emotional component takes hold in the second temple. It involves our relationship with the self and with others, teaching us the wisdom of the body and, by extension, the radiating etheric body that acts as an early warning system. It is in the belly, in the gut, that we learn whom to trust and whom not to trust. It's not the psychic information of vision or words, but primal intuition and instinct: this is safe or unsafe. It goes beyond the physical survival safety of the root, and into emotional and personal safety. Will this one nourish me and care for me, or will it harm me, drain me, and use me?

Most often, our gut-level instincts serve us well. Yet sometimes our immediate responses are dead wrong. Other times they are completely right, but we don't listen to them. When the lines of communication between our belly wisdom and our rational mind are polluted, we mix up our messages. Sometimes primal fears, memories, or past patterns cloud our belly's intuitive wisdom. Other times our rational mind won't accept what our belly is clearly telling us. Fearing we are clouded, we ignore it. Emotions, good or bad, can be so intense that they color our judgment. Though we encourage a "positive" and optimistic mind and tend to discourage a "negative" or pessimistic mind, we truly need to learn how to shift into the neutral mind, to know the reality of the situation rather than sense what we hope or fear.

The only remedy for this miscommunication is purification. The more we can perceive ourselves and our inner communications objectively—by making all our unconscious energies conscious and eventually removing the unhealthy patterns—the clearer our inner communication becomes. Water is the element of the second chakra, and thus the purification of our water, our emotion and unconscious mind, becomes a primary concern for us. Ritual bathing, fasting, particular diets, censing/smudging with sacred smoke, scourging, and other physical purification rites are used to simultaneously purify the energy bodies and bring greater inner clarity. Then the water element and its psychic instincts can truly serve you. When you look through clouded lenses, you have a hard time clearly seeing yourself and those around you. The material of this lesson is less technically complex than that of the other lessons, but don't let its primal nature fool you. With the extra time you have, truly process these emotions and purify yourself.

The Mystery of the Measure

When the goddess Inanna descends into the depths of the Underworld, the second-to-last item she gives up, before her ritual robe, is her lapis measuring rod and line. I always found that to be an interesting set of tools, and must admit that at first I didn't understand it, or its significance to modern witches. Lapis is a stone referenced a lot in the ancient world, and today we relate the gold-speckled blue stone with Jupiter, the planet alchemically associated with the belly chakra. Crystal healers will use lapis and other blue stones on the belly chakra, using the idea of opposing colors to heal, as blue is the opposing color of orange. The measuring rod and line is also a tool of geometry and measure, of masonry. It is used to lay out the dimensions of both sacred temples and the cities. Inanna's father, Sin, also carries the measure and line. Metaphysically, it could be said to measure the hearts of people and to execute justice, much as the scales are a measure of justice. The line and rod is like the weaver's spindle or distaff, used to weave fibers into threads. The great fate goddess weaves your life into a thread, weaving your thread into the pattern, the *wyrd*, of creation. In a metaphor popularized by Dion Fortune, the soul is sometimes described as a string, and the body like a bead or pearl on the string. As we move from incarnation to incarnation, we add pearls to the string of our soul.

The measuring line is also like the cord, the cingulum of the witch. Cords are used in many forms of magick. Knots have been tied in them to focus power. Weather witches "knot" the wind and untie the knots to release the wind when needed, particularly those working with sailors. Knots are used like a rosary or meditation beads in a tool known as the witch's ladder. Cords are used, with an athame, chalk, or salt, to mark out the edge of a circle. They are a sign of initiatory rank, and used to tie the robe of a priest/ess. The Temple of Witchcraft system uses a five-cord cingulum as a belt. Cords are symbols of initiation.

Many self-initiated, modern, and eclectic witches miss the significance of the cord, because it is not often used in self-initiation ceremonies. From our list of correspondences, it is linked with the fifth ray of Theosophy, the ray of concrete science, requiring measurement and knowledge. Yet it's more than that. The cord is said to be the tool of binding your will in the material world, and of setting boundaries, but it is truly a tool of trust.

Initiation rites vary in the lineage traditions, but most share some similar points concerning the use of cords. There are the binding cords and the measuring cords. In the "ordeal" of the initiation, the initiator takes a short cord and ties it around the right ankle of the initiate, making his or her feet "neither bound nor free," but really symbolic of being between the worlds. That is the nature of a witch, as priest/ess. We are free from slavery, as *The Charge of the Goddess* says, encouraged to be naked in our rites, yet we are bound by our oaths, and our most important oaths go to the gods, to the service of divine will. With a longer cord, the hands are tied behind the back and pulled up so that the arms form a triangle, a sacred symbol of the elements, and the cord is tied around the neck, with the end dangling in front of the initiate as a cable tow, to lead him or her around. Such initiates, particularly at the lower degrees, are blindfolded and need to be led in the circle. These are the binding cords.

Initiation rituals continue with presentation to the four powers, the fivefold kiss, ritual anointing, and possibly scourging. All act as blessings and/or purifications, as well as ritual teachings. At some point, the measure is taken. The initiate's height, and the circumference around the forehead, heart, and genitals, are all measured and marked with knots in a cord or string. The three centers are the primary power points of traditional forms of witchcraft: the brow, heart, and sexual center, omitting only the throat and feet as points on the Qabalistic Middle Pillar, which are already bound.

The measure is taken for several reasons. On the loftiest level, the physical measure, taken between the worlds, marks the initiate to the gods as being linked, corded, to the temples between the worlds and forever more recognized by the powers as a walker between the worlds. The less lofty reason that a measure was kept was so that if the initiate ever broke oaths, a tangible, strong link would be held by the initiator and coven to magickally curse the traitorous initiate, guaranteeing the secrecy of the coven. Once you learn the arts of magick, you would never want to cross one who held such a powerful connection to you. Gardnerian covens traditionally kept the measure, while Alexandrian ones gave it back to the initiate, to show the mark of trust and faith the group had for the initiate.

The practice doesn't seem in keeping with the passwords for the circle, "Perfect Love and Perfect Trust," yet to put yourself in the situation of being ritually bound and measured is an act of trust, of both your initiator and the gods. Many witches use the phrase "in the lap of the Goddess" to simply say that they put all their trust in the Goddess, for they, like children, have no control over the situation, but they trust that they've been led this far for the right reason. The first time I heard the phrase was in reference to Robert Cochrane, who reportedly said right before his death that his fate was in the "lap of the Goddess." I know many who were not prepared for such experiences of initiation, and had to trust in the magick, coven, and gods, because when a blindfold and robes come out, it is easy to assume the worst. In advanced initiations, the initiate, in turn, then binds the initiator, and scourges the initiator, where the trust must then be reciprocated. Unfortunately I know several cases where both the Perfect Love and Perfect Trust were not upheld by initiators who held measuring cords, and they used them unjustly against the initiates. In this day of the Internet and published books, there is very little that is kept from the public eye, and very little could and should be considered an offense worthy of a crippling or killing curse. Wounded egos of initiators and teachers should be put aside.

So the cingulum, the measuring line, is ideally the tool of building trust in the coven and the tradition. Our self-initiatory work in the Temple of Witchcraft does not involve the same binding, but it involves a trust and promise between us and the gods. It is symbolized by the five-braided belt of initiation, for each of the five levels and mysteries. Wearing each of the colored cords signifies, between you and the gods, that you did that level's work to the best of your ability. Making your nineteen-knot witch's ladder for this course with a secondary cord signifies that you have done the work of each lesson. As you do what others have done, a power builds up, connecting you to a tradition. If those in a tradition are all initiated in the same way, be it bound and measured or through other means, then the archetypal cord is like a chain of ancestry, connecting them all. It is like an umbilical cord, connecting them to the Goddess through the belly, through her womb to your belly. Here is where we get the greatest source of intuitive wisdom, direct from the Great Mother.

Here is the place we build our first trust, with the Mother, and through the Mother, to those who have come before us, in blood and with spirit. The Moon rules the belly, and the flow of blood mysteries, genetics, and birth. The Moon is the great measurer, marking time and tide with such precision.

The next exercise is designed to take you back through the cord, from the umbilical cord to the great chain of DNA. Rather than go to your soul's origin, as you did in the last lesson, you will be going through the blood's origin, working with the ancestors and in particular looking for the ancestors who might have shared your gifts, your talents, and your calling for the arts of magick. You are seeking out your own witchblood, those in your lineage who have shared this persuasion. Somewhere it is in the blood, and you can find it. Making links to your ancestors in general, but your witch ancestors in particular, is a powerful method of learning the mysteries of this temple.

EXERCISE 7

Ancestral Womb

Explore the power and memories you carry in the chain of DNA through your blood relatives. Even if you do not know your own parents or family, an exploration of the blood through the ancestral womb can reveal a lot about the blessings and difficulties you carry.

1. Perform Exercise 1: Inner Temple as a Mystery School Meditation (page 45), steps 1–5, to go to your inner temple. Feel your inner temple dedicated to be a mystery school. Feel it permeated with the energies of the Belly Temple. You might feel it all around you, or be guided to go into another chamber, a separate room that is your Temple of the Belly.

2. Ask to meet with the ancestors of your blood who have something to show you, particularly the ancestors of your witchblood. Ask that this be for your highest good, harming none. If possible, ask for the first of the witchblood in your line.

3. Go to the gateway of ancestors (*ITOW*, chapter 14). Before you open it, you need a special key to gain entry. In your spirit vision, cut your hand with the Sword of Truth (*TOHW*, chapter 8). Place a bloody handprint on the door

and that is your key to open the gateway of ancestral memories. The blood expands around the gateway, until you are entering a portal of dark red liquid. You might feel as if you are diving into a cauldron filled with blood. As you enter the path, you are entering the dark womb of genetic memory. Feel yourself entering the womb of your mother, through her blood, to her mother, your grandmother. Move through to your great grandmother and onward, deep into the blood, moving from womb to womb. Lose yourself in the blood of the ancestors, going back through the generations and bloodlines. You may hear the whispers of those who come before you, and realize that they are the familiar voices you hear when you dream and meditate.

4. Eventually the dark tunnel gives way to the light, and in the light something takes shape and form, the form of a person in your lineage. You find yourself communing with a strong ancestor who has much to share with you. Commune with this ancestor. Ask the ancestor what you inherit, for both good and for ill. What are the blessings you have, particularly in the ways of magick and healing? What are the burdens you bear because of your blood? What must you heal in yourself, so that your whole line will be healed and redeemed? What must you use from your ancestors, and what must you do for them, to heal them?

5. This ancestor may give a gift to you, representing all of the knowledge of power and magick he or she has. You have it too—it's in your blood, and the gift will act as a key, to safely unlock it. Feel this gift activate the fire in the blood, the secret witchfire that illuminates and empowers. Feel the fire flow through the blood, beating in your witch heart. Feel the threads of ancestry awaken within you. The ancestor might ask you for something in return, to honor him or her, or to do something for the family line. If you are up for the challenge, accept the gift, give thanks, and take it into you. Make sure you honor your pledge to your ancestor when you return.

6. Say farewell, knowing you will be able to make contact again much more easily if you both so choose. This could be the beginning of a much deeper relationship. You might start including items on your ancestor altar for this

particular ancestor. Direct items might be difficult, as the ancestor might stretch too far in the past for any personal photos, objects, or direct links, but you will know what is appropriate for this ancestor the more you work together.

7. Return to the inner temple. Close the gateway of ancestors.

8. Finish exercise 1, steps 8–11, to return to normal consciousness.

Purification is necessary to truly use the powers of instinct built in the belly center. In the alchemical teachings, the second process is known as dissolution. The calcinated ashes of the first operation are exposed to a fluid, to remove impurities that will not be dissolved by the solvent. Magickally, the solvent is elemental water, emotions. The second procedure is hidden in the Emerald Tablet as "Its mother is the Moon," following the fires of the Sun. Its associations are with the Moon—not the purified Moon metal of silver, but shiny tin, and its planet, Jupiter. The initiate is first burned in the fires of the will and then dissolved in emotions, bringing to the surface emotional wounds, subconscious memories, and patterns that cloud us. That which can be purified and integrated is, and that which no longer serves is cast out. This is very similar to the process of shadow work in *TOSW*. You almost drown yourself in your shadow emotions, to integrate the best aspects of them and to release those that no longer serve. Much of our healing work, in all alternative, energetic, and spiritual modalities, is referred to as "cleansing" because the water of dissolution clears us of these unhealthy patterns that are the source of many illnesses.

The Egyptian temple of Kom Ombo (or Ko Mombo) corresponds with the belly chakra. One of the gods of Kom Ombo is Sobek, the crocodile deity. This reptilian figure deals with our lower, gut, instinctual self. Crocodile mummies have been found at Kom Ombo. While the crocodile was feared, worship of the beast was to placate the danger it posed, and soon the crocodile, naturally associated with the Nile water, became a symbol of fertility and nourishment because the town of Kom Ombo is an agricultural center. The other side of the temple was dedicated to Horus the Elder. Edfu is also associated with the belly chakra. The Temple of Edfu was dedicated to Horus and was a center of his worship. It is interesting that both of these belly-chakra associations are with a god that has both a wise, elder manifestation and a childlike, younger manifestation. The belly is the chakra of the child, who is learning whom and what to trust by exploring the world.

The second castle is that of Caer Fandy-Manddwy, known both as the "Castle on High" and the "Castle of the Sea," associated with the sea god Manawyddan, similar to the Irish Manannan. Again we have the water and sea imagery for dissolution, for the belly and the gateway of the womb and water. One must pass through this realm before going deeper.

Planting the seed corresponds well with the mysteries of the belly chakra, as the belly/womb holds the growing seed of human life. The seed must be put into the ground—sheltered, nurtured, and protected by the land—so it can grow in darkness and eventually sprout toward the light.

In the path of Left Hand initiation, the second stage, following wandering, is the first shock. Something happens to the initiate to demonstrate that the world is not what it really appears to be. The initiate's foundation is shaken, or even dissolved away. This is similar to the awakening stages of the first temple, but for Left Hand initiates, it is truly the shock of it, the integration of this knowledge as being real on some level, and not a flight of fanciful imagination, that brings them to the edge, the boundary of the magickal. This brings them to the seashore or forest edge metaphorically, where they might decide to go deeper or continue their wandering. The shock is often of an emotional nature, such as a breakup, death, or betrayal, forever altering the initiates' worldview. In such cases, it shares quite a bit with the dissolution of the alchemist. Those who recover from such a shock with their will intact move on through initiation. Those who do not go back to sleep and wander. The virtue of the stage is quantifiable pride, as the initiates do recover from something difficult through their own merits and work. The vice is hubris, as they may falsely believe that they are more special than they are because of this shock and recovery. It's only one step of many.

All of these mystery teachings demonstrate the need to clear the pathways of energy exchange from all unprocessed emotions, thoughts, and feelings. By working with the energy directly, rather than relying on talk therapy alone, you can clear away the things that cloud your instincts in a much more effective way. It's not to say that talk therapy isn't helpful, or in some cases necessary and an extremely valuable part of the process, but working with the energy as well as verbalization is far more efficient in my counseling and teaching experience.

EXERCISE 8

Seven-Body Healing

In *ITOW*, we experienced a purification through the clearing and healing of the aura (exercise 24). If done regularly, it will have had a tremendous benefit to you over the last four levels. These are skills for general health and well-being, meant to ease us through the stresses and strains of both mundane and magickal life. In that first level, we focused on the overall aura, rather than work with all seven specific subtle bodies. Now, with your greater experience and knowledge, we will repeat the exercise, but do so in detail with the seven-body system—physical, etheric, astral, emotional, mental, psychic, and divine. When we are aligned in the seven levels, like the seven chakras, seven heavens, and seven hells, our magickal abilities expand with our consciousness, and we can discern the truth from our fears and desires. Then, our instinct serves us.

The basic meditation involves repairing the violations to the boundary of the aura, perceived as rips, tears, and leaks. Then we remove unwanted thoughtforms, packets of dense energy containing programs, stories, and "tapes" about us that no longer serve a higher purpose. Then we remove the unwanted attachments to other people, places, and time periods that hold us back, drain our energy, or allow us to drain others inappropriately. We'll continue to use that familiar terminology, but realize that it might now apply to all of the subtle bodies. The higher bodies don't have the same sense of boundary as the lower ones, yet they can still feel violated. Technically *thought*forms don't exist beyond the mental body, but we still find dense packets of unwanted energies in them. Use the imagery, and see what information you receive for each subtle body.

1. Perform Exercise 1: Inner Temple as a Mystery School Meditation (page 45), steps 1–5, to go to your inner temple. Feel your inner temple dedicated to be a mystery school.

2. Ask to find the gateway of healing. Open it. Call upon your highest healing guides. If you know their names, name them. Ask for all healing guides that are correct and good for you at this time to come forward. Ask them for healing and purification at this time and place. Ask to completely cleanse and heal the energy system, with ease, grace, and gentleness.

3. Enter the Gate of Healing. Feel your healing guides' presence. They might simply guide you, or do a lot of the work for you, depending on your needs and the relationship you have with them.

4. Begin an aura healing and clearing, as you would from *ITOW*, exercise 24. The aura clearing consists of three parts: first, healing any rips, tears, or leaks in the boundary of the aura; then removing unwanted thoughtforms; and finally removing and releasing the unhealthy energetic cords from the aura that link you to harmful people, places, or times. We are now going to apply those three steps to each of the seven subtle bodies.

5. Focus on the divine body, surrounding your entire energy field. It is truly infinite, and out of all the seven bodies, it should have the least amount of damage, if any. Scan the divine body. Do you sense a color for it? If so, what does that color mean to you? Scan this body from top to bottom. Does it have any holes, rips, or leaks? If so, fill it with a ball of white light, allowing the light to change to whatever color is needed to heal this subtle body. Scan the body from top to bottom again. Does this body have any unhealthy, dense energy patterns floating in it? If so, reach out to them with your will. As you grab them, you might be able to sense their program and origin. Either way, push them out of the aura and dissolve the dense patterns with white light, like sugar dissolving in water. When you have cleared out all the dense energy patterns, scan the body again, from top to bottom, to look for any cords rooted in this body. If you find any, psychically grab the cords, perhaps sensing their origin and who or what they connect you to. Gently pull out the cords. Fill them with white light, dissolving them all the way back to the source, and release the source with

a "blessed be." Fill any holes made by the cords with white light. Feel your divine body, healthy, clear, and balanced.

6. Focus on the psychic body. It is the body of visions. Repeat the instructions of step 5, with the focus on the psychic body.

7. Focus on the mental body. It is the body of the mind, thoughts, and ideas. Repeat the instructions of step 5, with the focus on the mental body.

8. Focus on the emotional body. It is the body of the heart, empathy, and relationship. Repeat the instructions of step 5, with the focus on the emotional body.

9. Focus on the astral body. It is the body of the self-image, self-esteem, and personal power. Repeat the instructions of step 5, with the focus on the astral body.

10. Focus on the etheric body. It is the template of the physical body. Repeat the instructions of step 5, with the focus on the etheric body.

11. Healing the etheric body directly affects the physical, and it will bring changes to the physical body. Scan the physical body for places of illness, imbalance, disease, and tension. Ask your guides for their aid in removing the etheric template of any ill organs or body areas, and replace it with a completely healthy template. Replace all organ and body parts that are damaged.

12. Bring the healing you have just done into total alignment; bring your physical body into alignment with your healthy etheric template and the other subtle bodies. Connect to the heavens, through your inner temple, and feel the stellar energy descend down through the crown, brow, throat, heart, solar plexus, belly, and root.

13. Finish exercise 1, steps 8–11, to return to normal consciousness.

Be aware that after this meditation, you might experience a period of physical cleansing, marked by coldlike symptoms or a digestive purge, as well as emotional cleansing, with vivid dreams and a need to express yourself verbally or creatively. Go with it, knowing that all these potential reactions are the energies moving through your system and are perfectly normal.

One student asked me if these energetic cords can ever serve a useful purpose. At the *ITOW* level, we focus on getting rid of the cords, for they are the mechanisms through which we get pulled off our center and pull others. They are inappropriate links. I describe healthy and appropriate links to my students as "bonds" or resonances. We are on the same vibration, so we don't have a linear relationship to each other, but a harmony, like two musical notes that ring well together. We might sense things about people to whom we are bonded, but we are not inappropriately taking or giving energy, or getting "stuck" to them and their situation. My questioning student didn't think all cords were bad, as she's seen some in visions. In this lesson, we've talked a lot about the cord, the measure, and how it connects us in a tradition, and the connection we have to the Great Mother. So how do you differentiate healthy bonds from unhealthy cords?

In my personal cosmology, I see the Great Goddess as the weaver, and everything in creation is made from her tapestry of webs. We are all strings of energy. A chant used in modern paganism for raising energy and cord dancing is "We are the Flow and we are the Ebb; We are the Weavers, we are the Web." Attributed to Shekhinah Mountainwater, other lines are sometimes added: "We are the spiders weaving our thread; We are the witches, back from the dead." In this chant we see the paradoxical concept of being both the weaver and the web, that divinity is both transcendent and immanent in its manifestation. As divine beings, we are both transcendent and immanent. Like the Goddess who is the weaver of all, we too are weavers. The cords that come from our divine source, that are us, and our reality, are really another way of looking at our bonds of resonance. They are our vibrations. They remain mostly invisible in this exercise, for we are asking to "see" what doesn't serve, to purify it. The pure strings that weave together to form our souls, and all of creation, not made in ego or harm, are the pure strands of the weaver and our weaver selves. If you choose to work with the Great Mother in the form of the weaver, she will show you how to work with the shining web strings of creation, and help you easily differentiate them from the dense cords of harmful connection that we seek to remove.

The Master-Teacher

To the priest/ess, there is no more important relationship than the one between teacher and student, initiator and initiate. This is the most sacred connection, through which the lines of power are passed. In the Temple of Witchcraft tradition, the lines of power are passed directly from the inner world to the outer world, through making a direct connection with the inner-plane adepts, our Hidden Company that guides the tradition of witchcraft as a whole. The most important thing a teacher can do, even in initiatory lineage traditions, is to help connect the student to the inner teachers and inner wisdoms, through guides and the higher self, and give the student the tools to access, discern, trust, and act upon the teachings he or she receives. The inner relationship is the most important.

Many kinds of guides aid us on the other side. We build up a team of spiritual guides, and they all have their own specialties. Sometimes the relationships are like lateral partnerships. We have guides that act as our friends, confidants, and companions in magick, just as we have those relationships in the physical plane. We also have non-lateral relationships on the physical plane, with those who act as mentors, teachers, and supervisors. We can have spirits that fulfill those same roles. I've found that, in the entire team of guides and guardians, one spirit takes the role of the Master-Teacher.

The Master-Teacher, like a physical spiritual teacher, is not here to be your friend, or to coddle you, telling you what you want to hear, but to teach you. Teachers all have different styles. Some create and maintain friendships, but it's not their primary purpose. They are here to teach, often to teach the tough lessons. This spirit is your guide from the inner planes, whose purpose is aligned with your purpose, and is here to educate you toward that purpose. Some teachers are like taskmasters. Others are gentle and benevolent. Some act like Zen masters, with riddles and mysteries to solve. Others give lots of intellectual work and direct information.

My own Master-Teacher is quite wizardly and Druidic, yet he has a head that continually shines and shapeshifts. It was a part of my training to discern his true nature and identity. He tends to be the trickster, giving me an assignment and not coming again until I've got something for him. Though we don't have a lateral relationship together, like other guides, we've grown over the years to have a more friendly and mentoring relationship than we did in the beginning.

Master-Teacher spirits can come from a variety of sources, from divinities to angels, ancestors and those ascended inner-plane adepts of the Hidden Company, enlightened witches, and magicians from another time and place. Usually the spirit is humanoid, not animal, plant, insect, or stone. Such spirits offer additional assistance, but are not the primary Master-Teacher. Some initiates have one or two spirits that fulfill all the roles of the team, while others have very specialized and individual spirits for each role. Your own Master-Teacher might be an entity you already know.

Don't confuse a patron deity with a Master-Teacher, though again, they could be one and the same. When in a patron-priest/ess relationship with a deity, you are the priest/ess of a Goddess or God, here to do the deity's work in the world in relationship with that deity. This relationship offers one kind of exchange of energy. Master-Teachers are here specifically to teach you for your own evolution and the evolution of your soul's purpose. They have experience with the path your soul is on, and they share this wisdom with you. Master-Teachers are the highest form of tutelary spirit, and their name directly implies that they have already mastered the work you are facing. Their work is in presenting it to us on this plane. The work between you and the Master-Teacher is more on the inner planes than in the material world. The two will be directly related, and your Master-Teacher can be quite a complement to your patron deity.

You can see the role of the Master-Teacher through history and legend. Most famous is Merlin's relationship to Arthur, as guide and teacher, depending on the version of the story. You can see a more difficult and severe relationship between Ceridwen and Gwion Bach, later to be Taliesin. Another hard relationship is between Cuchulain and the Morrighan. So hard in fact, that it doesn't appear to be a teacher-student relationship at all at first glance, but in many ways it is. Our teacher relationships are not always what we think they will be.

Use this exercise to make contact with your own Master-Teacher.

EXERCISE 9

Finding Your Master-Teacher

1. Perform Exercise 1: Inner Temple as a Mystery School Meditation (page 45), steps 1–5, to go to your inner temple. Feel your inner temple dedicated to be a mystery school.

2. Open the gateway of guidance. Ask to connect to your Master-Teacher of this lifetime, of this place and time, for your highest good, harming none. Declare your intention to sincerely work with this spirit for your spiritual evolution.

3. Perceive a teacher, a figure, coming out of the gateway.

4. Commune with this teacher. Ask your questions of the teacher, about the teachings and your work together.

5. Ask the Master-Teacher for the next step in your spiritual evolution. You could receive your first lessons, or preparation and a schedule for your lessons.

6. Thank and release the Master-Teacher, who will go back through the gateway of guidance. Now that you have openly invited the Master-Teacher into your inner temple, there will be more direct contact initiated by the spirit when appropriate. You will both be building a relationship together.

7. Finish exercise 1, steps 8–11, to return to normal consciousness.

HOMEWORK

- Do exercises 6–9 and record your experiences in your journal or BOS. Pay particular attention to detailing the lessons of your Master-Teacher and the messages of your blood ancestors.

- When you complete the trials of this chapter, tie your second knot in your cord in a ritualized manner.

- If you have not obtained the four cords from the previous levels—red for *ITOW*, green for *OTOW*, blue for *TOSW*, and yellow for *TOHW*—do so and loosely weave them together, using them as the binding cord for your robe. Generally they should be at least the height of your body. I prefer double the height of my body, to give enough length for when I braid them. If you are unsure, I've found that about twelve feet of cords will braid down to nine feet, which is an appropriate length for your cord. Obtain, but do not yet use, your fifth cord, which can be black, white, or violet.

- Students following this course with me are asked to take their own measure, around the neck, and knot a cord with the measurement of their neck, so I can make a necklace for them in accord with the tradition of the witch's jewels (see Lesson Five). This shows that in the Temple of Witchcraft teachings, we all must take our own measure of skill, determination, and drive, and we are only measuring ourselves against ourselves to improve.

TIPS

- Continue to build an integrated meditation and ritual practice.

- Speak with your Master-Teacher regularly. Build a relationship.

- Be more aware of your gut intuition, your ability to access and take measure of someone, some place, or some thing.

- In exercise 7, you could find yourself going back to the primal fount, to the Goddess, taking form as the cauldron goddess of rebirth, like Ceridwen, the goddess of the silver wheel, or like Arianrhod, or the Queen of the Blessed Isles who has many names and forms. If you do, speak with her and ask her to help you find the right ancestor, unless she has something else in store for you.

- For exercise 7, you can ritualistically prick your own finger, add the drop of blood to a bowl of water, stir it nine times, and then either leave it on the altar as you meditate or pour a circle of water around you, particularly if doing this exercise outside. It's not absolutely necessary, but it's a powerful way to connect with the ancestors. Many modern witches are squeamish about using blood, particularly their own, in ritual, but this is one situation where it's particularly appropriate to use some of the more traditional methods of communing with the ancestors.

- You can use the full chant by Shekhinah Mountainwater as a focus for exercises 7 and 5, specifically working on past lives of blood and spirit where you worked magick and were potentially persecuted for it. Many modern witches today are working through persecution complexes, in part stemming from identification with past selves who were also persecuted for magick and witchcraft, or at least the appearance of such.

- Exercise 8 can combine well with Exercise 4: Skeleton Meditation to bring healing to the physical body.

- Exercise 7 and Exercise 5: Exploring Your Spiritual Origin in the Great Ages can be put to use to heal both strands of your past lives—ancestral past-life energy you carry in your blood, and soul past-life memories brought by spirit. Apply these ideas along with the healing techniques of *TOSW*, chapter 14: Past-Life Healing.

LESSON THREE
TEMPLE OF THE SOLAR PLEXUS: POWER AND FEAR

The third gate, the Temple of the Solar Plexus, brings our consciousness up to a new stage, beyond the dependence of the root and belly, toward the first steps of independence. The solar plexus embodies the level of consciousness where we come into our own power—yet power always has its price. If our relationship with power is not balanced, we can stray into extremes. We can seek out so much power, afraid that we don't have enough, and feel we need to take it from others to be independent and powerful. We can be afraid of our power and give it away, letting others control us because power is too difficult to handle. Fear that is out of control manifests as anger. Only when power is balanced, when fear is acknowledged but not succumbed to, do we realize that power and control are really over ourselves, not others. Only then do we realize that the fears are ultimately not from others, but most often from within. Through this balance, we find the still center point of knowing when to take action. Like the seas, we learn when to rise and when to ebb. Both forces are needed to work effective magick.

Set up your altar using the correspondences of the solar plexus chakra. Use a yellow or gold candle and stones such as pyrite and citrine. Also, fiery Mars attributes, such as iron, can work well for this temple. And as with the previous chakras, build a direct relationship with this inner star through a contemplative meditation.

EXERCISE 10

Contemplation of the Solar Plexus

1. Sit quietly in a comfortable position and enter a meditative state. Call upon higher guidance, through your own spirit guides and the Goddess, God, and Great Spirit.

2. Place your hands on the upper belly area, just below the diaphragm, on the solar plexus.

3. Feel the energy of the solar plexus chakra. Start with your hands, but let any sensations move through your entire body. You might feel as if your entire energy field is surrounded in golden yellow light. Ask the solar plexus chakra to reveal its mysteries and guide you.

4. Observe the thoughts, feelings, visions, and insights you have, as well as messages you receive, while attuning yourself to the Temple of the Solar Plexus. These will guide you in this lesson to your own personal work.

5. When done, return yourself from the meditative state. Thank the energy of the solar plexus chakra as well as your spiritual guidance, and give yourself clearance and balance.

Magickal Teaching: Intensity
Force: Combustion
Chakra: Solar Plexus
Function: Power
Body: Astral

Tool of the Goddess: Gold Bracelet

Alternate Tool of the Goddess: Ring

Colors: Yellow, Gold

Ray: Third, the Ray of Active Intelligence

Element: Fire

Planet: Mars

Metal: Iron

Sign: Scorpio

Emerald Tablet Rubric: The Wind Carries It in Its Belly

Alchemical Operation: Separation

Totems: Owl, Beaver

Plant: Nettles

Sephiroth: Hod and Netzach

Tarot, Lunar: Trump III—Empress

Tarot, Solar: Trump X—Fortune

Tarot, Stellar: Trump XVII—Star

Life Stage: First Initiation (*ITOW*)

Hermetic Principle: Gender

Musical Note: E

Day of the Week: Tuesday

Castle of the Underworld: Caer Goludd—Castle of Gloom, Castle of Death, Castle of Trials, Fortress of Frustration and Riches

Egyptian Temple Sites: Luxor/Thebes, Karnak

Left Hand Initiation: Daydreaming

Vice of Initiation: Forgetfulness of Past Orthodoxies

Virtue of Initiation: Sense of Humor

Stage of the Bread Miracle: Green Corn

Challenge of the Temple: Anger

Blessing of the Temple: Power

Explorations of power can be difficult, yet we've chosen a path of power. A lot of people who identify as witches are uncomfortable with that fact, with power, yet it is a fundamental part of our tradition. Our paths are the paths to power. Our worship is rituals that direct and raise power. Our magick is backed with a certain power, and our magick is the way we commune; we pray with the universe. We don't have a worldview where we are disengaged from the universe, but are active and empowered participants of creation.

The Mysteries of Power

When I teach this lesson to a group of students, I usually start with the question, "What is power?" and I'm always surprised by the answers I get. Like so many things in witchcraft, you can get as many different answers as the people you ask, if not more. We, in our modern Western society, have a very strange relationship to the concept of power and its use. Keywords that come up in the discussion include *control*, *will*, *ego*, *abuse*, *fear*, *anger*, and *defense*. Usually the conversation takes a negative tone, and that is because we often have a negative view of our own power, an unhealthy relationship with it, like we have with many natural things. I have personally found witchcraft to be a remedy for many of the ills of our society, helping me reframe my relationships to find balance, rather than accept the unbalanced and unhealthy paradigms that are dominant in society.

Power is a necessary part of life. Power is the energy to get things done. Without it, nothing would happen. Power is a part of our psychic makeup, and is as necessary as the brain or liver to our physical makeup. The mysteries of this third temple, of the solar plexus, are a part of a chain. Without these mysteries of power, you cannot go on to the higher temples. On its most basic level, power is neither good nor bad. It is not inherently evil or benign; it simply is. You have power in your body, it fuels your body, but what you choose to do with your body is up to you. There is power in natural phenomena, such as electricity. We've learned to harness electricity, but how we use it is up to us, not the electricity. We can light a room, heat a home, or provide power to a life-sustaining medical device. Overall these are seen as "good" uses of power. We can use power to purposely kill someone, or we can accidentally leave a wire exposed, which could electrocute someone. Both can be seen as a "bad" use of power. Yet, to a staunch environmentalist, using electricity to excessively light a room or heat a home is "bad." Perhaps a life-saving device is keeping someone alive who would be better off dead. And if an electric chair is used on someone who murdered a loved one, and it prevents that criminal from ever harming another, it might be seen as a "good" application of electric power. Power, like nature, is neutral. It's our personal value judgments on its effect that cause us to label it "good" or "bad." Our judgments are subjective.

It is in our judgment of power where people develop an unhealthy relationship with it. While many people go one way, seeking out power over others, looking strictly for temporal and material power, rather than seeing any value to spiritual inner power, other witches move in the opposite direction. Rather than risk misusing power and hurting themselves or others, they avoid and relinquish power. It's too much responsibility. There is a certain wisdom in this concept, yet as a long-run strategy, it's faulty wisdom. I must admit, I structure my classes and tradition to dissuade those who are seeking only material power. If you can get through *ITOW*, with all its introspective meditations, and you have developed the ability to contact guidance, then you are ready to do the spellcraft of *OTOW*. But if you can't sit still and meditate, then I'm not anxious to teach you spellcraft. Yet both are necessary on the path of the witch.

Power and spirituality go hand-in-hand in our tradition. Spiritual wisdom without the power to act upon it is ineffective. Without power, you cannot change yourself or change your world. Material power without the wisdom of knowing when and how to use it is folly, for it leads people down a path of misfortune and heartache. The power itself did not do it, but the unwise choices in how they applied the power did. Just because you *can* do something doesn't mean you *should* do something. Ours is a path of doing, or action, as well as listening and being receptive. One way of learning to work appropriately with power is through the concept of will. Your will is what guides the power, and through using your power, you learn to distinguish your personal will from your True Will, your divine will (*OTOW*, chapter 10). From this knowledge, and acting upon this knowledge, comes wisdom.

In the descent of Inanna, the Goddess's fifth possession relinquished to the keeper of the gate is a golden bracelet, a symbol of the mystery of power in this third temple. The gold relates it to the solar plexus, the golden yellow chakra. The concept of a bracelet, on the wrist, so close to the hand, is an ornament decorating the part of the body that is used to direct power, to direct energy. In ritual magick, healing, and even day-to-day body language, we use our arms and hands to direct the flow of energy. By giving up her bracelet, Inanna is giving up her ability to direct her power, her energy generated at the solar plexus level and disseminated throughout her body. Though some tales give us a golden hip girdle, better matching the placement of the solar plexus and the concept of feminine power and self-image, the bracelet offers us some deeper insight into the ways of power.

In many traditions of initiatory witchcraft, priestesses and priests are entitled to wear a bracelet with their witch names in a cipher such as Theban script (*TOHW*, chapter 8) and grade sign (*ITOW*, chapter 17) engraved upon it. They are worn out in public as a sign to other witches, but something that the uninitiated would not recognize.

As a ritual tool, the bracelet means many things. Since it is earned as a part of initiation, it is symbolic of the power the witch has gained. Different traditions entitle the wearing of the bracelet at different elevation ranks, and many reserve it for third-degree high priestesses only, while others include high priests. The bracelet may change as the initiation rank changes, so keep in mind that some traditions encourage this practice at other ranks, and many traditions do not include the practice at all. The material of the bracelet is as diverse as the traditions that practice this custom. One line of reasoning says that women wear silver, Moon metal, while men wear gold or, for those with limited finances, brass or copper. Another school of thought says that women should wear gold, brass, or copper to better attune to the God, while men should wear silver to attune to the Goddess. Another choice is to use a bracelet of woven metals, usually gold, silver, and copper, or brass, silver, and copper. The copper, in particular, is said to have medicinal properties when worn, being good for arthritis and other joint problems.

A twisted or braided open bracelet or neck ring is considered to be a *torc* or *torque*. The ends are marked with ornaments, either a ball at each, or an ornate metal image of animal heads, plants such as thistles, or abstract designs. As a Celtic tradition, torcs were ornaments of nobles, warriors, and others of a high social status. Later, Romans adopted the use of the torc for distinguished soldiers. The torc has divine attributes, as Cernunnos, the horned image on the world-famous Gundestrup Cauldron (*TOSW*, chapter 5), is shown both wearing and holding a torc. Though many high priests will use the torc neck ring as their witch necklace, in place of the amber and jet of the traditional priestess, I wear the torc as a bracelet.

The bracelet is a mark of servitude, of "bondage" to the Goddess and God, similar in idea to the slave bracelet. It's an interesting concept, as *The Charge of the Goddess* says we shall be free from slavery. Yet we are in bondage to the oaths we have taken, and the most important of these is to be priest/ess to the Goddess and God. The bracelet is designed to be open-ended, to both allow the flow of energy and show that we can take it off at any point. We do so for practical purposes, but it is symbolic of the choice we have to walk away from the responsibility. We are not enslaved. Though some would disagree and say, "Once a priest/ess, always a priest/ess," many do walk away from the responsibilities of their oaths and vocations, at a heavy personal price. But the freedom is there. To be effective priest/esses, we must really choose to be in service, choose to dedicate ourselves to the Craft, and choose to be vessels for the Goddess and God in this world.

The interesting question to ask, in relation to the mysteries of power and the bracelet, is on which wrist was Inanna wearing it? Was it the left side or the right side? And on what side do you wear your witch bracelet, and why?

The Ethics of the Left Hand and Right Hand Paths

The concept of dividing magickal paths into Right Hand and Left Hand Paths is well known, though many modern pagans are not familiar with the concept or how it fits into modern witchcraft. And, like power, when you talk about dividing the applications of power into a polarity, into two groups such as Right and Left Hand Paths, you will get as many definitions for the terms as the people you ask.

Left Hand Paths are often equated with Satanism, yet there are many philosophies dubbed "Satanism." In an effort to distance ourselves from anything even remotely considered Satanic, most witches do not bother to learn any of the more subtle points, and latch on to the label of Right Hand Path, if being forced to pick between the two.

Some of the potential roots of these terms come from cultural uses of the hand in areas where water for washing was scarce. The left hand was used for issues of hygiene, while the right was used for food and social greetings, to reduce the chance of contamination. The term *sinistrality* means "left-handedness," and it comes from the Latin word *sinister*, as culturally, left-handedness was considered inferior, unlucky, or even wicked, and it was suppressed at various points in history in favor of right-handedness. A variety of "negative" associations and ill omens have become attached to the left-hand side, while positive ones go with the right.

In the most limited set of definitions, simplistic practitioners will define a Left Hand Path as an evil path and a Right Hand Path as a good path. One is using magick for harm, or for selfish purposes, while the other is never using magick to harm, and is for selfless purposes and personal development. It's the classic black-magick-versus-white-magick battle that most witches and magicians do not subscribe to anymore. Others will take it a step further, with the definitions of white, black, and gray magick (*ITOW*, chapter 3).

A more subtle, yet still oversimplified, approach to the two is to look at the Right Hand Path as creative, healing, and growing magick, while the Left Hand Path is the destructive, lessening, weakening, and cursing aspect of magick. At first glance, that might seem the same as the good/evil paradigm split, yet I know many a "good" and wise witch who might take the approach to curse the illness that plagues a loved one, and ultimately bring healing. Destructive is not necessarily evil. It's often quite good, for you need to destroy to create. It's a part of life. By these definitions, waning Moon and dark Moon magick could be considered Left Hand Path. When I began my witchcraft practice, most of my spells were waxing Moon. I wanted things. I wanted to manifest my desires in my life. As I grow older and hopefully wiser, more and more of my spells are waning Moon spells, to remove the "deadwood" of my life, and to make room to grow, without having a specific manifestation goal in mind. I knew I had to get rid of anything that no longer served me, like clearing out the garden before deciding what to plant next.

The two paths are also divided in terms of gender. In general esoteric schools, when doing magick and energy work, the right hand is principally considered the dominant, projective, yang, and masculine hand, while the left is the recessive, receptive, yin, and feminine hand. Particularly in the Eastern traditions, those paths that were more masculine, disciplined, ascetic, and martial, like many spiritual warrior yogic traditions, were considered Right Hand Paths. Traditions that were more devotional to the feminine, that celebrated the body and pleasure, and explored sacred sexuality, were considered Left Hand Paths. In mainstream society, it is much easier to describe the Right Hand Paths and get general acceptance than to explain to the uninitiated the concepts of sacred sexuality or dark goddesses. The classification of left as evil might find its root in a misunderstanding of these practices.

Lastly, we have a set of definitions supplied by those who identify as modern Left Hand Path practitioners. Those on the Left Hand Path are not seeking to merge with the source of all that is. They are on the path of the individual, finding their divinity by an exploration of the self. The model they use is the divine rebel, be it Prometheus, Malek Taus, Set, Azazel, Cain, or Lucifer. All are figures that go against the grain of traditional divinity to find their own path outside the scripted "rules" given to them. That is the pattern the Left Hand Path seeks to emulate, feeling those who simply want to merge their identity with the divine and become "one" are fools. Author Don Webb, in his book *Uncle Setnakt's Essential Guide to the Left Hand Path*, describes the difference using an oak tree. Those on the Left Hand Path want their acorn to take root and grow independent from the oak tree, rather than rot and feed the roots of the original oak. They seek to become divine beings in their own right, becoming equal with the source as a part of their evolution, rather than feed the source. Left Hand Path practitioners do not identify as evil, yet they do not feel constrained by the same rules that society has put upon us all. They have their own personal rules and moral codes. Don Webb is a guiding member of the Temple of Set, one of the most elegant purveyors of Left Hand Path theology, elevating it far beyond what most people think of when they think of Satanism.

By their definition, such Left Hand Path practitioners see most practitioners of Wicca as following a strictly Right Hand Path, but they would consider many of the New Age practices inspired by Madame Blavatsky and the Theosophical movement to be at least partially Left Hand Path oriented, with the goal of becoming an ascended master a self-deifying step. I'm sure this label would horrify most practitioners working within the Theosophical paradigm, who think of themselves as the "white lighters" and holy knights of the New Age movement. Many people mistakenly believe Aleister

Crowley to be a Satanist and/or a Left Hand Path practitioner. The Satanism comes from a misunderstanding of his writings, though you could argue he's somewhere in between the Right and Left Hand Paths. In his own cosmology, he was nothing but a Right Hand Path white magician, and he warned readers of the "black brothers" or evil magicians. Ironically, while the Dionysian current is most strongly associated with the dark, and the Apollonian with the light, it appears that modern Left Hand traditions are pointing out that, ideologically, they are far more Apollonian, as in their "light bringer" mythologies of Lucifer and Prometheus. The New Age of traditions of the light worker, while self-perceived as Right Hand, theologically want to merge with the divine, following a more Dionysian or Left Hand Path.

Does the Left Hand Path have a place in modern witchcraft? Many of the stereotypes and misconceptions put on the Left Hand Path also get put on witchcraft. In an effort to distance ourselves from those misconceptions and gain public acceptance, are we sacrificing some of our wisdom, wisdom that has been a part of witchcraft, predating our modern revival in the twentieth century? If so, what exactly are we sacrificing?

If our goal is acceptance, we must be accepted for who and what we are. Witchcraft, even in its most palatable forms, was not meant to be mainstream and easily accepted. It's not a mass-market path for everyone. In fact, we don't proselytize because we know it's not for everyone. It takes a level of awareness and responsibility that is not easy to mass-produce, despite what some might think. If we are only accepted by washing away the "dark" parts of our wisdom, it's like homosexuals being accepted because they "act" straight and subscribe to societal images that are not necessarily for them, or black people who are accepted because they conform to "white" culture and deny their cultural roots. That is not acceptance. To celebrate diversity, mainstream society must accept the diverse parts that it doesn't necessarily like or easily understand.

Just as I don't describe my magick as being black or white, or even gray, but filled with all the colors of the spectrum, I say that my magick is not Right Hand Path or Left Hand Path, because I need both hands to effectively use my tools, not just one. This might seem surprising to many people, as I'm often viewed as pretty mainstream when it comes to the ethics of the Craft, but I do feel that everybody needs to find their own way, and what works for me might not work for you. I believe that the true mysteries are found in the paradox of opposites—how both things can be true, such as witchcraft being influenced by both the Left Hand and Right Hand Paths. Some call it the Crooked Path, or Serpent Path, as it undulates between the two sides, like a snake.

I love the oak tree explanation of the two paths, because I love oak trees. They have taught me and continue to teach me a lot. The paradox for me is that some acorns do grow to be their own trees. Some never do and simply rot, feeding the land and plants around it. Even the oak that grows mighty and strong, like its parent tree, must eventually fall and feed the larger entity of the Earth, merging with it. The Earth itself is a single part of a larger universe. The paradox is in both individuality and union. Both are truths, yet one does not negate the other.

Left Hand Paths are considered evil, yet divine evil has no place in the witch's cosmology. We don't believe in an ultimate source of evil. We have no devil figure in polar opposition to the all-beneficent good-god figure. Our polarities are in masculine and feminine, embodiments of God and Goddess, in complementary relationship, not conflict. We believe in nature, and it's neither good nor evil—it's simply a cycle of life, death, and rebirth. We might label such phenomena as good or bad to us personally, but they are not inherently evil. A storm that destroys your house is bad. One that waters your crops so you can live is good. Same storm. It just depends on your perspective. And neither case is a punishment or reward from God, simply a natural process, like birth, life, and death. Death is not a punishment or reward, but the natural conclusion to a life cycle. How you die, and your view on death, frames how "good" or "bad" the experience is for you. It might surprise quite a few witches to know that most Satanists, particularly those of the Anton LaVey–style Church of Satan philosophy, don't believe in an ultimate, personified figure of evil either, but in the laws of nature.

Those involved in paths that are considered Left Hand are not averse to doing curses, yet most modern witches would be aghast at such a thought. Are curses a part of witchcraft? Up until fairly recently, they were a much larger part than many people like to admit. Though there has been a lot of propaganda about the witch from medieval stereotypes, stereotypes have a kernel of truth to them.

Witchcraft traditions that predate the very public Gardnerian/Alexandrian revival lack the Wiccan Rede ("An' ye harm none, do as ye Will") as an ethical guide. In what many call Traditional Craft, they tell us that it was quite traditional to do curses when you felt justified to do so. Though many witches believe the Wiccan Rede to be traditional, there are no real credible sources of origin before the modern revival of witchcraft. As the Craft entered a public light and received more initiates than it was used to for the last few hundred years, the Wiccan Rede was brought in to provide a guideline. Though it's unfashionable and critiqued in many pagan circles, I believe it's a good ethic and principle, particularly if you look to explore its deeper meaning, influenced by Thelema, concerning the alignment of your personal ego will with your divine True Will (*OTOW*, chapter 10). The Rede has been assumed to be an immutable law by many modern witches, but its very name, the word *rede*, means something given as good advice. It's a guide, not a law. It's a place to start, and a wisdom that can aid you, keeping you from making foolish mistakes until you truly understand your power, your motives, and the consequences of your actions.

Some would use the yardstick of the Wiccan Rede, whether you accept it or not, to measure if you are Wiccan or a witch. Though I think it's a good guideline, and what is considered British Traditional Wicca is a part of my practice, I identify with the words *witch* and *witchcraft* above all others.

Witches have judged the Wiccan Rede as too "Christian" or too judgmental, yet you find similar wisdom teachings in many other religions, beyond the Golden Rule of Christianity. The concept of energy returning to its source is not one of judgment, but it comes from our Hermetic Qabalistic concepts of divine emanations. The power flows down to form the Tree of Life. The lowest sphere eventually returns to the top, returning to its source. The magician issues from Kether and returns to it. In the microcosm of our lives, it creates what witches call the Boomerang Effect or the Law of Return. We are each our own microcosm, our own Tree of Life, emanating energies out and having them return to our source. An alternate interpretation proposed by author Gerina Dunwich is that your actions don't return to you threefold, but on all three levels of existence—physical, mental, and spiritual.

If you look at the Rede as an absolute, rather than a guide, you realize that it's ridiculous to follow it in a literal sense. You can't do "no harm." Every action you take carries some harm, seen and unseen. To eat, you must kill. Though many would like to say that vegetarian options negate this death, when you pick something, you are damaging it, harming it, by not letting it take its normal course of events. Plants have a hormonal and chemical response when they suffer any kind of trauma or injury, similar to the nerve response and endorphin release found when animals experience fear, pain, and injury. Driving your car has an impact upon the environment. Walking outside can crush small insects. Healing the sick kills viruses and bacteria. You can say that this is not what the authors of the Rede meant and that we are being ridiculous, yet this is the teaching. So the guide means that we are at our best when we do as little harm as possible. We have to make decisions on what constitutes "as little harm as possible" for us at any given moment, and act upon it. In that way, the Wiccan Rede becomes our guide.

I had a student once ask me why, if we focus our affirmations and statements on the "positive" outcome, we would use the phrase "harm none" so much in our magick? Isn't that evoking the power of "harm" even though that's not our intention, just like an affirmation would be for "wealth," not "no poverty," because our mind would just hear poverty? I answered too glibly at the time because I didn't really know, but upon further reflection, I realized that it's to remind us that everything we do has the potential of harm, and all we can do is minimize it. Repeating "harming none" keeps us vigilant on the conscious level to make the wisest of decisions.

Some forms of Traditional Craft have other wisdom teachings guiding the use of power, if not the Wiccan Rede. Author Orion Foxwood is fond of saying, "Whatever you touch, touches you back." Like attracts like, and the spirit of what you do does return to you. He purifies himself in Florida Water, a spiced and sweet cologne, so whatever he does will manifest "sweet" when it touches him. With such teachings in mind, we are urged to think about the consequences of our actions, and be prepared to face them, whether we subscribe to the Wiccan Rede or not.

So, in that light, do curses play a role in witchcraft? Is it better to curse someone or something to prevent it from doing further harm? If a criminal is loose in your neighborhood, can you curse that person to be caught? If a criminal is on trial, can you curse that person to be convicted? You're obviously hurting the criminal, yet is the good you are doing for society outweighing that hurt? Should magick be used at all?

One of the less-quoted sayings in the Craft is "To heal, you must know how to hex. To hex, you must know how to heal. They are two sides of the same coin." I have to admit, I had a hard time with that bit of wisdom, but it's true. Creation and destruction are two sides of the coin. You can have the knowledge of hexing, understanding it by not fearing it, to enhance your ability to heal and to banish and uncross the hexes of others.

If you are afraid to learn about hexes, then you won't be able to easily identify one. Technically, a hex is usually defined as a ritual, often with a charm, candle, or herbal component, while a curse can be a ritual, or simply a spoken spell cursing the target. A good doctor knows more ways to kill you than to cure you, yet it doesn't mean the doctor is acting on that information. It's simply a part of his education. A martial artist knows how to attack in order to defend. The herbalist's knowledge of making a healing tea or tincture is the same knowledge used to make poisons. I can know how to do something without actually doing it.

Author and teacher R. J. Stewart made an amazing and insightful point in a lecture at the PantheaCon 2005 convention regarding blessing and cursing. Today we don't talk about the two; we talk about healing and purification. Cursing is a part of purification. New Age traditions that would never talk about cursing talk quite a bit about purification, purging, and healing release, but without those terms, it would seem quite like a curse. Such experiences, framed as curses, "bad" karma, or purification serve us in the challenge by eventually making us better people. The ritual kiss of initiation is partnered with the scourge, which, in theory, is like a curse. When the scourge is presented, initiates are told, "This is a sign of power and domination. It is also used to cause purification and enlightenment, for it is written, 'To learn you must suffer and be purified.'" A kiss is given, and then the initiate is asked, "Are (thou) willing to suffer to learn?" The postulant replies, "I am." Here we have the idea of power, suffering, purification, and enlightenment all linked, yet most witches like to think of our Craft as a tradition of life and pleasure. But in any tradition that honors the life force, we must also acknowledge and work with the forces of death and pain, or our cycle of life is incomplete. Along with the scourge, one finds mention of the blasting rod in traditional witchcraft sources. A blasting rod is a long wand, cudgel, or walking stick traditionally made from blackthorn or yew (even better if it's from a graveyard), and used for curses and banishing. It could be paired with a blessing wand, often of birch or whitethorn (hawthorne). The scourge and the kiss, blasting and blessing, show how the pair go together in myth and magick. When we look to the heroes of legend, under a curse or Celtic *geis* (sacred prohibition), the gods are usually the ones doing the cursing. They are not necessarily malicious or personal in the bigger scheme of things, even though they appear to be, but they are a necessary step in the purification and enlightenment of the hero.

Those practicing the pre-Gardnerian traditions of the Craft might be called upon to do a curse for several reasons, including as a part of healing work to curse the illness, to break a curse by cursing the person who sent it, and to prevent harm or right an injustice. Many traditional witches would do it simply because their clients asked them to do so, with the ethos that it is not their actions, but the clients' actions. They are simply the ones giving the knowledge and power. The clients are the ones who bear the responsibility for their choices and actions with the magick. The same is said of many of the African diasporic cultures that practice ritual cursing. The magickal practitioner is much like a gun, and the client wields the gun, and ultimately uses it, either for defense or harm. The gun is not responsible. Be it the African slaves in the New World or the rural poor of pagan and later Christian Europe, such methods are for those who feel they have no access to power or justice. How do the rural poor deal with the upper classes of empires and kingdoms? Curses were a way of seeking justice and retribution when the law did not serve the good of all.

Though it's an unpopular, politically incorrect notion for our Western core shamanic practitioners and holistic healers, tribal shamans and medicine people were not above placing what we would describe as a curse upon someone to rectify a situation or defend themselves or their tribe. I know at least one shaman who felt he was poisoned by another shaman with "bad medicine" simply because he was more well known and better liked. Many shamanic traditions have various "death prayers." Though we see them through modern New Age eyes, filling them with an enlightenment we don't possess, shamans, like the witches of old, know how to heal and hex. For some reason, we elevate the tribal traditions of the Americas, yet look with scorn upon the old traditions of witchcraft, Voodou, and Santeria.

Some witches believe the Law of Three is a call to send harm back to the source threefold. Our job is to bless and curse, and we do a whole lot of blessing, but few of us do an equal amount of cursing. Folk sayings tell us that a witch will not suffer evil or any injustice. One of my favorite thoughts in this arena came to me from a Feri student of Victor Anderson, T. Thorn Coyle, from a non-Wiccan Rede tradition, who says, "You must be free of the sin you would curse someone for." If you are not, your curse will backfire, and not have the intended results. Here sin doesn't refer to a Christian concept, but the misdeed or quality that makes you believe someone is worthy of the curse. In many ways, blessings and curses are conduits of energy from the divine into the world, and are not personal. If you get too personal, it gets you personally involved. If you are not attached to the situation on a personal level, the results are much "cleaner." I think it's a good policy to follow, and while I wasn't taught it that way, I think I've held to its spirit.

Some Wiccans who have a very conservative interpretation of the Rede might even look at certain binding, banishing, and neutralization spells as curses. I know I've done quite a few spells intended to stop the actions of another, or remove that person from a situation. But in those instances, there was no malice, simply what needed to be done at the time. Any time thoughts of malice and revenge come up in regard to using magick, I've had to stop and question myself, my motives, and review my role and responsibility in the situation. When I'm motivated so strongly by shadow emotions, I mustn't deny them, but I also have to look at how the situation and people involved are mirroring my shadow back to me. Doing a curse might take care of the short term but magnify the things I don't like about myself, without giving me the effective introspective tools to work with them. Some Wiccans have a much wider range of interpretation, with one version of the Rede having the line, "...ever mind the Law of Three unless in self-defense it be...," giving permission to use magick to defend yourself, even if it involves cursing.

Another concept is one of divine anger. Many of our gods are angry war gods. One need only look at the "witchiest" of dark goddesses to see that few are exclusively devoted to love and light. Their stories are filled with battles and curses. As priest/esses of the gods, should we not be enacting their will in the world by righting these wrongs? Such divine retribution is Qabalistically the sphere of Geburah, a sephira above Tiphereth, the higher self, on the Tree of Life. To really think of yourself as an agent of the gods in this way, you have to be in touch with your divine essence and have worked through a lot of your shadow. Traditional cunning folk were called to find stolen objects and psychically ferret out criminals in the community, and many of us feel that past-life call. Many others, unfortunately, think they are the retribution of the gods, without doing much personal introspection work. They can't separate a divine call from their ego's desire to punish those who made them feel bad. When we get to a point where we are upset enough to curse someone, we are usually very personally involved. I know that any time it's crossed my mind passionately, I was not in a clear space. We dislike others for the things they mirror about ourselves. If we curse them from that perspective, we are certainly not free from that "sin." Those who carry out any form of divine retribution for the gods know that it's not a personal decision. Divine anger and divine justice are very different from personal anger. In the end, I think it's best to leave the gods' curses to the gods.

Some witches I know believe that in certain situations, the curses, and their backfire, is worth it. Others have strict ethics about when and how to curse to prevent themselves from needlessly cursing, or unconsciously cursing. Ever get really upset with someone and silently wish that person ill, and misfortune befalls the individual right away? You are potentially not in control of your thoughts. If you are going to do that, you should be completely conscious and decide to do it, being aware of the situation rather than letting your energy fly wild. One witch I know has a three-warning rule. He will sincerely speak to the offender about the problem three times for a peaceful resolution, and if all attempts fail, then he feels justified to curse. He stipulates that the curse must match the offense against him, and it would be intended to give the offender something else to deal with as opposed to bothering him. Others will put a lock into the curse, so it won't activate unless the target of the curse does something to activate it. You should, of course, make it abundantly clear that the curse is in effect. A curse against an abuser that will not activate unless the abuse is repeated is a good example of this. Such ethics put the target of the curse in active engagement, so that like healing, the person involved is responsible for the outcome. Others think that a curse, a one-time tactic, is far better than many of the bindings that are available, to prevent a person's power from doing anything. Binding spells truly interfere with the person's free will and fate more than any curse. The binding spells learned in the Temple of Witchcraft tradition simply impede the person's harm and malice, not the individual's total power or will.

Though it's fashionable to berate the Wiccan Rede in favor of more "Traditonal Craft" ideals, I can't help but look at the history of witchcraft and wonder how Traditional Craft ideals have been serving us. I truly believe that the inner-plane priestesses and priests, the Hidden Company of witch masters, have guided the revival of witchcraft in our era, with all the old prohibitions of secrecy being broken. I also believe that all the ingenious contributions that were unfortunately added with a potentially dishonest account of their true origin have actually served the Craft. More of our traditions are in print now, and I wonder if they could ever be stamped out or driven underground as thoroughly as they once were. I wonder if part of our traditional morality of healing and hexing led to the fear and revulsion of witchcraft, rather than our celebration and acknowledgment by the community we served. The rebirth of witchcraft with the Wiccan Rede so thoroughly stamped across it has served us, giving us a basis from which to guide those new witches who might not be tempered by a moral code from repeating the same mistakes that lead to fear and revulsion, while giving us aspects of a theology with which to have a dialogue with non-witches.

The subject of curses is not even broached in lower levels of training, for there needs to be an understanding of both the forces of power, of magick, and of our own spiritual development. Though you have had the Wiccan Rede as a guide, I'm sure that if you are anything like me, you have made your share of mistakes—the love spell that you cast on someone specific, but asking it to be for the highest good, harming none—yet you mumbled the last part and got exactly what you asked for, but not really what you wanted or needed. Or the moment of anger when you didn't neutralize your thought, and something went awry with the one you were mad at. Or the time you called for "justice" from the gods when you felt justified, yet in retrospect, you were probably just angry and not in need of divine retribution. There's always a temptation to curse once you have the power. With this knowledge of how the power can work, and of your own spiritual unfoldment, you can maturely look at our history and nature in regard to curses. Then we have to decide, individually and as a community, if the times of unequal power are over, and if there is the potential for justice and protection in this society without having to resort to curses.

This, however, is not a call to perform curses, but an exploration in understanding our relationship to power. If you have completed all the previous courses and made it this far in the Temple of Witchcraft tradition, you have both the ability and knowledge to curse. You should give thought and understanding to all aspects of the Craft, even the ones you don't like or are uncomfortable with. "Where there is fear, there is power" is the pagan saying, and when we fear something needlessly, we lose our power. This is a lesson to learn to claim our power and decide for ourselves what exactly to do with it. Most people I know who perform curses at the drop of a hat for very personal reasons, without lots of introspection, have pretty unpleasant lives. If I needed any proof of the Law of Return, I see it there. Their magick isn't pretty, and when it touches them back, it's not pretty. I always look at the end results. I don't feel called to be the embodiment of divine justice. If I want someone to go away and leave me alone, I do a spell for that person to go away and leave me alone, asking that I immediately and gently learn anything I need to learn from him, to not attract someone else like him into my life. If I feel there is danger, I do a spell to neutralize the danger or the dangerous person. I don't do it with malice. If the criminal in town gets caught, has a change of character, or gets hit by a truck, I know that I did the spell in the spirit of the highest good, in divine will, and I let the details of it work their way out. Though it could be considered a curse, I still consider it an act of theurgy. The more you practice theurgy, the more you understand when you are that divine channel, and you start to see how your every thought, word, and deed becomes a divine act of magick, in service to the gods. Yet it is easy to think that's what you are doing when you are upset. That's why it's so important to keep up a regular introspective and meditative practice, no matter how "advanced" you might think you are. I don't think you should even contemplate that you are a justice bringer until you really assume the duties and responsibilities of the high priest/ess through doing the personal and community work. It's far easier to go around cursing people than it is to build something tangible in your community.

As we are all ultimately responsible for our actions, whether we subscribe to this Rede, or any other, we know as initiates of the mysteries, that we are not separate from everyone and everything. We are all interdependent and connected. To attack another is to attack yourself. Each of us is the divine in another perspective. I love the Native American saying, "It is a foolish tree whose branches fight among themselves." We are all part of not only a human family tree, but a universal tree, all fed and nourished by the same source. When we forget this, one branch fights with another, to the detriment of the whole tree. Our desire to curse someone in anger or fear comes when we feel we are separate from the greater whole, or deem our enemy completely separate from the greater whole. It comes when we have an illusion of lack, that someone is taking something vital from us. We know that if we all perform our True Will, there will be no lack. Resources will shift so that everybody has what they need for that given moment. Our creed as witches is not "turn the other cheek," which is what some feel the Wiccan Rede amounts to, nor is it "an eye for an eye." Both extremes come from our biblical culture. Perhaps there is a middle path, and it's up to witches to implement it. I greatly admire martial artists and Eastern mystics. You are not going to walk all over them or violate them. They are warriors, physical and spiritual, yet they do not neutralize the threat in anger, malice, or fear—they simply neutralize it.

Our exploration of the Left Hand Path can put a lot of magickal goals into question. Along with hexes or curses, glamours, enchantments, and mesmerism all fall under a similar gray area of magick, yet all are a big part of witchcraft, then and now. If you use your abilities to get out of a traffic ticket, when you were knowingly speeding, is that black magick? Is that harm? Are you unduly influencing the will of the officer? If so, then if you are simply flirting with the officer, is that harmful as well? Magick to manifest your will comes about in many ways. It depends on your frame of reference and your own moral code, and how you do it. I know a non-witch crystal healer who would "fill an officer's heart with love," so he would feel compassion for her and let her go with a warning, and she would think that this was done "in the light." Yet it has the same result as the magician who might push his mental will onto the police officer, which she would see as black magick. Things are not always black and white, and that is why we can't always classify ourselves as good or evil, or Right Hand and Left Hand Path. A famous magickal saying, with variations attributed to both Robert Graves and Victor Anderson, tells us, "White magick is prayer/poetry, and black magick is anything that works."

Our Left Hand symbolism might not be as easily recognized, but it is there. The traditions that wear the bracelet of initiation most often put it on the left hand. At one point in my spiritual exploration I was involved with the Sikhs, yet once I found out their sacred bracelet was both made of steel, a metal toxic to most faeries, and worn on the right hand, I realized that they were not compatible for me with my roots in witchcraft. While some traditions blend easily, others do not. While iron can be used in certain forms of magick and tools, I don't think I could wear it continuously, and this tradition required adherents to wear it always.

One of the Christian theologies that puts us in harmony with the Left Hand Path comes from Matthew 25, verses 31–33: "When the Son of man shall come in his glory, and all the holy angels with him, then shall he sit upon the throne of his glory: And before him shall be gathered all nations: and he shall separate them one from another, as a shepherd divideth his sheep from the goats: And he shall set the sheep on his right hand, but the goats on the left." The sheep are then given the reward of heaven, and the goats are given to everlasting punishment. We are not a religion of sheep, following a good shepherd blindly, but a tradition of horned ones, blazing our own trails up the mountain. We don't seek to be taken care of solely by others, but go our own way. Unfortunately, the image isn't as effective as goats become more and more domesticated, but there is a definite difference in the temperament, style, and spirit of the goat when compared to the sheep. The goat god, as the horned god in the image of Pan, is very important to us. On one level, Pan is the "all" and life force of the cosmos, a god of Chokmah, to the Great Mother figure of Binah on the Tree of Life. Even the image of Baphomet, for ceremonial traditions, plays a role in our work. The fearsome image of Baphomet is used to confuse the uninitiated. If you are afraid of the androgynous and phallic goat god, which in essence is the spirit of all nature, male and female, human and animal, then you should not go on to deeper levels of magick. Only when you confront your fear do you find your power.

In the end, modern witchcraft is neither a Left Hand or Right Hand Path, and yet it's both; just as in life, we use both hands. We don't seek union with the source above all else, nor do we seek separation from the source above all else. We seek to serve as priestesses and priests, serving our True Will, which is also divine will, in a magickal paradox of separation and union. We do whatever the path calls us to do, using whichever hand is appropriate. This is the paradox of the Aquarian Age, where we are called to be individuals, yet called to the greater good. The witch's god is dual, light and dark, Apollonian and Dionysian. We learn that we can serve the greater good only by being our true individual selves, in harmony with the divine in all worlds, above and below. Our path is ultimately a middle path, drawing on both sides as needed.

Some practitioners simply sum up the differences between the Left Hand and Right Hand Paths with the phrases *"My* will be done" and *"Thy* will be done" to describe each, respectively. In my view of witchcraft, a better phrase would be "Our will be done," as we seek to merge personal and divine will, knowing nothing is truly outside of ourselves.

Exercise 11

Directing Power with the Hands

This exercise is very similar to those touched upon in a lot of the previous levels, but here, I want you to really pay attention to the sensation of power, and to truly be able to build power. As you breathe, draw up energy from the earth and/or down from the sky. Have it meet in your heart or solar plexus. Build up a ball of energy, a ball of power there. Use whatever methods—will, intention, breath visualization, vocalization—that work best to build the power. With your will, intention, breath, visualization, and any vocalization that works for you, project that energy down and out your right hand. Like a martial artist building up *ki*, you should experience a notable shift in your body, and possibly in your environment. If you project it toward others, they should feel it. I've done exercises with my students where we're able to sway and even push back one another with this energy. Repeat the exercise, using your left hand. Explore both hands, and get to know what qualities come out in both hands for you. Though we learn that the left hand is receptive and the right hand projective, or feminine and masculine respectively, a good witch knows that both hands can be used for both functions whenever needed.

Certain shamanic traditions encourage the student to learn to work with both hands, both sides of the body, and both sides of the brain. Exercises to balance the functioning of the brain and body range from benign meditations to the more extreme measure of tying your dominant hand behind your back. Such work helps you experience your magick from both perspectives, not favoring either. Such dominance for left or right side is not found in nature, and for those following a nature religion, it can be helpful to emulate nature's bi-dexterous quality.

Those who are initiated in a Gardnerian-style tradition know that the power, the current of initiation, can only be passed through the use of two hands. The initiator places the left hand under the initiate's knees and the right hand upon the head, forming a magickal link. Then with the words "I hereby will all my power into you," the current is passed. In the tradition of the Law of Return, the initiator knows that his or her power will not be lost, but return multiplied. Those witches who have initiated the well prepared (as opposed to those who initiate simply to say they have a large number of initiates) find their power expands and increases. Such initiations are like the final key to be turned in the third-degree elevation process. Like a Reiki Master, the process isn't quite complete until the Master has attuned another to Reiki. Though it's not absolutely mandatory, I've found that an initiatory witch finds a process complete only when the initiation is then passed on to the next generation.

THE EGO SELF-IMAGE

The proper application of power—right, left, or both—requires an understanding of the ego self, for it's in the ego self where we are most likely to abuse or give away our power. To effectively and appropriately use our power, we must have healthy self-esteem. The yellow ray is not the ray of power for this temple, as one might think, as red is the ray of power and will. Yellow is the ray of active intelligence, the ability to discern when to use power, and how to apply it, creatively or destructively. It's about our ability to make appropriate judgments.

The third temple is aligned with the astral body. This is the subtle body that forms the emotional pattern for the etheric and physical bodies, but takes shape based on how we see ourselves, or how we think others see us, rather than what is truly there. The self-image can derail our life efforts far more than we realize, and only through changing our self-image and self-esteem do we overcome long-standing problems. If you've ever made a physical change, such as losing weight, and intellectually you know you have lost it, but when you look in the mirror, you still see your larger self, you have changed your physical body, but not your astral body. It will be pretty easy for you to gain the weight right back, and most people do, because they didn't change on all levels.

Due to the large Eastern influence upon New Age metaphysics, many of us have the idea that to be spiritual, we must destroy the ego. "Destroy" is probably not the best metaphor. We need our ego, but what we don't need is to solely identify with the ego, to be trapped by it. The ego is one of a number of selves we have, and when we recognize and identify with the higher self, the Holy Guardian Angel (HGA), we are no longer trapped.

To "destroy" the ego, we have to have an ego to destroy, and many people come to magick with low self-esteem and a poor self-image. Destroying what little they have does not lead to the higher self, but leaves them directionless. "Transcend" is a better image for our spiritual path than "destroy." We reach beyond the ego, realizing that it is one of many tools, one of many possessions we have.

Part of the witch's training is to go beyond limits. We stand between the worlds and are capable of many things deemed impossible by those around us. We have to be open to having a wide range of possibilities, going beyond the ordinary, yet remaining grounded in reality. One foot in both worlds is necessary for this.

To move beyond your limitations, ask yourself some questions. These questions will help you see the blocks in your personal power and in manifesting the life you are called to create. They might not resolve in the way that you desire, but contemplation of them helps you understand your relationship to these issues and the most effective use of your energy in your daily and magickal lives.

Are you limited by your physical body? If so, how?

Are you limited by distance in your life? If so, what would you experience differently if not limited by distance?

Are you limited by time? If so, how?

What do you feel powerless against? Why?

Working beyond our limits is best done through working on the astral plane. Anything imagined is possible on this level of consciousness. You are not bound by space and time, or the law of physics. You can create and recreate yourself. Much of our awakening to magick as a reality is through dreams, visions, and psychic experiences that work through our connection with the astral plane. When we realize that everything is connected through the subtle planes, some of our limitations in regard to time and space dissolve away. Others simply are reframed in ways we can deal with more effectively. We move through some of our self-imposed limits and see how powerful we can truly be.

Many of our formative magickal experiences are things we previously thought were impossible—either wholly impossible or simply impossible for us to do. Things like psychic energy, past-life recall, traveling to other realms, spiritual entities, the higher self, and the shadow were once beyond our reality, but they have become a part of our worldview, now that we have moved past our limits.

In the alchemical teachings, the third stage of initiation is separation. Once the ash of calcination has been made into a solution, the parts that are insoluble are separated from the solution. That which doesn't serve is removed from the mixture, making it more pure and refined. Much of the third stage is the power of the warrior, the inner warrior who has to fight the expectations of others, as well as fight to stalk the inner fears. One begins to separate from the personal self, to see and identify with the higher self. Unhealthy limits are removed. One, like the spiritual warrior, who is an aspect of the magician, realizes that we are not the body, emotions, will, or mind, but those are things we own. They are tools on our path. We also begin the process of realization that we are different from those around us, and feel separate from society, friends, and family. Ultimately, as the magician you walk a solitary path, even in a coven or lodge, for no one can do the work for you. They can only support your process, and most people who are not going through a similar process have difficulty doing that.

The process of separation relates to the planet Mars and the metal iron, though we think of the realm of the solar plexus as Sun oriented. Both have the fire correspondence, but in alchemy, the Sun, and its metal, gold, are reserved for the highest operation. Iron is protective, and when we think of the tools crafted of iron, the athame and sword, we use them to direct energy, create boundaries, and break links, though paradoxically, the most common use of the athame is to join together, as in the Great Rite. Interestingly enough, the traditional element for the third alchemical operation is air, for it is a filtering process. Most of our self-imposed limits are in the mind, our air element. In the Emerald Tablet, the line "The Wind carries it in its belly" is the teaching of separation. Much of our discussion of the Left Hand Path centers on the process of separation, being separate and independent, or seemingly so, from the divine. For many, it's a very intellectual process, yet primal and fiery as well. Ultimately, though, it's one part of a much larger process of separation and recombination occurring from an alchemical perspective. It is through separating ourselves from that which holds us back that we see how far we can go.

This next meditation is designed to take your consciousness beyond preconceived limits and expectations of what you can and cannot do. It works with your astral body, your self-image. If you've been working with the Temple of Witchcraft material, you've already been working with the astral self. We learn to go to the inner temple and look in the reflective surface (*ITOW*, chapter 14, exercise 31) to take stock of ourselves and our astral self. We see beyond the astral self, into the past, future, and our true nature. This exercise is a bit different, expanding that image of the self to encompass all things, and then, using the alchemical process of separation, separating ourselves from what no longer serves our highest good.

EXERCISE 12
Going Beyond Limits

1. Perform Exercise 1: Inner Temple as a Mystery School Meditation (page 45), steps 1–5, to go to your inner temple.

2. Find the reflective surface where you can truly see yourself, your astral self-image. Look at yourself in the reflective surface. How do you see yourself? What do you project to others?

3. Once you have accurately taken stock of your self-image, your self-esteem, affirm your wish to move past your self-imposed limits, claiming your spiritual power.

4. Rise up out of the inner temple, moving at the speed of light. Imagine yourself moving into space. It can be the space of the physical universe, going by recognizable planets, or the space of a higher plane, with nothing remotely corresponding to the physical world.

5. Travel faster than the speed of light, moving faster and farther than you thought possible.

6. Travel beyond your wildest ideas of a destination, throughout the space-time continuum.

7. When you are ready, take a look around. Where are you and what do you perceive?

8. If you could go to any place, to any dimension and time, where would you go? Why? Go there now, using your will to stretch across the cosmos. Visit your target destination.

9. Explore your ability to direct your consciousness wherever you want to go.

10. When ready, return to the inner temple. Take stock again of your self-image. Has it changed at all? If so, how?

11. Finish exercise 1, steps 8–11, to return to normal consciousness.

THE POWER OF FEAR

In the process of purification, of separation, to move beyond all that doesn't serve, our biggest obstacle is fear. Fear is the greatest limitation. Many teachers would boil down our two basic principles not as love and hate, but love and fear. While love expands consciousness, fear contracts it. Like healing and hexing, both love and fear are the providence of the witch's world. Why else would so much of our lore be so scary?

Fear motivates so much of what we do and how we operate. When we fear something, we don't always know it. We let go of our power, and let it run wild, creating a scenario based on fear, rather than reality. We fear when we are out of control, yet we know that in life, we are never fully in control. Still, we create illusions about being in control and when those illusions are broken, we enter fear. Fear leads to anger, for we want to do something with our power, but when we have no channel for it, we become angry. At certain times fear and anger can be quite helpful. Fear tells us when we are in danger and helps preserve our lives. Anger helps give us momentum, and it also helps us draw boundaries and set limits. Staying in a continuous state of anger or fear is unhealthy, though. When we are in unhealthy fear, it is rooted in the ego, for the ego is what creates the illusion of being in control. The fear of the ego is that it will end, either through literal death or the loss of self-identity, ego death. The ego doesn't always serve our highest good. It often creates stagnant situations where rather than being forced to grow and shed an aspect of the ego, we keep our consciousness contracted in fear and retain the ego in its contracted form. It is a part of our self-sabotaging mechanism, and only by identifying it through introspective practices can we transcend it and get it working for us. You can think of the ego as the middle management in your life that likes to think it's the boss. When we identify with the boss, the higher self, we are truly in charge. When we identify with the middle management, we feel like we are run ragged in a poorly staffed company with no real leadership or vision.

The Left Hand Path initiation stage for the third level is known as dream walking. This speaks to me more of not yet facing the third temple's mystery, where one enters a fantasy world with a magickal theme, but with none of the discipline and self-awareness. The initiate has not yet identified with the higher self. Many experienced pagans and witches get frustrated with those not on the path, or with those who are stuck on the path, who find themselves in a stage that seems to be all about playing pretend, dressing funny, shocking people, and losing their grounding in reality. They want to have another lifestyle, and they embrace the outer trappings of paganism, or what they think is paganism, without necessarily having the theological understanding. They forget or reject the more orthodox lifestyles of the past, but they do not necessarily think through their new choices. They try on new identities, new self-images, and new personas.

In the Miracle of Bread, the Green Corn might initially signal a correspondence with the green chakra, but the Green Corn is symbolic of the immature plant—younger, growing, and not yet matured into golden wisdom. It corresponds with the solar plexus, the raw power, yet it lacks the true wisdom to temper that power. Like energy ascending from the solar plexus to the heart, the grain must ascend from its immature state to a more mature state.

We must remember that this is a stage and we all go through it at some point and in some way. Those who go through it gracefully usually have a sense of humor and don't take themselves or their new path so seriously that they can't see how unorthodox it is. As I began my coming-out process as a witch to my friends and family,

I started with, "I know this will sound kind of crazy, but..." Humor helps keep us grounded and able to relate to others. Humor defuses the unhealthy ego we might build with this new self-identity. Without it, we're in danger of becoming fundamentalists. One need not be Christian or Islamic to be a fundamentalist. You can find them in all spiritual traditions, including paganism, witchcraft, and magick. Be aware and on guard against becoming one yourself.

The biggest fear we have, collectively as ego-based humans, is the fear of death. Fear of death comes in many forms, such as fear of the pain and suffering involved. We have fears of deathlike experiences, of being different and cast out, or of being persecuted. I know I feared being disowned, which is like a familial death. We have fear of failure and fear of success, for we learn that we are not who we thought we were—we are not our ego when we become something new, killing the old self-image. The ego death is one of the biggest fears, but only when we identify with the ego alone. And most importantly, we fear literal death with all the unknown factors of what really happens to our sense of "self" and our consciousness after death. We create religions to tell us about it and assure us, but the shamanic experiences let us walk the paths of death before we die, and let us commune with the spirits and ancestors while we are alive, giving us some direct knowledge and assurance rather than a hollow promise.

As witches on a path to power, we must move past our fear, and ironically because we do, and we claim our power, we are in turn feared. Our spiritual iconography is scary. Our rituals have an element of fear to them. Opening the gates, speaking to the dead, astral travel, skulls, bones, horns, toxic herbs, wild animals, caves, deep forests, and the crossroads at midnight are all beyond most people's everyday, ordinary experience. We surround ourselves with this seeming death-and-fear fetish, or at least at particular times of the year, to confront our mortality and fears head-on. The idea is to face our demons, and while the imagery still carries a "charge" psychically, we are desensitized to our personal fears, robbing them of the energy, in effect separating from them. Certain Eastern initiations of "death" cults are done in crematoriums, just as the witchcraft stereotype is the ritual in the graveyard. It's to confront fear. If you've never done a ritual in a graveyard, you don't know what you're missing. Quite a powerful experience, though I know it's not for most witches. Yet I'd encourage you to try, because it breaks your own fears and stereotypes of what a witch is or isn't. Death is at the heart of magick. One of my most favorite ideas comes from the comic *The Invisibles*, where the South American shaman-witch says, "I am a sorcerer and death is my ally." We walk hand-in-hand with both life and death, for it takes both to make change.

Once we have a certain mastery and separation, or at least can identify our fear, we gain a greater power. The witch's temporal power and seeming fearlessness over what scares others is precisely what makes us scary to the general populace. We become so different that it's easy to become "inhuman" as we work with otherworldly forces and are perceived as demonic. We often mirror back other people's relationship with their fear of death, mortality, and power. If it's unhealthy, they transfer that fear to us. Only in our culture, which doesn't have a role for the community mystic, do we have that fear grow. If our culture was not so fearful in the first place, and if it realized that there were channels to tackle these issues, we'd be seen as the priests and priestesses that we are. Though we must admit, some of the fear comes from those learning the temporal power of magick and abusing it with a lack of wisdom about how and where to use it. In either case, we need to get over our complexes and fear of persecution, and work within our society in this new age, but not water down our mysteries to make them more acceptable to the masses. They are not for the masses.

In our Egyptian temple system, the solar plexus relates to Luxor. Luxor is the site of the ancient city of Thebes, and it holds the temple sites of both Luxor and Karnak. On the west bank of the Nile River is the Valley of the Kings and the Valley of the Queens. The Luxor Temple was originally built by Ramesses II with additions by Amenhotep III. Amenhotep III is the father of the radical reformer Akhenaten. Amenhotep depicted his wife as the goddess Neith, in what some would see as an act of vanity and arrogance, exactly the type of corruption Akhenaten sought to purge. Yet Akhenaten's zeal to force his will upon his people was also an act of arrogance. Decorations were also added by Tutankhamen, whose image still appears at the temple, but whose name has been erased. Karnak is associated with the Theban triad of deities, each with its own precinct. In the temple complex of Karnak, there is precinct dedicated to Amun-Re, a sky and Sun god; a precinct dedicated to Montu, the war god; and a precinct dedicated to Mut, the mother goddess of the triad. The Temple of Amenhotep was dismantled by his son. Together, these figures, human and divine, represent some of the more memorable in Egyptian history, and they highlight the themes of fire, war, and creation. Studying of these temples encourages you to reflect on how you perceive yourself and how people perceive you, as well as your mortality, and potential immortality through how you are remembered.

In the Celtic rings of Annwn, Caer Goludd is known as the Castle of Gloom, the Castle of Death, the Caste of Trials, and the Fortress of Frustration and Riches. It is a place of rewards, but only after great trials. It's the archetypal witch's castle of darkness, yet within it lies a light. It's the scary place you don't want to go to. Like the perils of this temple, we are faced with death, but the death of the ego. Well, perhaps not the death of it, but attempting to transcend it on any level can bring a host of difficulties, depression, and frustrations. Yet the reward for learning to move beyond the ego self, the fears, angers, and need for control is immeasurable.

In the Merlin mythos, the Tower is embodied by the solar plexus. As a tarot card, it's ruled by Mars. In the tales of a young prophetic Merlin, the Tower of Vortigern would not stand, for no apparent reason. It collapsed and was rebuilt repeatedly. Vortigern's mages stated that mixing the mortar with the blood of a child with no earthly father would fix the problem, so Merlin, the child of a human mother and either a faery or demonic father, was summoned. Vortigern was angry because the symbol of his power was falling, and he was willing to sacrifice that which he didn't understand for the sake of appearance, for his ego self. Merlin the child made prophecies, describing a lake beneath the tower, which we can think of as the belly chakra temple, and within the underground lake a rock, the root chakra temple, with red and white dragons fighting within, rumbling. The two dragons are like the serpents of kundalini rising through the chakras. King Vortigern had the land dug up, and all was as young Merlin said. The stone was cracked, the dragons came out, and the white dragon killed the red. Merlin then prophesized that Vortigern would be killed and he was. King Vortigern was like the ego of the people dwelling on the land, and his death prepared the way for higher kings to come, from Aurelius, Uther, and most famously, Uther's son, King Arthur. Death and destruction preceded a more enlightened time for the land and its people. In later stories, Merlin goes through a period of separation, via madness, wandering the woods. He later returns as the magician, with his wisdom and insight. But it takes the period of seeming destruction to bring him to that place.

Working with the worlds of the dead helps prepare us for ego death, initiation, and the actual physical experience of death, for we know it is only rebirth in another world. Death becomes a less fearsome prospect because we have some understanding of it. I must admit, I think our shamanic understanding might be idealized compared to the actual process of it, but it doesn't make the concept so foreign as it is to those who do not have skills in working in the Otherworld. Near-death experiences, or NDEs, become life-changing initiatory catalysts for many people who live in a culture that doesn't recognize the call of the spirits to the shamanic traditions. Shamanic traditions would follow an NDE with an education from the spirits on how to heal, how to make medicine, and how to traverse the worlds of spirit. Many traditional shamans guide the souls of the dead across the world personally, and the instructions on how to do that eventually became the Books of the Dead, such as the Tibetan Bardo or the Egyptian Book of the Dead. Eventually the practice of shamanically guiding the dead was given up for reading the text, placing it in the funeral trappings, or carving it on a wall. Many think the trainings of some mystery schools in the ancient world were intended to engineer NDEs in initiates. Many New Age practitioners don't think of the pyramids as burial chambers at all, but initiatory temples aligned with the stars. Though modern archaeological interpretation would disagree, perhaps they have a point, for we don't really know the ancient Egyptian mind from our twenty-first century reference point.

Once we truly experience the realm of the dead in some way, we can change our relationship with fear, as our fear of death is the root of all our fears. Though experiences such as ancestor communication and past-life recall can help, the visceral experience of undergoing death in the Underworld can be life changing. The classic shamanic initiation is to have the shaman stalked by fearsome creatures—gods, monsters, or demons. These beings rip the would-be shaman apart and, through a spirit resurrection process, he or she is reborn, often with a new component such as a bone or crystal added by a divine figure—a deity, angel, or ancestor. That new component is indicative of the shaman's new power. The process of experiencing the death of your self-image, of watching your own death and becoming separated from it, shows that your consciousness is not dependent upon your body or the image you have of the body. This shamanic death is played out in a variety of mythologies, and it becomes the basis of the pagan mystery schools.

Though they typically happen spontaneously in shamanic culture, you can engineer such experiences as a part of the mystery training. That is what an initiation ritual is, in essence. The Tibetan Chöd rituals, where a demon goddess is summoned specifically to devour the practitioner, are in the same vein as these devouring shamanic initiations. Qabalistically, it's the crossing of the Abyss, of Da'ath, and facing the devouring demon Choronzon, and the demons of the reverse of the tree. It's the Goetic demon rituals done all at once (*TOHW*, chapter 13). Mexican sorcerer initiations can consist of digging one's own grave and spending the night in it, to be claimed by the spirits and face the demons. You can work with the spirits and totems. Ask for death and resurrection directly. It's taught in advanced core shamanism classes.

Part of the experience that is hard to reproduce in textbook trainings is the real-life danger factor of the mystery schools. The possibility of actual death is a motivating force to heighten the experience. The toxic herbs, the sicknesses, and mock burials are all things that could potentially lead to death. Danger is a gateway to magick, though what is appropriate in an ancient mystery school, with its guidance, preparation, and support, is not appropriate for one on a self-study course. I know of only one modern open witchcraft school that exposes its students to such potential danger, and I question if it does enough to prepare the students adequately. There is also the psychological risk involved in any case. These are real and powerful forces working on many planes. Those who are not suited for this path can be scarred by such initiations. You have to want it, and you have to be properly prepared. *Properly prepared* means more than cleansing and fasting. It means being trained in the magick of the Otherworld. If you have been following this tradition, using all of the instructions in the four previous books, then you have been properly prepared for this working.

EXERCISE 13

Facing Your Death

1. To begin your shamanic death experience, start by making a list of all the things that you fear. Be thorough. Even if you think you have tackled it and overcome it, if an idea, situation, person, place, time period, or concept

comes to mind, write it down. Write it down on a separate piece of paper that can be burned, like a mini–shadow journal (*TOSW*, chapters 15–17).

2. Create a sacred space. Put on journeying music that is appropriate, such as the rhythmic track from *The Temple of Shamanic Witchcraft Meditation CD Companion* or other drumming music.

3. Burn the list you have created in a cauldron or other flameproof container.

4. Perform Exercise 1: Inner Temple as a Mystery School Meditation (page 45), steps 1–4, to go to the World Tree.

5. Journey to the Underworld.

6. Seek out the spirits ruling your greatest fears. Stalk your fear spirits like a hunter.

7. Surrender to the fear spirits, allowing them to kill and devour your spirit form, but know that your consciousness lives onward.

8. Feel the still nothingness, with no fear, no pain, but a oneness with your environment.

9. Through the power of your will alone, or with the aid of a patron, ancestor, or totem, rebuild yourself. Resurrect yourself in perfection, with no illness, no imbalance, and in perfect health on all levels.

10. Finish exercise 1, steps 8–11, to return to normal consciousness.

To be a successful witch or magician, you must learn how to die and resurrect yourself. You will be called upon to do it regularly if you plan on having a long and inspired life. Failure to do so ends in burnout. Those who can do it know when to end cycles and patterns and reinvent themselves successfully. The death is just that part of the outmoded ego patterns and the successful creation of new patterns that better serve you.

Successfully navigating the mysteries of the third temple requires an intuitive understanding of the paradox of ego. We must have an ego to survive in the world, yet we must know that the ego isn't real, or at least it's not really us. We are individuals, and we have to explore our individual gifts, talents, and fears. Yet we know that we are part of a larger whole, and what we desire and do, or don't do, affects the greater whole. Everything everybody does affects us, yet ultimately we are responsible for our own fate. This chapter provides a lot of questions and a lot of provocative ideas, but it doesn't provide any easy answers, for there are no easy answers. It's meant to make you think about your power, your fears, and push your buttons and induce you to take action.

Homework

- Do exercises 10–13 and record your experiences in your journal or BOS.

- When you complete the trials of this chapter, tie your third knot in your cord in a ritualized manner.

- Obtain a bracelet. Consecrate it and begin wearing it, either daily or in ritual, to build a connection to it. Think about how your hands and arms guide and direct power. If you don't feel drawn to work with a bracelet as a ritual tool, think about the ring (*OTOW*, chapter 17) and its role in directing energy with both the left and right hands.

Tips

- Continue to build an integrated meditation and ritual practice.

- Speak with your Master-Teacher regularly. Build a relationship.

- Be more aware of your fears and your attitudes toward power in your daily life. When you have the option to exercise your power in your life, do you? Why or why not?

- Learn about hexing and curses, even if you choose to never cast one. Learn the history of curses from an intellectual and scholarly point of view, from ancient Egypt, Sumer, Greece, Rome, and medieval Europe, and from folk traditions such as Hoodoo. Understand and be able to recognize them. I suggest starting with the book *Utterly Wicked* by Dorothy Morrison (Willow Tree Press, 2007).

- The wisdom of "Where There Is Fear There Is Power" is most often associated with the writings of Starhawk and the Reclaiming movement. Starhawk has created an entire chant with this title and it can be easily found online and on recordings from the Reclaiming movement. Contemplate the words, use them in ritual, and learn the deep meanings of fear and power.

Lesson Four
Temple of the Heart:
Love and Balance

To enter the fourth gate, one must find balance between the upper and lower realms. As the Temple of the Heart, it functions like the heart chakra itself, as the connection between the lower chakras of primal needs and the higher points of more lofty pursuits. The key to this temple is love. When given initiation into the magick circle, two passwords are given, "Perfect Love" and "Perfect Trust." It is through the ideal of Perfect Love that we create a temple between the worlds, experience the initiations of the gods, and explore the mysteries. Perfect Love doesn't always seem like love, because it is not our sentimental ideal of love. Perfect Love can be harsh and cruel, but necessary. Perfect Love can tell you and show you things you don't like, but need. Perfect Love is the balancing force of the initiate, doing what must be done to bring forces into equilibrium so the deeper mysteries can be experienced.

For this month's lessons, set up your altar using the correspondences of the heart chakra. The colors green and pink are appropriate, as well as the following stones: emerald; rose quartz; peridot; green aventurine; green, pink, or watermelon tourmaline; and pink kunzite. Venusian correspondences, including copper and roses, are also appropriate for the Heart Temple.

EXERCISE 14

Contemplation of the Heart Chakra

1. Sit quietly in a comfortable position and enter a meditative state. Call upon higher guidance, through your own spirit guides and the Goddess, God, and Great Spirit.

2. Place your hands on the sternum, at the center of the chest. I've had one teacher, who was instrumental in helping awaken my heart chakra to deeper levels of love, insist that tapping the area above the sternum, the thymus, like you are playing a drum, awakens the thymus and consequently the heart chakra. You can tap on your chest before you meditate.

3. Feel the energy of the heart chakra. Start with your hands, but let any sensations move through your entire body. You might feel as if your entire energy field is surrounded in green or pink light. Ask the heart chakra to reveal its mysteries and guide you.

4. Observe the thoughts, feelings, visions, and insights you have, as well as messages you receive, while attuning yourself to the Temple of the Heart. These will guide you in this lesson to your own personal work.

5. When done, return yourself from the meditative state. Thank the energy of the heart chakra as well as your spiritual guidance, and give yourself clearance and balance.

Magickal Teaching: Empathy
Force: Balance
Chakra: Heart
Function: Love

Body: Emotional

Tool of the Goddess: Breastplate

Alternate Tool of the Goddess: Girdle

Colors: Green, Pink

Ray: Fourth

Elements: Earth, Air, Water

Planet: Venus

Metal: Copper

Sign: Taurus

Emerald Tablet Rubric: Its Nurse Is the Earth

Alchemical Operation: Conjunction

Totems: Rooster, Deer

Plant: Vervain

Sephira: Tiphereth

Tarot, Lunar: Trump IV—Emperor

Tarot, Solar: Trump XI—Strength

Tarot, Stellar: Trump XVIII—Moon

Life Stage: Handfasting/Second Initiation (*OTOW*)

Hermetic Principle: Cause and Effect

Musical Note: F

Day of the Week: Friday

Castle of the Underworld: Caer Rigor—Royal Castle, Castle of the Royal Horn, Castle of Interminability

Egyptian Temple Sites: Dendera, Abydos

Left Hand Initiation: Shock

Vice of Initiation: Despair

Virtue of Initiation: Openness

Stage of the Bread Miracle: Yellow Corn

Challenge of the Temple: Imbalance

Blessing of the Temple: Compassion

To me, the way of the witch has always been a heart path. As we align with the green world, with nature, and venerate nature as the physical manifestations of the divine, we are aligned with the green that has become associated with the heart chakra. Many mystics have found their spiritual awakening through nature and through the awakening of the love that connects all things. Though we tend to call the omnipotent force that is creation the Divine Mind in Hermetic philosophy, for we are thoughts within the Divine Mind, we could just as easily call this force the Divine Heart, for it is love that creates all, binds all together, and releases all to be transformed anew.

THE MYSTERIES OF LOVE

The fourth temple is the gateway of love, for love has been almost universally associated with the heart, the center of the chest. In our chakra model, the heart is the bridge between the lower and upper chakras. One who is balanced, who lives the middle path between extremes, is anchored in the heart, so ideally his or her consciousness can ascend or descend as needed, but the place where all action begins is the heart. Above the lower three chakras, it is the first energy center where the concept of empathy, of understanding the other's point of view, regardless of how it personally affects our survival, is developed. Here, we learn what it's like to be in others' shoes, to feel as they feel, and to sympathize. We learn how to make loving attachments to friends and family, as well as develop romance.

In the ideal world, we also learn to develop boundaries, knowing how to maintain an open heart chakra and love unconditionally, yet protect ourselves from giving unconditionally to the detriment of ourselves. Though understanding the nature of sacrifice is one of the Qabalistic lessons of Tiphereth, the heart center, we must first learn to care for ourselves. Sacrifice is only a part of the divine mysteries when it's motivated unconditionally, in service to the divine and divine will, not in service to the ego. Many people sacrifice, thinking themselves selfless, but they are immersed in the issues of the lower three chakras. They do so because they feel unworthy, have low self-esteem, or are expecting a reward. We have to heal and master the lower gates before we truly know our motives for sacrifice. For many initiates, the hardest lesson is to learn how to remain in that state of unconditional love, of Perfect Love, but not live in unconditional relationships, where we allow ourselves to be used and harmed, thinking that we are being spiritual.

Of all the descending Goddess's possessions, the one that makes these mysteries known to us is the breastplate. When I first heard the term *breastplate*, I thought of a piece of armor, like a knight would wear to cover the chest. And yes, the breastplate can be a piece of armor like a medieval knight would wear, but I'm sure that is not what Inanna was wearing. An older meaning for the breastplate is a piece of clothing, like a leather or goatskin shield, tied over the torso. It has both magickal and religious significance. Inanna's breastplate is called "Come, man, come." In the Old Testament, the breastplate is a square device holding the twelve precious stones of the Tribes of Israel, from which we derive much of our gem lore and zodiac associations. It is also referred to in the Bible as figuratively protecting someone from unrighteousness. The following are the stones most commonly associated with the breastplate (figure 7), but there is debate about their zodiac and tribe associations. The second table (figure 8) gives us modern associations of birthstones with zodiac signs, rather than the more common birthstones by month.

sardius topaz carbuncle
emerald sapphire diamond
ligure agate amethyst
beryl onyx jasper

Figure 7: Biblical Stones of the Breastplate

Aries: ruby / garnet / diamond
Taurus: emerald / rose quartz
Gemini: agate / carnelian
Cancer: moonstone / pearl / beryl
Leo: citrine / topaz / diamond / amber
Virgo: agate / sapphire
Libra: peridot / jade
Scorpio: diamond / obsidian / jet
Sagittarius: sapphire / lapis / turquoise
Capricorn: onyx / garnet / jet
Aquarius: opal / aquamarine
Pisces: amethyst / aquamarine

Figure 8: Modern Witch's Birthstone Chart

In Greek myth, the breastplate finds a prominent place as the Aegis (figure 9), armor notably used by the god Zeus and his daughter Athena. Medusa, the snake-headed Gorgon whose gaze turned people to stone, was depicted on the Aegis, with tassels that were said to be the serpents. Many myths are associated with this breastplate, as it has magick powers to strike fear in the hearts of enemies, control the weather, and protect the user from harm. The origin of the Aegis might be a strap to hold a shield, or a garment borrowed by Greeks from Libyan women, potentially being a shamanic pouch, like our witch bag, to hold ritual objects. The monstrous image and snakes were to frighten the uninitiated from opening it.

Figure 9: Aegis

In all these associations, it's a magickal device, usually worn over or near the heart, used for protection. The breastplate is used to protect the heart, one of our most sensitive and vulnerable centers of magick. Yet at the same time, the mystery of the breastplate is knowing when to have it on and when to take it off, or, more simply, knowing who and what to let into your heart, and who and what to guard against. When Inanna gives up her breastplate, she is exposing herself, her heart, to her dark shadow sister.

In British Traditional Wicca initiations, the initiate is brought to the point of a sword before entering the circle, and is asked, "O thou who standeth on the threshold between the pleasant world of men and the domains of the Dread Lords of the Outer Spaces, hast thou the courage to make the assay? For I tell thee verily, it were better to rush on my weapon and perish miserably than to make the attempt with fear in thy heart." The heart is vulnerable and exposed. There is no breastplate of protection. The sword is the symbol of justice, of Lady Justice embodied by Venus in Libra, a combination corresponding to the heart chakra. The potential witch must answer with the two passwords that were given to her earlier, saying, "I have two passwords: Perfect Love and Perfect Trust." The sword is lowered and the initiator answers, "All who approach with Perfect Love and Perfect Trust are doubly welcome." The initiating priest circles behind the initiate, blindfolding her, and puts his left arm about the waist and right arm around the neck, drawing her back and says, "I give you the third password, a kiss to pass through this dread door." He pushes her forward into the circle, sealing the circle behind him and truly beginning the rite.

You must have the defenses of the heart down to receive initiation, yet with Perfect Love and Perfect Trust, the breastplate becomes a part of you, a permeable, rather than rigid, shield. Eventually the breastplate energy becomes a part of the heart chakra, keeping you simultaneously open and vulnerable to that which you need and want, and protected from that which doesn't serve. It's an interesting paradox to become so secure in your relationship with yourself, and your gods, that you can make yourself vulnerable, and at the same time know that ultimately nothing can permanently hurt you if you do have that strong relationship with yourself and your divinity. Only when we have this openness, as we did as children, can we be reborn. Inanna was open to Erishkigal, and therefore learned all of the mysteries of the Underworld. She wasn't closed to any of them, and she learned them not just intellectually, but from the heart.

She was thus able to be resurrected and gain self-mastery over the three realms. You can love unconditionally, but not necessarily have unconditional and unhealthy relationships with people in your life. The magick of the breastplate is knowing when and how to draw emotional boundaries, and how strong to make those boundaries. It's part of the magick of life, and many never learn how to be both open and protected.

In alchemical teachings, the fourth stage is known as conjunction, the union of opposites. You find the teaching in the Emerald Tablet through the line "Its nurse is the earth." From our astrological point of view, the Earth is the third force that connects the Sun and Moon to produce the conjunction of two seeming opposites. In witchcraft, the Earth, Moon, and Sun are the primary heavenly bodies we observe. The Sun and Moon are really complementary, and stronger when in union. We see that union occur in masculine/feminine, soul/spirit, and light/dark. It is the stage beyond shadow work and knowledge and conversation with the HGA, but the union of the two polarities into a new whole. This rebirth is known as the lesser stone in alchemy, the birth of the conscious Overself, the aspect of you that can exist in the world as a spiritual being consciously human and divine, using the intelligence of the heart and integrating the elements. Conjunction is sometimes mistaken for the final stage of coagulation, where a seeker believes the lesser stone to be the Greater Stone of enlightenment.

The fourth stage of the Bread Miracle is the Yellow Corn, for the golden grain signifies a ripening and preparation for fullness. We relate this stage to the heart, because when the heart chakra is open, we have "ripeness" or maturity of emotion, and we are capable of moving to higher levels of consciousness.

I find it interesting that the heart has various elemental associations. It is seen variously as water for the seat of emotions, fire for passion and romance, air when associated with Venus and Libra, or earth when Venus and Taurus are dominant. The alchemical operations put it with Earth and Taurus, further linking the green of the heart chakra with the green of the planetary vegetation and nature. Yet, the associations with all the elements are because the fourth temple of mysteries represents integration not only of opposites in polarity, but of opposites in quadruplet.

The elements manifest in our inner world as personal embodiments of their nature. Just as you can manifest a higher self/Bornless Self/HGA and a shadow self, the elements can manifest as being of your fiery, earthy, watery, and airy natures. Your elemental guardians from the four directions in ritual help you explore and manifest these aspects of yourself, even if they have not coalesced into a distinct form for you. You started in *OTOW* to explore the elements and call upon them in ritual, journeyed deeper in the realms in *TOSW*, and then worked to master the four elemental tools in *TOHW*.

The manifestations of your four elemental selves should not be confused with any sort of personality disorder. In modern magick, we manifest many aspects of ourselves to commune with, from the higher self and shadow self to the anima and animus. This is simply an extension of the concept. In some modern shamanic traditions, such exercises are called *balancing the medicine shield*. The process of alchemy is working with these elements and embodying these elemental energies. Personifying them is simply one way to further refine them.

The relationship these different selves have to each other define much of your day-to-day life and temperament. But by manifesting these selves in your inner temple and, as the magician, bringing balance to them, you consciously create the life you desire, and can be aware of the aspects of your consciousness, your imbalances, for they are demonstrated before you in the words and behavior of these inner selves.

Fire
The form the fire self takes is usually a warrior, protector chief, or form of royalty—an emperor or empress. As the embodiment of will, power, passion, and drive, this being will be the part of you that holds the Spear or Wand of Victory.

Air
The air self comes to us as the student, or for those learned, the teacher or sage. Sometimes it will take the form of a knight, for this is the self that holds the Sword of Truth, embodying your ability to learn, to communicate, and to hold your truth.

Water
The water self manifests as a healer or counselor or even a child, one who holds our heart and the Cup or Cauldron of Compassion. This self is soothing, healing, and flowing with the powers of love.

Earth

Coming to us as a caretaker or nurturer, a physical provider, or mother figure, the earth self holds the Stone of Sovereignty, manifesting our physical health and well-being, as well as our place in the world, our daily lives.

The four selves can manifest as a family unit, of parents and siblings, or not manifest as an aspect of the self at all, but their messages can be conveyed by the elemental guardians you work with, be it the four archangels, power animals, elemental kings, or deities for the four directions. In any case, it is important to recognize that the fifth being in this set, for the element of spirit, is you, your conscious and fully aware self. As you move through this work, you will integrate these four beings more and more, until you are the only one to hold these four sacred objects and use them in daily life.

Exercise 15

The Balanced Heart

1. Perform Exercise 1: Inner Temple as a Mystery School Meditation (page 45), steps 1–5, to go to your inner temple.

2. Open the gateway of guidance and ask for your Master-Teacher. Call your Master-Teacher by name and ask for aid in this task. Your Master-Teacher will guide you and instruct you as needed, but for the most part will let you do all the work. The Master-Teacher is simply there for backup and support.

3. Open your doorway to the realm of fire and invite your fire self into the temple. What does it look like? How does it act? How does it hold the Spear of Victory? Speak together. Ask if it is happy and healthy. Ask what you can do to help form a healthy relationship with it. Ask it to tell you any messages you need in order to more fully master this element. This elemental self might ask for healing and direct you in what to do to heal it. Do any healing work on this being as needed.

4. Open your doorway to the realm of air and invite your air self into the temple. What does it look like? How does it act? How does it hold the Sword of Truth? Speak together. Ask if it is happy and healthy. Ask what you can do to help form a healthy relationship with it. Ask it to tell you any messages you need in order to more fully master this element. This elemental self might ask for healing and direct you in what to do to heal it. Do any healing work on this being as needed.

5. Open your doorway to the realm of water and invite your water self into the temple. What does it look like? How does it act? How does it hold the Cup of Compassion? Speak together. Ask if it is happy and healthy. Ask what you can do to help form a healthy relationship with it. Ask it to tell you any messages you need in order to more fully master this element. This elemental self might ask for healing and direct you in what to do to heal it. Do any healing work on this being as needed.

6. Open your doorway to the realm of earth and invite your earth self into the temple. What does it look like? How does it act? How does it hold the Stone of Sovereignty? Speak together. Ask if it is happy and healthy. Ask what you can do to help form a healthy relationship with it. Ask it to tell you any messages you need in order to more fully master this element. This elemental self might ask for healing and direct you in what to do to heal it. Do any healing work on this being as needed.

7. Introduce all four elemental selves to each other. Bring them together, like a family. Do they know each other well? Are they in harmony or do they have conflicts? Do they need reconciliation? Notice who is attracted together and who is not.

8. Ask them if there is anything you can do to aid them and their development as a group. You might need to mediate conflicts between them, acting as an arbiter and peacemaker. They might collectively require healing. Ask them for any messages they might have, as a group, for you.

9. Ask for their aid in living in balance with the four elements. Ask them to work with you in daily life as well as ritual and meditation.

10. Thank these four elemental selves and release them to their separate spaces. They may not want to leave the inner temple, and that is perfectly fine. Let them choose what is correct at this time.

11. Thank and release your Master-Teacher, who might depart through the gateway of guidance, or remain in the temple, or go with one or more of the elemental selves. Take notice of what the Master-Teacher does.

12. Finish exercise 1, steps 8–11, to return to normal consciousness.

The fourth gated castle of Annwn is known as Caer Rigor, the Royal Castle. Also known as the Place of Otherworldly Hospitality or the Castle of the Royal Horn, it is a place where one finds respite and healing. Mythic tales tell us of places where the heroes rest and regenerate through feasting, dancing, singing, and games. They are healing through finding the joys of the heart. It is also translated as the "Castle of Interminability," inferring determination in the quest, and seen as the otherworldly, or underworldly, counterpart to the royal castle of Britain in the material world.

The Temple of Dendera is one of the Egyptian sites associated with the heart chakra. Dendera is best known for the Temple of Hathor, traditionally known as the Temple of Tentyra. Hathor is the ancient Egyptian goddess of music, pleasure, and joy, though originally she was thought of as goddess of the Milky Way. She was linked with the cow-headed goddess Bat, absorbing some of Bat's associations with pleasure. Hathor became identified with the lion-headed Goddess Sekhmet, as the gentle, pleasurable side of the goddess, while Sekhmet was the anger and fire. This dual association did not last long in Egypt, but it has become popular among modern witches as an Egyptian view of the dark and light sides of the Goddess. Hathor was also considered Thoth's wife, and she took some attributes of Thoth's first wife, Sheesat, such as associations with records and judgment, but she is still primarily known as a goddess of love, pleasure, the arts, and enjoyment—all qualities that open the heart.

Abydos is the second Egyptian site to have associations with the heart chakra. Considered sacred to the god Osiris, the heart associations are not as apparent. Much of the history and structure is concerned with honoring past kings and their journey to the afterlife, yet the journey to the afterlife, and the remembrance of those who have gone on, is a form of love. Osiris is resurrected due to the love his wife-sister Isis has for him, and only through his love for her does he become the lord of the dead. While not reflecting the pleasurable side of life associated with Hathor, the tale of Isis and Osiris shows the depths of love, through the "better and worse" that comes with true commitment of the heart.

Interestingly enough, the Theosophical fourth ray, the green ray, is known as the ray of harmony through conflict. That confuses a lot of us interested in the ray sciences. Harmony and conflict? Together? That doesn't seem to make sense, but the idea is that once one experiences conflict, inner or outer, then the resolution of that conflict leads to a greater sense of peace, connection, and belonging to the greater world. The green ray is also associated with nature and herbal healing, faery spirits, elementals, devas, and the creative arts. The power of the heart does attract conflict, as our need to empathize, to receive empathy, and to build emotional relationships attracts us to people who are very different from ourselves, and the misunderstandings that can occur bring both great learning and potentially great conflict. The powers of the heart can force us to grow, to stretch beyond ourselves, which can hurt and even injure us, but as we heal, we grow stronger and more wise for the experience.

The Left Hand Path initiations again focus on what might be the inverse of the fourth temple. It is labeled as "second shock." The initiate becomes open to new possibilities, yet open to such a range of possibilities that conspiracy theories can abound. I have gone through this phase myself, and have seen how many in the New Age movement, without a lot of grounding practices and traditions, but with a desire to focus on the heart through "love and light," get stuck in this stage, fearing the government operations conspiring with shadowy figures of evil. The focus from the heart to the conspiracy, sometimes leads to depression and despair. The remedy for it is the openness of the heart, grounded through the real world, through the green ray of nature, of the material reality, of what is before you, solid and assuring, rather than the phantasms of the night. That is not to say that conspiracies can't be real. As the saying goes, just because you're paranoid doesn't mean they aren't out to get you. But when initiates focus on paranoia, they fall off the path and lose their way. This is a condition that needs healing.

As the heroes of our own stories, we rarely take time out at the Royal Castle to experience healing and rejuvenation. When we reach the level where we are desiring to be clergy, to be high priest/esses, we so intently seek to serve, and have the program of self-sacrifice to be "spiritual" embedded in us due to the dominant Christian culture, that we lose ourselves, our own health, and our enjoyment. As followers of a religion affirming the sacredness of the material world, witches are here to enjoy the material world as well as serve. The games played by the warriors in the sacred castles are fun. They are meant to be enjoyed. In *The Charge of the Goddess*, the Earth Goddess reminds us of this through the lines, "Sing, feast, dance, make music and love, all in My presence, for Mine is the ecstasy of the spirit and Mine also is joy on earth. For my law is love unto all beings." And the Star Goddess states, "Let My worship be in the heart that rejoices, for behold—all acts of love and pleasure are My rituals."

We are here to enjoy the world. I have a friend who was looking at a book of spiritual rituals and exercises, prescribing all the things you should do as a magickal initiate upon rising, at midday, at night, and throughout the year. His first thought was, "If I did all that, I wouldn't have time to eat ice cream. Sometimes the most sacred thing you can do is enjoy eating a big bowl of ice cream." There's another cute proverb where you fill in your favorite thing, particularly to eat or drink— ice cream, beer, whisky, etc., and say that it is proof that the gods love us. We are meant to enjoy the senses, enjoy our bodies, enjoy our hobbies and passions and our time off. The most spiritual people laugh, sing, and enjoy life. They are not filled with seriousness. They still get their True Will, their mission, accomplished, but they enjoy doing it and don't have an attitude of putting off fun until later. Putting off ecstasy until later, until the afterlife, is a Christian concept, not a pagan concept.

If you aspire at all to the healing arts, one of the first lessons to learn is that we must find healing and balance for ourselves before we can ever help others. Visit the Royal Castle, the inner temple, often, and rejuvenate, but also take this wisdom out into life. Enjoy life and all that is has to offer. Everything in moderation, including moderation. Wisely follow your passions and pleasures while you pursue your mission.

Here is a meditation to help you enjoy the feeling of Perfect Love.

EXERCISE 16

Gateway of Perfect Love

1. Perform Exercise 1: Inner Temple as a Mystery School Meditation (page 45), steps 1–5, to go to your inner temple.

2. Open the gateway of guidance and ask for your Master-Teacher. Call your Master-Teacher by name. Ask to open the gateway that will bring you to the mysteries of unconditional love, of Perfect Love and Perfect Trust. Any of the twelve gateways (*ITOW*, chapter 14) might open, but usually it will be the gateway of peace.

3. Feel the peace of unconditional love, or Perfect Love and Perfect Trust, as you enter through the gateway, or feel its energies spill out and fill your temple.

4. Become one with the Perfect Love and Perfect Trust. Feel the true power of balance.

5. Stay as long as you like, but when you are done, close the gateway and thank your Master-Teacher. Your Master-Teacher might have a final message or lesson for you. Communicate now with this guide. When done, say your farewells.

6. Finish exercise 1, steps 8–11, to return to normal consciousness.

This exercise is not always what you expect. One student had difficulties, feeling that she was fluctuating between being in the gate and out of the gate; she couldn't remain anchored in that state of consciousness for any period of time. Several other students have reported that they didn't go through the gateway of peace, but the gateway of Perfect Love opened up within them, through their own self image's heart chakra, and they were drawn into it, being both the gate itself and the consciousness entering the gate, which was powerful, but initially disconcerting.

THE POWER OF HEALING

The way of the witch is the way of the healer. Our strongest positive folk image of the witch is the cunning man or wise woman at the edge of the village whom people seek out for cures and remedies for their illnesses, as well as advice and counsel in matters of the heart and home. Physical health is strongly related to our emotional health, and whether it was explicitly taught or not, our spiritual ancestors knew this truth.

Today, modern witchcraft is a healing path. Many people who cross my doorstep in search of classes and training, or buy my books, will eventually find that witchcraft is but one step of many on their healing path. Because it's a healing art, many confuse the need for healing with a desire to be a witch, to be a healer. Though the path is not for everybody, training at the earliest levels can give life skills that anybody can use, while the deeper mysteries are reserved for subsequent training.

I came to witchcraft with a need for healing, yet I didn't know it at the time. I came to it as a skeptic, wanting to debunk it, at least on a conscious level, but I really came as a wounded soul, upset with my traditional spiritual upbringing, filled with self-doubt and low self-esteem. My desire to experience magick, if it was real, challenged me to find self-esteem and personal power. My healing was emotional and spiritual, but as I progressed, it tackled physical and karmic issues as well. As I continued on the path, in an eclectic but definitely structured study, I pinpointed and worked on my weaknesses at that time, and I learned that the healing journey never ends. Many healers describe the healing process as layers of an onion. There is always another layer to go, and you never quite get to the center, yet the tools you learn to use make each layer, each step on the healing path, easier to cope with. Though healing might never become easy, the tools we gain help us understand, process, and integrate the experience, making it a part of our evolution.

I was speaking to a priestess of the Craft from the United Kingdom, from a much more formal lineage and training than mine, who expressed her surprise at the state of physical and emotional health of so many American witches. She told me that such people would not have been brought into the Craft and initiated in her day, for an initiate must be fit and healthy on all levels. Though I agree, I sometimes think that if modern witches, and in particular, American witches, had that same standard, there would be few of us indeed, myself included. Witchcraft as a healing path has adopted the image of Chiron, the wounded healer, or the lame shaman-sorcerer as well as the elder wise one. Those who are called to it are welcomed, and the process of unfoldment determines where they stop. Many move on, as their desire to be witches, or even to be healed, was a fad. Others take the tools, and continue the journey, called to be seekers for now. Many people who learn witchcraft are never witches, and that's okay. If our teachings help them in some way, then we've been of service to the greater good and helped heal the world. Those who are called to be witches will dig those roots in deep and connect with the Mother's power and wisdom for their own healing, and the healing of the world.

The first step on the path of the healer is self-healing. You have to get yourself to a place of health and well-being before you can counsel anyone else. I think that was really what my priestess friend from the UK meant. A potential initiate might be called to do a certain amount of personal work before being brought into the tradition, and many would not complete it. In America, we put a lot of that initial personal work under the umbrella of training the witch. We get candidates with a whole range of issues and problems, ranging from the minor to the deeply serious. They are seeking healing, often soul healing. We have to do that work before we can be ready to be of service, if in fact, that's our calling. That doesn't mean you have to be "perfect" to be a healer. You simply need to be aware of and actively working on your own healing issues. You must walk your talk, and if you can't say you are taking the steps to become more healthy, how can you ask others to do what you have not done?

Once you attain a certain level of self-mastery, you are ready to help others. You might not believe you have reached that mastery, but others will notice it in you, and come to you for healing. Part of our job as aspiring high priest/esses is to be healers, though how we do this work comes in many forms.

The most important form is to model a healthy way of life. That is the first requirement, and nothing else is necessary. By living a happy, healthy, and sacred life, we create a living model for others. Much of our healing work will occur by being open to questions from those who see our lifestyle and want to emulate it, finding their own way in harmony with the earth.

Others walk the secret path of healing, dedicating much of their spells and rituals to the healing of the planet and its people, for peace, environmental healing, quelling wars, crossing over souls trapped in disaster zones or war-torn areas, and working with the spirits of illness that affect a great number of people. You might never know they are healers, for they have no shingle on their doors advertising their services, and they have no personal relationship with their "clients."

Lastly, we have those who work with individuals on a personal level. They might literally have a shingle on their doorstep, or a professional office and a vocation of some sort that allows them to offer healing services to their world. They work in counseling, body work, herbalism, and energy healing vocations more widely accepted in the world than witchcraft. A few make their vocation as witchcraft ministers, offering a variety of services publicly under the umbrella of witchcraft.

Most of us don't have the opportunity or calling to dedicate our full-time careers to public ministry, and we find the role of the high priest/ess more in our interactions with the community and coven. Our healing work comes through the interactions we have before and after circles and gatherings, through a kind word and sympathetic ear, and through advice asked for and freely given. It comes through conversations over tea and walks in the woods, as well as over tarot cards and astrology charts. Healing works in many ways.

Our relationships might not be as clear and clinical as those of the counselor, for we are immersed in our community—our local community, our pagan community, and our circle of witches. When doing healing work with witches, we must realize that we are a religion of clergy, of priestesses and priests, and we cannot look quite the same way at our sisters and brothers in the Craft as we would outside of our circle. Many of us don't give time and thought to our healing work, formal or informal, and the relationships we forge through it. These are very sensitive and sacred relationships, and they deserve much thought and attention if you are going to pursue the path of the healer and high priest/ess.

When walking the path of healing and offering your services in the healing arts to others, it is important to remember that you are not entirely responsible for healing another person. The client must be actively engaged in the healing process. The phrase that has been the single most helpful bit of wisdom I've learned was not from a witch, but from a Reiki Master, yet I teach it to all witches who study with me. The phrase is "healing facilitator." Though not as inspiring or romantic as the title of healer, shaman, or witch, it is the most accurate. Anyone who aspires to be a healer is really a healing facilitator, and that second word reminds us of who is really doing the work. A healer is really like a coach. We cannot truly heal anybody else. Our magick can have great effect, seemingly without the effort of the recipients, but if that healing is to take root, the recipients must accept it, and make corresponding changes in their physical, mental, emotional, and spiritual lives. We cannot heal anyone else. We can only help others heal themselves. Even those involved in modern medicine cannot heal one another. Their techniques can cure disease and provide nutrients and chemicals that will promote specific effects and reactions, but ultimately the individuals and their bodies do the healing. Their bodies do the work; doctors simply direct the process and help it along. Forgetting this fact has given us a culture where doctors are deified as miracle workers and patients feel like they have no power or part in the process of healing.

Modern therapists and analysts are famous for not giving their clients the answers, but having them figure out their problems by asking the clients questions, to show them their own thought processes and emotional patterns. The counselors act as coaches, for they know if they simply give them the answers, without the necessary work, they would not be understood or appreciated, and their wisdom would not be put into practice. We all have friends to whom we've given advice or pointed out a problem, and although they heard our words, they were not in a place to really listen to them. Then, months later, someone else said the same exact thing, and they acted like it was a brand-new solution to their problem. They finally processed enough of the experience to see the information that was obvious to us. It's obvious to the facilitator, who stands outside of the process, looking at it more objectively. We rarely find the answer to our personal problems as easily because we are immersed in them and can't see the entire picture objectively. In the end, counselors are facilitators of healing.

Witches do the same. We use our tools to bend and shape the healing process, helping others heal. We use our magick to guide the forces of healing along, but the most effective healing is that which fully engages the recipient of the healing in the process. As clergy to those who seek out our aid, we know that in times past our ancestors have done this work. It's only in the modern age that we divide the disciplines, specializing those with knowledge of the body, of the stars, of the herbs, of the spirit world, and of the soul. The root of the word *psychology*, now considered to be the study of the mind and behavior, comes from the Greek goddess Psyche, and the Greek term for the soul. *Psychic* has the same root, referring to listening to the messages of your soul, your intuition. Rather than divide the disciplines, witches work in a holistic paradigm, drawing from a wide variety of tools in our toolbox. To me, witchcraft became the paradigm that held together a wider range of tools and techniques that I use in my healing practice. Students and clients who were interested in healing work wondered how I could work with so many different modalities and address issues through talking, energy work, herbal remedies, stones, and religious rituals. To me, they all fall under the wide brim of the witch's hat. The witch's worldview organized all the things I was interested in, providing a structure, yet also a flexibility that none of my other tools and techniques could.

Though you don't have to be a witch to be an effective spiritual healing facilitator, I certainly think it helps. I encourage all witches to give thought to the healing arts. You might simply need it for yourself or your immediate loved ones, but most healers don't set out to be healers—they are called to the path, often against their ego's will.

Here are some skills and systems you might be called to explore on the healing path, to integrate into your "toolbox" of techniques:

Physical Healing

This involves learning basic first aid and CPR, or a deeper understanding of anatomy, physiology, and even bone setting. Ancient shamans and priest/esses, responsible for funerary rites, were the ones most knowledgeable about anatomy.

Body Work

Body work is the application of your knowledge of physiology to manipulate the tissues of the body, usually through massage or related skills. Most body work techniques require intense training to make sure no physical injury occurs, and they are regulated by state and local government.

Herbalism

While magickal herbalism is a powerful skill for the witch, coupling that knowledge with medicinal knowledge is even more effective. Even though witchcraft is a path of nature, many witches unfortunately do not know basic herbalism or even how to identify the basic medicinal plants that grow wild in their area. Choose a few herbs appropriate for a wide range of illnesses, and learn how to make medicinal preparations such as tea blends, tinctures, syrups, and salves. Learn how to properly identify and harvest wild plants. Use herbal healing in your daily life when appropriate. One doesn't need to be an herbal expert to use some simple and effective remedies.

Magickal Cooking

Though few think of cooking as a healing art, the use of magick in food preparation is an amazing way to work healing into another avenue, and it is a time-honored tradition. My friend Jessica cooks for magickal retreats, and she uses her magick as a part of her cooking, to support the healing going on through the workshops and sessions. Magickal cooking is balanced on one side by the science (knowing the power of nutrition, proportion, and food combination) and on the other by the art (using color, texture, and scent) to create change within the person who consumes the food. Knowledge of the magickal properties of spices and herbs that are used in cooking is essential to the art.

Counseling

Counseling skills can also be used, either through training and licensing in psychology or psychiatry, or through spiritual and personal counseling programs and life coaches. Many high priest/esses who have legal credentials to perform spiritual counseling as ministers are not necessarily trained and licensed counselors, and they must make that clear to potential clients. They counsel by applying the spiritual theology of their tradition to the situations at hand with their clients, and advising the clients using these guiding principles.

Divination

Through the use of divination techniques, such as the tarot or runes, as well as systems such as astrology, one can do a reading to help guide the seeker on an appropriate course of action. Often divination sessions lead to spiritual counseling sessions and other modalities of healing.

Guided Imagery

Learning to guide others through meditative imagery, what many would consider hypnosis, is an effective technique to engage another in the healing process. Images can be used to de-stress, to heal, or to solve life's problems. Exploration of past lives and spiritual skills can be handled through the use of guided imagery. While many witches pick up this technique through teaching others (see Lesson Five) and through their own personal work, training in hypnotherapy is also very beneficial.

Energy Medicine

Energy medicine refers to healing techniques that use life-force energy to heal the body and psyche. The use of visualized colors (*ITOW*, chapter 10) or techniques such as pranic breathing (*TOSW*, chapter 5) or Reiki are just a few forms of energy healing available.

Vibrational Healing

"Vibrational" refers to the use of remedies that are not necessarily known for their chemical properties, but are said to change the energetic patterns of the recipient when used in healing. Crystal healing, ranging from a large layout of stones upon the body to carrying a stone with you, is a form of vibrational healing, because the stone is said to work through its energy, its vibration. The stone can also be made into what is known as a gem elixir, and taken orally. Far more common is the use of flower vibrational remedies, known as flower essences (*TOSW*, chapter 13). Training and certification programs in flower essences and crystal healing are available at holistic training centers, but they are also techniques that can be learned easily through self-study and practice.

Spiritual Healing

Spiritual healing refers to any ritual of healing, from shamanic medicine healing and soul healing (*TOSW*, chapters 12–15) to spells and rituals of empowerment.

Spell Consultation

Sometimes a client will come to a witch not to be healed directly, but to obtain a desired spell. Sometimes the need for a spell will arise naturally through other services, such as a divination that ends with a poor outcome, but others simply seek spells for love, money, uncrossing (curse breaking), or healing. Sometimes less successful witches, in terms of spellcraft, will come to more successful witches to find their "secret." While this doesn't appear to be counseling at the onset, such spell consultations can turn into counseling. While we can give information on spellcraft, correspondence, and magickal timing, we have to point out when people's intentions are not in harmony with their actions, and not in harmony with their overall health and well-being.

People, even witches, expect magick to do the impossible, with no follow-through. I've had people in my office who want a love spell to find a monogamous lifetime mate, yet they sleep around with everybody they meet. Though there is nothing wrong with sex, they are not focusing their energy on what they say they want. I've had clients do magick to become writers, yet they never sit down and actually write. Their spells are not necessarily for the inspiration or discipline to write, but for the fame and fortune. They don't have a stronger purpose for their goal.

By crafting a spell with someone, and getting to the heart of the matter, and their true personal intentions, you help create a self-fulfilling prophecy for the future. If you leave clients with a very "negative" outcome at the end of a divination, and you give them no options, they will have a hard time creating a future that is any different from what you've predicted. If you frame your reading in terms of free will, you empower your clients. Your reading can only tell what is most likely to happen at this moment. Now armed with such information, clients can change the outcome if they so choose. If your clients are open to it, you can construct a spell to help them change their reality to fulfill their goals and live a better life. Though not every difficult trial can be changed through magick, it gives them a worldview of empowerment and working with the energies of the future in partnership, rather than leaving everything to fate.

Mediumship

Although the classic name for this service of the witch would be necromancy, most prefer to call it mediumship today. Mediumship refers to spirit communication, as the practitioner is the medium, the go-between, for the client and the spirit world. Most mediums connect the living with the dead (*TOSW*, chapter 9), though technically the term *medium* can be used for communing with any spirit. Witches can prefer the term *death walker* for those who work specifically with the realm of the ancestors, but most outside our tradition don't like the term. The mediumship traditions have changed over time, from the shamanic tribal ancestor reverence to temples and home shrines, and then the popular séances of the spiritualist church. In a culture generally devoid of true ancestor reverence and a connection to the land and Underworld, many people have great fears surrounding the dead, and they cannot move on when a loved one has left the physical realm. Although a medium can bring forth specific information about a deceased loved one's life, the process usually serves to reassure the living querent that there is life after death and that the loved one is all right. Though technically not parts of mediumship, one who does this work should be prepared in other ways—a medium may need to provide grief counseling, refer serious cases of grief to licensed counselors, and work with the spirits of those who have not crossed over but remain as the earthbound dead.

While we've divided the modalities into several categories, many of them cross the lines, not fitting neatly into any one category, and many are complementary. A witch who acts as a medium, for example, might give a client a crystal, elixir, or essence to aid in grief, as well as a candle spell to bless the ancestor. A body worker might use relaxation techniques and guided imagery to fully heal a client at the end of a session.

Many of these are techniques and skills you have already learned in your training as a witch, and hopefully you have learned to apply them in your daily life. To incorporate them in a healing practice, you have to take them to the next level, and learn how to use these tools when working with other people.

I highly recommend that if you want to pursue the path of healing, for others or simply for yourself, you should get training in at least one more modality outside of witchcraft to give you another tool and perspective in the healing arts. The healers you personally see for your own evolution will pass on their style, techniques, and wisdom to you. Then you will be able to integrate these things into your own personalized practice.

EXERCISE 17

Overshadowing with Your Healing Guide

1. Begin the Pranic Breathing Exercise (*TOSW*, exercise 6). Draw energy from below and above into your heart chakra, and expel it through the shoulders, arms, and hands with the intention of Perfect Love and Perfect Trust. Let the energy flow through you, and then close your eyes and begin to do the meditations.

2. Perform Exercise 1: Inner Temple as a Mystery School Meditation (page 45), steps 1–5, to go to your inner temple.

3. Open the gateway of guidance and ask for your healing guide. At this point, your Master-Teacher might be your primary healing guide, or another spirit can fill this role.

4. Together, open the gateway of healing. Feel the inner temple fill with healing energy. Notice the colors and forms in which it manifests. As you breathe in the inner temple, feel the healing energies mix with the energies above and below, flowing through you.

5. Ask your healing guide to overshadow you. Feel the guide step around you, possibly giving you a hug, or hugging you from behind, and with that hug, your self-images merge. You are invoking (*TOSW*, exercise 19) the healing guide into your body.

6. While still merged with the healing guide, bring yourself back through the World Tree, back to the Middle World. You have left the gateway of healing in the inner temple open. Still feel the energy of the healing gateway flowing through your body, as well as the power above and below. Feel your consciousness merged with the healing guide that overshadows you. The

guide helps you moderate the flow of energy. For now, put one hand over the heart, and the other over the belly. Feel the energy flow and circulate around you. If you have any pain, illness, or disease, note its location and let it fill with healing energy. Do anything your healing guide urges you to do.

7. When done, return to the inner temple, release the healing guide, and separate yourself. Close the gateway of healing and then the gateway of guidance, saying farewell to your healing guide.

8. Finish exercise 1, steps 8–11, to return to normal consciousness.

You can use this technique for both self-healing and energy work, and when working with others. Practice with it should allow you to be overshadowed by your healer and connect to the healing gateway without having to go deeply into vision and to the inner temple. You will be able to do it in session with a client present, and also release the guide with the client present as well. The healing guide will assist you with every step of the healing, sometimes with silly requests and aid, but you will often get spectacular results. The union of the two of you is much like the alchemical process of conjunction we attribute to the Temple of the Heart. Two forces, a physical person and a healing spirit, fuse together making a divine instrument of healing, capable of doing much more than either one could do alone.

HOMEWORK

- Do exercises 14–17 and record your experiences in your journal or BOS.

- When you complete the trials of this chapter, tie your fourth knot in your cord in a ritualized manner.

- Though it might be difficult to obtain a breastplate, think about what jewelry you have that guards your heart. It might be your pentacle necklace (*ITOW*, chapter 17) or some other charm. Contemplate how it acts like a breastplate for you.

- Another option for a ritual breastplate is to make your own stone charm emulating the powers of both the Hebrew and Greek breastplates. Make a small pouch or bag on a necklace that will hang at the heart level. You can paint a Medusa head on the front of the pouch. You can build it all at once, filling it with twelve stones for the zodiac, or build it gradually. As you complete all the lessons in Volume Two, based on the zodiac signs, obtain, cleanse, and consecrate the appropriate stone for each zodiac sign and add it to the pouch, one per month. I like small chips of stones, the size of a bead for a necklace, not larger polished stones, so that I can make sure the pouch will fit neatly under my shirt without a bulge. Wear it whenever possible, to help you in understanding how the "stars" are within your heart, protecting, healing, and guiding you.

TIPS

- Continue to build an integrated meditation and ritual practice.

- Speak with your Master-Teacher regularly. Build a relationship.

- Contemplate peace through Perfect Love and Perfect Trust. Do you have a sense of peace in your life? Do you live through Perfect Love and Perfect Trust? If not, why not?

- Write about a healing experience you have had helping another—formally or informally. I bet even if you think you never have, you will find at least one case where you have been in the service of healing. Write it down in your journal or BOS. If you have not done healing work with another, be open to the experience, and when it occurs, write it down.

- Think about your own healing and balance. What are you doing for your own healing? Do you think you are not in need of healing? Have you seen a healing facilitator? If not, why not? Make sure you are in a healthy place before you even begin to think about working with others. When you are truly ready, people will seek you out.

LESSON FIVE
TEMPLE OF THE THROAT:
COMMUNICATION AND TEACHING

Ascending to the higher temples, the fifth gate guards the opening to the throat. It is one of the few gates that actually is a physical opening as well as a spiritual opening in our body. It is the gateway through which the nourishment of food and breath enters us, and through which our words, our power, are expressed. Though an upper point of the chakra system, the throat is strongly connected to the lower chakras. Many who come to the path of the witch find themselves either with great power at this temple, or great weakness and a need for healing the throat. Its power lies in its dual nature, of both expressing and receiving, for you can only have true communication when the powers of listening and speaking are engaged.

Set up your altar with throat chakra associations—blue candles, stones such as lapis or turquoise, and flowers—to work with the powers of the throat and its mysteries over the next month. Mercurial correspondences work well for the power of air, as well as Jupiterian correspondences, because blue is the color of Jupiter. Anything that works with the element of air, the sky, and the power of breath is a tool for the tasks you face in this temple.

Exercise 18

Contemplation of the Throat Chakra

1. Sit quietly in a comfortable position and enter a meditative state. Call upon higher guidance, through your own spirit guides and the Goddess, God, and Great Spirit.

2. Place your hands on your throat. Rather than take a position where you appear to be choking yourself, place the base of the hands, near the wrists, together, and then place one palm on either side of the throat, to cradle the throat without creating too much tension in the arms.

3. Feel the energy of the throat chakra. Start with your hands, but let the sensations move through your entire body. You might feel as if your entire energy field is surrounded in blue light. Ask the throat chakra to reveal its mysteries and guide you.

4. Observe the thoughts, feelings, visions, and insights you have, as well as messages you receive, while attuning yourself to the Temple of the Throat. These will guide you in this lesson to your own personal work.

5. When done, return yourself from the meditative state. Thank the energy of the throat chakra as well as your spiritual guidance, and give yourself clearance and balance.

Magickal Teaching: Expression
Force: Vibration
Chakra: Throat
Function: Communication
Body: Mental
Tool of the Goddess: Double-Stranded Necklace
Alternate Tool of the Goddess: Necklace

Color: Blue

Ray: Second

Element: Air

Planet: Mercury

Metal: Quicksilver

Signs: Leo, Capricorn

Emerald Tablet Rubric: Separate the Earth from Fire, the Subtle from the Gross

Alchemical Operation: Fermentation

Totems: Snake, Wolf

Plant: Skullcap

Sephiroth: Geburah, Chesed, and Da'ath

Tarot, Lunar: Trump V—The Hierophant

Tarot, Solar: Trump XII—Hanged Man

Tarot, Stellar: Trump XIX—Sun

Life Stage: Third-Degree Initiation (*TOSW*)

Hermetic Principle: Vibration

Musical Note: G

Day of the Week: Wednesday

Castle of the Underworld: Caer Fredwyd—Castle of Perfected Ones, Castle of Carousal, Castle of Mead

Egyptian Temple Site: Saqqara

Left Hand Initiation: School

Vice of Initiation: Attachment to the Thoughts of Another

Virtue of Initiation: Moderation

Stage of the Bread Miracle: Stones

Challenge of the Temple: Muteness

Blessing of the Temple: Voice

The power to effectively communicate is essential for any magus. As witches, we are magick workers, and magick is ultimately our ability to communicate. We work magick in communicating with ourselves and the hidden parts of our psyche, with the spirits, with our gods, and with the living world around us. But communication is twofold. We must also learn to listen and we must always remember that if we want to effectively walk the path of the witch.

The Mysteries of Communication

Communication is the essence of magick. Our rituals, spells, and words of power are all tools that allow us to effectively communicate with the world around us, to make change. We communicate with ourselves, with the open and hidden parts of our own soul. Through our communication, we enter a better relationship with ourselves. When we communicate with the people around us, we improve our relationships with others. Sometimes the most effective magick is simply asking someone for something we want. We communicate with the spirits of the living and the dead, of nature and supernature all around us. We communicate with angels, faeries, demons, and the gods. We might not even see a persona behind certain forces, such as the weather or elements, but our ability to communicate our desire, our will, to the patterns of the world is what effectively changes them. All magick is about relationships, and relationships are built upon our ability to communicate.

In much of our old medieval magick, we find the concept of pacts. Witches were accused of making pacts with the Devil, gaining power in exchange for their souls. Because of our desire to distance ourselves from anything even remotely associated with Satanism, many witches do not understand or make pacts with spirits today. Many forms of modern energy-work magick do not engage directly with entities. Other styles of magick command or bind spirits to do their bidding, or consider spirits to be simply mental constructs, not individual entities in their own right. Witchcraft is different.

In witchcraft, spirit relationships are essential, and making pacts, which really amount to promises and agreements, is also essential. We are not just manifesting our own lives, but at this level of training, we are really ambassadors from the human realm to the various spirit realms. We make contacts for our own benefit, but also for the benefit of the spirit world. Think of pacts as treaties, both on a personal and individual level, and also on a community level. No spirit I've met has wanted my soul. I don't think of a soul as something you can possess, except for your own, but spirits, particularly nature spirits, have asked me to do things to maintain and strengthen the links between our realms, and

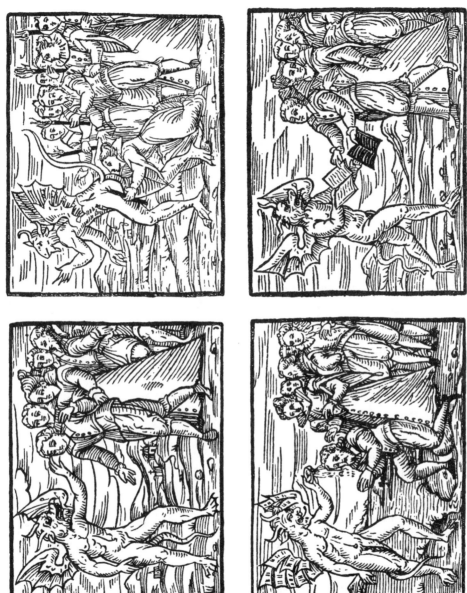

Figure 10: Woodcuts from R. P. Gauccius's Compendium Maleficarum, Milan, 1626

to act in the interest of those spirits' overall good. The essence of understanding a pact is that spiritual magickal relationships are two-way streets.

The series of woodcuts in figure 10, from R. P. Gaucius's *Compendium Maleficarum*, depicts what was believed to go on at a witch's gathering with a demon or devil. When the same images and information are looked at without the Christian lens, you can gain an understanding of the pacts witches and sorcerers most likely made and learn how you can apply them to your own work today. The demonic figure could be a demon, as in the Goetic sense of working with demons to understand both your shadow nature and the collective shadow of humanity (*TOHW*, chapter 13). It could be another spiritual entity simply depicted as a demon because in the Christian view there were only angels, saints, ghosts, and demonic beings. It could also be a human initiator, wearing a mask, invoking a spiritual entity, and acting as the mediator for the spirit world and other witches.

In the first panel, we have the entity bestowing a blessing. We are blessed and re-born in the initiation process. A blessing from the Otherworld symbolizes an exchange or acceptance. One might be consecrated with items pleasing to the spirits he or she is working with, such as blessings with particular herbs and oils, to resonate with the spirits more strongly or to be accepted as one of them. Sometimes we receive names in the tongue of the spirits we work with—our faery name, angelic name, or witch name—to signify our acceptance into their fold. Witches were once considered the kith and kin of the spirit world.

The second panel is the scandalous ritual kiss of the devil's buttocks. Though seen as horrific to the medieval Christian for it involved sexual images, let alone sexual images that were not aimed at procreation, the kiss is a powerful ritual tool. The kiss is the third key to the initiation circle, after Perfect Love and Perfect Trust. The kiss is used multiple times, including the famous fivefold kiss for blessing, initiation, and invocation. This is also a symbol of intimacy, and would mark intimacy with the spirit world and the potential to have a "spirit lover." The kiss, and with it the mouth, is the opening to the throat chakra and the rest of the body, appropriate for the mysteries we learn in the Temple of the Throat. Of all the seven chakra centers, only the root and throat have actual openings to the body, with the sexual organs/anus and mouth respectively. All the others are more symbolic openings. It is interesting that these two power points would be paired in this panel. We can also imagine such pairings in sexual initiator rites in the ancient pagan temples of the Goddess, as well as modern sexual initiation rites, where in the moment of passion, the secret names of the gods are whispered into the initiates' ears and fused with their energy systems, forever altering them, bringing them into the world of the witch. I was told by one traditional witch that the old covens would have a test: once your blindfold was removed, you were standing before the hindquarters of the goat and urged that the next step of your initiation was indeed to kiss it. If you did not protest, you were diverted from the goat and brought to the lips of the fairest maiden or most handsome lord of the group to kiss instead, and that willingness to take the plunge into what is strange and taboo is rewarded with sweetness, then true initiation. If you refused, then the initiation ended there in failure. I'm not sure if that was a true practice, or a clever play on what remains in the evidence of woodcuts such as this, but the idea has a certain romantic appeal.

The third panel is much like the first, but instead is an anointing, a ritual baptism of sorts. This is seen as a mockery of the Christian baptism, but rites of purification, water blessing, and rebirth are as much a part of the pagan tradition as the Christian traditition (*OTOW*, chapter 11).

Lastly, we have the exchange of knowledge. The final panel depicts the Christian giving up the Gospels for a book of black magick. Without the Christian bias, it is the exchange of knowledge and power between us and the Otherworld. We share our human magick and power and receive spirit magick and power, and both races are strengthened by the exchange, forming a bond.

All four panels really represent an exchange. In the first we are given a blessing by the spirit world. In the second we give trust and intimacy. In the third we are given baptism and the pact is affirmed. In the fourth we have a true exchange and a relationship is built. But, for that relationship to be maintained, there must be continuous communication and exchange between both sides. These woodcuts can show us the way with both individual spirits and spirit races, as well as an entire attitude and protocol for relating to the universe. There must be reciprocity.

Many work their magick, and in effect, live their lives, continuously talking, asking, and expressing, and they believe they are good at communication. They are only good at one-half of the equation. True communication is not only about speaking, but also about listening. Others are great listeners, but they never speak up for themselves and express what they think or want. Sometimes they don't know. Other times they simply can't say it. There is a block. They are not effective communicators either. The throat chakra rules the throat, the mouth, and the ears, for they are all the instruments of communication, speaking, and listening, and both skills must be developed in the use of this temple. When we look at magick, it's a two-sided coin, with our spellcraft helping us speak to the universe, while vision work and meditation help us listen to the universe.

In the descent of Inanna, her double strand of beads, hanging by her breasts, is the tool of this fifth temple. Not much information on this necklace is given, other than that it is double stranded. Some describe it as lapis, though lapis lazuli is used to describe the next tool, the single-strand necklace for the sixth temple. The double strand is symbolic of the two currents of the throat chakra, of communication, both speaking and listening. Envisioning a double-stranded necklace down to the breast, I think of the image of Eastern mala meditation beads, which are used as a tool for mantras and affirmations today.

The witch's ladder can double as both cingulum and knotted prayer rope, as ancient sacrifices, often believed to be willing offerings of their people to the gods, had nooses around their necks, even when hanging was not the method of death. Modern witches believe it doubles as a symbol of service, a collar, symbolizing their sacrifice of their lives to the gods. Some of us emulate the practice with knotted or collared necklaces to denote our service to the gods.

Today, witchcraft traditions vary as to what a witch's jeweled necklace consists of. Many high priestesses wear a necklace of alternating amber and jet. These two organic stones embody the powers of Sun and Moon, God and Goddess, projective and receptive, life and death. They are the double powers of giving and receiving, like the power embodied by the double strands of Inanna. I wear, and encourage graduates of the Temple of Witchcraft tradition to wear, a choker-style necklace of amber and jet, with collar symbolism, like the noose, to signify that we are in service to the divine. Our personal will is subservient, in service to the divine will of our higher selves and our patron gods. The necklace is symbolic, and when used as a set of prayer beads, literally, a focus for our mind, to project our consciousness toward divine will.

The use of mantras or affirmation meditations, repeated phrases said silently or chanted out loud, is a method of focusing the powers of the mind. The throat chakra rules the mental body, our mind, which permeates all the bodies before it—the emotional, astral, etheric, and physical. Our thoughts change our feelings, our bodily sensations, and eventually our long-term physical health. Mastering the mind helps us in mastering our reality, for our thoughts and words do so much in creating our reality. We learn the power of the magick word in our spell casting, and to neutralize the unwanted things we accidentally say (*ITOW*, chapter 8).

Through work with the element of air, initiates learn that we are not our mind, but our mind is a tool of our spirit. Most people live their lives believing they are the mind, and never learn to master it. They serve the mind, rather than the mind serving them. Through our work with the Sword of Truth, we know that there is little difference between the magus and the spiritual warrior, for both have to master the mind. We must learn the difference between reaction and response. While some instinctual reactions are very magickal and life saving, like fight or flight, most of us have that same immediate mentality in situations that are not life threatening. We let other people and situations push our mental and emotional buttons, rather than observing the situation and responding effectively. The difference is between a conscious response and an unconscious reaction. Responding doesn't mean you don't express yourself, or that you don't get angry, but you handle your response through your conscious will, expressed however you choose to communicate it. Yet you choose—your mind doesn't choose for you. Your mind is the tool that helps you get the response across to others.

To master the mind, we must spend time alone with it. In the Eastern traditions that focus on mastering the mind, meditation is not the familiar pathworking that witches and magicians do, but an exercise of occupying the mind, honing it to single-pointedness, free from distracting thought. The aim is to clear the mind of images and thoughts, to simply experience pure consciousness. Only then can one truly understand the nature of his or her consciousness. Counting the breath, focusing on a visual mandala known as a yantra, chanting, and using a silent mantra are all ways of focusing the attention to achieve this meditative state.

Mantas, specific sacred words, often in Sanskrit in the yogic tradition, are used, and many people believe that the very words have the power to change your consciousness.

Different mantras, sacred to different gods and goddesses, are used to achieve different effects. In some ways they are like spells, because they focus the mind, but specific goals are not usually voiced. They can be compared to the divine names in Hebrew, for the sephiroth of the Qabalah. The mantras are repeated, and a beaded strand known as a mala, acting similar to the Catholic rosary, is used to keep track of the number of mantras. One hundred and eight repetitions is traditional, with mala strands having one hundred and eight small beads and one larger bead to let you know when you've reached the end of a set.

Western mystics, witches included, often have a hard time with such meditations. We want to "go" somewhere, or "do" something in our work, with a sense of experience or accomplishment. Such activity is part of the Western mystery tradition, but the line between activity and receptivity is a fine distinction. One cannot look at the exercises of a yogi or martial artist and say that nothing was done. Nor can one look at a witch communing with a tree without words or pictures and think anything was really accomplished. Yet all of these experiences denote potentially profound spiritual results.

To truly master the mind, and understand how the mind plays a role in communication, we must first look at how we communicate with the mind, and how it communicates with us. We must spend time in silence observing the mind. Even such observation has an intrinsic mental quality, showing us how difficult it is to separate our airy function from our spirit. In fact, many languages have a connection between the words for breath and for spirit or life force.

EXERCISE 19

Time of Silence

For this meditation, there is no explicit set of instructions. There is no journey or visualization. There is no invocation or spirit guide. There is no energy work. Set a timer that will let you know when the exercise is done, but don't use music, as the point is silent meditation. I suggest starting this exercise for fifteen minutes, though it is good to work up to at least a half hour regularly. For some the time will fly by; others will feel as if it's crawling. Light a candle. Turn out the electric lights. Get comfortable and sit. Be with yourself. Pay attention to your breath, counting a series of breaths and then repeating. If you know a mantra, you can use it, but many witches will use their magickal name, or their patron deity's name, as a mantra, silently reciting it on the inhale and exhale. Watch your mind. When it wanders, bring it back to attention. I have a wonderful yoga teacher, Stephanie Rutt, who says, "Thank your mind for sharing, and tell it to go sit on the couch. There's plenty of room." Acknowledge that the mind is wandering, but gently bring yourself back to the moment. Don't judge yourself. Don't get mad at yourself for not doing it "perfectly." Simply observe and come back to the present moment. It's all part of the process. Learn to be silent with your mind. To separate from it. Observe it. And then gain greater mastery over it. When the timer goes off, ground yourself if necessary, snuff the candle, and turn on the lights. Reflect. What kinds of thoughts came up for you? What was expected? What was unexpected? How did it feel? What is unsettled in you that you can work on through your other magickal and meditative practices?

I've had a profound experience practicing something that was called "White Tantric Yoga." Though we usually think of tantra as sexual, this practice was a long meditation with the arms raised over the head, reciting a mantra out loud to a partner. I know when I was first given the instructions, my mind thought, "No way. I can't do that." My mind made a judgment before checking in with my body, or checking in with "me," the true spiritual consciousness that directs the mind. I reacted without really reflecting. I felt quite empowered after holding that pose for fifty-two minutes, the allotted time of the exercise. I realized that I can do things I never thought I could. I had a teacher who was famous for doing this ritual of silence, yet introducing a fearful element to it, like holding a tarantula, a hissing cockroach, a rat, toads, or a snake. They are creatures associated with the dark, with our fears, and then when you take time to be with them silently, you find they are not what you thought they would be. The fears of your mind were disproportionate to what the reality was. They are not as dangerous, slimy, icky, or painful as believed. To move past these preconceptions, you had to detach and observe the inner dialogue, and allow your actual impressions to enter into the equation, not just your assumptions. It turns out that the experience can actually be more pleasant than you realized. Many physical exercises in spiritual traditions, from yoga and martial arts to walking high ropes and climbing mountains, even fear-inducing exercises, are intended to show you that what your mind holds as truth is not always your reality. Then you can move beyond what the mind, the ego, thinks about a given situation and break through barriers. You are the master of the mind, rather than it mastering you.

The throat chakra has a number of dark associations, despite being a part of the upper three chakras, deemed "good" by many healers who see the lower chakras as base, material, and "unspiritual." The mind is a link to the rest of the body, and it is the root of many of our ego associations of judgment, perception, and misperception. The throat shares associations with the root, as both are the chakras with physical entry points into the body. Color magick links the throat and the belly, for the colors blue and orange are opposites on the color wheel, and used together. Orange, being the color of the sephira Hod (*TOHW*, chapter 8), the ruling sphere of language, has a throatlike magickal quality when looked at Qabalistically. Blue is the second ray of Theosophy, the ray of divine love, and it is considered one of the three primary powers of creation, along with red and yellow. The throat and the solar plexus are also linked, as they both express themes of power. The solar plexus is potential power, while the throat expresses that power in the world. The mouth feeds the stomach and starts the power of digestion, giving the entire body its fuel. The ego level of the solar plexus is connected to fear and control, echoing similar themes to the mental body of the throat chakra. The throat also feeds the lungs air, oxygenating the blood that is pumped by the heart. The diaphragm is the part of the body supporting the breath, and our ability to speak, sing, and express ourselves with full lung capacity, but it lies between the solar plexus and heart. Though all the chakras are connected to one another, the throat has some special connections to all those beneath it.

The power of our words, tied to this intense chakra, has its drawbacks too. The more we learn the power of our words, the more we see the need to neutralize the words we do not want to create with. Those skilled in the power of words, of communication, realize soon that our words can reach out and grasp the thoughts of others, projecting and implanting our ideas into their minds, even when we don't really mean to do so. Though this technique can have a great effect for the teacher or healer in cases when we are aware, it's not always the effect we are striving for in day-to-day life. The power of mesmerism—the use of words, sounds, cadence, and power, to seduce, compel, and entrance—is linked with the throat chakra. The bardic mysteries of the Celts frequently show us the power of words and poetry to make magick and to change both individuals and reality. We find the same power in the cult leader and con man as we do in the witch and magician, and we therefore have to be quite vigilant in not abusing this ability once we develop it. It's one of the reasons why witches are considered to be dangerous, like cult leaders, deceivers, and con artists. We often impose our will on others through the power of the word, without even realizing it.

The throat center is Qabalistically linked with the non-sephira Da'ath, the sphere of Knowledge and the Abyss. It is knowledge and power, but not necessarily the wisdom to use it properly. It is the chakra of life and death according to my student Kim, who sees the power of both primal breath to give life and the fear of losing breath, of losing voice, akin to death.

The temples of Saqqara, or Sakkara, correspond with the throat chakra. Saqqara was a necropolis for Egypt before the rise of Giza in popularity for royal burial. It contains the world's oldest step pyramid, a potential prototype for the later pyramids, designed by Imhotep for King Djoser. Saqqara represents the first encounter with the higher mysteries, and the mistakes we can make on the journey. Not to say the step pyramid is a mistake, by any means, but it is less perfected than the pyramids of Giza. In this way, it represents the blessings of the throat, and Qabalistically, of Da'ath, and then the energy rises and the vision becomes clear.

In alchemy, the dark powers of the fifth stage are associated with fermentation. Fermentation is a chemical change caused by enzymes. It's transformation. Grapes and water are transformed into wine. Honey water is transformed into mead. Grain water is transformed into beer. Each of these substances results in a spirit, in an alcohol, a magickal mixture with properties quite different from its source ingredients. Alcoholic spirits are aptly named, because they can be used, intentionally or otherwise, to open the gate to the spirit world. In many folk practices, alcohol is used as an offering to disembodied spirits to "feed" them, thereby strengthening their connection to the physical world, keeping the gateway open.

The spiritual experience of fermentation is the dark night of the soul, the doubts and questions of faith that can result in a stronger, greater sense of self and purpose. It's the classic "If it doesn't kill you, it makes you stronger" experience. Like the chemical reaction, the spiritual process has two basic parts. First is putrification, where the substance is decomposing, digesting, or rotting. This is the blackening phase of alchemy, akin to shadow work. It is the initiation of the Abyss. The second phase is the actual fermentation, the spiritization of the mixture, and of the initiate, by introducing something new to the union of the higher, lower, and middle selves. It's the yeast of the brewer that makes fermentation possible. The new aspect introduced can be new information about the self. As in Exercise 19: Time of Silence, if a teacher introduces a new element into the exercise, such as putting a spider, snake, or roach into the student's hands, that catalyzes a new series of perceptions, and the sense of self ferments, becoming something new and potentially stronger. Alchemists describe this resulting material as the *peacock's tail*, because many mixtures get a floating residue with an oily hue, like oil and water on the pavement, creating a peacock-like rainbow. From the darkness is birthed the most brilliant and royal of colors. The Emerald Tablet says, "Separate the Earth from Fire, the Subtle from the Gross," as the two steps are aligned with Leo, the fiery chemical process of putrification, and Capricorn, the new substance, the earth that emerges from the process. Both steps are needed in this dual process to reach a higher level of awareness, just as both aspects are needed in the double strand of the goddess's necklace.

The Stones in the Miracle of Bread are related to the throat chakra, and they refer to both the mill stones and oven stones, the bread stones used in the baking process. The grain is harvested and milled, separating wheat from chaff. For the initiate, it is the process of separating what serves from what no longer serves, like the alchemical separation process of the solar plexus. But it is raised, and the milled grain is then mixed together with the dough ingredients, including yeast, and baked in the oven. The transformation process has begun. As the throat is related to the Abyss of the Tree of Life, this baking process is much like facing the Abyss, the potential for destruction, but if all is done right, it means a chance for redemption and resurrection on the other side.

The fifth castle of Annwn is Caer Fredwyd, known as the Castle of Perfected Ones or the Castle of Carousal or Mead. It is where troubled souls engage in feasting and forget troubles, including troubles of the past or past lives. The very titles seem contradictory. How can it be the castle of "perfected ones" if they are there to feast and forget? That doesn't seem very perfect to me. Yet the forgetting is much like drinking from the river of forgetfulness in the Underworld, where one is made pure and perfect, innocent again, in order to return to the world of men reborn. The feasting is much like that of the tales of the Wiccan Summerland, the place of perpetual feasting and abundance, for that is heaven in a culture dealing with the woes of winter and the toils of the harvest. Abundance of food, drink, dance, and sex, without worry or work—carousing—is heavenly. Yet the true initiate seeks more, to penetrate deeper into the mysteries, to return to the world in service rather than rest, feast, and forget. It is the deeper experience of the previous castle, Caer Rigor. Here the initiate seeks to penetrate beyond. As this corresponds with the level of Da'ath and the Abyss, many don't make it past this realm, to the deeper realms. It's like a test, somewhat like the initiate and the goat. Without pressing further, you don't go deeper in the mysteries. Though this option is quite a bit more pleasant than kissing the hindquarters of a goat, many would simply want to enjoy their time rather than press forward into the mysteries that await in the next ring. The witch, magus, and mystic have to claim the power of the fifth gate to move forward. Those who are not ready to claim it get to journey again into the world, in a new body, place, and time. The gate to the next level is the magician's "door that hath no key."

The Power of Teaching

On the Left Hand Path of initiation, the fifth step is "school," meaning that the initiate finds a teacher and system of metaphysics with a proven track record of successful graduates who have applied these philosophies and workings in their own lives, and the initiate begins to study. Many become zealous in this phase and need moderation in their studies. They must not neglect the pleasure and responsibilities of the rest of their lives, because the modern mystic is rarely cloistered. And for the witch, who needs to be in the world, cloistering would not be advisable. Zeal can also lead initiates to form attachments to the thoughts and ideas of another, the teacher, or the school, rather than use them as a springboard for their own inner teachings and personal philosophies. The mystic's teachings should not be transformed into dogma, but should allow for both personal and cultural evolution. If the school stagnates, it dies.

It's wholly appropriate that the fifth stage of initiation be schooling, for the powers of communication readily lend themselves to education. As the chakra temple corresponding with Da'ath, it is the temple of knowledge. A teacher can impart knowledge and information, and facilitate experiences in the application of that knowledge, yet only the student can learn it and, in his or her own subtle alchemy, transform that knowledge to wisdom. Facts and figures do not make someone wise. There are many educated scholars who do not have the wisdom of the witch. And although it's very important, there are many wise witches whose knowledge doesn't come from books, facts, and figures, but from the school of life and observation of the natural world. One must receive what is being offered by a teacher, digest it, ferment it, and make it new. Only then does it become integrated wisdom, rather than a recitation of facts.

Teaching the Craft is an important part of its continuation. As a tradition of wisdom, we are continually seeking out new information and experiences, to learn, grow, and transform ourselves. There's a great responsibility among those who would consider themselves clergy to pass on the knowledge they have learned at least once, before it grows stagnant and corrupt within them. The power is meant to be passed, meant to be shared with others. We come from a mythic, spiritual, and sometimes literal lineage of teachers and students, a chain linking us to the past and forging our future. We are a link in the chain, but not the final link. Students teach us as much as we teach them, if not more.

We live in an age in which the interest in witchcraft might be at a global high. Though there could have been times in ages past where it was more widely believed in and more readily accepted as a part of life, populations were smaller. With our ever-growing population and our mass media, more books and information are available than ever before. At times, this is arguably a good thing. At other times, less so, because the material is presented without proper context and great misunderstandings can occur. We live in a time when the number of students looking for witchcraft far outstrips the number of teaching coven positions to train them all. Our age is also one in which perhaps the old methods of training are not appropriate for everyone, so new methods must be devised. Students of today who will be the ministers of tomorrow must be a part of the new teaching solutions.

One of the problems with our modern era is the vast amount of information available. It takes the industrious student a long time to sift through it and find what is a magickal teaching and what may be the sole invention of commerce, for some would seek to cash in on the "coolness" of witchcraft, particularly with the younger population. Yet even in some of these less-than-stellar teachings will be keys that unlock the mysteries for you. The process of searching and sifting takes a lot of material out of sequential order. Truly, the mysteries are cyclical, and a teacher might choose to start anywhere in the cycle. Some old covens wouldn't let students talk to other students of different covens, feeling that it would cause problems if they compared notes and learned they were not being taught the same thing at the same time. But a flesh-and-blood teacher will give you a foundation and be able to answer questions. Books are topic-specific, and rarely convey a system, lineage, or body of lore in its complete form. Many authors will write the mysteries in code, keeping essential information out of print, information they feel is too dangerous to put into print. If you have a teacher, or know the mysteries in some other way, it's easier to see these blinds and holes, but if you don't, you might never know there is something missing. Some teachers believe that essential information should only be passed from teacher to student, keeping the oral tradition alive.

I struggle with the conundrum of book learning and formal teaching. I am a teacher by profession. I facilitate experiences that are profoundly helpful for my students. If I didn't, I don't think they would keep coming back. I myself have had amazing experiences with my own teachers, and I wonder if I would be able to be where I am without them. They have been an amazing support and resource. Yet I am also a writer. I have had amazing experiences and insights from books and rituals presented in books. I know many great witches who never had a true teacher, mentor, or lineage, but a natural talent, an eye for the mysteries and the daring to put things into practice, with successful results. Can you learn from only books? Yes. Does this suit everybody? No. Should you have a flesh-and-blood teacher? I think it's wonderful to have one if possible, and I'd highly encourage it. But a teacher is not the be-all, end-all answer to your magickal problems. It is better to have no teacher than to have a long relationship with the "wrong" teacher, one who is incompatible with you and your spiritual health. But keep in mind, compatible does not always mean easy or agreeable, for what is good for you might not always be a salve to your ego.

I agree with much of the wisdom of Thelemic writer Lon Milo DuQuette. He speaks of teachers in his book, *Angels, Demons & Gods of the New Millennium*:

I still believe that it is very important to seek out and find a flesh-and-blood personal magical mentor, and I urge anyone who is serious about the work to tenaciously pursue the quest. The psychological edge of knowing you are a part of a serious and illustrious spiritual brotherhood is often the only momentum you will have to get you through the inevitable dark nights of the soul. It is well to keep in mind, however, that no individual, no matter how enlightened, can project power or illumination upon you. More often than not, you will learn your greatest lessons in spite of your teacher's efforts, and not because of them. (p. 9)

I've created the Temple of Witchcraft tradition and the accompanying teaching manuals upon inner-world guidance and through the needs of my students. It's designed for this generation of eclectic witches. We are crafting the new global traditions of witchcraft. Some people have the job of keeping traditions separate, while others have the job of synthesizing things together, with respect to the past and an eye toward the future. Those are the witches that I teach. Those are the witches I have in mind when I write. Here is a system that is fluid enough for the solitary witch who is reading, for the eclectic teacher seeking to pass on a system, and for those who wish to find a spiritual lineage connecting them to witches across the world. Nothing in particular is held back, but the writings work on two levels—the overt and explicit step-by-step instructions, for those who need them, and the little gems buried in the text, deeper points and the ideas of how to act upon them. Thus the modern tradition of openness is honored and maintained, as well as the hidden tradition of secrecy, woven together as one for those who have the eyes to see.

Many flesh-and-blood teachers are in favor of keeping the mysteries a mystery, and would prefer nothing to be written about them in print, and nothing said in public. I understand the sentiment, but I think that's happened for so long in the modern witchcraft movement that many do not realize that it is a mystery tradition, a school for the soul, and they see it simply as a craft. That doesn't derail the power and wisdom of our folkways, but there is more to be had. If people's main method of learning is reading and if few are writing about the mysteries, then no one of the next generation will really seek them out and understand them in the context of witchcraft. I know that was part of the reason that I searched so much outside of witchcraft. I wanted more. I knew intuitively that there was more, and all that I was studying in herbalism, ceremonial magick, Theosophy, and shamanism led me right back to my foundation of witchcraft, but it let me look at the old legends and myths with new eyes. There is a danger of learning too much, too quickly, without the proper support when you are on your own. Some are "blinded by too much light" when they delve in without a teacher, drowned by the experience, and they never quite achieve a functional life. But in the dawning of this new aeon, we are each called to be our own guru, and must make choices and bear the responsibilities of them. I am in favor of writing about anything and everything, complete with all the warnings, suggestions, successes, and failures that are possible. Once you give students the information, they can make an informed decision as to whether to continue or not, and how fast to go.

Though this section on the mysteries of teaching will give you a lot of ideas on how to teach, what to teach, and why to teach, each minister must decide how this falls into his or her vocation, if at all. There are many ways of passing on wisdom and mentoring, and not all of them involve formal teaching. I like to keep in mind the words of Robert Cochrane (Roy Bowers) from the Clan of Tubal Cain and 1734 tradition, on teaching styles and teaching the self, in his third letter to Joe Wilson, dated February 1, 1966:

> We teach by poetic inference, by thinking along lines that belong to the world of dreams and images. There is no hard and fast teaching technique, no laid down scripture or law, for wisdom comes only to those who deserve it, and your teacher is yourself seen through a mirror darkly. The answers to all things are in the Air—Inspiration, and the winds will bring you news and knowledge if you ask them properly. Trees of the Wood will give you power, and the Waters of the Sea will give you patience and omniscience, since the Sea is the womb that contains a memory of all things. There is no secret in the world that cannot be discovered if the recipient is ready to listen to it, since the very Air itself carries memory and knowledge.

Teaching and mentoring are not necessarily for everyone. Traditions and wisdom can be passed on in many ways. There are many styles of teaching, many of which do not appear to be overt and formal. Many people will not choose to teach, but be called to teach in this critical time. I know it was not my aspiration to teach, but out of all my "titles"—such as writer, minister, reader, healing facilitator, herbalist, and Reiki Master—teacher is the one that has become the most dear to me, for it is involved in all of the others. Yet my professional aspiration before this phase of my life was musician, not teacher. They say that when a student is ready, the teacher will appear. I think that also works on the other side of the equation. When the teacher is ready, the student will appear. Very few spiritual teachers actually think they are ready to take on students, yet the gods have a funny way of sending you what you need, rather than what you want or expect. All you have to do is be open to the designs of higher will and your role to play in the manifestations of True Will.

In terms of when you are truly ready to be a teacher, I would suggest that those who are exploring the lessons of the Ethical Triangle, Tiphereth-Geburah-Chesed, on some level will not only be ready to teach, but will start to attract students. At this point, a certain mastery over the elements has been achieved, and while you are contemplating the deeper wisdoms and challenges, such as questioning power and things like the Wiccan Rede, you are able to teach with experience to new students. In fact, the entire learning-teaching process can be likened to the Qabalah.

When you are learning something, you experience things physically (Malkuth), feel them (Yesod), know them (Hod), and process the energy (Netzach), but until you have "mastered" them, in the sense of a basic adept (Tiphereth), you can't really teach. We always continue to master them in greater detail, but you achieve a minimum level of competency. Once you have "mastered" them, you have to use them appropriately in the balance of power (Geburah) and love (Chesed), and you move to truly understand them (Binah) and cultivate wisdom (Chokmah).

When preparing to teach and searching for your own style and methods, ask yourself a few questions.

- What did you like about your own training? Was it formal, in-person training, casual in-person training/mentoring, or book learning? What did you enjoy about it, and how would you pass that on?

- What about your own training did not suit you? Why didn't it suit you? Was it because it didn't work magickally, or was it because it was difficult and it challenged your boundaries? Even if you didn't like it, was it something important and worth passing on? What would you change and how?

- Do you want to work one-on-one or in groups? If in groups, how small or how large? There is a reason why traditional covens don't go above thirteen. Twelve students is a large number to handle at one time and still give each enough individual attention.

- How much traditional material do you want to teach? Do you have an easily accessible resource, such as a formal tradition, an in-depth book, or a series of lessons to guide you?

- How much personal material do you want to teach? Do you want to use traditional techniques, or have you pioneered some new ideas you wish to share with others? Do you want to create your own guidelines and curriculum from scratch? If so, what pattern or theme will you use? I've used the elemental pattern in the Temple of Witchcraft series.

- How does your own personality fit with teaching styles? What kind of relationship will you have with your students? Will it be intense and personal? Will it be more detached? Will it be carried out in public venues or private homes? How much involvement do you expect in their lives and in your life? How do you set up boundaries to reflect these intentions?

- How much of your personal time will this involve? Most of us are not asked to be full-time teachers, so we must keep day jobs and family relationships, as well as our teaching responsibilities. Set a regular schedule, and make sure that schedule is clear to potential students and yourself.

- What are your criteria for accepting students and continuing with them? Will you accept anyone with sincere interest? Will you have a set requirement or things to do before training begins? Would you have to personally like a student to take that person on, or do you see teaching as something separate from personal preferences?

Through this training I want to teach not only witches, but also witchcraft teachers. In doing so, I'm not hoping to create clones of myself, but inspired individuals. I have some students, in person and readers of the books, who ask what this tradition is called, and have affectionately offered "Penczakian" as an option. I jokingly say I prefer "Christopherian," but in all seriousness, I think the time of traditions named after one individual is over. The new traditions will be amalgams of many different cultures and voices. I think of my tradition as the Temple of Witchcraft tradition, simply because it relates to the sacredness of what is important to me, and because it is inclusive and not as tongue-twisting as saying I'm a Shamanic-Hermetic-Chaos-Theosophical-Green-Folk witch.

The Temple of Witchcraft series of books is intended to help you teach in this system, if you so desire. You don't need my permission to use the books for your own personal classes and groups. And you don't have to use them for your own students if you don't want to. You can use the series as a complete system, in part, or not at all—whatever works for you. Other popular books to give you a structure are Janet and Stewart Farrar's *A Witches' Bible* and the Silver RavenWolf series that includes *To Ride a Silver Broomstick*, *To Stir a Magick Cauldron*, and *To Light a Sacred Flame*. Ann Moura has a very popular training series on Green Witchcraft. Each has its proponents and critics, and all of our styles are very different. Anything that takes you through a series of lessons, and that you have found personally helpful, is great as a teaching manual or required reading for your students. Create your own curriculum. Use what works best for you.

Teachers have specific temperaments and attract students that are suited for those temperaments. We can divide our temperaments using the archetypal systems, such as the planets, that we have learned from our magickal studies. When we think about the planetary temperaments, we can describe ourselves and others very well. Originally, I taught the teacher archetypes as the five "higher" planets of Jupiter, Saturn, Uranus, Neptune, and Pluto. Each is said to be a higher octave, a higher self of the more personal planets of the Sun, Moon, Mercury, Venus, and Mars. Together each pair makes a link through a spiritual principle, and these principles can be a guiding force in our learning. The trick is matching our own current needs with the right temperament. Sun-Jupiter focuses on the development of the self. The Moon-Saturn axis focuses on clearing karma. The Mercury-Uranus pair focuses on the mind. Venus-Neptune works through the principle of love. Mars-Pluto develops the will.

If you identify strongly with any of the planets, you have a clue as to the type of student you have been and what kind of teacher you will be. As with any system, it's important to realize that this is a symbol. Just as we are each more than our zodiac Sun signs, as teachers we are more than any one planetary archetype. But certain archetypes will be more dominant than others, and they will give us better insight into our teaching style and student relationships. The planetary archetypes might not all display the qualities listed earlier. For instance, the Saturn taskmaster can seem lacking in compassion, play, and flexibility at times, but if students understand the archetype, they will know why and be able to work better with that teacher. Good teachers can be dominant in one archetype, but they are able to display the needed skills of any of the five "higher" planets when necessary. Can you understand and at least partially identify with each of the five higher planets?

Jupiter

In the Eastern traditions of Vedic astrology, Jupiter is the planet of the guru, the spiritual teacher. A true guru is one who puts you in touch with your higher self, your own inner guru. The archetypal nature of Jupiter is of the father god, associated with benevolence, caretaking, opportunity, and expansion. Jupiterian teachers are good natured, using humor as a tool. They are generous with their resources and knowledge, and they seek to expand consciousness to see the broader global perspective. Jupiter is described as the spiritual light of a thousand suns, and while astrologers have generally considered it a beneficial influence, that light does act as a spotlight, illuminating areas of life and showing us things we don't always want to see.

Saturn

Saturn is the planet of karma, and it is known as the great taskmaster. Magickally it is said to manifest the lessons we need to learn and force us to face them. We can tackle these lessons head-on or try to avoid them; we can pick the hard way or the harder way, but in either case, Saturn makes sure we take responsibility for our past. Saturnian teachers are taskmasters. They are disciplined and often martial. They force you to confront your limits and your past actions. They are not merciful, benevolent, or understanding like Jupiterian teachers. As the embodiment of limits, they actually push you past your limits, so you can see the truth about your self and reality. They push your buttons, emotionally and mentally, and use each difficult situation as a lesson. Though they are great teachers, it is difficult to form a personal attachment with them. You may not like Saturnian teachers, but you can be very appreciative of the lessons they give you after they are over.

Uranus

Uranus is the planet of the eccentric and the insightful, the power of the higher mind to see things in a different way and gain a deeper understanding or inspiration. Uranus creates the unconventional teacher. Its archetype is the divine rebel, the trickster who "tricks" you out of your ego self, your safe, limited identity, and provides the light or bolt of enlightenment from the heavens. Such teachers work through paradox, using riddles and poetry. Their actions and words can seem contrary until you contemplate them. Uranian teachers will not give you the answer, but will ask you to figure it out. They might even push you in the opposite direction or give you an unexpected clue to jump-start your process. Uranian teachers will encourage you to be yourself, trust your intuition above all else, and find your own individual path. They discourage dogma or too much structure. As we enter the Age of Aquarius, the sign of Uranus, we might need Uranian teachers over all other teachers at this time.

Neptune

Neptune is the planet of dreams, illusions, creativity, and at its highest level, unconditional love. The Neptunian teacher works through stimulating your feelings, your creativity, and your dreams. Art, music, dance, and stimulation of the senses are expressions of this archetypal teacher. Although named after the sea god Neptune, with his oceanic unconscious imagery, the archetype of the sacrificed god is another strong Neptunian principle. Dionysus, as the Greek god of poetry, madness, wine, theater, and rebirth, is Neptunian, as is the figure of Jesus Christ. Although this archetype is often presented as martyrs or tragic figures, a powerful current under the Neptunian force is healing. Neptunian teachers dive to the depths of the unconscious, of the Underworld, and resurrect themselves and rise back out again healthy, whole, and enlightened. They encourage a sense of merger with the Great Spirit, with the all, just as Dionysian mysteries force us to merge through the senses.

Pluto

The planet Pluto is named after the Roman lord of death. The planet rules the higher will, and the destructive power wielded when someone is not in alignment with the higher will. Pluto is the destructive power of the Underworld, the shamanic initiation of being torn to shreds, only to be rebuilt again. Plutonian teachers explore the riches of the depths that go beyond material wealth, into a richness of spirit serving divine will. They are very shamanic in nature, taking you to the Underworld to face your shadow and guide yourself out. They are testing you, as Pluto is the higher vibration of the warrior Mars. Plutonian teachings, when they don't kill you, literally or metaphorically, make you much stronger. Plutonian teachers bring you into the mysteries, to investigate the unknown and occult, but they do not provide all the answers. Experience is the teacher. Strange rituals, sexuality, trances, and facing death are all part of the training. The traditional Greek schools of the Eleusinian mysteries and the Orphic mysteries are very Plutonian at their core.

When you look over the teacher archetypes, do you see aspects of yourself? Do you see people who have already been attracted to your light and the patterns between your energy and/or temperaments? Each person is really a combination of energy, not a single archetype or temperament, but the predominant forces can be visible for you to understand and explore. As you develop as a teacher and as a student, your own temperament and archetypal mixes will change. The material you teach in life, within witchcraft and beyond it, can shape your character and style, as some traditions are more aligned to specific archetypal energies.

Sometimes teaching archetypes don't come in physical form, a human teacher, or even a spiritual entity. Events in life, places, or a period of time can all act as teachers. Certain jobs, schools, residences, and events such as illness, injury, or winning a boon or contest can all be teachers. We can enter a period of depression that results in a very Plutonian-style teaching, or we can have a career that acts as a Saturnian taskmaster. Time spent in a place in nature will show us the lessons of Neptune. This learning is not limited to linear teachings conducted through exercises and words; it also comes from the experience of life. Think about this the next time you feel you are learning a "lesson" in life, and ask yourself what kind of archetypal teacher is this. Perhaps it will give you a whole new perspective for the situation.

As you teach, you will discover your own personal blend of styles and energies. The types of students you attract will help inform you, and recognizing their temperaments will help you understand how best to reach them. In the end, your only job is to help them develop their skills and find the methods by which they connect, which might not be the same way you do it personally. A teacher has to be aware of a wide range of techniques and skills. You act like the light of the wandering stars, and can guide the way, but the students must take the steps to walk the path; you can't do it for them.

With the teacher archetypes there is a strong foundation for understanding the dynamics of the teaching process between teacher and student. But some practical advice is always helpful too. Here are some points to keep in mind when teaching and preparing to teach.

Beginners Are Beginners

Whenever you take on a new student, try to remember the wonder, excitement, and nervousness surrounding your first journey into magick. Things that are as simple as breathing is for you now had to be learned. Remember that, and don't get frustrated or bored when teaching new students. You might be surprised when they teach you something new about a technique you thought you mastered long ago. Don't skip anything, even if you think it's too basic. If you lay a strong foundation now, you will be able to teach them more advanced concepts, but if you rush into the concepts that are currently exciting you, you will lose the beginning student.

Practical Preparation

On the practical side, make sure you have all the material things you will need with you before you begin the lessons. If you need ritual tools, notes, handouts, or anything else, have it ready. I tend to ritualize teaching, even in a public lecture setting, and usually wear black clothing, accented by whatever jewelry that is in harmony with the class at hand. Some students are surprised to discover that I have other colors of clothes when I'm not working, but keeping in basic black reminds me of the ritual of teaching, and that it is a part of my ministry. I also have a quartz crystal point that I keep either on the class altar or in my pocket, charged with a spell to help me communicate clearly and effectively, and to transmit the information on all levels, not just the conscious level.

Setting Up the Space

The setting in which you teach can be very important, and I've found that various set-ups can either hinder or help my teaching practice. I like to teach in a circle and have an altar in the center whenever possible. I also like to set up the space energetically, having a few moments in the room alone, and do a cleansing and intention ceremony. I've filled the space with violet light for purification and then whatever color I feel is most appropriate for the topic (*ITOW*, chapter 10). I've done the shamanic smudging ritual (*TOSW*, chapter 3) when I could burn incense in the space, or my version of the Lesser Banishing Ritual of the Pentagram, or LBRP (*TOHW*, chapter 6 and appendix II), when burning incense was not appropriate. If a lot of other magickal work is done in the space, working with energies I am not familiar with, or are not appropriate for my work, I follow the LBRP with the Lesser Banishing Ritual of the Hexagram, or LBRH (*TOHW*, chapter 10 and appendix V).

When I don't clear the space, particularly for more public lectures, I always regret it. I have a friend who imagines that he is psychically "writing" his name on the walls, marking the space as his, and then psychically erases it at the end of the night if the area is not under his sole ownership. It helps you keep control and sovereignty over a space, particularly when dealing with the public and not longtime students. If I have the time, I like to meditate for a few minutes in the space, opening myself up to guidance and listening. Sometimes I will gain an insight into the direction I need to take a particular class, or be more open to on-the-spot inspiration once it's begun. Once I've set up the space for myself, I try to start most lectures, workshops, and classes with something to involve everybody in the space, such as a simple opening evocation or prayer, breathing exercise, or grounding/centering meditation.

Public Speaking

Get comfortable with your own speaking skills. Learn how to communicate clearly and effectively. You will develop your own style of speaking, but when you begin, think of the speakers who have been more effective for you. Why were they effective? What did they do that worked for you? Emulate aspects of their style as you develop your own. If you get nervous speaking publicly, practice as you would for a presentation, or "test" material out on smaller, more intimate groups or one-on-one before you present it to larger groups or strangers. Use your own experiences as you speak.

Free-Flowing Structure vs. Syllabus and Outline

When you begin teaching, you'll have to experiment and see if you are the type of teacher who lets each moment bring out the appropriate teaching, flowing from one topic to the next as the situation, students, and inner guidance bring them to you, or if you are the type to have a structured linear format, with topics arranged sequentially and each point planned out. Most teachers have a mix of the two, but determining how much of a mix can be difficult. Some situations require structure and format, while others are more open and free. Teachers working with students one-on-one, or in environments such as during a hike in the woods or up a mountain, have more of an opportunity of letting the spirits and nature lead the teaching, while those of us in the classroom have to be more prepared with an outline. Having an outline, but not being completely attached to it, is helpful, because it helps you make sure to cover the major points you intended, and it can bring you back to the topic when you wander. However, when you wander, you can learn a lot too, so it's nice to take little teaching sojourns off the path.

Questions

Be prepared for questions. I encourage questions because they make everyone think, including me, which only helps the teaching process. Be prepared not to know the answers to your students' questions, and don't ever be shy about saying, "I don't know." Sometimes you can point them in the right direction or learn together, but the worst thing you can do is pretend to know something that you don't. Students respect an honest teacher, and they will know that when you do answer something, you are speaking from authority. If you work within a lesson plan structure, be prepared to curb questions and comments when they totally take you off the topic, and particularly when they focus repeatedly on the problems and issues of one individual student. Sometimes a student will try to use a group setting for personal counsel, which doesn't benefit the group, particularly in a setting with limited time. I will often limit my query to, "Does anybody have any questions on what we just covered?" If they bring up something off topic, I tell them I'd be happy to discuss it after class, or another time, but we must remain focused on the lesson at hand. Some teaching styles are based entirely on questions. One of my first teachers would simply have me read books and come back with questions and points to discuss. There was no formal lesson plan, but a figure-it-out-as-you-go approach. If I didn't ask any questions, there was an assumption that I completely understood the material and put it into practice, and the next book would be given. I learned to ask questions to make sure I truly understood the entire lesson, and the experiences my teacher imparted to me.

Storytelling

Storytelling is a great way to get information across to students. When we follow a lesson plan, we can often come across as dry and dull, not engaging the students. When the lesson is peppered with personal experiences of our application of the material, it makes the lesson come alive. Storytelling techniques can also include nonpersonal stories—myths and folktales—that relate to the topic. The use of parables is a key method of teaching. Being able to relate esoteric information in a personal or engaging way teaches the students how this information actually benefits them in life.

Pace

Make sure to be aware of your pace in both a specific lesson and in the overall course of training. We each tend to have a natural pace and style. I tend to work fast. Others are very slow and methodical. You have to be aware of your pace, and how effective it is for your students. I often need to slow down, because what is easy and old hat for me is brand new for my students, and I need to give them time to really explore it. Yet I teach quickly and intensively because all of the material is meant to be practiced at home as well. That is how I was taught. I wasn't spoon-fed every lesson, and I don't do that for my own students. Everybody goes at a different pace, and you might find that when you teach a particular lesson, some students might not "get it" the first time because of where they are in the learning process. Such students will come back to the lesson later, when it is more personally meaningful to them, and suddenly the material "clicks" for them. Some people will be afraid if they are evolving too far too fast with magick. Sometimes they just need reassurance, while other times, consciously or unconsciously, they are looking for permission to get out of a level of training. Before I start a level of training, I perform a prayer, asking the gods to bring those who need to do this work to the class, while asking anybody who is not ready, who has not met the criteria for this work internally and externally, to not sign up for the course. While I encourage people who have made it to continue to completion, if particular students make it clear to me that they are not ready, I usually do encourage them to leave the course and master the previous material, so they can come back when they are ready.

Repetition

Don't be afraid to repeat material. Though it might bore you, a student is not going to get all the subtle details of everything. Repetition drives it home. Each time the level of understanding can deepen. In publicity, the common wisdom of the trade says it generally takes people three times to remember and recognize something, and five times to really know it.

Taking on New Students

The decision to take on a new student is always a momentous one, regardless of the context and level of intimacy. I generally believe that a teacher should be open to a potential student interviewing the teacher before taking classes. Though this is not always possible or appropriate for one-night lectures, discussion groups, and weekend intensives, it should be done for long-standing students who plan on studying a tradition or program with you over an extended period of time. Likewise, the teacher has a right to interview a potential student, getting a better understanding of where the student is coming from, what the student expects, and how the student's intentions match the teacher's. Don't be afraid to decline a potential student if you don't feel you are the appropriate match. There is no rule saying you have to take on everybody who comes to you. You can also have criteria that need to be met by students before you take them on in a long-term capacity or continue onward to the next level of training. Be aware of your own motives, of why you are declining, or accepting, a potential student. Sometimes the ones we want to decline are our greatest teachers, for the student always has something to teach the teacher. Our roles are not always as neatly defined as we'd like to think.

Exchange

Like healing and psychic readings, I'm a big believer in exchange between teacher and student as a means for keeping the balance in the relationship. Some methods of exchange are financial, and come under some scrutiny from the pagan community (see Lesson Nine in Volume Two), while others are more energetic. I think that at the very least you have to make it absolutely clear what you are and are not offering to a student, and what you expect in exchange. Many students wish to attend and become a part of a group, but not do the work. If you are working hard to prepare lessons, the student must work hard to master the lessons. Only then do you have an equal relationship. Without equality, you will grow resentful if you are putting so much into the practice and into the education of the student body and not receiving any sense of compensation for your time, effort, and energy. Lack of exchange leads to energetic and spiritual burnout because you enter a pattern of continual giving without any receiving. A lesson that I've found helpful to apply to all relationships as a spiritual teacher is that unconditional love is not a license for unconditional relationships. Just because you are a spiritual being aspiring to unconditional, Perfect Love, it doesn't mean you let others take advantage of you. Perfect Love for yourself calls you to do just the opposite, and love yourself enough to stand strong against those who would intentionally or unintentionally harm you.

Previous Education

Most students are not coming to you as a blank slate, but will have had other teachers, other traditions, books, and experiences that color their point of view. Some traditions insist that you start at the beginning, for each tradition is separate and complete, and you need to build its foundation. Others let those of equivalent experience jump in at higher levels. At one time there was a lot of initiation swapping between lineage bearers. A high priestess of one tradition would initiate into her tradition a high priest of another tradition, on the promise of this initiation being reciprocated. That high priest might not have had a lot of education in her tradition, possibly assuming that an HP in one is equivalent to an HP in another. Unfortunately, these reciprocal initiations created a lot of high priest/esses who were not particularly well versed in all the traditions in which they held a lineage title, and when they passed on those lineages, their students were even less prepared.

The decision to force experienced students back to the beginning isn't easy. I've let some students jump into higher levels, and while it's worked out well a few times, there have been other times when it was disastrous. I've started study at the beginning of other traditions, and I've sometimes been frustrated, but ultimately I understood and appreciated why the teacher took me from the beginning, regardless of my previous training. You can't always assume that something that was basic training for you, in your tradition, is the same for another. You can't assume previous knowledge without talking to your students first. You must also be aware of imprinting, as students often imprint the first symbol systems and ideas they are exposed to as being "right." They will resist new symbol systems and ideas as "wrong," not simply different. For witchcraft, it occurs particularly around the associations of air and fire with the directions and elemental weapons, but also in relationship to concepts of deity, magickal ethics, psychic techniques, and a whole host of other imprinted teachings. You have to honor what students have learned as being right for them, yet open them to the possibilities to see things differently.

Special Cases

Some students will not respond to traditional techniques. Many potentially great witches are differently abled, and would correspond with patterns diagnosed in modern medicine as ADD, ADHD, and dyslexia, among others. You have to determine if you are prepared to work with such students and investigate new methods of teaching, as long reading assignments or strict lectures will not impart the necessary information to them. Techniques and tools such as experiential exercises, stories, parables, and pictorial teachings—for example, using tarot or other oracle cards like *The Well Worn Path* and *The Hidden Path* by Raven Grimassi and Stephanie Taylor—can be particularly helpful.

Higher Guidance

I truly believe that good spiritual teaching doesn't come from the teacher alone. Quite literally, the spirits teach through us, consciously and unconsciously. When you join a tradition, even a broad, eclectic tradition, you tap into the ancestors and guides of that tradition, who work through you to continue that tradition. As a magickal practitioner, you can evoke these spirits and ask for their direct aid. Your Master-Teacher is an excellent source of support, and so are your patron deities. You become a channel for this higher knowledge when you make this connection. I find words flowing out of my mouth that I had no conscious intention of saying, yet they were the most perfect words for the situation. It's not quite channeling or invocation of a specific entity, but opening to the flow of divine wisdom. Witchcraft elder Maxine Sanders calls it the "Seat of Solomon." In meditation, my guides called it the "Lap of Aradia." If you open up to this wisdom, your divine teacher will whisper into your ear whatever you need to share with your students. While many teachers will draw intellectually upon experience and memory, a teacher in touch with this current of wisdom will have lessons come out that she was not consciously aware of herself. This is true wisdom. Be open to your guidance. Use your intuitive gifts to know when to start discussions, when to take questions, when and how to guide pathworkings, and when to bring students back. There is an immense support from the other side guiding teachers who are willing to listen and flow with it.

Oracles

Pay attention to signs and omens when teaching, as your higher guidance may be trying to give you a message, but not a direct telepathic message. If you burn incense or candles during pathworkings, watch the patterns of the flame flickering and smoke wafting. I've noticed that the smoke usually gathers around the person having the most intense and challenging inner experience, and I can lend some of my psychic attention by sending light to support the student in that experience. The candles might change their pattern or intensity of flickering when it's time to end a meditation or move on to the next part. Outside noises, be it in nature, the building, or an urban environment, can also provide clues for the teacher to move onto the next step in a pathworking meditation, or bring people out of it altogether. If I'm in doubt, I use muscle testing (*ITOW*, chapter 13) to ask my guides if it's time to bring the meditation or healing to an end.

Group Consciousness

When you teach a set group of students over a long time, you will find that it develops a group consciousness. If you use intention to guide this group consciousness, you have an additional ally to aid you in teaching. Many students will report that they are capable of experiences—acts of meditation and magick—that they are incapable of at home. The group energy lends its support, as does your energy as a teacher to open the way, but a student must be versed in working with groups and working solo. While the group consciousness can develop naturally on its own, without intention, it can sometimes run wild. Doing group journeys, building astral temples together (*OTOW*, chapter 16), opening and closing evocations for the class, and sharing personal experiences after exercises are all ways of promoting a harmonious group consciousness. In the case of permanent study groups, naming the group, and creating a sigil or symbol for it, is another way to add to its overall effectiveness and power, because it creates an identity for the group from which the individual members can draw strength.

Humility

Out of all the qualities a teacher can have, humility is one of the best. Be humble. Remember that your way doesn't necessarily constitute the "right" way. Be open to other points of view and remember that you don't know it all. It's easy to get into a mind-set that you are always right when you are usually the most experienced, yet often the most inexperienced student will have the most inspiring observation on a topic. Though it takes a certain confidence to teach, which is strongly attached to the ego, a good teacher has a healthy ego, not an overbearing, unbalanced one.

All Things to All People

You must learn quickly that people will project their own images of who you are, and who you should be, upon you. Some of their images and expectations will coincide neatly with your own. Others will not, but such conflict might not be readily apparent. There is a desire when you are a minister, teacher, healer, or reader to be all things to all people, never wanting to disappoint others but to completely live up to their expectations. You can't. Don't even try. The only expectations you should be living up to are your own. If you can learn this early on, then you will have a far easier time than I've had.

Performance Anxiety

Be aware that both you and your students can suffer from performance anxiety. When we are put on the spot, with people watching, things that are normally easily and effortless become real challenges. Our minds get in the way and sabotage our training. Patience and perseverance are key for both you and your students in working through these anxieties.

You Are a Student

Don't forget that, as a teacher, you are always a student. There is always something new to learn. Just because you are a teacher doesn't mean that your own practice and evolution should grow stagnant. We are each on a spiral of growth, and if we don't continue to grow, we'll not be moving forward with our students. Most importantly, remember that your students are your greatest teachers. They will continue to teach you about magick and about yourself.

While these points don't cover everything there is to keep in mind as a teacher, they are a good place to start, and they represent some wisdom I wish I'd had when I began.

Each experience will teach you something new and give you something to add to this list.

Teaching with Your Master-Teacher

Your most valuable ally in the task of teaching is your own inner teacher, your Master-Teacher spirit guide. Your Master-Teacher will continue to guide your development in all things and be the greatest source of wisdom and aid you have, beyond your own divine higher self.

Your relationship with your Master-Teacher is comparable to a relationship you would have to your physical teacher, and the relationship your students will have with you. Don't assume anything about your teacher, but let your experience inform you. Just as you wouldn't want assumptions being made about you as a teacher and student, don't make them about your Master-Teacher. I put all my assumptions about what a true spiritual teacher, a guru, would be upon my inner ally, the Welsh wizard god Gwydion. In many ways, I divorced myself from some of my own teachings and advice. I would only go to him for mystical, spiritual lessons and help. When I really needed help and advice, to apply my lessons to issues of money, family, and sex, I didn't think to consult him or ask for help. I thought that was less spiritual and beneath a Master-Teacher. One day he scolded me, telling me those things are not different from magick, healing, and enlightenment. The divine is in everything. Energy is energy, and we are here in this incarnation to master our energy. In essence, that is a Master-Teacher, a master of energy, something we are all striving to be. Gwydion reminded me of the story of his myth, and his nephew Lleu. He helped his nephew get a name, weapons, and a wife—all earthly pursuits, but all with great life significance.

Don't judge your Master-Teacher by your own concepts of what is enlightened or holy. I've known a few Western students dismayed at the behavior of Eastern masters, yogis, Zen masters, or shamans because they didn't live up to the students' sentimental expectations of a guru. Even witches sometimes expect the kind of teacher who is always peaceful, wearing long and flowing robes, never raising his or her voice, never having a vice, and never doing anything controversial, but most spiritual teachers are not like this. They do have balance, but they know when to be on the side of mildness and when to be on the side of severity. They are peaceful inside, but they know how to be formidable warriors whenever necessary. We are not a tradition that believes in meekness unless that is a part of an individual's own path and nature. It's not a norm to be expected and cultivated in everyone. We each must heed the call of our higher will.

Since you began working with your Master-Teacher, do you see one or more of the higher planet's archetypes being expressed? Think about it. What you learn from your Master-Teacher will influence how you teach your own students.

Exercise 20

Dream Work

You can have an intuitive dream lesson with your Master-Teacher. You can go to the inner temple in dreams and make contact with your inner teacher, learning while you sleep. This concept is found among the inheritors of the Theosophical and Spiritualist traditions, who believe that we are learning while we sleep. They believe that the most active global teachers of the ascended masters, the withdrawn order or Hidden Company, have astral ashrams, to borrow a term from the East. Think of them as psychic temples, the masters' own inner temples, set firmly in the Otherworld and inviting all of their students for evening classes.

Though this is a powerful technique, I advise you not to do it every night, as some nights you need to rest both body and spirit, rather than spend all your time learning.

1. Get comfortable in bed. You can ritualize this process if you'd like, and take a cleansing bath, light incense, or wear appropriate oil before climbing under the covers. Just make sure that the incense and candles are safely extinguished before you do.

2. Perform Exercise 1: Inner Temple as a Mystery School Meditation (page 45), steps 1–5, to go to your inner temple.

3. Open the gateway of dreams and ask to go to your Master-Teacher's temple. Call your Master-Teacher by name, and ask for the way to be open. Enter

the gateway and let yourself drift into sleep. You will go to the temple and learn the Master-Teacher's wisdom.

4. When you wake up, there is no need to count yourself up and out of the temple. The awakening process will do that automatically for you. Make sure there is a notebook by your bed for you to write down any direct messages and impressions you've had to contemplate later.

People who do this dream teaching with their Master-Teacher regularly, such as once a week or once in a Moon cycle, find they are intuitively growing by leaps and bounds, even if they do not always consciously remember anything from the dream.

Exercise 21

Class with Your Master-Teacher

1. Perform Exercise 1: Inner Temple as a Mystery School Meditation (page 45), steps 1–5, to go to your inner temple.

2. Open the gateway of guidance and ask for your Master-Teacher's presence. Call your Master-Teacher by name.

3. Ask your Master-Teacher to formally teach you. Each Master-Teacher has a different style, so you might be receiving a formal lecture and lesson, a discussion, a puzzle, or a journey. Interact with your teacher as you feel called to do so. Things will be revealed in these lessons about magick, philosophy, theology, and your life. Pay attention. They are the most important keys to integrate and pass on to your students. If you are ever in doubt, ask your teacher if you have permission to share a particular lesson with your students.

4. Finish exercise 1, steps 8–11, to return to normal consciousness. Record any material you receive from your teacher that you feel needs to be written down.

If you are concerned about teaching, ask your Master-Teacher how you can best work together with students. First ask if you are ready to start teaching, and if it's even your calling in this life. I think it's good for everybody to have a little experience teaching, even if it isn't their vocation. You can ask your teacher if you can work directly together, through invocation (*TOSW*, chapter 9) or through a lesser form of invocation known as overshadowing. The teacher will guide you as to how, where, and when this should be done in a setting with your own students.

HOMEWORK

- Do exercises 18–21, and record your experiences in your journal or BOS.

- When you complete the trials of this chapter, tie your fifth knot in your cord in a ritualized manner.

- Obtain a necklace for your double-stranded cord, perhaps something akin to the meditative mala beads. My first choice would be an amber-and-jet choker to be prepared now but not worn until the completion of this course. The cost of amber and jet can be prohibitive, and like the taboos against buying your own tarot cards, many believe you should not purchase such a gift, but be given it. In the age of self-initiation and solitary work, we often have to be both the giver and receiver. Other taboos state that it is only for the high priestess, but due to its dual, versatile nature and immense power for both protection and magick, I recommend that all high priests and high priestesses wear one. They are phenomenally helpful when working with the public as a reader, healer, and most importantly teacher. If amber and jet are not right for you, necklaces beaded with oak acorns are appropriate, as well as snake vertebrae and holey stones (rocks with naturally occurring holes in them—a.k.a. faery stones or hag stones). I know some initiates of the modern Feri tradition who use necklaces or prayer beads of alternating pearl and hematite for their rituals known as the Pentacle of Pearl and the Pentacle of Iron. Other crystal beads are also appropriate, particularly quartz or lapis lazuli. Typically the number of beads on the necklace has magickal significance, done in sets of 9, 12, 13, 19, 21, 22, 24, 28, 29, 32, 33, 64, 72, 78, or 108 beads.

- Design a basic teaching outline. If someone came to you and said, "Teach me witchcraft," what would you do? Where would you start? What would you prepare? Prepare notes for at least three meetings, as detailed or as basic as you would require in order to teach. It need not be formal training but it should include a general overview of what witchcraft is and isn't, and explain the basic beliefs and structure.

Tips

- Look to appendix III for a teaching curriculum for the Temple of Witchcraft series.

- Continue to build an integrated meditation and ritual practice.

- Think about your own learning experience in this life, from both physical teachers and spirits.

- Review the Dream Magick of *TOSW*, chapter 10.

- Speak with your Master-Teacher regularly. Build a relationship. Ask your Master-Teacher what lessons you need to learn, and ask to be taught them.

- If you plan on being a teacher or mentor, I strongly recommend *Spiritual Mentoring* by Judy Harrow, a pioneering book for teachers on a pagan path.

Lesson Six
Temple of the Brow:
Vision and Knowing

When seeking out the mysteries of the witch, many are allured by the gifts of the brow, of the third eye. Believing witches to be able to see beyond the veil of space and time, to discern visions of the past, present, and future through preternatural sight, would-be initiates are drawn into the mysteries. And they are absolutely right. We can perceive things others cannot. We know things others do not. Yet these gifts are not the end in and of themselves. They serve a purpose. Knowledge without wisdom is useless. Sight without true vision, the ability to put it into perspective, is worthless. We serve a higher power, and the gifts of the third eye not only serve that power, but help us to see that power so we can better serve it.

For the lesson of the brow chakra, set up your altar in deep purples and indigos. Planetary associations of the Moon and of Neptune are appropriate, as the element of water rules our psychic abilities. Crystals such as amethyst and sugilite are appropriate. Trance inducing oils and incense are appropriate for the workings of this temple.

Exercise 22

Contemplation of the Brow Chakra

1. Sit quietly in a comfortable position and enter a meditative state. Call upon higher guidance, through your own spirit guides and the Goddess, God, and Great Spirit.

2. Place your hands on your forehead. I prefer the position of my left hand on my brow and my right hand over my left hand, to focus on the center of my forehead. This exercise can also be done lying down to prevent any strain on the arms.

3. Feel the energy of the brow chakra. Start with your hands, but let any sensations move through your entire body. You might feel as if your entire energy field is surrounded in indigo, blue, or purple light. Ask the brow chakra to reveal its mysteries and guide you.

4. Observe the thoughts, feelings, visions, and insights you have, as well as messages you receive, while attuning yourself to the Temple of the Brow. Contemplate your own psychic gifts, and how they feel in your body. These insights will guide you in this lesson to your own personal work.

5. When done, return yourself from the meditative state. Thank the energy of the brow chakra as well as your spiritual guidance, and give yourself clearance and balance.

Magickal Teaching: Information
Force: Light
Chakra: Brow
Function: Vision
Body: Psychic
Tool of the Goddess: Lapis Necklace

Alternate Tool of the Goddess: Scepter

Colors: Indigo, Purple

Ray: Sixth

Elements: Air, Water, Spirit

Planet: Moon

Metal: Silver

Signs: Virgo, Libra

Emerald Tablet Rubric: It Rises from Earth to Heaven and Descends Again to Earth

Alchemical Operation: Distillation

Totems: Pelican, White Buffalo

Plant: Mugwort

Sephiroth: Binah and Chokmah

Tarot, Lunar: Trump VI—The Lovers

Tarot, Solar: Trump XIII—Death

Tarot, Stellar: Trump XX—Judgment/Aeon

Life Stage: Fourth-Degree Initiation (*TOHW*)

Hermetic Principle: Rhythm

Musical Note: A

Day of the Week: Monday

Castle of the Underworld: Caer Pedryfan—Revolving Castle, Four-Cornered and Revolving Sky Castle

Egyptian Temple Site: Giza

Left Hand Initiation: Shock

Vice of Initiation: Obsession with Magick

Virtue of Initiation: Synthesis

Stage of the Bread Miracle: Resurrection

Challenge of the Temple: Ignorance

Blessing of the Temple: Vision

The basic talents of "the sight," learned by some, inherent in others, are a part of the traditions of witchcraft, though we think the experience of vision will be quite different from what occurs. Psychic vision, the messages from our psyche, occurs all the time, bringing us information, though we don't always recognize its gifts as such, believing that those talents in vision work must involve seeing grand images that are three-dimensional and fully "real," rather than quick psychic glimpses that can occur in daily life. All visions, grand and mundane, serve our higher purpose.

THE MYSTERIES OF VISION

The very study of the Craft opens you to the mysteries of vision. Personal initiatory experiences, self-initiation rituals, and formal lineage initiations all can be conduits for opening the third eye's visionary powers. Some people have experiences that cause the awakening of the third eye without prompting, while others have to seek it out. Some witches are naturally gifted in seeing "between" the worlds and beyond the veil, and it is that gift that prompts them to seek guidance in the Craft.

Psychic vision is both an allure to the path, and a reason why people fear witches. The purple/indigo of the third eye is connected to the yellow, its opposing color on the color wheel, of the solar plexus, where we deal with fear and power. The solar plexus is the raw power applied to the other chakras. In the brow, this power becomes psychic power, yet the fear of psychic power is still present, both for the witch using this gift and for those around the witch. There is the fear of power abused. *Will a witch see something I don't want seen? Will a witch know and reveal something I want to keep private?* The witch with active gifts can fear these things as well as fear being different and outcast, fear seeing something tragic, and ultimately fear the responsibility of using this gift, yet the use is ultimately in service to the divine for the high priest/ess. The fear of our gifts can block their manifestation and use, for once we cross the threshold into seeing, and then knowing, it is hard to cross back and block out this knowledge. We are reminded again of the teaching, "Where there is fear, there is power." That is why in this progression of temples, we work through many of our base fears in the lower temples, to claim the gifts and face the challenges of the upper temples.

Eyes, literally and symbolically, are prominent in folklore and mystic traditions across the world, and they are a sign of power. Eyes are said to be the window to the soul. We look someone in the eye to know if that person is telling the truth. The binding of eyes in initiation rituals, and the use of blindfolds and darkness, are powerful techniques. We shut our physical eyes to awaken the hidden third eye. Magickal charms are shaped as an eye, in the theory that the eyes both receive and direct power. One who can cast the evil eye on another draws the power of his or her gaze and ill will toward a target. Eye charms "catch" this evil, providing a "false" target. The opening of the inner eye to see the true nature of reality is part of the mystery school training, as various rituals and practices are used to awaken the eye, which tends to slumber in most people.

Shiva is the great god of the Hindus, and some have linked him with the god of witches and the image of the Christian Devil for he holds a trident, like the Roman sea god Neptune. Though depicted as the third in a trinity of divinities, embodying destruction or dissolution, along with Brahma the creator and Vishnu the sustainer, the three points of the trident show he is master of the three principles of creation, sustainment, and dissolution, as the three gods are all aspects of each other. He also has three eyes, with the third being the eye of wisdom that sees beyond the obvious. The third eye is linked with the dissolution power, the untamed energy that dissolves and destroys, bringing us back to oneness to begin the cycle of creation again.

In Irish Celtic myth, the fearsome Balor of the One Eye, king of the giant Fomorians, could kill anyone he looked upon. His lid was kept closed and he required other men to lift the lid and direct his gaze upon his enemies. Balor was killed by his grandson Lugh, now one of the Tuatha de Danann, who turned the evil eye's power upon the Fomorians and won the second battle of Magh Tuiredh. Balor is similar to a host of mythic beasts whose gaze kills, paralyzes, or petrifies, such as the Gorgon Medusa. Linked to the Aegis, the breastplate of Zeus and Athena, and possibly related to the early Minoan snake goddess, her gaze might be symbolic of the experience that occurs when we turn the powers of vision upon and within ourselves.

The Udjet (figure 11), often known as the Eye of Horus, is a popular symbol used by witches and magicians today, tracing its history back to Egypt. Traditionally, the right eye is associated with the Sun, and both the Sun god Ra and his grandson, the avenging Horus. The left eye is associated with the Moon and the lunar god Thoth. Though one would assume that a goddess would have this position, Thoth was considered a Moon god in ancient Egypt due to his magick and his precise timekeeping like a lunar calendar. Today we associate him with Mercury. In ancient Egyptian myth,

Figure 11: The Eye of Horus or Udjet

Horus's left eye was torn out by his uncle Set and restored by Thoth. Some versions of the tale state that Horus eventually made a gift of this eye to his father, the deceased Osiris, so he could rule the Underworld. The plucking of Horus's eye on one hand can be seen as a myth explaining the dark Moon, plucked out of the socket of the night sky each month. Horus's story, when taken beyond the realms of good versus evil, shows Set as a tester, or an initiator, and it is a tale of sacrifice and transformation—to know the mysteries of the other side, of receptivity, healing, and lunar magick. The two eyes together can be viewed from our modern perspective as the forces of yin and yang, of female and male, lunar and solar. The symbol of the eye is used in protective amulets and as a sign of wisdom.

Odin undergoes a similar loss, but rather than having his left eye plucked out by an enemy, he voluntarily sacrifices it to Mimir, to drink from the Well of Wisdom. Mimir accepts his eye as an offering, and it now lies at the bottom of the well. When he drank its waters, Odin saw the past, present, and future—all the trouble of men and the gods. Paramount in the myth of the Norse, and in our lessons here, is the greater good. The Norse gods make sacrifices for the greater good, applying their knowledge and magick to the preservation of the whole, rather than the desires of the one.

So much eye lore, when concerned with the physical eyes rather than the etheric third eye, involves the left eye, being receptive and associated with the Moon. In alchemy, the sixth process of transformation is distillation, and it is associated with the Moon's metal, silver. Distillation occurs when a substance, the fermented material from the previous operation, is boiled, evaporated, condensed, and then purified as any part of the substance that will not evaporate is removed. The retort, often called the pelican retort for its long neck, is the vessel used in this work (figure 12). The retort has modern associations with the Ibis-headed Egyptian god Thoth, a god of magick, alchemy, and, as we

Figure 12: Retort

discussed, the Moon. Magickally, the process involves removing the ego, purifying the self from the ego for the final stage. One removes the vestiges of attached emotions and thoughts, moving beyond the sentimentality of the emotional bodies or the contemplation of personal theories and ideas in the mental body, to identify with the higher archetypal divine forces. Initiates can identify so strongly with divine forces that they can lose touch with everyday reality—the reality that the initiates are still grounded in as human beings. Some experience mystic delusions, and undergo savior illusions, that only they can save the world, or they identify with other powerful archetypes and lose touch with their daily human lives. The sixth ray of the Theosophists, indigo, is the ray of devotion to the divine. Devotion is wonderful, but through their zeal, some people become fanatical. Having much in common with both the Moon and Neptune, the boundaries of identity can blur between human and divine. The ideal of the distillation process is to identify with the divine self, the higher self or Bornless Self, and distill away any blocks and impurities that prevent you from orienting your identity with the highest self. Then the divine self-identity is grounded in daily life.

In the Eastern tradition of Taoist inner alchemy, a practice of circulating and transforming bodily energies and the biochemical changes that result from these manipulations, the energy of the lower centers rises up to the brain, to the pineal gland, which is associated with the third eye, and then circulates back down again. This flow is also mimicked in chakra work and the ceremonial magician's Circulation of the Body of Light (*TOHW*, exercise 10). This line, from the Emerald Tablet, describes the distillation process of evaporation and condensation, emphasizing that the united powers are then grounded in the earth, the body, and the daily life of the initiation: "It rises from Earth to Heaven and descends again to Earth, thereby combining within Itself the powers of both the Above and the Below."

In the descent of Inanna, the tool of the second gate she encounters, the sixth as we follow them upward, is quite confusing. Most often it is described simply as a necklace, or a lapis necklace, assumed to be single-stranded to differentiate it from the double strand of the last lesson. Why does she have two necklaces? And how does this one differ symbolically from the last? Some have gone out of their way to describe this tool differently, as lapis earrings or a diadem headdress, to bring it closer to the third eye, yet there is still not a great match between the sixth tool and the third eye.

I do find it interesting that sometimes the primary energy point is not associated with the brow, but with the back of the head, closer to the neck, where the top of the spine and the base of the skull meet. A term from the Huichol Indians of Mexico was introduced into my early training in the Craft, the *nierika*. Laurie Cabot describes it in her book *Power of the Witch*: "The Huichol Indians of Mexico tell us that the mind has a secret doorway that they call the *nierika*. For most people it remains closed until the time of death. But the Witch knows how to open and pass through that doorway even in life and bring back through it the visions of nonordinary realities that give purpose and meaning to life" (p. 16). I have always associated the nierika with this point at the bottom of the skull, though it's not explicit in the teachings of the Huichol Indians. It just seems to buzz when we talk about it. In Chinese acupuncture, this point is known as the *feng fu*, translating as the "wind mansion." It is one of the thirteen ghost points in acupuncture that are used to treat problems difficult to define, like mania, depression, fright, and dementia. All of these are issues that aspiring shamans face. In Hinduism, the point is known as the *Lalana* chakra. Not being one of the seven major chakras, there is some confusion as to its location, cited at the back of the head, behind the throat chakra, just above the roof of the mouth and behind the nose, or even between the brow and crown, but it is said to be the source of a secretion, a divine soma, which drips to the throat chakra. The throat chakra separates poison from nectar and "feeds" the yogi, who must practice a mudra known as the "space-walking seal" or the *khecari* mudra, with the tongue on the soft palate to receive the proper effect.

In Taoism, the point is known as the Heavenly Pool, where the tongue is also pressed to the palate to create a circuit of energy and offer divine blessings to the Taoist. Both are said to confer healing and immortality. The base of the brain deals with our primal powers and reptilian brain.

In certain shamanic traditions, it is where the "medicine" or healing energy comes through. Reiki traditions emphasize this point, both in healing and in initiation or "attunement" practices to connect the recipient to the universal life force, to become a healing practitioner. One of the Reiki "master symbols" is placed in this point. In New Age philosophy, I learned it as the Well of Dreams, from where we get our deepest impressions and understandings.

For some, the reptilian nature of the lower brain would immediately relate it to the Qabalistic point known as Da'ath, the fallen sephira of knowledge and the doorway to the reverse of the Tree of Life. The path of the Moon tarot card, joining Malkuth and Netzach, with the letter Qoph, meaning "back of the head," also is related to the nierika. Reptilian primal powers, ghost points, Moon paths, immortal elixirs, and space-walking all seem to point to the reality of the shaman. This energy center is the gateway between worlds, the secret doorway of the witch.

The necklace of this temple is closer to the nierika point than the third eye, but both share a lot of similarities as gateways to inner vision. Like the cord or noose around the neck, both relate to the wisdom of one who goes through the death and rebirth process, returning with knowledge from the world of shadow.

The color of the necklace, lapis blue, seems to link it to the throat, as most people think of the third eye as purple, yet the third eye is described as indigo, really a deep shade of blue, the color of the sky at midnight. Some psychics envision the third eye point as a black star, drawing in psychic light as the color black absorbs the colors of the light spectrum. It is the light that grants visions within us, being absorbed by the dark star.

Robert Cochrane described five forms of inner vision available to a witch, as outlined in his *Pentagram Magazine* article called "The Faith of the Wise" (*Pentagram* 4, August 1965, reprinted in *The Robert Cochrane Letters*). They describe the deepening of the mysteries for those seeking to open to inner vision. He describes the following forms of vision:

Poetic Vision, *in which the participant has inward access to dream images and symbols. This is the result of the unconscious being stimulated by various means. Images are taught as part of a tradition, and also exist (as Jung speculated) upon their own levels. They are, when interpreted properly, means by which a lesser part of truth may be understood.*

The Vision of Memory, *in which the devotee not only remembers past existence, but also, at times, a past perfection.*

Magickal Vision, *in which the participant undertakes by inference part of a Trial of Service, and therefore contacts certain levels.*

Religious Vision, *in which the worshipper is allowed admission to the True Godhead for a short time. This is a part of true initiation, and the results of devotion towards a mystical aim.*

Mystical Vision, *in which the servant enters into divine union with the Godhead. This state has no form, being a point where force alone is present.*

Through exploring these five different forms of vision, you experience the mysteries of this temple. They can seem vague in their descriptions, but as you delve deeper into their lessons, you realize that words, part of the mental realm of the previous lesson, often fail when we enter the psychic realm of the third eye and inner vision. You have probably already experienced the poetic vision regularly in your pathworkings and meditations. The Vision of Memory has been actively sought in our past-life work in *ITOW* and *TOSW*. We are now working on the next three levels, entering service and deepening our inner-world contacts. We may have experienced religious vision in our pathworking exercises of *TOHW* and other divine meditations and shamanic journeys where we commune with divinity. This is really the type of vision associated with alchemical distillation. Mystical vision is what we seek to attain in union with the top sphere on the Tree of Life, Kether, as well as the final gate of the crown chakra.

By working with your Master-Teacher, you can experience one or all of these levels of mystic vision. The following meditation will help awaken you to the powers and gifts of inner vision.

EXERCISE 23

Initiation of the Third Eye

1. Perform Exercise 1: Inner Temple as a Mystery School Meditation (page 45), steps 1–5, to go to your inner temple.

2. Open the gateway of guidance and call upon your Master-Teacher.

3. Ask for a third-eye initiation, to open you to the true mysteries of vision.

4. Cooperate with your Master-Teacher in the facilitation of this vision.

5. When done, ask your Master-Teacher any questions you have about this experience.

6. Thank and release your Master-Teacher through the gateway of guidance.

7. Finish exercise 1, steps 8–11, to return to normal consciousness.

The third-eye initiation experience is different for everybody, ranging from simple and pleasant sensations and imagery to incredible challenges. Sometimes it's slow, and other times blazing fast. Sometimes it's gentle, and other times painful.

My first experience with this form of initiation occurred during an illness precipitated by an unintentional shadow working, an emotionally cleansing experience. In fevered dreams, an archangel stabbed me with a great sword through the third eye, and it was one of the few visions where I have felt physical pain. When the ordeal was over and I recovered, I noticed not only a greater acuity to my psychic senses, including clairvoyance, but also clairaudience, clairsentience, and the psychic equivalents of the other senses. I began to awaken to a great sense of purpose in my life, and I found myself guided to my spiritual path.

My students have had similar experiences that have included a gentle touch on the forehead by the Goddess, a hot finger burrowing into the brain, a surgery-like opening of the brow, brain tissue removed and other substances put in its place, or a direct transference of psychic energy from the Master-Teacher's or another divine being's third eye to the student's third eye. Some have been told that they are not ready and must go back to this exercise at a later date. Others are told that it is already open, and they have already received this initiation and don't need to do it, but they talk with their guides about its meaning in their personal lives.

The Power of Knowing

Psychic vision, hearing, touching, tasting, and smelling are all facets of a larger ability, the ability of clairsentience, to simply sense, to know information beyond the physical senses. We interpret psychic information through a variety of corresponding psychic senses, for that is the way we are used to receiving and interpreting information. Yet psychic knowing, while less flashy, is more powerful and goes beyond the information of other psychic senses, which must be interpreted, with their symbols decoded. Psychic knowing most often occurs when the information simply seems to "download" into us, like a computer file, and suddenly we become aware of something we did not know. Mystics are fond of saying that everything we need to know is already inside us, but what clairsentience does is give us the key codes to access the information we need when we need it.

The process of developing psychic knowing through the other senses actually refines our ability to use extrasensory knowledge. When students are first exploring psychic sight, they wonder what to do when they see something they don't like, whether it's about the future, about health, about themselves, or about someone they love. They fear the random access of information pouring into their vision at inopportune times, creating personal and moral conflicts for them.

I've found that for myself, and for others who have delved into psychic awareness, a calming of the skills occurs as clairsentience grows. People assume that if you are developing psychic ability, you are seeing visions—ghosts, spirits, gods—all the time, hearing their voices, receiving their messages. Though some practitioners work that way, and seem to be between the worlds constantly, and they learn to live their lives in that state of consciousness, most of us do not. Though I'm continually aware of the "energy" of vibration and the energies of the environment around me and the people I'm with, I don't have continuous precognitive flashes, or psychometric readings on all the objects I touch. If I did, I wouldn't really be able to get anything done. I find that direct messages, visions, and knowing comes when I need it, because that knowledge serves my overall mission. I don't shake someone's hand and suddenly know their deep secrets. If I wanted to do a reading on them, I probably could and gain some knowledge about them, but it would take effort. If I meet someone and get a message through words, images, and knowing, then I know that information is something I need to use. It came to me for a reason. One of the strongest trials is to move through a period of simply developing your intuition, getting messages and insight about everything, and to shift into a mode of service, so that you don't get messages about everything and everyone, but recognize that when they do occur, they are messages for you to act upon. You need to sift through the superfluous to get a sense of when a message is real, when it is important, and not simply random information.

When I do read for people, clients will ask, "Will you tell me everything you see? Even if it's bad?" "Of course," I answer. The information isn't for me. It's for them. It's not my job to shield them from the unpleasantness of life, but to give them information they can use. I've dedicated myself and my psychic ability to the service of the gods, to the greater good, so if something comes through in a session where I am of service, though I have the ability to choose how to express it (and learning tact is a hard but wonderful thing), it is not the job of my ego to determine what is best for someone else to know. If it comes through while I hold the intention of service, then it comes through in service.

As ministers, witches are called upon by others in and out of our community to act as readers, counselors, and advisors. Psychic insights and divination skills are part of the reason why we are sought out, because we can provide a perspective that most people do not have. We can read the patterns of the universe, but also ground our advice and insight in real-world action. We can offer spellcraft, meditation, and healing advice to change the situation. Simple knowledge of the past, present, and future is not always helpful, even when it's accurate. We need wisdom to apply the knowledge, wisdom to know when to take action and when not to. Knowledge without wisdom is not always a great thing. In the Tree of Life, we learn that knowledge alone is a gate to the reverse side of the tree, but when we aspire to understanding, wisdom, and union, we can cross the Abyss of Da'ath.

One technique beyond simple intuitive readings or divination techniques, used to get not only information, but a greater context to put that information in, is through reading what is known as the akashic records. The term has been popularized by the New Age inheritors of Theosophical lore and Edgar Cayce material, referring to a spiritual databank of all knowledge. *Akasha* is an Eastern term sometimes used for the element of spirit, and such records are said to be the sum total information of creation. Seers from across the ages who have knowledge of the greater happenings of the world in the past, and prophecies of the future, are considered to be readers of the akashic records. All the past, present, and future, for the planet and every individual, is said to be "written" in the ethers of these records. They hold information on our various incarnations throughout history, and they tell the story of our soul. Edgar Cayce read from these records in his healing sessions, to explain karmic roots for his clients' illnesses.

Though the akashic records don't seem particularly "witchy" or connected to the traditions of witchcraft, I know many witches, some who act as professional psychics, who use the concept of the akashic records. Some have learned it from other psychics. A few have spontaneously experienced something similar and then learned the term for this vast library of information later.

Interestingly enough, like many things in the spirit world, the form that the "place" takes in our inner vision will reflect our own beliefs and experiences. Most claim to visit a place that appears like a library, filled with books and even librarian spirit beings who guide them to the right volume and page. Some have more science-fiction concepts of the library, from computer disks to "Atlantean crystals" that record and transmit information through pictures, words, or direct downloads into their consciousness. I know a few witches who simply go to the old temple with the single scroll or book that contains all information needed. Others go the wizard's laboratory and tower library. Tribal practitioners might find the information written in cave paintings, while a modern urban practitioner might see what is needed through the lines of graffiti.

The most famous of Egyptian sites, the Sphinx and the Great Pyramid of Giza, are said to be the sites of the brow chakra. Like the brow, they are said to be keepers of inner mystery and a vision of the new world. While traditionally thought of as burial chambers, many initiates of the modern mysteries speculate that the pyramids were actually initiation chambers designed to align seekers with the energies of the earth and stars. Some modern prophecies state that a chamber of ancient records will be discovered beneath the Sphinx, giving us a new perspective on our past and our future. It is the "physical" location we most associate with the ancient akashic records.

In the castle of Annwn, the next gate to cross is of Caer Pedryfan, described as the Revolving Sky Castle, or the Four-Cornered and Revolving Castle. From this starry, heavenly, revolving castle, one can see anything and everything. It is the hub of the cosmic wheel, detached from the motions of time and space, where all of time/space can be looked at as a continuous whole. Caer Pedryfan is where nine goddesses guard the cauldron. Like Mimir's Well of Wisdom or Ceridwen's Cauldron of Inspiration or the akashic records, it is the place where all knowledge is kept.

The concept of this castle, these akashic records, being at the center of the wheel, is very powerful. Some think of the akashic records at the center of the Earth, in the core of the planet, or the electromagnetic field around the planet. Others think it is in the Sun, or center of the galaxy/universe, if a physical location is given. I think of it as the center of the great cosmic web, as we are each in our own center. But the idea of the center, revolving and rotating, repeats time and again. The term *caldera*, or *kaldera*, from the Spanish, meaning "cauldron," is used to refer to the center. Usually it is the center of a volcano or explosion point, as a volcano crater is cauldron-like. It matches our mythic imagery of a well, pool, or cauldron in the center of this plane, and the potential power, and danger, associated with the center, with the cosmic ground zero. Being outside of the cycle of time and space, from a still point in the center, and watching the world turn and change around you gives you the perspective of all knowledge. It gives you the perspective of divine vision, detached from the proceedings. For a moment, you become separate from that which you observe. You know truly that you are not separate from anything, but it gives you that illusion to serve your vision better. You get to read it from a more detached state than if you were immersed in the action. One of the most important things a reader needs is detachment from the vision, from the information, at least at the time of the reading. The more involved you are, the more you are in the spinning cycle and can't see clearly. When you are on the road, you can only see as far as the next bend. When you are above the road, you can see the entire road, yet it loses its personal meaning and perspective.

I had a student who had a vision about the 2004 presidential election in the United States. She was certain of the outcome, but also personally hoped for the outcome she had predicted. When it didn't occur, she felt betrayed by her vision, her psychic ability, because she was sure, and wondered how she could trust it again in the future. The key is learning to recognize when you are in the still center of the Revolving Castle, and when you are not. Magick, both spellcraft and divination, involves the strange paradox of detachment and will, which seems contradictory. You have to want what you want in order to create change, yet be detached from the outcome to let it occur, without losing your will. You do this from the higher perspective, to create from the center of your web. You circumvent the ego will and focus on working with the higher will. That is why when you try to read from your middle self's personal will, it's muddled, yet when things are personal, it's hard to make that shift to a higher perspective. Going to someone else can give you a clearer reading.

The difference between traditional forms of intuitive reading/divination and reading the akashic records is the depth and detail that seems to be available in this hall of records. Though much of the information doesn't always have a practical use, it gives the client and yourself a deeper spiritual insight into the forces at play in a situation. The records can give information on life lessons, past relationships, and more about the secret history of the earth, as well as your relationship with various spirits, guides, and gods between the physical plane and the Otherworld. Reading the akashic records usually requires a level of trance that is deeper than what most experience in a regular reading. It is that level of detail that can be very helpful in orienting the information you receive in a long-term spiritual context.

Unlike the Theosophical concept of the akashic records, there appears in the older mythologies a sense of danger, sacrifice, or guardianship associated with knowledge. Not just anyone can go in and gain this knowledge. They must prove themselves worthy to the guardian. Once they have met the test and proved their worthiness, then the knowledge of the cauldron, well, or castle is theirs to take.

Those who develop skills of psychic ability must be vigilant. The volcanic nature of the cauldron, the sacrifice required by the guardian, is to ensure the forces are used for a higher purpose. Much of our work up until this point has been about the higher good and greater will. Those who don't have a sense of greater purpose in their psychic development run many risks. Our stray thoughts and daily neuroses must be purified, for as we claim more power, we empower those thoughts. They seem little and inconsequential at the time, but as my student Dennie said, enough small pebbles thrown can create an avalanche. That is why when first developing, we learn the power of neutralization (*ITOW*, chapter 8), to neutralize our stray and unwanted thoughts. The more we order our thoughts, develop our will, and dedicate ourselves to the role of the high priest/ess, the less neutralization we need, for all our thoughts become more and more devoted toward our True Will and purpose.

Those who develop great skills but have not cleared out their consciousness become the worst psychics. They are the worst because rather than simply being wrong, they have a lot of genuine information in their reading, making you take them seriously when you receive it. Yet the information is filled with their own fears, desires, and preconceived notions. If they haven't had training in interpersonal skills and communication, boundary and disempowerment issues become common.

Judging boundary issues, particularly concerning psychic skills, is always tough. One student, Christian, asked if we have a moral responsibility to help people when we have the knowledge to help them. Yes and no. He has experienced quite cold climates and his example was if someone you see is running around with frostbite on his face but is too numb to realize it, aren't you obligated to tell him? And if so, isn't some psychic information the equivalent? Someone is walking around with a potentially dangerous condition. You know it and he doesn't. Shouldn't you tell him? I don't think psychic impressions are as cut and dried as a physical injury like frostbite, or other physical dangers and diseases. I encourage you to use your discretion, and if you feel called, by your own will, to approach someone, then do so. But be vigilant that you do not become one of those witches or readers who have so much unbidden information for others, yet obviously need to be working on themselves. Generally, I think you can make yourself available to others, yet let them approach you whenever possible. If you feel the need to approach others first, you should always preface such information by asking them if they would like it, rather than blurting out psychic impressions or giving whole unwanted psychic readings for those who are unenthusiastic about them.

I was taught that witches make the best readers. Why? Because ideally we go through mystery school training to clear out our psyche and learn to be detached. We've learned to sacrifice aspects of the personal self to attain the perspective of the higher self. We are grounded in the world, in self-empowerment, and in sound spiritual principles. We explain and offer tools for change. We read in the spirit of service, in the vocation of ministry. We believe reading for another is a sacred trust and aren't afraid to say we don't know or don't understand the message. We embody the principles of spiritual counsel over simple fortu-netelling. I say "ideally" because there are a lot of readers who are witches who don't do this, and we have to remember that there are a lot of readers who do all this, and do not identify as witches. Anybody who holds to this level of integrity and perspective is poten-tially an excellent reader whose advice should be honored.

Performing psychic readings—through tarot cards, runes, scrying, and eventually reading the akashic records—can be the first step on a path of ministry, healing, and service. Be open to the opportunities to serve in this way if you feel called to do so.

EXERCISE 24

Reading the Akashic Records

1. Perform Exercise 1: Inner Temple as a Mystery School Meditation (page 45), steps 1–4, to go to the World Tree.

2. Hold the intention of going to the akashic records, to the starry castle at the center of the wheel. Then ascend the tree to the Upper World however you see fit. Some move inside the tunnels of the tree, spiraling upward, while others climb the outside. You can even shapeshift (*TOSW*, chapter 7) to a fly-ing animal and ascend without climbing.

3. Enter the great starry record house, the great castle or library of all knowl-edge. It will appear differently to everyone, but it will have the feeling of a wheel rotating in some way, as it rotates outside of space and time.

4. Enter the castle and seek out the library. You might be stopped by guardians asking you questions or asking for an offering. Do as your inner guidance and wisdom bid you. There might be more than one guardian, so be prepared.

5. Once you are in the records and understand how to interface with them, as they can manifest as paintings, scrolls, books, crystals, computers, or any-thing else, ask your questions. They can be about yourself, about another,

or about a specific issue. You can ask things like, "What are the unresolved patterns from my past lives?" Or you can say, "Show me the patterns in my relationship with...," and name a person who is involved in an issue in your life. You can simply ask to be shown what you need to know at this time to fulfill your True Will.

6. When done, thank the records and put them back as you found them. If any spirit beings, acting as librarians, aided you, thank them as well.

7. Return the way you came. You can make a detour to your inner temple and discuss these records with your Master-Teacher, or other guides, if you so choose.

8. Finish exercise 1, steps 8–11, to return to normal consciousness.

†rue Purpose

Application of divine knowledge leads to an awareness of your true purpose. Many mystical traditions believe that everyone comes to life with a divine purpose, and no matter how grand or small by society's standards, each individual has a unique role to play in the larger pattern and purpose of the universe. The first quest of the mystics, after awakening, is really to know that purpose, and the second is to actively pursue it in every moment.

When you first talk about will and purpose, people assume you are talking about your desire, about what you want to do. But your purpose, your higher will, can be very different from what your personal self wants. This is the difference between personal will and divine will, or what we have referred to as your Magickal Will or True Will (*OTOW*, chapter 10). This is the teaching of Aleister Crowley's tradition of Thelema and the deeper meaning to the Wiccan Rede's "An' ye harm none, do as ye Will." Finding your higher will requires a certain degree of surrender to the higher self, the Bornless Self that sits at the center of the Revolving Castle, attached to you, yet detached from space, time, and form. When others talk of surrender, particularly in mainstream religions, it's seen as the supposed abandonment of personal will and desire in lieu of serving the creator god. In magick, you cannot abandon your personal will and desires, or demonize them, for they are your teachers and bring you to a greater understanding of your True Will. They contain both the seeds and fertilizer for the development of True Will.

Other mystic traditions understand this concept of True Will and have different names for the concept. One of my favorites is the word *dharma*. Dharma is used with a wide range of meanings in both Hinduism and Buddhism. From an American yogi, I learned about dharma and savadharma. Dharma is your life purpose, or mission in a general sense—the right action to be taken to be in harmony with the divine. The term *savadharma* refers to your own personal purpose to help fulfill the greater dharma.

Dharma is intimately linked to karma, a concept widely accepted by modern neopagans, likewise borrowed from Hinduism and Buddhism. Unfortunately, while karma has been adopted, most pagans and modern metaphysicians have never heard of dharma. Many erroneously believe that karma is reward and punishment. If you do something good, you will get something good. If you do something bad, you will get something bad. From an Eastern perspective, it's more like the law of gravity. If you throw something up in the air, it will naturally fall down. Energy returns to its source. Whatever type of energy you send out, it returns to you in a similar fashion. If you deem it "good" because it's pleasurable, then it's good. If you deem it "bad" because it's painful, then it's bad. It's really neither of those things, good or bad. It simply is. Some think the Eastern concept of karma, and modern pagans' adoption of the concept, indicates buying into the moral structure outlined in Christianity, of reward and punishment, heaven and hell. Many believe that those who work with the concept of karma are seeking to wipe out "bad" or "negative" karma and accrue "good" or "positive" karma, as many look at these polarities in banking terms, using the phrases "karmic debts" and "karmic credits."

While those who misunderstand the teachings of karma might be seeking "good" karma, those who work with it realize that the true dual action is not between good and bad karma, but between karma and dharma. A mystic seeks to have a zero "balance" free of good and bad karma, as it is so deemed by humans, because any karma keeps us shackled to a certain level of consciousness—karmic consciousness.

Karmic consciousness is operating at the action/consequence level of awareness. Though we never can really escape the consequences of our actions, it means our awareness is really rooted in the Middle World, if we are to use shamanic cosmology, rather than the wider perspective of the Upper or Lower Worlds. When we are in karmic consciousness, we are fairly blocked from the other two worlds and our other two selves.

Dharmic consciousness means that you are operating beyond simple cause/effect and are united with your true purpose. When you are united with your true purpose, your savadharma, in any given moment, you are aligned with the will of the divine, and the powers of creation back your every thought, word, and deed. When you are in dharmic consciousness, you are operating in part from a realm beyond the Middle World, seeing the bigger picture and united with higher powers, just as the alchemist who undergoes distillation is united with higher powers. Karmic consciousness prepares and purifies us. It's a necessary step to reach dharma. With dharma, you are operating beyond personal attachment. The consequence of your actions does affect the material world, and your material life, but the greater result of acting out your dharma is the opportunity to act out more of your dharma, more of your True Will and purpose.

My yoga teacher, Stephanie, says, "If you are not in dharma, you are in karma." We pass in and out of both levels of awareness, as we find moments to work our True Will. Yet it can be hard to maintain a place of True Will twenty-four hours a day, seven days a week. You can be in your dharma in one part of your life—say, your vocation—and be in karma in your personal relationships. You can have one aspect of life, one relationship, be very dharmic and clear, while the other is very karmic, attached, and sometimes difficult. The process of life and enlightenment is to actively work to be more in your dharma, fulfilling your mission here in the physical plane. Finding your purpose sounds like an easy, one-time thing, yet it isn't. While your purpose might be described in cosmic archetypal terms, with broad artistic strokes of interpretation, you must determine how that purpose is applied in every moment. You must choose how to manifest it every day. The process of learning how to manifest is the road to magickal enlightenment. I say the following as a part of my daily altar devotionals (*OTOW*, chapter 9):

I ask the Goddess, God, and Great Spirit to guide my every thought, word, and deed. By your divine will, so mote it be.

Dharma has been largely associated with the caste system in India, and it is considered the "right action" expected of one born to a particular class. Though modern mystics generally denounce such class systems and in the Aquarian Age seek ways to show the individuality and value of each member of society, dharma does have a family-like connection to it. Caste systems did have an inherent purpose, even though their application is not appropriate today. Many witches, espousing the evil and inherent prejudice in the Indian caste system, fail to realize that many of the Celtic traditions had a similar caste system. They simply didn't survive into the modern era because pagan Celtic culture didn't survive into the modern era, as Hinduism has. Celtic society was divided into warriors, leaders, farmers, tradesmen, and religious leaders. In the Druidic caste of religious leaders, there were the bards and poets on one level, the judges or ovates on the next, and then the archdruids, or high priest/esses that guided Celtic culture.

Today, the modern witch defines family, or caste, in a much broader sense than the societal class into which one is born. Your family caste and ancestry can be defined in genetic terms, physical location, social status, spiritual links, and karmic heritage, such as the Great Age in which you first incarnated (Lesson One), and the first root race into which you incarnated. Modern mystics talk about a concept called the soul family, or soul group—a collection of individual spirits with a similar mission and purpose, though each might have a different role to play in that purpose. Sometimes members of the soul family choose not to incarnate at the same time, so one can act as a spirit guide from the Otherworld, while another is incarnated to do work in the physical world. Soul families are described in terms of vocation. Journalists might all come from a similar soul family, and doctors from another. Each member of a soul family has a vocation that shares broad archetypal qualities, yet each individual job is very different. All of these vocations are necessary for society, and they have evolved over time.

You can have a particular divine dharma, but have free choice as to how it is expressed. Your dharma can be teaching, and you can express it as a schoolteacher, Reiki Master, coach, professor, personal instructor, tutor, or witchcraft teacher. If you are a leader, you can be a leader of an organization, a leader of a smaller team, an explorer who leads the way for others, or perhaps a scientist, leading new research and discovering new areas.

The twelve zodiac signs give us a model for looking at both literal and spiritual vocations, an understanding of dharma from both a practical and archetypal perspective. This is not to say that your Sun sign reveals your dharma, based upon this chart, but understanding the place of astrology in your life can indicate how to express your dharma. I highly encourage all witches to have a thorough astrological reading of their natal charts, and to consult with an astrologer regularly, say once a year, to understand the spiritual patterns inherent in their lives, and coinciding with the current movement of the sky, to know how best to work with these forces. Your astrological natal chart can give you a greater understanding of how you will fulfill your dharma.

Aries: Leader, Explorer, Warrior, Athlete, Adventurer
Taurus: Builder, Craftsperson, Earth Steward, Artist, Singer, Planner, Laborer
Gemini: Speaker, Writer, Scholar, Student, Researcher, Social Planner, Trickster
Cancer: Caretaker, Protector, Counselor, Chef, Domestic
Leo: Entertainer, Artist, Leader, Creator
Virgo: Servant, Healer, Counselor, Domestic, Analyst
Libra: Creator, Artist, Social Engineer, Judge, Lawmaker
Scorpio: Investigator, Mystic, Healer, Shaman, Guardian
Sagittarius: Explorer, Administrator, Philosopher, Teacher, Spiritual Leader
Capricorn: Community Leader, Manager, Coordinator, Engineer
Aquarius: Pioneer, Inventor, Creator, Social Activist, Rebel
Pisces: Mystic, Artist, Dancer, Musician, Healer, Ecstatic

As the zodiac is very archetypal, we find our dharma and our magickal spirituality expressing itself in other archetypal manifestations. Pagans can each choose a magickal name that is not so much who they are, but who they aspire to be. The mythic name embodies the concepts they want to develop. In many ways, it's the archetypal myth they want to live. Such names and stories help you manifest divinity in your daily life, in your personal identity, as we learn that the gods are both immanent and transcendent, both within you and beyond you.

Sometimes you can better define your personal vocation, archetype, and "mission statement" or goals by understanding what you are not. By process of elimination, what you are becomes much clearer. For a while I was bogged down in the *business* of my business, too focused on publishing and teaching, selling merchandise and hand-made products, organizing successful community events, and looking to branch out into new businesses in the pagan arena. I was scattered and conflicted, until a medita-tion helped me refine my focus and acknowledge what I didn't want to be. I don't re-ally want to be a businessman, or at least I don't want to be focused on business. I don't want to make products. I don't want to coordinate or employ other people. Those things might happen in the future, but it became clear that at this time my job was to teach, and also to teach via writing. Anything that wasn't involved in teaching the mysteries for a vocation fell away, and all the other pieces fell into place to support my vision of self as a witchcraft teacher.

Pagans have adopted the phrase "Thou Art God/dess" as both a greeting and a rit-ual statement to empower people to see their divinity. Originally this came from the novel *Stranger in a Strange Land* by Robert Heinlein, and it was made popular through the pagan organization the Church of All Worlds (CAW), which was highly influenced by that book. According to the church's material, the statement "implies that each one of us must define our own specific purpose. There is no excuse; no shelter from the awesome responsibility of total freedom." Thou Art God/dess is applied not only to people, but to everything in nature, from trees to insects to the planet itself. It's a powerful thing to hear in ritual, awakening us to the fact that, yes, we are divine, and magickal spirituality is the process of awakening to, recognizing, and claiming our divinity consciously. Yet, know-ing that divinity is immanent, we must claim our humanity as well.

We, as pagans, will therefore choose names of figures that share whatever purpose we aspire to fulfill as a part of our dharma, our True Will. I thought I understood the concept and its ramifications, but it wasn't until I spoke with Oberon Zell-Ravenheart, the co-founder of the Church of All Worlds, at a Starwood festival that I really did un-derstand it. We were talking about his fabulous clothing; for anyone who meets him, he dresses like the archetypal wizard. In a different time and place, you could easily mistake him for Gandalf from *The Lord of the Rings*, or Merlin from Arthurian myth. He talked about why he chose this motif, and about his friend, the highly influential pagan musician Gwydion Pendderwen. He told me how Gwydion identified strongly with the slain god archetype, and he was killed in a car accident in 1982. Oberon soon decided that he wanted to identify with an archetype that lived a long and enjoyable life, so he chose the wizard archetype. He asked me to think about the archetype I identify with strongly, the one that guides my life, and if it's serving me, or if I need to reshape my own fate.

I am still pondering my own archetypes as I write this. For me, I don't think any one image embodies me entirely, though having one to hang my hat on, so to speak, would be helpful. In the same conversation, LaSara FireFox, pagan author of *Sexy Witch*, talked about how the image of the sacred whore, or of the Thelemic goddess Babylon, helped guide her to her life's work, as she learned to embody sacred sexuality. Another friend of mine described the influence of Vulcan in his work as a builder and craftsman. I look to the modern system of archetypes introduced to the popular culture through the book *Sacred Contracts* by Caroline Myss. She outlines a twelve-archetype system based on the zodiac wheel of twelve houses, or areas of life. Though her system doesn't fit me entirely, I began to look at my own astrological chart not only in terms of modern psychological processes, but archetypal forces that guide the twelve areas of my life.

The prominent amalgam figure that worked its way into my own mythos is the witch king. Just so there is no mistake with readers thinking that I aspire to Alex Sanders's title of King of the Witches, the image of the witch king, for me, blends the issues of masculine and feminine, solar kingship, and earthly sovereignty with magick, ritual, and religious calling. Rulers are really servants of the people, but they take it upon themselves to guide and accept responsibility for larger institutions. Personal sovereignty, ruling your own life, rather than letting others rule you, has been a huge issue for me. I've also struggled with the idea of attracting the "divine fool," the one who points out things to you, usually in jest; these are things that you need to hear, but you might not want to hear them because they are unflattering to your ego. Though they are infuriating at times, these divine fools have become valued friends and confidants, and they are helping me develop a healthy, balanced sense of self, while keeping in check the less attractive aspects of ego. The witch king embodies the light, yet goes into the dark. It's a mixture of the archetypes of the witch, the Solomonic sorcerer king, warrior, counselor, and priest. At least it is for me.

I've also had a fondness for the three wise men of early Christian lore, as I see them as sorcerer-kings, yet wanderers. They are each a king without a land, where all lands must be home. As someone who travels much of my life teaching, the wandering king, sovereign wherever he goes, is an important image. Sovereignty is not tied to one place, but it's a state of being. There is a Wiccan wisdom teaching (appendix VII) that says, "Remember the Passwords: Perfect Love and Perfect Trust, so trust the Universe and be at Home everywhere." I'm reminded of this teaching by the image of the wandering witch king. I also think of the image of St. Christopher, the renounced saint of Christian theology, who is a wanderer and guide. He bears Christ, or the principle of unconditional love, yet the church does not love him.

The simple mage, folk witch, healer, or teacher didn't embody everything that I felt I was struggling with, working with the red ray as well as the green and violet. It did embody the tarot archetypes of the three zodiac signs that are most prominent in my chart—Taurus as the horned god and priestly hierophant, Virgo as the hermit and wanderer, and Cancer as the seeking grail knight. There are no real tragic associations with the witch king image for me. It has aspects of the old, wise wizard that Oberon is fond of, yet it's different. I realize now that, as a younger man, I was attracted to quite a few self-destructive archetypes, and wished to shed them. Perhaps I was unknowingly aspiring to it while in a rock band, trying to emulate figures such as Ozzy Osbourne and Alice Cooper. Not a completely classic archetype, the witch king gives me a bit of freedom to define it myself. As you explore your True Will, feel free to make new terms and images that suit what you are called to do.

Sometimes by finding an image that works for us, we can transform ourselves and our relationship with both our Craft and our lives. One student, Colleen, who was feeling low self-esteem about her practice, found the key to transforming it through exploring a new personal archetype. Her class was filled with herbalists and wild witchy women with great psychic skills for working with plants and animal spirits. She did not feel that same connection, nor was she drawn to the more wild ecstatic arts. It was only when she realized that she was really a bard, connected to goddesses such as Ceridwen and Bridget, and talented in the use of the written and spoken word, that she found her confidence. She has written amazing ritual poetry. Another student in the same class, Jerusha, found her power in the archetype of the literal crafter—doing sewing and stitching projects with her magick, rather than personifying the classic image of the potion maker. She makes beautiful cross-stitch magick. Another student, Mark, has been on the path of the sacred fool, exploring the archetype of the clown, and much of his own magick and ritual explores humor. He delved into the history of clowns to find their magickal origin in the roles of the shaman.

We can look to our spiritual leaders and ancestors in the modern era and try to see the archetypes that have guided their lives. In a discussion with other priestesses and priests of the Craft, we made some guesses about some of our favorite public witches. Tarot is one of the great systems to start with in the exploration of archetypal roles. One suggested, without malice, that Doreen Valiente embodied the Fool archetype herself, moving happily from one tradition to another, with an open mind and open heart. She was quite a joyous woman. She played both the Fool and foil to the serious Hierophant image of Gerald Gardner. Maxine Sanders is guided by the consummate role of the Priestess, in service to the Goddess. Carl Weschcke can be associated with the figure of the Hermit. Though these are views from the outside, we never know what personal archetypes, if any, the individual truly identifies with. For instance, a few people in this discussion group have identified me with the Devil, yet it's not the one I identify with personally. This exercise gets your mind working to understand your own archetypal patterns, when you look in reference to other teachers of the Craft.

We are drawn to embody certain divinities. They call to us in our magickal working, and they manifest in our daily lives. One need not be a mystic to see the display of mythic images in popular history. It's easy to see JFK as the sacrificed king, or Marilyn Monroe as the Venusian enchantress. Einstein was the Mercurial or Uranian divine genius, while many of our dark gothic rock stars embody the shadow trickster. One can see Dionysus readily in Jim Morrison of the Doors.

The sixth stage of the making of bread is known as Resurrection. We relate it to the brow chakra, for the grain now has a new vision of itself, as bread, entirely transformed. The separate ingredients have come together through the fiery, abyssal baking process to become something new and far more nourishing.

Some witches note that the more you work with such forces, the more you embody them, and the less they appear in our meditations and visions, for you are already embodying them. The archetypes that are less like you make themselves known in your personal magick work. But in your ministerial vocation, many people seeking to connect with the forces you embody will come to you, making you the link and touchstone to get in contact with the divine forces. I know that many connect to my patron goddess Macha through me by attending my rituals and classes. I have a friend, Matthew, who is a priest of Hecate, and he connects many to her through his rituals and readings.

Your bliss, your passion and pleasures, will often lead you to your life's purpose, even if it seems impractical. What are you called to do? You may have many different expressions of your dharma throughout your life. You can have more than one dharma in your life, and more than one at a time. Many dharmas cannot be classified or categorized. Don't feel locked into one place. Your expression of your dharma will change as you change. Your personal archetypal images are only guides and tools. The truth of you is much bigger than any one archetype. Allow yourself to change from one label to the next, unattached when it no longer suits you. Joseph Campbell, the famous modern mythologist, said, "We must be willing to let go of the life we have planned, so as to have the life that is waiting for us." That is one of the best ways of describing your True Will, yet you have to actively let go of what you planned and be open to your guidance. We learn how to listen to the promptings of our psyche so we will know when we are being guided toward our dharma. There are no hard and fast rules; as everyone is unique, their dharma will be unique.

Yet sometimes, with our archetypes in mind, it can be helpful to create a mission statement of your dharma, a constant theme and thread that has run through your whole life, guiding you like a North Star, even if you didn't recognize it until now. For me, the thread has been a gateway of consciousness to the unseen. That's my broad job description. Through art, I opened to that world and shared it with others. Then I went into science, seeking to understand how it all worked, the invisible structure behind our familiar world. Then music took over, as I learned to channel the energy of performance, the spirit of the song, for others. At the same time, I started my study of magick and healing, learning to channel a variety of otherworldly forces to aid myself and others. I now teach people how to do the same. "Opening the gates" has been my north star, my mission statement, and it keeps me in harmony with my witch-king archetype.

In the Left Hand initiation system, the sixth point is not dharma, but the shock that can occur before finding the True Will. The initiate, in touch with the divine aspect of our distillation, then believes that all involved in the magickal arts are superhuman, devoid of ego and faults. The teachings have not been grounded in the material world.

While we aspire to be free of ego and faults, we go through the stages of initiation over and over again, each time refining our consciousness. The initiate is shocked to find that magicians are still people, with their own faults and failings. The shock might initially start because the student, being disappointed in a teacher or spiritual brother or sister's actions, feels the school, tradition, or teacher is corrupt. The student might become obsessed with magick, rather than the healthy application of magick to daily life. Those who learn to healthily overcome such shock realize that people are always people. No one in a body is perfect, and eventually students must synthesize, taking the best from all that they learned, to create their own take on the teachings, because no one else's perspective will ever fit them perfectly. Once you reach a certain level of mastery, you also reach a certain level of flexibility.

To the true pagan reconstructionist, who feels that Eastern terms have no place in the theology of European witchcraft, we have the concept of fate. Fate, like karma, is a difficult concept—it is confusing, and when taken out of context, misunderstanding occurs. Unlike the Hindu's karma, no complete core doctrine on fate has survived to our time. We look to the myths to understand, but myths can be tricky.

Fate is usually seen as a predetermined course of events, controlled by some higher power. Belief in fear implies that there is a natural order to things, and thereby everything must follow the natural order. The question among magickal practitioners is how much of that natural order is open to interpretation, or can be changed, and how much is permanently set in stone, unchangeable?

Fate and destiny are used interchangeably, but the term *fate* has more negative connotations, linked with the word *fatality*, while *destiny* implies the participation in such events. I tend to use terms such as dharma, True Will, Magickal Will, and purpose rather than fate or destiny to emphasize the personal decision and to de-emphasize any sense of fatality in all actions. Fate has such a finality to it, for mythically, the concept of fate is linked to the Greek *Moirae*, the Apportioners or Fates. They were responsible for the "threads" of life for every mortal, god, Titan, and monster, from birth, life, death, and beyond. The Moirae include Clotho, the spinner who spins the thread of life from her distaff onto a spindle; Lachesis, the allotter, who measures the thread of life with her rod; and lastly, Atropos, the inevitable, who cuts the thread of life with her shears. In Rome they were known as the Parcae, or Fata, and Nona, Decima, and Morta respectively. They are similar to the Norse Norns, or Wyrd Sisters. The Norns live beneath the roots of the great World Tree Yggdrasil, though some say they dwell on the arch of the rainbow bridge Bifrost. Like the Moirae, they weave the threads of human, god, and monster. Urd is the sister of the past, Verdandi the present, and Skuld what is to come. They are associated with the Well of Mimir, as its waters feed the World Tree, and the Fates are the ones to water the tree. Even the images of the three witches in Shakespeare's *Macbeth* are based on the triple-Fate image. These personifications of the ultimate powers of birth, life, and death have been strongly associated with all forms of witchcraft and have played a vital role in the rebirth of witchcraft in the modern era, giving us the basis for the maiden, mother, and crone triple-goddess image.

All of this sounds very fatalistic. Are actions and events predetermined, without any chance of change? Does what we do matter? If we adhere to the strictest interpretations of the myths, and of fate, it appears we have no choice in the matters of our lives, and we are at the whim of this triple goddess. How can someone who believes in magick, in the power of change and spellcrafting, agree with this? Doesn't it fly in the face of all our other teachings in the Craft? Why would our ancestors do magick, and petition the gods if there was no point to it? What is, is. What will be, will be, regardless of our action or inaction.

The Moirae in Homeric text are not inflexible goddesses, but seem to be influenced by both the gods and humans. They are inflexible in the sense that they are goddesses of birth and death, and those two points cannot be avoided. They are said to dole out good and evil to people, but what people choose to do with those portions is up to them. In certain versions, they are the daughters of Zeus and the Titan Themis. In others, they are older, as the daughters of Nyx, or Night. They are not always impartial. The Moirae took several actions in the battle of the Titans to assist Zeus and the Olympians. While in the legends of the Norns these three sisters generally seem far more inflexible and impartial, critics would say that the fatalism comes from the later Christian influence, comparing the Norse Ragnarok to the Christian Apocalypse. Even if that's true, which is debatable, the difference could simply be in culture and climate. Those who live in a far more hostile environment tend to be harsher in their overall religious outlook than those in more temperate climes.

I find it interesting that the image of fate used across varying cultures is string, thread, and weaving. It appears to me that if things were immutable, then perhaps the image of stone carving would be used, being more permanent. But even the strongest stone can be recarved and reshaped into something new. Threads can be woven, rewoven, broken, and tied back together. When you are up close to a tapestry, as when you are up close and immersed in your own life, you can't see the bigger patterns that the individual strings create. The Fates are the divine powers that see the bigger patterns.

For many, fate, or destiny, appears immutable. Most people don't have the skills to step out of the personal and see the bigger picture. When we do, we are merging a part of ourselves with the great weavers, and sharing in the weaving of our lives. That is magick. Most people don't realize they are connected to this great weaver, taking part in the weaving of their lives, so to them it appears that they are being battered around, with little control to make changes. The more "enlightened" you become, the more magick-ally aware, self-realized, or any other term you have for it, the more you are working in communion with these forces that seem to go even beyond what we think of as the gods. They are the true generating, organizing, and destructive principles of creation, given name and form. When you are in union with them, you can do anything.

In modern tarot imagery, the Fates are said to use the Wheel of Fortune, trump X, as their loom. The true mystery of the wheel is not good luck, as some would have you believe, but the ability to identify with the center of the wheel, the divine self, rather than the part of you on the edge of the wheel, going up and down, the personal self. The center of their wheel is like the center of the Revolving Castle, of Caer Pedryfan. From the center, you see the greater pattern and fulfill your part in the pattern. You know there are ups and downs, and that is part of the pattern, yet not for you, because your true self is in the center of the wheel. The pattern manifests on many levels. Forces do have a natural order and tendency, but we can each choose what level, what octave of manifestation to work with. You can be called to be that teacher, and you can be a depressed grammar-school teacher or an inspired grammar-school teacher. You might teach other subjects, and move into institutions that support a higher vision of educa-tion, or work to change education wherever you are. Your "destiny" might be under a particular archetype, but you have room to manifest it in whatever way you want. Remember our chant from Lesson Two: "We are the weaver. We are the web." We are both that which weaves and creates destiny, and that which is woven. When you be-lieve in the paradox of both immanent and transcendent divinity, the only separation between you and any other being, any god or force, is your perception. Change your perception and you change your life.

I once had a teacher, in music school, rather than witchcraft training, who always said that destiny was when opportunity and preparedness come together. The "Fates" can offer you a great opportunity, but if you don't take it, then such a destiny won't manifest. Fate can throw you a curve ball, but if you are prepared for it, then you can avoid a "tragic destiny." Nothing is set in stone. Good things won't happen if you don't work for them, and it's not inevitable that you will or will not work for them. You must choose. Bad things are not unavoidable. You create your destiny by the way you react to both the good and bad. Since I learned this at the same time as I learned magick, it highly influenced the way I see fate, destiny, and karma, and it has been extremely helpful in understanding the role of the fate goddesses in my life.

Rather than use the term *fate* or *destiny* as a witch, I much prefer the term *wyrd*. Though the use of the term in a modern context is probably quite a bit different from that of its ancient origins, wyrd speaks to our spiritual heritage in the Indo-European traditions, and it also relates to our modern word *weird*. Originally related to the strange and extraordinary happenings associated with witchcraft and magick, it now refers to the odd, strange, eerie, bizarre, or mysterious. All of these meanings appeal to modern witches, for in many ways, we're all a bit weird for pursuing this path. My friend Christopher Giroux lovingly refers to those magickal people who don't fall neatly into the categories of witch, magician, or mystic as "wyrdos."

Wyrd relates to the Norns, the Wyrd Sisters, and comes from an Indo-European root word meaning literally "to turn." Wyrd refers to that which has become, and how the past continues to affect the future, connecting to our "fate." Though fate has a sense of predestination to it, wyrd is not only the effect of past actions, but it is also continually created by how we respond to the situations at hand. In that sense, it can be interpreted much like our karma/dharma concepts of the East. Some might see it as the spiritual equivalent of the Eastern concept of the Tao.

Nothing is free of wyrd, for all the past affects the present and future. It influences your actions now. One can also think of it in terms of the Principle of Cause and Effect (*ITOW*, chapter 8) in the Hermetic Principles. The two strongest poetic images of wyrd are the Well of Wyrd and the Web of Wyrd, both associated with the Norns. The "dew" or energy of past actions collects on the branches and leaves of the World Tree, and it drips down and fills the Well of Wyrd. The well, in turn, feeds the World Tree, with its waters nourishing the new growth and fruit on the tree. The past nourishes the present and creates the future. The past would also include the influence of our ancestry upon us—our family, our genetic and personal predispositions, where we grow up, and how we grow up. It's interesting that the Well of Wyrd and the Well of Mimir, as the Well of Wisdom, both seem to serve the same function, and are sometimes considered to be the same well, showing how our past contains all the wisdom to know our future. When we look across cultures, the Well of Mimir/Wyrd serves a function cosmically similar to the various Goddess wells and cauldrons, such as the Cauldron of Ceridwen.

The weaving Norns turn the loom of the Web of Wyrd. Every strand is connected in some way to every other strand, in the overall pattern of the tapestry. All actions will influence the overall pattern, affecting everybody's pattern. Such a concept is similar to the Hermetic Principle of Correspondence, telling us how all things are connected, existing within one thing, the Divine Mind. In many ways, wyrd seems to encompass both your actions and your divine purpose and pattern, so it could be said to involve both karma and dharma.

Though the concept of absolute free will entered Germanic cultures with the spread of Christianity, and seems in direct conflict to the concept of wyrd, for everything is influenced by the past, the concept of choice and influence to change the future is not alien to either ancient Anglo-Saxons or modern day heathens. Though some myths see wyrd as something inexorable, and perhaps in some circumstances it is, most see it as a force you continually work with to shape your life. There's a ritual known as a *symbel*, involving drinking and boasting about the future, with the gods and ancestors in witness to the boast. Through this ritual, the actions are placed within the Well of Wyrd. When the act is completed, victorious boasting at another symbel is done, to ensure the actions are remembered and become a part of the Well of Wyrd.

In modern Germanic teachings, *orlæg* or *ørlög* refers to the "primal layer," and in terms of wyrd, means the sum total of your past deeds. While intentions are important, from this tradition, the actions, your actual deeds, define who you are and your coming life. You can change your wyrd through performing different actions, as wyrd is the process of becoming. You have a measure of control in your personal wyrd, somewhat akin to weaving with the Fates. But it is difficult to change the course you are on. By being aware of your past deeds and the web of fate where all things are interrelated, you can assume responsibilities for your actions, and change the quality of your character and life through your actions. From such a pagan perspective, fate is not something you embrace or escape, but something you are. You are what you have created yourself to be, through your actions.

Since I personally connect the image of the triple goddess to the Fates, and see my images of the divine feminine as the weaver, I don't like to dismiss the concept of fate out of hand, but I also don't like to equate it with predestination and fatalism, for that has not been my experience of magick. One could argue that free will is really a concept emphasized in Judeo-Christian literature, with its focus on choosing sin, while most Indo-European pagan cultures believed in some form of fate. They also all believed in magick, showing us their concept of fate was not fatalism. Things could be changed. Nothing was predetermined. For me, it seems like "fate" has many different octaves of manifestation, higher and lower manifestations of certain themes, based on your choices and actions. You might be "fated" to experience certain things, but how you manifest and react to those experiences is within your control. Rather than thinking of fate as completely predetermined, thinking of it as wyrd, as the web and the well, as a force I work with rather than am ruled by, I can follow its strands to better know my true purpose, my dharma, and go about fulfilling it. I think the paradox, the mystery of freedom and fate, is part of the winding way of the witch. Part of mysteries is to become "free from fate" by learning to weave our fate with the goddesses.

EXERCISE 25

Opening the Gateway of Purpose

1. Perform Exercise 1: Inner Temple as a Mystery School Meditation (page 45), steps 1–5, to go to your inner temple.

2. Open the gateway of guidance and call upon your Master-Teacher.

3. With your Master-Teacher's aid, perform a cleansing and purification. Use the elements of fire, air, water, and earth to purify yourself. Imagine the four elements passing through you, clearing you. You can do *OTOW* Exercise 8: Elemental Cleansing Meditation while in the inner temple.

4. With your Master-Teacher, find and open the gateway of purpose. Enter the gateway. Experience whatever vision, words, feelings, or knowing that it offers

in regard to your purpose, your True Will or dharma. You might experience the presence of deity, your patron guiding you, the weaver, the web, or the well. You could find yourself in the center of the Revolving Castle, the center of the web, the akashic records, or any other place appropriate to reveal your purpose.

5. When done, step back out through the gateway and close it. Ask your Master-Teacher any questions you have about this experience.

6. Thank and release your Master-Teacher through the gateway of guidance.

7. Finish exercise 1, steps 8–11, to return to normal consciousness.

Once you have your vision of purpose, your task is to put the information, the knowledge, into practice. You must claim it. You might be set with a long-term, wide-ranging goal, but there will also be an overarching theme. What is the archetype of the theme? How can you be true to it, and fulfill it, for this very moment? What are the long-term steps? Do you need help interpreting your vision? Seek it out from the wise ones around you. Let your vision guide you, but also be open to new visions and further information. Set your goals and work, for destiny is fulfilled only when opportunity and preparedness conjoin. You must prepare yourself for the work, and when you are in harmony with your True Will, fate will open all the doors you need. There is a reason why triple-goddess figures, like Hecate, associated with the Fates, have the key as their symbol: They are the keepers of the ways, the guides at the gate. They open and close the doors on the path. They are the keepers of the mysteries.

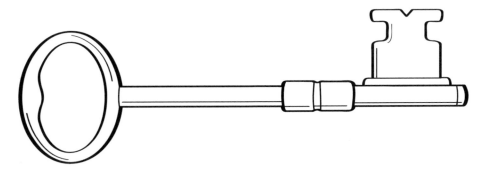

Figure 13: Key

Homework

- Do exercises 22–25 and record your experiences in your journal or BOS.

- When you complete the trials of this chapter, tie your sixth knot in your cord in a ritualized manner.

- Obtain a tool for the sixth gate. It can be a necklace as in Inanna's descent, or a pair of earrings. Another possibility is the skeleton key on a necklace, symbolic of Fate goddesses and opening the nierika, the inner door between worlds.

- Make a list of all the aspects of psychic work with which a high priest/ess should be familiar. Are you familiar with these things? If not, rank them in order of importance to you and your ministry, and become familiar with them. Have you experienced any of them? Experiment. Reflect.

- Review appendix VII and the wisdom teachings contained within. What are the phrases, sayings, and bits of wisdom that guide you? What are the things you would like to pass down to your future students, or to your descendants? Do they come from witchcraft sources, folk sayings or other religions? Make a list of such sayings, and if possible, trace the source. Record your list in your Book of Shadows.

Tips

- Continue to build an integrated meditation and ritual practice.

- Speak with your Master-Teacher regularly. Build a relationship. Ask your Master-Teacher what lessons you need to learn, and ask to be taught them.

- If you realize you are working with personal archetypes that are unhealthy for you and have chosen a new image and new mission statement, do a ritual to release the old image and invoke the new one into your life.

- Imagine you are in the center of the Web of Wyrd. You can start this awareness in meditation, but bring the awareness into daily life. Do you feel the vibrations of certain strands, certain directions? What are your impressions of them? Do you feel a tug, a pull, from certain directions? Do you feel pulled by the webs or currents of wyrd to take one direction over another? Watch how wyrd manifests in your life. Try to feel its subtle pull on you, and learn to work with it directly. You might work directly with the Great Weaver Goddesses, and they may instruct you in working with the Web of Wyrd directly.

- If you are having difficulty working with the mysteries of the third eye, make an oil- or water-based potion to aid you. Ingredients such as mugwort, eyebright, loosestrife, chamomile, Queen Anne's lace, bay, blueberry, and vinca are all excellent to aid your inner sight.

- When working with the akashic records, you can feel overwhelmed by the amount of information you receive. You can use a quartz crystal to help store and process the information, in the same way you can use it to store past-life information, as described in *ITOW*, chapter 16.

- Be on your guard for "soul weariness," both for yourself and in your elders. Those who have been fulfilling their dharma often experience a soul weariness, or a desire to rest. Being awakened to your true purpose further separates you from most of the people around you. It can be difficult to be the only "spiritual" person in a family, office, or community of those who are unconcerned with spirituality or magick. We are all spiritual, but we don't all acknowledge it or live it. There is a responsibility, and for some, it feels not like a joy, but a burden. Mystics can feel like they have done so much work, both personally in their own healing process, and for the world, that they can feel older than their physical body or peer group would merit. Yet ironically, such mystics often have the most healthy bodies because of the work they have done. The weariness is not in body, but in spirit. Sometimes we discover the conflict between our ego desires and our divine desires, and although we follow the divine desires, it doesn't mean we aren't a bit mad that things didn't work out the way we wanted. We can be mad at the divine, at the gods and Fates, for not giving us what we want when we've been faithful servants, and start looking at dharma/karma as reward/punishment, not simply energy. These bouts of weariness happen when we are not taking care of ourselves or continuing with our own spiritual practice, or when we need to take a break from the responsibility of our spiritual practice to simply enjoy life. If divinity is immanent, then we are meant to enjoy every moment in life. Meditation becomes an experience of enjoying every moment, every bite of food, every drink, every touch and movement, the light across our skin, the music we listen to, the entertainment we watch. It's all divine, and appreciating all things, to really enjoy every moment of life, is just as much a part of the path of the witch as all the rituals and formulas. Enjoying the world is a part of the path, and it rejuvenates us from the weariness of carrying the burden of our spiritual responsibilities.

• You can use Exercise 24: Reading the Akashic Records in conjunction with the psychic healing of *ITOW*, chapter 15, to not only read a person's illness, but to understand any past lives and karmic reasons behind the illness, in a method similar to that of Edgar Cayce. Experiment and see how to make it work for you.

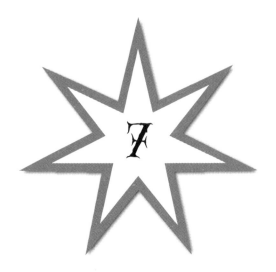

Lesson Seven
Temple of the Crown:
Union with Spirit

The seventh and final gate in this cycle of teachings is actually the first gate for Inanna. Descending from the top backwards, she is first forced to relinquish her crown. It is upon the crown chakra that we base this lesson. The crown is the chakra of spirit. While the root is defined as physical survival, being the lowest of the chakras, I think of the crown as spiritual survival, rooted in the transcendental source rather than in the physical world. The crown is the culmination of the seven chakras, unifying their lessons into a cohesive spiritual whole that connects us to the source. The top of the Qabalistic Tree of Life, Kether, means "crown," and although we think of it as the top of the tree, through the Tree of Life glyph, many teachings state that the Tree of Life is an upside-down tree, with its roots in heaven, nourishing it. The crown is the root of the tree, while the material realm, the base chakra, or Malkuth to use Qabalistic terms, is the fruit. The fruit contains the seed, the potential for the entire tree. Both the crown and the root chakras contain the other, for we know the spiritual law "As above, so below."

EXERCISE 26

Contemplation of the Crown Chakra

1. Sit quietly in a comfortable position and enter a meditative state. Call upon higher guidance, through your own spirit guides and the Goddess, God, and Great Spirit.

2. Place your hands on the top of your head. Feel the weight of your hands on the crown of your head.

3. Feel the energy of the crown chakra. Start with your hands, but let any sensations move through your entire body. You might feel as if your entire energy field is surrounded in clear, white light. Ask the crown chakra to reveal its mysteries and guide you.

4. Observe the thoughts, feelings, visions, and insights you have, as well as messages you receive, while attuning yourself to the Temple of the Crown. Contemplate the spiritual laws encoded within the crown. Understand the laws of spiritual survival. These insights will guide you in this lesson to your own personal work.

5. When done, return yourself from the meditative state. Thank the energy of the crown chakra as well as your spiritual guidance, and give yourself clearance and balance.

Magickal Teaching: Insight
Force: Unity
Chakra: Crown
Function: Spirituality
Body: Divine
Tool of the Goddess: Crown

Alternate Tool of the Goddess: Crown

Colors: Violet, White

Ray: Seventh

Element: Spirit

Planet: Sun

Metal: Gold

Signs: Gemini, Aquarius, Pisces

Emerald Tablet Rubric: Glory of Whole Universe; Greatest Force of All Powers

Alchemical Operation: Coagulation

Totems: Eagle, Phoenix

Plant: Chamomile

Sephira: Kether

Tarot, Lunar: Trump VII—The Chariot

Tarot, Solar: Trump XIV—Temperance/Art

Tarot, Stellar: Trump XI—World/Universe

Life Stage: Elderhood/Fifth-Degree Initiation (*LTOW*, vol. 2)

Hermetic Principle: Correspondence

Musical Note: B

Day of the Week: Sunday

Castle of the Underworld: Caer Sidi—Castle of the Sidhe, Castle of the Zodiacal Wheel, the Revolving Castle

Egyptian Temple Site: Heliopolis

Left Hand Initiation: Work

Vice of Initiation: Emotional Servitude

Virtue of Initiation: Cunning

Stage of the Bread Miracle: Consumption

Challenge of the Temple: Hubris

Blessing of the Temple: Humility

The light of the crown is described as violet, orchid, white, or shining with the brilliance of a thousand suns. While many envision it as white light, and use the concept of white light as an all-purpose form of magick, it is not opaque white light. Many witches echo the teachings of Tibetan Buddhism, referring to the highest light not as white light, but clear light. I imagine it as what I call "crystal white light," white that is not really white, but translucent like a crystal, reflecting the colors of the spectrum brilliantly, like a diamond in the Sun.

Prepare your altar for this month's lesson using the correspondences of the crown and the element of spirit. White and crystal-clear objects, such as quartz points and spheres, as well as diamonds, are appropriate. Ambergris is the scent of the crown, but any incense of a high vibration will do. I like to use Kyphi incense, a complex blended incense from the Egyptian tradition.

The Mystery of Spirit

The mystery of spirit is the paradox of union and separation. The divine power seeks to expand outward and create itself anew in a variety of forms, adding to the diversity of life. It also seeks to return to its source, finding union and completion. These two currents are again an apparent contradiction as spiritual principles, yet the interplay between them is what creates, sustains, and destroys the worlds as we know them.

No sooner does divine energy expand outward, or descend downward, than it seeks to rise and return to the source. The Hindus see this yearning embodied in the love between Shiva, the great dissolver god descending, and Shakti, the great goddess of the world rising. They are seen in the creation of the universe in the macrocosm, but also in the microcosm as the spine of the yogi, as Shakti rises from the root chakra and Shiva descends from the crown chakra. In this sense they are seen as primal powers, like yin and yang, or positive and negative currents. Modern witches capture the essence of this theology, of creation and return, in the popular chant of Z. Budapest, "We All Come from the Goddess" (www.ZBudapest.com):

We all come from the Goddess
And to Her we shall return,
Like a drop of rain
Flowing to the ocean.

The great creative force is personified as Mother, as Goddess, and like the Qabalists' realm of Binah, she is the cosmic mother of oceans, and the ocean is seen literally and metaphorically as the source of life and creation, be it the waters of the planet or the dark ocean of the outer spaces. We all come from that Goddess source and, like the cycles of water, we are separated from the ocean through heat and rise like vapor, condense in clouds, and fall like rain, flowing through the land, through the streams and rivers, eventually returning to the source. Like water returning to the ocean, we have many adventures, and we become a part of many other things—plants, animals, lakes, trees, wells, and people—along the way.

The power of creation and destruction and the love that joins them together is magick. Witchcraft, and in fact almost any magickal or mystical tradition, is about this change and, through change, evolution. That which is created learns more and more complex forms. It yearns to rejoin the source to share that complexity with the whole, which by its very nature is simpler. Together, both the individual and the entire creation evolve. Witchcraft is a tradition of life, and of life force. We can be considered a somewhat Darwinistic tradition, but we are spiritual Darwinists, looking for the evolution of both body and soul, and every part in between the two. The desire for us to rise through these seven temples, or to descend down through the seven gates, is the desire for evolution.

As witches, we know that even though we personally might not like it at times, everything that exists serves a purpose. Everything. There are no mistakes in nature. There are no spare parts to the universe. Everything has a purpose, even if we don't understand or agree with it. It's not our job to give approval to things we don't understand, but it is our job to serve our own purpose. Groups, events, and people we don't approve of, like, or agree with still serve a purpose, from the large scale of world politics to the smaller arenas of personal interactions. We are tempted to invalidate others, even in our own traditions of witches, as not being "real" witches, or not being spiritual or not being genuine. Perhaps we're right, but they are serving a purpose. A bad teacher teaches many lessons to those who are ready to learn. A bad leader teaches us to think for ourselves. Who knows? It could be that the purpose of the ones who get you angry is to get you angry, so that you take action and change the world, evolving it to the next step.

If we subscribe to immanent divinity, and "Thou Art God/dess," then it applies to everyone, not just the people you like. Yet, that explains one of the mysteries of the old myths. Many look strangely at the stories of the old gods, feeling that to be "spiritual," each god should be kind, beneficent, and lovable. Like people, there are a lot of gods I don't like, yet I know that they too serve a purpose, and their stories show the purpose they serve. Without change and discord, nothing would be created.

SPIRITUAL LAWS, PRINCIPLES, AND CODES

As spiritual power seeks to both rise to be one with the crown and descend from the crown to create, this center of consciousness, from a cosmic perspective, is said to be where divine law originates. While the root is the realm of material laws, the laws of physics, chemistry, and biology, the crown is the realm of spiritual laws. People hear the terms *divine law* or *spiritual law* and get a little concerned, thinking of a prophet's arbitrary proclamations of a god upon high. Divine laws are more like the laws of physics. The laws of science are simply models for scientists' observations on how the universe, the physical universe, works. The spiritual laws of age-old traditions are the same, but the models are based on the observations of sages, mystics, philosophers, and magicians. A surprisingly consistent body of ideas has been simultaneously discovered and maintained, yet each culture has used them with different labels and colored them in different cultural symbolism. They are the operating principles of our magick, and if you have been a practicing magician for any length of time, you have learned these laws in theory and practice.

When you contemplated the crown chakra, what came up for you in terms of spiritual laws? What concepts passed through your consciousness when you tuned into the crown chakra and contemplated the thought of spiritual laws governing existence? Reflect on what seems like a "true" spiritual law, a guiding principle in the operation of the universe, and what appears to be dogmatic programming. We often accept ideas from religion and society that are not really found in our crown chakra. Some we accept because they are tradition, and the tradition serves us. Others are limiting programs, embedded in us at the highest level, and we need to recognize them to break them. Exercise 8: Seven-Body Healing can do great things to find and heal such programs, but sometimes when they are not within our conscious mind, when we haven't recognized them as harmful programs, we remain blind to them.

For me, the prominent "laws" that come up are the seven Hermetic Principles (*ITOW*, chapter 8). Though they are only one way of looking at the universe, they have provided me with a solid, nondogmatic structure with which I can build my other ideas and frame my own experiences. Everything I see as a "law" relates back to this structure, from the complexity of the Tree of Life to understanding the patterns of the magick circle. There are many other complex and complete magick theory structures. We tend to favor whatever we first "imprint." Some magicians favor the magickal axioms found in Isaac Bonewits's classic text, *Real Magic*.

Anything else that does not fit into the sense of spiritual "laws," I find, is really a guideline for my life. Some are things I need to release, for they have not guided me well. Others are quite helpful, and though I realize that they are not laws and absolutes, they still guide me, in a conscious choice of self-programming. The Law of Three is a hotly debated concept of witchcraft. Though many scoff at it today, this Wiccan teaching has served me well as an excellent guide, reminding me of the consequences of my actions in all things. Another has been the words of Mahatma Gandhi, "We must be the change we wish to see in the world." My mother's own wisdom on hate guides me too: "Hate hurts you far more than anybody you're hating."

Spiritual guidelines have been mistaken for laws, for metaphysical truths, for as long as religions have been around. While they can help guide and shape a society, they shouldn't be misconstrued as metaphysical laws. Those who seek direct experience know that even our metaphysical laws are not absolute, but are theories and expressions of our experience and understanding formulated in a way that makes the most sense to us now. Like scientific theorems, they will change and refine as our understanding becomes clearer.

Dogma evolves out of mistaking one's moral codes and metaphysical principles for absolute truths. Unfortunately, Wicca is no different, even as a mystery religion. We have our own laws and codes that have become dogma for some. The important thing to realize is that any of these laws is simply a model, a map, and any of our codes of conduct is a rede, a form of advice, not an absolute law. Each of us must take responsibility for our actions. Advice can only guide us in the spirit of the tradition. Structures that seek to legislate all possible scenarios, and fill us with "thou shall nots" restrict our own personal evolution and moral understanding of the universe.

The first time the laws of witchcraft came under question in the modern era was the addition of a section known as the "Old Laws," or "Ardanes," to the Book of Shadows by Gerald Gardner. In the opening paragraph, it states:

> The Law was made and Ardane of old. The law was made for the Wicca, to advise and help in their troubles. The Wicca should give due worship to the Gods and obey their will, which they Ardane, for it was made for the good of the Wicca.

The Old Laws are broken into a series of 161 statements including rules, advice, warnings, theology, and proverbs for the witch. It appears that they were not in the earlier versions of the book. While Gardner claimed them to be laws of old given by the gods, and passed to him through the New Forest coven, many believe they were later added when Gardner was losing control over the tradition, and the "laws" were a means to establish his authority. This document appears in response to a set of "Proposed Rules of the Craft" offered by his conveners, including Doreen Valiente. They felt the need for such rules after Gardner's multiple interviews with the media, because they felt he was not following the laws of secrecy he applied to everybody else. Gardner rejected the proposed rules because he said that Wicca already had its laws and didn't need any more. Soon he produced the Old Laws. He may have cobbled them together from various sources, and many of the basic concepts appeared in his books, but the Old Laws gave him an opportunity to codify his own personal beliefs, biases, and prejudices into the Craft and claim they were tradition. Today, most find these laws sexist, ageist, homophobic, and paranoid. Those who break these laws are said to be "cursed by the Goddess" or "condemned to Christian Hell," contradicting much of the general spirit of Wicca. Valiente doubted and disputed the authenticity of the laws, and they contributed to her falling-out with Gardner, particularly concerning the section on the older high priestess gracefully stepping down for a younger priestess because "youth is necessary to be the representative of the Goddess." Somehow old men were perfectly fine to represent the God. You can find a version of the Old Laws in appendix IV.

Though these laws do not suit the religion now, or perhaps ever, codes of conduct, virtue, and ethics help shape the tradition. Most eclectic and solitary pagans don't come across the Old Laws unless they search them out. Even then, they don't often think about codes and laws, and how or if they fit into modern witchcraft. I think the idea of codes shouldn't be thrown out with Gardner's laws wholesale, though I don't think any one code will suit all witches. I don't think of any of them as spiritual laws, but as potentially good advice and wisdom. Pagan traditions are filled with great advice and good wisdom. We should look for it in the poetry, myths, and traditions we have, and build upon it for the future, yet remember that it's only advice, and not absolute law.

You can deconstruct *The Charge of the Goddess* to find a set of guidelines for pagan spirituality. Summed up in its practical points, *The Charge* would look like this:

Ritual once a month when the Moon is full to adore the Goddess.
Be naked in your ritual to show you are free from slavery.
Sing, feast, dance, make music, and make love, in life and as a part of your rituals.
No sacrifice is needed to practice witchcraft.
All acts of love and pleasure are rituals sacred to the Goddess.
Cultivate the traits of beauty, strength, power, compassion, honor, humility, mirth, and reverence.
Seek your answers within, not outside of yourself.

The following eight traits are also known as the Eight Wiccan Virtues in some circles. You could correspond them with the eight holidays. I put the pair of concepts listed in *The Charge of the Goddess* with the Sabbat holidays, having each pair on one axis of the Wheel of the Year. Though these are my personal associations, they are by no means traditional, and you can make your own. Your Wheel of the Year rituals can reflect a theme of each virtue, and you can strive to learn more about and embody that virtue at the appropriate time of the year.

Beauty   Imbolc
Strength   Lammas

Power	Litha
Compassion	Yule
Honor	Ostara
Humility	Mabon
Mirth	Beltane
Reverence	Samhain

I've also found the Nine Noble Virtues from modern Germanic paganism, known as Heathenry, to be a great set of guidelines. Modern witches focus so much on our Celtic lore, they forget that the Germanic, Norse, and Saxon traditions have greatly influenced our understanding of witchcraft in the present age. Modern witches, Wiccans, and pagans can learn a lot from our counterparts in the Teutonic traditions. The Nine Noble Virtues are drawn from the Poetic Edda, Icelandic sagas, and Germanic folklore. Codified by John Yeowell and John Gibbs-Bailey in the 1970s for the Odinic Rite, they now serve as an ethical code for modern practitioners. I have found them quite inspiring, and I aspire to these virtues in my own life and encourage my students to do the same. They capture the essence and spirit of European pagan traditions.

Courage

Truth

Honor

Fidelity

Discipline

Hospitality

Self-reliance

Industriousness

Perseverance

In the modern role-playing game *Mage: The Ascension*, a supplemental book known as *Dark Ages: Mages Grimoire* has a list of Pagan Virtues for those of the Old Faith. Even though it comes from a game, it is a very magickal game, written by some very magickal authors. This particular section, written by pagan magician Steve Kenson, sums up many core ideas of pagan life. They echo many of the same concepts in the Eight Wiccan Virtues and Nine Noble Virtues, yet reduced further to four key concepts. The four attributes are:

Vitality

Vitality is the celebration of life force, experience in the world, enjoyment of earthly pleasures, and experience of the cycles and seasons of life. Those who celebrate life must therefore be able to embrace death as a cycle of life. Earth is the element of physical vitality.

Courage

Courage is the ability to do what needs to be done, despite the danger. Courage is not foolhardiness, but the virtue of doing what is necessary, even when what is necessary is not easy. Courage is celebrated in pagan society, but its opposite, cowardice, is a stigma. Fire is the element of courage.

Honor

Honor is the action of living by a code of ethics, of being trustworthy and dedicated. It is almost a tangible commodity, and it's better to die with honor than to live without it. A key concept of honor in the pagan societies and in magickal cultures is the oath, the word, being your bond, and it must be honored. Honor is connected with the element of air.

Generosity

The ability to freely give to others is the last virtue. Those who have more than others, and share it, are looked upon favorably by humans and the gods for their generosity. Hospitality to strangers and beggars in particular is considered a pagan virtue, as many myths tell of the gods disguised as beggars or travelers. The principle of generosity is aligned with water.

While many of us hold the archetypal Eastern ideals of peace, compassion, and noninterference as the keys to enlightenment, when one looks to the pagan myths, the violent yet courageous and honorable warrior is more apt to receive the rewards of the

Otherworld than the nonviolent monk. The violence was not the key or the barrier, but how and why such acts are committed. In defense of the village and honor, combat is a virtue in ancient pagan spirituality, and blessed by the gods.

Another set of guidelines, created more for the general public than for witches, is the Principles of Wiccan Belief, as established by the Council of American Witches in 1974. Though created to help combat the general misunderstanding of Wicca, witchcraft, and neopaganism in America, these thirteen statements have become the introduction to paganism and guiding principles for many beginning witches in America. Though the concepts might not be new to you at this stage of your education, modern witches should be familiar with this document as a set of guidelines to witchcraft beliefs. The statements themselves serve as an overview, not attached to any one tradition or system. They can be found in appendix V.

Popular American witch Scott Cunningham gave us several documents much beloved by modern witches in his books *Wicca: A Guide for the Solitary Practitioner* and *Living Wicca*, including "The Thirteen Goals of the Witch," "The Law of the Power," and "The Nature of Our Way." I particularly love the Thirteen Goals of a Witch and give them zodiac correspondences in Volume Two of this book.

The Thirteen Goals of a Witch

1. Know yourself
2. Know your Craft
3. Learn
4. Apply knowledge with wisdom
5. Achieve balance
6. Keep your words in good order
7. Keep your thoughts in good order
8. Celebrate life
9. Attune with the cycles of the earth
10. Breathe and eat correctly
11. Exercise the body
12. Meditate
13. Honor the Goddess and God

The Law of the Power

The Power shall not be used to bring harm, to injure or control others. But if the need rises, the Power shall be used to protect your life or the lives of others.

The Power is used only as need dictates.

The Power can be used for your own gain, as long as by doing so you harm none.

It is unwise to accept money for use of the Power, for it quickly controls its taker. Be not as those of other religions.

Use not the Power for prideful gain, for such cheapens the mysteries of Wicca and magic.

Ever remember that the Power is the sacred gift of the Goddess and God, and should never by misused or abused.

The Nature of Our Way

As often as possible, hold the rites in forests, by the seashore, on deserted mountaintops, or near tranquil lakes. If this is impossible, a garden or some chamber shall suffice, if it is readied with fumes or flowers.

Seek out wisdom in books, rare manuscripts, and cryptic poems if you will, but seek it out also in simple stones, and fragile herbs, and in cries of wild birds. Listen to the whisperings of the wind and the roar of water if you would discover magic, for it is here that the old secrets are preserved.

Books contain words; trees contain energies and wisdom books ne'er dreamt of.

Ever remember that the Old Ways are constantly revealing themselves. Therefore be as the river willow that bends and sways with the wind. That which remains changeless shall outlive its spirit, but that which evolves and grows will shine for centuries.

There can be no monopoly on wisdom. Therefore share what you will of our ways with others who seek them, but hide mystic lore from the eyes of those who would destroy, for to do otherwise increases their destruction.

Mock not the rituals or spells of another, for who can say yours are greater in power or wisdom?

Ensure that your actions are honorable, for all that you do shall return to you three-fold, good or bane.

Be wary of one who would dominate you, who would control and manipulate your workings and reverences. True reverence for the Goddess and God occurs within. Look with suspicion on any who would twist worship from you for their own gain and glory, but welcome those priestesses and priests who are suffused with love.

Honor all living things, for we are of the bird, the fish, the bee. Destroy not life save it be to preserve your own.

And this is the nature of our way.

Through his influential letters, Robert Cochrane unofficially outlines a "code" that has been adopted by witches who follow his more primal wisdom, such as those from the 1734 tradition. His code, summed up by those who follow his way, is:

- Do not do what you desire—do what is necessary.

- Take all you are given—give all of yourself.

- What I have—I hold!

- When all is lost, and not until then, prepare to die with dignity . . . and return to the womb of the Dark Goddess to give life another try until the wheel of rebirth is finally broken.

Author Rhiannon Ryall, in *Weaving a Web of Magic*, gives us the following seven principles:

Learn This as if It Were a Law

1. Love all things in nature.

2. Suffer no person to be harmed by deed or even thought. Thoughts vibrate into the Silver Web.

3. Go quietly and confidently among the ways and paths of the World.

4. Be mindful always of the Unseen Guardians.

5. Knowledge comes through application and the surety that the Universe will uphold and support you.

6. Contentment comes with knowing that a thread runs through your life, and all is for the ultimate good.

7. The truly wise grow never old, even though they age in the physical realm.

There is no one theology and set of "rules" and guides that fit all witches and all witch-craft traditions. Perhaps the Council of American Witches' statement comes the clos-est as a unifying document, but even that divides us from witches in other parts of the world, or traditions that hold to pre-Gardnerian practices. Even in seemingly similar traditions, such as Gardnerian and Alexandrian witchcraft, and even different genera-tions within those traditions, there are theological differences. Some blame it on the miscopying of the Book of Shadows, yet if the "mistaken" practice works, is it really a mistake? If it's all you've ever known, then it's right for you.

What brings us together is far stronger than our differences, when we look out to the rest of the world. We are set apart, walking the edge when looking at the rest of society. Regardless of the tradition, at heart, we are a mystical, magickal people for whom personal experience is the key component. What is different is to be celebrated. We share, we study, and we absorb, keeping the tradition alive with new fertile wis-dom, nourishing our roots and growing new branches. What is the same between us might be too elusive to put into any list of beliefs or document of "laws," yet it still bonds us. Any guides and rules we come up with must be for ourselves and our own traditions, for we know how horrible the world can get when one dominant religion forces its own worldviews upon everybody.

EXERCISE 27

What Are Your Own Spiritual Laws?

What are your own spiritual laws guiding your life? Which are unhealthy programs, and which are true wisdoms aiding your evolution? Make your own list of spiritual laws and guidelines. Refine it. And when ready, copy it into your BOS.

Soul Anatomy

Just as mystical philosophers divide the universe into operating principles in their exploration of the mysteries of spirit, so they also look at the spirit of an individual and draw dividing lines, seeking to understand the whole better by examining the part. They create a form of "soul anatomy" for the metaphysician, to aid in the healing process. From a modern perspective, soul anatomy might be better labeled as soul psychology, looking at the various nonphysical forces in our makeup and understanding how they affect our daily lives and spiritual evolution. Soul psychology has become a primary focus of Theosophists, with their system of "ray psychology." It's interesting to note that those most involved with such teachings are aligned with the esoteric seventh ray, the violet ray of ceremonial order. We relate this power to the crown, to healing, and to alchemy, magick, and witchcraft. Those of the seventh ray, and of the seventh chakra, seek to understand the mysteries of spirit as it manifests in the universe and as it manifests in the self.

You have already learned quite a bit about soul anatomy, with various models of the soul. The simple model is the three-soul cosmology, one for each of the three main realms of the shamanic World Tree. There is the middle self of the personality and ego, in the world of space, time, and process. It is the part that names and divides, and interestingly enough, it is most concerned with the precision of soul anatomy. There is the higher self in the upper realms, filled with divine insight and wisdom, watching from "above," beyond space and time. The lower self is the most intuitive, childlike, and animalistic self. It serves as the bridge, the messenger, between the higher and lower selves, and helps us shape our reality, based on both our conscious intentions and unconscious motivations. Understanding the relationship between these three selves, and how they are communing, we can remedy "soul issues" that are impacting our lives in a difficult way and learn the secret science of magick, which is truly communication with ourselves and the universe, to create the life we desire.

In the initial training of the inner temple, we called these selves the three minds—the divine mind, conscious mind, and psychic mind—yet they really are three complete selves, complete souls. In the shamanic mysteries, we call them the three selves. One of the difficulties for many when studying soul anatomy is understanding that the soul is not one thing, but it can be expressed as many things. You are a many-souled, or many-bodied, individual.

There are many names for the three selves beyond higher, middle, and lower (figure 14). The names I've adopted and adapted from the traditions of witchcraft teacher Adam Sartwell are the Watcher, Namer, and Shaper, and I prefer those terms when not using the simple higher/middle/lower or divine/conscious/psychic mind names.

Another example of soul anatomy comes from the exploration of the subtle bodies. In the inner temple, we studied a model of dividing the energy field into seven layers, each corresponding to the nature and function of a chakra. They also correspond neatly to all the lessons in this text, based upon the seven gates, seven chakras, and seven alchemical processes. In these seven layers, we have one gross or material body of function and form, and six other subtle bodies, composed of energy. The further away they move from the physical body, the more sublime and difficult they are to express. The names for these seven bodies are physical, etheric, astral (lower astral), emotional (higher astral), mental, psychic, and divine.

	Higher	*Middle*	*Lower*
LTOW	Watcher	Namer	Shaper
ITOW	Divine Mind	Personal Mind	Psychic Mind
Hawaiian	Aumakua	Uhane	Unihipili
Siberian	Ami	Suld	Suns
Greek	Logos	Thumos	Epithymia
Roman	Diamon	_	Psyche
Voodou	Gros Bon Ange	Petit Bon Ange	N'ame
Egyptian	Sa (Ba)	Ba (Sa)	Ka
Hebrew	Neshamah	Ruach	Nephesh
Arabic	Sirr	Ruh	Nafs
Alchemy	Sulfur	Salt	Mercury
African Feri	Ori	Emi	Vivi
Cora Anderson	Gamma	Beta	Alpha
Victor Anderson	God Self	Human Self	Animal Self
Starhawk	Deep Self	Talking Self	Younger Self
T. Thorn Coyle	Sacred Dove	Shining Body	Sticky One
Orion Foxwood	Star Walker	Surface Walker	Dream Walker
Serge Kahili King	Kane	Lono	Ku

Figure 14: Three Selves

Some systems simplify the division, using a pattern of four or five, based on the qualities of the elements rather than the chakras. Their divisions are earth (physical), water (emotional), air (mental), and fire (spiritual). The four elemental divisions of the self are very similar to the Native American teachings of the medicine wheel, orienting four aspects of the self with the four directions.

The Qabalistic Tree of Life is not only a map of the universe but, if the axiom of "As above, so below" holds true, a map of the individual. Each sephira describes an aspect of the self, giving us an even more precise soul "map" with ten parts of the self, and twenty-two processes that connect these parts. The Jewish concept of the soul has evolved over time from a three-part, to a four-part, and then to this ten-part model of our inner forces, influencing our modern Hermetic Qabalistic teachings. As our understanding of the self evolves, so do our ideas of the soul.

One of the most complex and comprehensive models of soul anatomy for modern witches and magicians comes from the Egyptians. Although this is another model that has varied over time and had many modern interpretations, it is generally held to be a nine-part soul system. As a tradition deeply concerned with both life and death, an understanding of the soul is essential to Khemetic spirituality.

The Egyptian soul model contains the following parts. A modern student of Egyptian mysticism should realize there have been many interpretations of this soul model. Here are the definitions of the various parts that have been most helpful to me.

Khat or Khabs: The physical body. The *khat* becomes the corpse when left to decay, or the mummy if preserved through embalming rites.

Ka: The spiritual double, similar in concept to the astral self. The *ka* is the soul part that remains in the tomb to receive offerings. It can wander about independently of the body.

Ba: The soul, appearing as a human-headed hawk (figure 15). The *ba* is connected with the ka and is similar to what we might call the higher self.

Ab: The heart. The *ab* is the conscience, the good and evil one is capable of performing in life. It is also the animal nature. The ab is weighed on scales against the truth of Ma'at at the end of life.

Khaibit: The shadow. The *khaibit* is the primal darkness of the self, seen by some as the repressed and unconscious emotions.

Khu or Akhu: The spirit. The spiritual body that is the opposite of the khat. It is the radiant, shining body that never decays. It dwells with the gods upon death. Some think of it as the union of the ka and the ba. Modern New Age lore refers to it as the Light Body.

Seb: The ancestral soul. The *seb* is the energy passed on from parents through the genetic lineage.

Ren: The name. The *ren* is the secret spirit name, or true name of a person. Names hold a lot of power in Egyptian lore. Isis was said to ascend to supremacy in magick

Figure 15: Ba

by obtaining the ren of the creator god Ra. The power of naming, and magicians keeping such names hidden, can be traced back to this lore.

Sahu: The spiritual body. The *sahu* appears after the individual is deceased and judged. It is the immortal imprint or image of the khat.

Sekhem: The vital life force. *Sekhem* is the energy of the individual. Some would relate it to the life energy known in various cultures as prana, mana, ki, chi, pnumen, or rauch. Sekhem is not always considered a soul "part," but the force animating and connecting the souls.

Some of the African diasporic traditions have a similar concept of nine souls and corresponding spiritual beings aligned with each part of the soul. This particular interpretation, along with its corresponding spiritual powers, can be found in the book *Voodoo Contra* by Robert Gover.

Universal Soul: The power that unites humanity with the universe. This is the universal god, the supreme force known as Olodumare or Olorun.

Human Soul: The earthly human form. The human soul gives us the ability to relate with other humans. Corresponds with Obatala.

Racial Soul: The spirit and characteristics of a particular ethnic race. European racial soul is ruled by Ogun. African racial soul is ruled by Olokun, and the Asian and American Indian racial soul is ruled by Eshu.

Sexual Soul: The energy of the gender, and the gender identity of the individual. The sexual soul, the ideal image of a man or woman for that individual, is influenced by the culture and by the racial soul.

Astral Soul: The motivating force behind particular talents, gifts, and abilities. Connected with the astral soul is the personal archetypal "god" who grants and encourages certain gifts.

National Soul: The spiritual quality of the nation where an individual is born.

Ancestral Soul: The inherited spiritual qualities from your direct personal family within your race and nation.

Historic Soul: The spirit of the age, or the time when an individual is born.

Personal Soul: The ego or persona. What we refer to as the middle self.

The Celtic tradition of soul anatomy has seven parts. Edred Thorsson outlines the Irish soul concept in his text, *The Book of Ogham*.

Delbh: The appearance or shape. The *delbh* is the outer shape and form, but not the literal physical body. It is the etheric template that the *duile*, the elements of the body, fills. The delbh is somewhat malleable and can be changed by actors, magicians, and others skilled in altering their appearance.

Duile: The elements that make up the body. There are six elements of the body, and each one corresponds to an aspect of the world.

Elements of the Body	*Aspects of the World*
Anál—Breath	*Gaeth*—Wind
Imradud—Mind	*Nel*—Cloud
Drech—Face	*Grain*—Sun
Fuil—Blood	*Muir*—Sea
Colaind—Flesh	*Talamh*—Earth
Cnaimh—Bone	*Cloch*—Stone

Although some similarities can be seen between this list and the classical five elements, it's important to note that the ancient Celts did not use the system of classic elements familiar to modern witches today. The *anál* is given special consideration, as a separate element in and of itself, for it is the vital animating principle, congruent with our concept of prana, ki, or chi.

Menma: The mind and will. The two are considered so close that one term is used for both, rather than dividing mind and will. The less focused and driven mind appears to be described as the duile, also known as *imradud*.

Cuimhne: The memory. The *cuimhne* is subordinate to the menma.

Féin: The self. This is the individual self and the primary daily consciousness.

Púca or Scál: The shadow or shapeshifting form. A divine part of the self, yet often unsettling or dangerous when activated in certain circumstances. The *púca* can manifest as an alter ego with the repressed shadow traits of the individual. The terms *púca, pucca,* or *pooka* are also used for a fearsome shape-changing faery being.

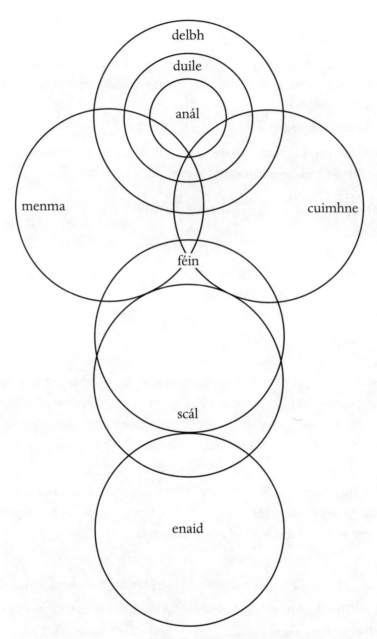

Figure 16: Celtic Soul Cosmology from The Book of Ogham

Enaid: The soul or shade. This aspect of the self is only manifest upon the death of an individual.

Thorsson does similar work exploring the Norse concept of the soul in his book *The Nine Doors of Midgard*.

Lík/Lyke: The physical body.

Hamr/Hyde: The "plastic" energy that gives shapes and form to physical objects, including the body. It is similar to our concept of the etheric energy and etheric body.

Önd/Athem: The breath of life or vital energy. It is similar to prana.

Hugr/Hugh and Minni/Myne: Reflections of Odin's two ravens, Thought and Memory, Huginn and Muninn. The *hugr/hugh* is the cognitive faculty and analytical part of our mind, like the left hemisphere, while *minni/myne* is the reflective faculty, the creative side, like our right hemisphere.

Ódhr/Wode: The power of imagination and enthusiasm manifesting in poetic thought, furious rage, or magickal reality. Though powerful, this force is beyond reason. The Hugr and Minni are brought together by the *ódhr*.

Fylgja/Fetch: A complex and somewhat independent entity in the soul complex. It can manifest as an animal, anima/animus figure, or geometric shape. It acts as a tutelary guide in terms of gifts and abilities, including magick. The *fylgja/fetch* might be better developed in some individuals and less developed in others.

Hamingja: An individual's luck, protective essence, and ability to cause change in the world.

Sál: The soul, in the sense of the shade that appears after death.

Sjálfr: The self. Self-consciousness, the personal ego self.

In our modern day, soul mapping is not that different. We simply call it psychology, but rather than thinking of it as soul science, we think of it strictly as a way of working

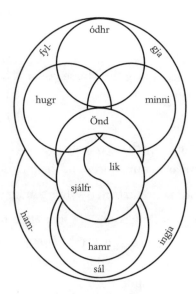

Figure 17: Norse Soul Cosmology from The Nine Doors of Midgard

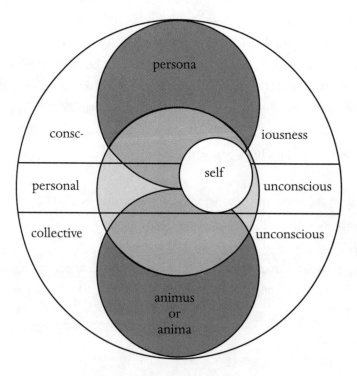

Figure 18: Jung's Map of the Mind

with the mind. Carl Jung's structure of the mind (figure 18) is not so different from any of the ideas explored in this section. Divided into three realms, like the three shamanic worlds (consciousness, personal unconsciousness, and collective unconsciousness), and divided into three selves that overlap and connect the worlds, like the three souls (the persona, self, and animus/anima), the modern psychological model strikes a similar chord. We would expect no less from the scientists who put so much value in the traditions of alchemy and divination, and gave us a modern understanding of many ancient esoteric phenomena.

All of these systems are simply that—systems. They are models attempting to map something that is essentially timeless, eternal, and unmappable. Just like our reality maps of *TOHW*, these soul maps give us a better understanding of the souls and how they work together, but they are not to be mistaken for the soul itself. Our perspective on the soul is influenced by our theology, our culture, our geography, and our ancestry. Though given cultural terms, each of these models is influenced by my own understanding, and by those whose sources I've drawn upon. The terms are so filled with subtlety and nuance that it's hard to be certain if we understand a concept the same way our pagan ancestors did. We live in a different world, with a different consciousness and exposure to new and innovative ideas from across the globe. But they do provide a foundation for understanding the nature of the soul.

Figure 19 compares some of the soul anatomy systems and terms, but each system is unique unto itself, and these equivalences are really gross generalizations. Each system has its own subtle cultural nuances.

This information provides you with a basis from which to contemplate the various systems of soul cosmology. As a modern witchcraft culture, we are challenged to create new models that will aid us in our own ministry to others. Based on this cross-cultural comparison and your own experience, what is your map of the soul? How do you see the various parts connected? Does one model appeal to you over the others as being most helpful? Or will you need to "map" your own, based on your own experi-

Qabalah		Egyptian	Celtic	Norse
Sephira	Soul Part			
Kether	Yechidah	sahu spiritual body home of akhu totality of self	enaid soul/shade after death	sjálfr and sál soul and higher self
Chokmah	Chiah	khaibit shadow self magic self	púca shadow	fylgja/fetch guide
Binah	Nesh- amah			hamingja luck, protection, shapeshifting
Chesed		khu spiritual soul blood/ intelligence	menma thought and will	hugr/hugh mind
Geburah				
Tiphereth	Ruach	ab heart/emotions	cuimhne memory	minni/myne memory
Netzach		ba heart soul astral/ghost	féin self/individual	ódhr/wode inspiration/ magic
Hod		sekhem will/power	anál breath of life	önd/athem breath of life
Yesod	Nephesh	ka double of body	delbh shape, appearance	hamr/hyde shape
Malkuth	Guph	khat physical body	duile body elements	lík/lyke physical body

Figure 19: Soul Anatomy Chart

Elements	Chakras	Theosophy	Voodou	Aztec
fire	Sahasrara spiritual body	atma	gros bon ange big angel life force	
	Ajna psychic body	buddhi		ihilia liver passion/ animal instincts
		higher manas	z'étoile star of destiny	
air	Vishuddha mental body			
		lower manas		
	Anahata emotional body			teyolia heart knowledge/ personality entered the afterlife
water	Manipura astral body	kama		tonalli head life force
		prana	petit bon ange small angel personal essence and aura	
	Svadhisthana etheric body	linga-sharira	n'ame spirit of flesh	
earth	Muladhara physical body	sthula-sharira	corps cadavre mortal flesh	

Figure 19: Soul Anatomy Chart

ences, ideas, and divine guidance, just as you "mapped" your perspective of reality in *TOHW*? My own "soul map" (figure 20) contains the following:

Higher Self: Known as the Holy Guardian Angel, Bornless Self, divine self, or Watcher, it is the essence of our soul expressed in the Upper World. This is our star self, the divine light that emanates from the Great Mother and Father into the world of form. It holds our true name, and incarnates globally across time and space, giving us a universal perspective. It is the part of us connected to the divine creative energy of the universe. The higher self is influenced by a god or spirit that can be considered the patron of the individual. This patron can work with the higher self through many incarnations.

Middle Self: The middle self is the ego, the personal self, or Namer. It is the core self that walks in the Middle World of space, time, form, and function. This is the self most people think of as the "self." It is our connection to the world, and it forms the core of our Middle World self. It is the part of us that seeks to understand the parts and the greater whole by identifying and naming them, and exploring their relationship in the context of the individual self, where the higher and lower selves experience the interconnection of everything much better. It is for this reason that the middle self must engage the higher and/or lower selves to do magick, healing, and divinatory work. The middle self, born of the Middle World, contains aspects known as the nation energies, the group energies of the nation where one is born, and the historic energies, or the group energies of the time and age when one is born. The middle self generally doesn't reincarnate. Most middle selves dissipate and break down, like all things in the Middle World. Disturbed middle selves become ghosts until they break down. Many strong-willed souls become one with the nature spirits and guardians of the land. The traditional spirit guides and healers work most closely with the middle selves, acting as guides, companions, and confidants.

Lower Self: The lower self is the instinctual self, the Shaper, connecting to us through the lower body, our "guts," but it is the part of us that is most at home with the Underworld. This the primal self, often considered to be the "blood soul," for it carries the genetic lineage with it, reincarnating through the family, or at least the overall ethnic group. Though rooted with the Underworld forces, it doesn't remain station-

higher self

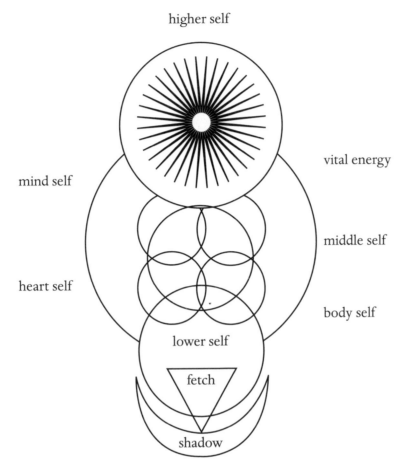

mind self

vital energy

heart self

middle self

body self

lower self

fetch

shadow

Figure 20: Modern Soul Concept

ary. It acts like a bridge to connect the higher and lower selves. The fetch, other totemic and tutelary spirits, and in particular the Master-Teacher, work with the lower self, and they are often equated with the lower self in other systems.

Fetch: One could argue that the fetch is not really a separate part of the soul, but a connection to a spiritual guide or a manifestation of the animalistic lower self. Though intimately connected with the lower self, this spirit is the animalistic nature of the soul, the core animal spirit/totem/familiar that lives in the center of the shamanic witch's medicine wheel (*TOSW*, chapter 3). This is the self most strongly identified with the individual in this current incarnation. Upon death, and even just prior to death, the fetch can leave the individual, acting as an independent animal spirit. Sometimes it will reincarnate in another soul complex, often following the lower self along family/tribal bloodlines. A group of related individuals might have the same type of animal as a fetch, or pass a fetch on from parent to child, or teacher to student, supplementing the receiver's original fetch. The fetch also helps connect the soul complex and the shadow self.

Shadow Self: The shadow is the repressed aspect of the lower self, initially divided off from the lower self, yet still immensely powerful. Part of soul healing is to bring the shadow self back into harmony and alignment with the entire soul complex, re-attaching it in a healthy and productive way. The shadow self can act as an alter ego for the middle self. When you have an unhealthy relationship with your shadow, its manifestation through the middle self is extremely unhelpful and often unexpected. When in a working and healthy relationship with the shadow, it can act as an aspect of the magickal persona that witches consciously conjure to do their Craft. In advanced souls, the shadow winds its way through the entire soul complex, like a web, empowering all aspects of the self. The shadow self is influenced by a variety of lesser spirits, most popularly codified as the Goetia of King Solomon, just as various angels are of influence and harmony with the higher self.

Vital Energy: While the three main selves act as the element of spirit divided in the three worlds, the Middle World has the remaining four elements manifested. The fire element is the vital energy of the self, the prana or life force. So often associated with the element of air, it is really the air that feeds the flame of the vital life force. This is the energy that fuels that action of the soul complex and provides the willpower necessary to do magick or accomplish any other task. Techniques can be used to build this vital life force, increasing health and magickal ability. Though the vital energy and its body work with the entire soul complex, it has a natural attunement to the upper realm. The personal self has access to vital energy that is manifested and processed, gathering it up from the food, water, air, and light, and it can use the lower self to manipulate the vital energy for daily life and magick. The higher self has a connection to a purer form of universal vital energy, unmanifest in the material world, but the personal self only has access to this through forging a strong connection with the higher self. The shadow self can horde vital energy for its own purposes, usually unconscious to the personal self. Only when one has a conscious relationship with the shadow is that energy freed for the vitality of the entire being.

Heart Self: The heart self is the emotional body, or astral body, that is the container for our strong emotions and our self-image in the material world. It contains our emotional memories and generates our intense feelings. The heart self can reach out to others to make connections. When it radiates outward, it makes healthy, nonlinear connections. When it creates lines of connection, it can make unwanted energetic cords to other people, places, and times in the past, draining you or them of vital life force and keeping you stuck to unhealthy influences. The water element and the Lower World are associated with the heart self.

Mind Self: The mind self, or mental body, is the generator of our ideas and language, as well as the container for our memories and education. The mind self contains all that we've ever learned in this life, and it can be divided into portions we consciously remember and unconsciously know. The air element and Upper World are both associated with the mind self.

Body Self: The body self is the actual physical body and the spirits of the elements and compounds that make up the physical body. While the middle self is the overall animating consciousness of the body self, linked with the vital energy, heart self, and mind self, the body self is the physical vehicle. It has a consciousness and awareness all its own. Connected to the element of earth, in many ways it is more strongly associated with the lower self than the middle self, being instinctual and survival oriented. The body self also contains the etheric body, the energetic shape, as well as the physical flesh.

Though not marked in the diagram, I also find relevance in such concepts as the inherited ancestral or tribal totem figure, the soul of the nation where you live, and the soul of the age when you live. They are all important parts of the self.

Understanding the nature of the soul gives us a very powerful perspective on what we might have considered psychology in days past. The soul parts have archetypal qualities, and through the study of both soul anatomy and mythology, we examine the fundamental forces of the universe, both outside ourselves and inside our con-sciousness. Though it doesn't give us the equivalent of a modern psychology degree, it does give us insight into the human condition, how we operate, and how best to ad-vise people who are finding conflict within themselves and no clear road to resolution. Working with the soul selves through ritual, meditation, shamanism, and even simple talk-style therapy, we can make significant improvements in our lives and the lives of those who seek out our counsel. I've found soul psychology to be a huge asset in my work as a pagan minister. Often a tarot reading, healing ritual, or class turns into a ses-sion of pastoral counsel, whether you realize it or not, and whether you are ready for it or not. This knowledge has helped prepare me for that work.

Soul psychology is not just a psychological model, but an energetic reality. Tradi-tions that work directly with the other world believe that the soul can be damaged, fragmented, or lost, and that loss interferes with the otherwise proper working order of the soul—just as if an organ within your body is damaged or lost, the rest of your body would not function as well. Thankfully, with shamanic healing techniques, we can heal and return lost parts of the self, using what is called soul retrieval. It is also known as "singing the soul back home." The process is covered in detail in *TOSW*, exercise 35. Many experience soul retrieval once, but then do not actively pursue com-plete soul integration. Soul healing is a difficult process, and it's easy to understand why many people don't pursue it with greater enthusiasm. It demands a lot of both the healer and the recipient, and doubly so when performing acts of soul healing on one's self. But integration of lost soul selves and healing any damage is an extremely important part of the path of the high priest/ess.

EXERCISE 28

Soul Retrieval

1. Start the process by reflecting first on your current life and the physical, emotional, mental, and spiritual experiences that you consider to be trau-matic. When you reflect on these points, do any of them still carry an ener-getic "charge" for you, or a sense that something has been lost? If you have

done much past-life exploration and healing, reflect on traumas from previous incarnations.

2. Prepare for a shamanic journey. Have drumming or other repetitive music available. Create sacred space. Enter an altered state of consciousness and travel to the World Tree with the intention of performing as complete a soul retrieval as possible at this time. Call upon your animal allies, and ask to follow the trail of your soul trauma. As if one continuous line links the past traumas, follow the trail, and at various points, you will encounter parts of yourself in need of return. They can appear inert, like fragments of glass or crystal, or personified, appearing as "you" from that time and place. Some will reassimilate quite easily, while others will need coaxing and reassurance that it is "safe" to return and that the trauma will not occur again.

3. Follow the trail as long as you can, reintegrating with as many parts of yourself as you can at this time.

4. When you have gone as far as you can, go to your inner temple. At the inner temple, seek out the gate of harmony.

5. Enter the gate of harmony and feel yourself expand out infinitely. Feel yourself expand to fill the universe, in all directions and all dimensions. Become one with everything.

6. Invite all the fragments of yourself you might have missed on the journey to return to you, assured by this feeling of oneness. Feel the various parts of your soul, now whole and complete, communing with each other fully. In this place of harmony, do you have your own vision of soul anatomy, of how the various parts work together? Does it conform to a culture you know, or is the vision unique to your own experience?

7. Allow your consciousness to contract, shrinking down to normal proportions, until you feel the boundaries of your arms, legs, torso, and head.

8. Exit the gateway of harmony. If you need guidance or counsel, open the gateway of guidance and speak with your Master-Teacher.

9. When done, close any gateways that remain open, bid farewell to any spirits remaining. Exit the inner temple in the usual manner, returning through the World Tree and grounding yourself back in the physical world.

While it would be nice to simply enter the gateway of harmony and have all the soul's parts return easily, I've found that many will not return unless individually tracked down and coaxed back. But the more whole you become, the easier it will be to return your soul fragments, as each part will feel more secure and comfortable with you.

If you received any insight or vision about the anatomy of the soul selves, make your own sketch. Use that as a basis for your own soul mapping project, imitating the process of the reality map in *TOHW*. Perhaps your understanding of reality will be reflected in your understanding of the soul. Having a method to understand and communicate about the deep inner nature gives you another tool in your ministry, both self-ministry and for the greater community.

The Power of Union

The power of witchcraft as a religion doesn't come simply from the magick, from the spellcrafting, though they certainly help. It comes from the concept that our gods reside both outside of us and inside of us, in our flesh and blood, bones and breath. The physical world, including our bodies, is divinity in its most dense form. Every aspect of us, from the most physical to the most sublime, and everything in between, such as our emotions, thoughts, and desires, is sacred. These are all simply different expressions of the divine energy. All our rituals, spells, and crafts lead to this understanding and experience of the divine.

We seek, and find, direct experiences with the creative spirit. Though we sometimes have to overcome cultural conditioning that says otherwise, we don't believe that we are separate from the gods. We all have access to the divine. Some seek out the divine in transcendent experiences, sending forth their sense of self, their spirit body, into the nontangible worlds and commune with the gods there. Others awaken to the spirits in the flesh and invoke the gods, bringing them through from the otherworlds to manifest in the body. Though it appears to be two separate and distinct practices—sending forth the self or drawing the divine to you—they are very similar. To the witch, there is little difference between "here" and "there," for we are all points within a larger whole. Both points really have the same address. Magickal enlightenment is about reconciling the paradox of here versus there, of the divine outside of us and the divine inside of us. To be truly magickal, multidimensional beings, we must open our perspective to include here and there, and all the points in between, simultaneously.

The final alchemical stage of enlightenment is known as coagulation. Coagulation is the fusion of the final substances. The matter congeals into a semisolid, homogenous gel, blending the traits of solid and liquid. This is known as the Greater Stone in alchemy, the Sophic Salt. It is symbolized by the pure and incorruptible metal gold, solid yet soft, the king of all metals at the top rung of our alchemical ladder. The final lines of the Emerald Tablet reveal this mystery: "Thus will you obtain the Glory of the Whole Universe. All Obscurity will be clear to you. This is the greatest Force of all powers, because it overcomes every Subtle thing and penetrates every Solid thing."

Coagulation yields a stone that blends the traits of mercury and sulfur, the alchemical powers, perfecting anything with which it comes into contact, transmuting and purifying. In the body, it is the achievement of immortal consciousness. The body becomes spirit, but the spirit is made corporeal. In Theosophical terms, this is known as the Light Body or Golden Body of Light. In the initiate's consciousness, this is the sensual and mystical state of ecstasy, to be both in the body and yet free from flesh. In this state, in this body, an initiate can exist in all levels of creation.

The final stage in the Miracle of Bread is the consumption of the bread. Through eating it, we become one with it, just as when we work with the crown chakra, we recognize our innate oneness with everything. Consuming sacrament is the key for any tradition seeking union with the divine.

In the Descent of the Goddess, this level is symbolized by the relinquishment of her crown. Inanna wears the *shurgarra*, the crown of the steppe, a symbol of her authority. She is the Queen of Heaven and Earth. Her motives for descending to the Underworld are unclear. Some believe that she simply wants her sister's throne, to add the realm of the dead to her lands. Others say she is simply visiting her pregnant sister. She could be paying her respects to her sister, as her sister's husband, Inanna's brother-in-law, Nergal, has died. Lastly, there are those who feel she is solely seeking knowledge of the mysteries, and only her sister's land can grant initiation into the dark mysteries. In many ways, her sister is her shadow. But before she can go further, she must give up her most valued item, exposing her head. Like the gold of coagulation, we most often associate crowns with this metal. The crown is a symbol of sovereignty, of rulership.

In previous teachings, we've associated sovereignty with the element of earth, yet now we relate it to the crown chakra. For most, the crown chakra seems the very antithesis of the element of earth. Earth is associated with the root, with grounding and the physical body, while the crown is ethereal and sublime. Yet our magick teaches us that flesh and spirit are the same. The root and crown are reflections of each other. One is physical survival and one is spiritual survival. Both are needed to embody sovereignty. Yet to truly reach this level, to wear the crown, so to speak, is to go beyond personal sovereignty and personal responsibility. The one who wears the crown must also be looking at the greater good of the community.

When we think about the image of the sacred king or sacred queen, he or she is not the ruler over the people and the land, but the sacred steward. The rulers truly serve the people, not the other way around. The royalty, as priest-kings and priestess-queens, mediate the forces of the land and spirits to the people. They must master the four elements, the four powers embodied by the four elemental tools—truth, victory, compassion, and sovereignty. The word *royalty* is related to the word *reality*, as those who are truly royal are masters of their reality. Yet there is a fifth critical element missing from the picture. For me, this critical fifth ideal, corresponding to the element of spirit, is humility.

In traditional initiation rituals, the initiator kneels before the initiate, saying:

In other religions the postulant kneels, as the Priests claim supreme power, but in the Art Magical, we are taught to be humble, so we kneel to welcome them and say:
"Blessed be thy feet that have brought thee in these ways." (He kisses her feet.)
"Blessed be thy knees that shall kneel at the sacred altar." (He kisses her knees.)
"Blessed be thy womb, without which we would not be." (He kisses the top of the pubic triangle. For a man being invoked, "womb" would be replaced by "phallus.")
"Blessed be thy breasts, formed in beauty and in strength." (He kisses her breasts.)
"Blessed be thy lips, which shall utter the sacred names." (He kisses her lips.)

The fivefold kiss, the blessings of these five points, is given. Then the measure is taken and initiation oaths are given. Though many looking into Wicca are titillated by the skyclad kisses, they miss one of the major points: humility. Humility is needed for a ruler to rule wisely, even if it's simply over the kingdom of the self. If you do choose to work with the greater community, humility is the trait that will serve you best, guiding the other four powers. We remember that the power is part of us, but it also moves through us. We are all a part of the greater web. It belongs to no one alone, and every act we take affects everything else. When looking at the "L" words that correspond with the elements—light/fire, life/air, love/water, and law/earth—liberty, the law of Crowley's Thelema, fits well as the fifth "L" word, as one who wears the Crown of Humility embodies liberty, the freedom to enact True Will.

In several witchcraft traditions, the high priest and high priestess wear crowns, circlets, or headdresses of some sort. The high priestess uses a silver circlet with the symbols of the Moon on it (figure 21) to empower the third eye. For a high priest, a golden circlet or a Sun crown can be used (figure 22), but a stag or goat horn headdress or mask is more common (figure 23). Natural crowns made from laurel wreaths, thorns, reeds, and flowers can also be used as ritual crowns, though they are not of a lasting nature. The Cabot tradition usually forgoes the actual crown in place of a crown ring.

As you did with the four elemental tools, seek out the Crown of Humility. If you are ready for it, the guardians will give it to you. If not, they will advise and teach you what you need to know to be ready for it. If you have not yet received the four previous tools, work on them before attempting to work with the Crown of Humility. Truly, the Crown is forged from the gold found in the quest for your own enlightenment. The allies and guardians can only help you forge from what you have already found within yourself. At this stage we forge the gold of enlightenment into an innerworld ceremonial object. In future workings, the allies and guardians may have you recast it into something of more practical value. It is an alchemical coagulation, akin to a Philosopher's Stone, formed from the work of the previous four gifts. There are many levels of attainment with this crown, and I'm not suggesting that simply succeeding in this vision working will grant you perfect health and immortal life, but the Crown's formation can create profound change in your life. A witch who draws together the

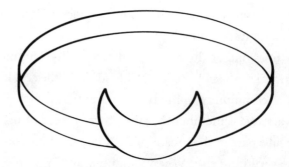

Figure 21: Moon Crown

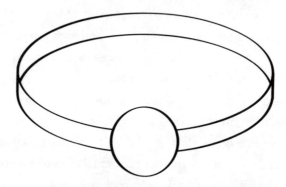

Figure 22: Sun Crown

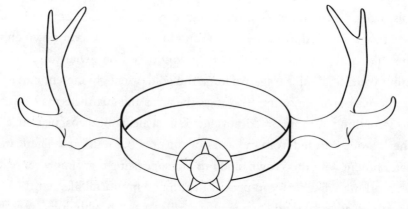

Figure 23: Stag Crown

powers of the five elements in the crown can use any one element as needed, as well as benefit from their union.

EXERCISE 29

Quest for the Crown of Humility

1. Perform Exercise 1: Inner Temple as a Mystery School Meditation (page 45), steps 1–5, to go to your inner temple. You must have obtained the four elemental tools from the *TOHW* course before you can truly receive the Crown.

2. Reflect. Open the gateway of guidance and call upon your Master-Teacher. Ask your Master-Teacher to guide you to the realm of spirit where the Crown of Humility resides. Ask to speak with the guardians of the Crown.

3. Your Master-Teacher will bring you to this realm, but will leave you to the challenges, blessings, and lessons of the Crown's guardians, returning to take you back when you are done. Ask to receive the Crown of Humility. The guardians and teachers of the Crown might give it to you, or test you first, making sure you are ready and worthy of it. Commune with the guardians of the Crown.

4. Return to the inner temple. If you received the Crown, feel all five of these powers residing with you, within your aura.

5. Ask your Master-Teacher any questions you have about this experience.

6. Thank and release your Master-Teacher through the gateway of guidance.

7. Finish exercise 1, steps 8–11, to return to normal consciousness.

In traditions of witchcraft that use the title of Lady or Lord before the craft name of a high priest/ess, the title signifies that person's spiritual "crown" being active and vital, and he or she is ideally sovereign, truthful, compassionate, victorious, and humble, aligned with the divine will in service to the highest good. That is the aspiration of the high priest/ess, to balance all the elements in service to the gods and people.

Once you are crowned, don't be surprised if your magick changes. Your relationship with your True Will deepens, and you might find that simple and base spells that once worked, but do not serve your highest good, don't work as easily. Your relationship with the guidance you receive might no longer appear to be coming from outside of you, but now from part of your own mental-emotional process, making it difficult to distinguish your personal will from your True Will until you integrate this new awareness.

I use the following meditation frequently to align with the five elemental powers in service. It can be done as a part of the Altar Devotional or the LBRP, or before any magickal working. It requires one to perform all the previous elemental exercises of *TOHW*, to obtain the Stone of Sovereignty, the Sword of Truth, the Cup of Compassion, and the Spear/Wand of Victory. When you first practice this meditation, you might not "feel" the Crown, because you might not yet have personally attained it in the previous meditation. As you complete this course, you will have earned the Crown of Humility. It comes as a part of final initiation in this tradition. Once you feel comfortable with all parts, you are welcome to alter the words or imagery to best suit you.

Exercise 30

The Five Gifts

1. Stand and center yourself. Take a few deep breaths to slightly alter your consciousness and create a focus. You don't have to be in a deep meditative state to do this ritual.

2. Bring your awareness to your feet. Feel the power of elemental earth, of sovereignty and its blessings upon you. Remember receiving the Stone from the elemental guardians. It still lies in your aura at the feet. Say out loud or think silently:

   I stand upon the Stone of Sovereignty.

3. Bring your awareness to the hip of your nondominant side. Feel the power of elemental air, of truth and its blessings upon you. Remember receiving

the Sword from the elemental guardians. It still lies in your aura, as if hanging from a belt, ready to be pulled. Say out loud or think silently:

With the Sword of Truth at my side.

4. Bring your awareness to the nondominant hand. Feel the power of elemental water, of compassion, and its blessings upon you. Remember receiving the Cup from the elemental guardians. It still lies in your aura, as if resting in your receptive hand. Say out loud or think silently:

I hold the Cup of Compassion in one hand.

5. Bring your awareness to the dominant hand. Feel the power of elemental fire, of victory, and its blessings upon you. Remember receiving the Spear or Wand from the elemental guardians. It still lies in your aura, as if resting in your projective hand. Say out loud or think silently:

And the Spear (Wand) of Victory in the other.

6. Bring your awareness to the top of your head. Feel the power of spirit and its blessings upon you. Think of the Crown of Humility and feel it within your aura. Say out loud or think silently:

Upon my head lies the Crown of Humility. May I serve with honor.

7. Be aware of twelve jewels on the crown, one for each of the twelve points, like the twelve stones of the zodiac (Lesson Four, figure 8) and the breastplate. If your spirit crown is of an organic variety, perhaps the twelve jewels are really twelve colored roses. Think of the blessings and challenges of each of the zodiac signs in order for a moment—Aries, Taurus, Gemini, Cancer, Leo, Virgo, Scorpio, Sagittarius, Capricorn, Aquarius, and Pisces. As you go through the subsequent twelve lessons, you can focus on one stone and sign as you do this ritual.

8. Bring your awareness back to your feet and feel yourself grounded, yet armed with the five powers.

If you have not obtained all five elemental gifts yet, but you want to practice Exercise 30: The Five Gifts, replace the statement for whatever gifts you have not yet received, with "I quest for the (Stone of Sovereignty/Sword of Truth/Cup of Compassion/Spear (Wand) of Victory/Crown of Humility)" at the appropriate point in the meditation.

By focusing on your body and the five elements, you are opening to the crossroads. At the crossroads, no one is alone. It's the nexus of powers coming together, and you might feel the presence of your spiritual guides and helpers—totemic beings, angels, and deities. We have the continual support of the Otherworld when we wield these gifts. I find myself, particularly in ritual, using the plural words we, our, and us rather than I, mine, and me, even when doing ritual "alone," for I have a continual sense of being in the presence of the spirits and working together. The evolution of this sense of self comes with the Crown of Humility, somewhat like the sense of the royal "we," when we are speaking with a larger group in mind, not just speaking for the personal self-interest. Our religion gives us not only the sense of continual support and companionship from the otherworlds, but the possibility of merger with our divinities.

The city of Heliopolis is the Egyptian site of the crown chakra. Heliopolis is the city of the Sun god Ra, the supreme deity of Egyptian cosmology. Not to be confused with a modern suburb of Cairo of the same name, Heliopolis is one of the most ancient cities of Egypt. While it was a major center of Sun worship, and known to the ancient Greeks as the City of the Sun, it was also where grain had been stored in the winter, and it was known as the City of Bread. At one time, it was a center of great learning, only eclipsed later by Alexandria. It is the spiritual "city of the gods," and where one has communion and fellowship with the *neters*, the Egyptian gods.

The last and final gate for the castles of Annwn is Caer Sidi, described as the Castle of the Sidhe, or faery race, the Castle of the Zodiacal Wheel, the Glass Castle, or the Castle of Arianrhod, the Goddess of the Silver Wheel and sister to Gwydion. Some accounts say that Caer Sidi is surrounded by four rings of fire, and in the center is the fountain, well, or cauldron of all knowledge. Through drinking these waters, we have a flow of knowledge, inspiration, and divine power that supports and empowers all that we do. This is the poets' *awen*, the divine inspiration that flows through us as easily as breath.

Caer Sidi is sometimes considered to be a collective term for the seven castles, with the mysterious Caer Wydyr (the Castle of Glass or Castle of Blue) being listed among the caers, though it is unclear if it is a separate castle or a synonym for another one. It is considered the joyous place of the dead, and it is often equated in meaning with Caer Rigor (the Royal Castle) or Caer Fredwyd (the Castle of the Perfected Ones). It is also in the same stanza as Caer Goludd, adding to the confusion. In such lists, Caer Wydyr might be associated with the crown, featuring glass like the dazzling light of the Otherworld, or with our Temple of the Heart, being the fourth caer listed in "The Spoils of Annwn," if you don't count Caer Sidi as an individual stop. If following this heart association, then the remaining castles would be adjusted. Caer Rigor would be associated with the throat, Fredwyd would be the brow, and Pedryfan would be the crown, all enveloped collectively by Caer Sidi. In any case, Caer Sidi is considered to be the ultimate expression of these powers, much like the crown is the ultimate expression of the chakras, containing the potential and patterns of the chakras beneath it.

Once making this connection, a witch can open and close the flow to a certain extent, fueling magickal gifts and inspiration, but it is always available. The flow does not come from up or down, but inward and all around, yet some witches perceive it coming from a direction based upon the nature of the divinities they serve. Those who work with sky gods will feel it more from above, descending down into the crown, while those who work with Underworld gods will feel it rise from below, but truly, it is the unified, connected field of life, surrounding and interpenetrating all things.

One of the blessings and benefits of bringing the initiate into the mysteries, uniting with the gods, is the revelations of the "secret names" of the Goddess and God. Different traditions have different names for the Goddess and God, said to be their "true" names, known only to their special and hidden children. The overt observer would not be able to garner these hidden names. The public images and names of the gods might put off seekers who are faint of heart in order to prevent those who would not respect the traditions. Those who could not get beyond the image of Baphomet (figure 24)—a hermaphroditic and bestial occult guard—as a manifestation of the divine, would fare no better in the inner mysteries. Witchcraft and occultism are not for everybody. The goat head (crowned with a candle), bare breasts, erect posture, and wings—the image is frightening. It plays into our fearful images of the "devil." But in the frightening image of Baphomet is the mystery of paradox, of Goddess and God, male, female, human, animal, flesh, and spirit all in one, as they are in us. The upside-down pentagram that outlines the head of Baphomet, or the horned god—commonly thought of as a Satanic symbol—actually shows the imbalance of the material elements over spirit, and the crisis

Figure 24: Baphomet

of spirit that occurs when we descend to the depths. The mystery play of the Goddess's descent is enacted in the second-degree initiation, and this reversed pentagram is a common symbol for the second degree. The mysteries of Baphomet remind me of one of the names the Feri tradition holds for the divine, "God Herself," which I rather like.

The power of names, magickally, is well known. If you have the true name of someone or something, it is a method of making a deeper connection. Names are used in healing and hexes to make contact. Even gods were said to have secret names, beyond the mundane. One of the most famous tales is of the Egyptian Isis gaining the true and secret name of Ra, the creator god. Ra had been a powerful creator god since the dawn of time, but as he grew older he became enfeebled, and new gods took over the world. Isis saw this as an opportunity to gain greater magickal power. The elder Ra drooled upon the sand. Isis took that fluid from Ra's body, and with the sand she fashioned a serpent. It was made of Ra, so it could hurt Ra, but only Ra could undo it. She hid the serpent on his path and it predictably bit him. Ra didn't recognize the creature as his own, and he didn't recognize his power over it. Isis came to him, promising to cure him of the painful poison, but she could only do that with his true name. After several attempts at keeping his name hidden from her, giving her false names, he gave in to the pain and gave Isis his secret, true name. With it, she had power over creation, just as Ra does. She used it to cure Ra but retained the power of his name, growing to be a mighty magician. The secret name of Amun, another form of the Sun god Ra in the time of Ramesses II, is described in the Papyrus Leiden I: 350 as follows:

One falls down with terror if his ineffable name is spoken.
Not even another god can call him by it,
He whose name is hidden.
Because of this, he is a mystery.

The hidden name gives you the key to the mysteries, and the name of the Goddess and God will naturally reverberate with its essence, bringing you closer. The true sound of creation, the true name of the creative force, Goddess and God, cannot really be comprehended, yet magicians and mystics approximate it with our formulas of OM, AUM, IAO, YHVH, and the hidden name of the Goddess and God.

In initiatory traditions, the use of secret names for the gods is meant to bring one closer to the inner nature of the gods, as interpreted by that tradition. It creates a particular face that works with the members of that lineage. The secret and sacred names would be revealed at various points in the initiation. Particularly prominent in Gardnerianism, a range of variations of the true names is used, changed by some high priests and high priestesses when a set of names is revealed to the public. Many lineage-based traditions have outer-court special names for the gods and inner-court, oath-bound names for the gods. I met a very early-generation Gardnerian priestess, very close to Gardner in the chain of lineage, who said that she would probably fail many modern Gardnerians' "tests" of proof because she did not have what they would deem to be the appropriate secret names.

One of the first revelations came from a book originally published as *The Devil's Prayerbook* by A. Witch and later released as *Rites of Shadow* by E. A. St. George, both potentially revealing a set of Gardnerian names for the Goddess and God, each starting with the letter *z*. Later it was said to be a hoax, with fictional names and rites, to prevent someone else from publishing a real Book of Shadows with the secret names and words.

Non-initiates pore over the writings of Gardnerians and Alexandrians, looking for clues and hidden meaning. Some believe that the names Azarak and Zamilak, found at the end of the Witch's Rune (*OTOW*, chapter 11) are the hidden names, along with the more overt Aradia and Cernunnos. One of the true names of God Herself in the Feri tradition has been publicly revealed: Quakoralina. Some witches claim a lineage of the practice dating back to initiator rites where the secret name would be whispered and imprinted upon the initiate during an act of initiatory sex magick during cave and forest rituals.

So where does this leave the self-initiate seeking the mysteries in a non-lineage-based tradition? Do the secret names of the gods apply to us? Do they serve a purpose? I believe they do. The secret names are a way we forge a personal link to the Great Goddess and Great God, who at heart seem so vast and nebulous. When a name is passed down to us through a lineage, we are inheriting and adding to the link that someone else has forged. When we are solitaries, we must forge that link for ourselves.

You must seek out the Goddess and God and ask them directly. What are their secret, sacred names for you?

EXERCISE 31

Receiving Your Secret Names of the Goddess and God

1. Perform Exercise 1: Inner Temple as a Mystery School Meditation (page 45), steps 1–4, to go to the World Tree.

2. Call out to a trusted guide to take you into the Otherworld.

3. Tell the guide you wish to visit with the Goddess and God, and ask for their secret names. Make sure you explain that you want to experience *the* Goddess and God, not a specific goddess and god from a cultural tradition. The beings you meet might conform to a specific godform, particularly your patrons, but through them will be flowing the powers of the divine all-mother and all-father.

4. Follow the guide to the Goddess and God. Though their manifestations might be familiar, they might not. Go with the experience. Commune with the gods and ask them their secret names. What do they want you to call them? Commit the names to memory. Thank them. Ask what service you can perform as their priest/ess and ask them how, when, and where these names should be used.

5. Return the way you came. Finish exercise 1, steps 8–11, to return to normal consciousness.

The Goddess and God will tell you if you are to keep their names secret. I share my names with my Witchcraft V students, so I've been given permission to share their names here. The knowledge of the names might not be of any use to you, unless you make the connection.

I know the Great Goddess as MachaKali Triformis. She appears to me in the somewhat frightening and nonlinear form of a many-armed, spiderlike triple goddess, phasing in and out of time and continually rotating around. Sometimes I'm swept up into her arms and I rotate with her. Her name is an obvious union of my patron Macha with the Hindu goddess Kali, yet her appearance is not like either of those as portrayed in myth. Other times she has appeared ninefold, not threefold, and she gives me the name Macha-Kali Ennead.

I know the Great God as KerPanAy Apotheosis. He appears to me as a many-horned man, with stag, goat, and bull horns together, and with both flesh and vegetation covering his bones. I infer that this name is a mixture of Cernunnos, the horned hunter stag god, guardian of the gates, and lord of the Underworld, and Pan, the "All" and the horned god of witches and wild things. The union of both, of death and life, and of the two major cultures that have influenced my Craft, Celtic and Greek, has proven powerful for me. He is Apotheosis because he is embodied in the world, both in the flesh and the green, but like us, he is transitory, always shifting shape from one incarnation to the next.

Though they are both very loving, they are vast and, at times, somewhat alien to my human consciousness. At those times, a more specific godform, more comprehensible to me, will appear through them. Yet rituals where they are specifically called upon, or even invoked within me, are extremely powerful and moving. Their names are like my own personal speed dial to the power of the Goddess and God. Names become an important step on the path of relationship with the divine, but through the mysteries we truly learn the universality of deity, not just intellectually, but in our experience.

The final stage of the sevenfold initiatory pattern, according to the Left Hand tradition, is work. Yes, work. Just like after graduation, you are called to use these skills, in your life and your community. Initiates are called to do their spiritual life work, following their true path, adapting and expanding the teachings as only they can, and passing on the experience. Those who experience the vice of this work experience emotional servitude, serving the needs of others without considering their own True Will. They are the people pleasers. Witches seek to be god pleasers, divine pleasers, not people pleasers. The egos of people's wants do not matter compared to your divine work in this lifetime.

Author Kala Trobe has taught me that if you are doing and saying something important, people will not always like, agree with, and accept you. But you are creating change. Change never comes easy, yet change is part and parcel of the way of the witch. Those who develop the virtue of this final stage develop cunning. Many spiritual seekers shy away from cunning, but cunning is a virtue for a witch. We have been the cunning men and cunning women. *Cunning* comes from the Middle English, from the present participle of *can know*, meaning that one who is cunning has special skill or knowledge. Wort cunning is knowledge of the herbs. Cunning refers to one who is dexterous or crafty, who uses his or her skills in attaining an end. Someone who is cunning has keen insight. Sometimes characterized by wiliness and trickery, the cunning one knows that everything is not as it appears.

The process of initiation is not simply sevenfold, but doubled. Inanna enters the gates going down seven levels, meeting seven guardians who instruct her in the mysteries of the Underworld: "The ways of the Underworld are perfect. They may not be questioned." But after learning the mysteries, she had to experience resurrections and climb her way back up through the gates again. The energy flowing down the seven gates and up again reminds me of the illumination process, what the Celtic tradition calls the fire in the head. It leaves the initiate changed, as the flow of awen, of inspiration, takes on incandescent qualities, ignited and fully illuminating the witch or seer.

We have mapped out the process from the bottom up. Your final initiation ritual, at the end of the coming twelve-month cycle of Volume Two, will mirror the descent and rise of Inanna, done ritualistically to clear, energize, and empower all seven centers, crowned by the twelve powers, leaving you ready for your work in the world.

Homework

- Do exercises 26–31 and record your experiences in your journal or BOS.

- Contemplate soul anatomy. What aspects of the soul have you experienced when you look at the various models and traditions? Do you have your own soul cosmology? If so, record your working model in your BOS.

- When you complete the trials of this chapter, tie your seventh knot in your cord in a ritualized manner.

- Obtain a crown, circlet, diadem, tiara, or headdress as your tool of the seventh gate.

• Make sure you have completed the basic requirements of the first seven lessons before you go on to Volume Two.

Tips

• Continue to build an integrated meditation and ritual practice.

• Speak with your Master-Teacher regularly. Build a relationship. Ask your Master-Teacher what lessons you need to learn, and ask to be taught them.

• Perform Exercise 30: The Five Gifts regularly.

• Explore the idea of your true name. Most pagan traditions use initiator names either in honor of a divinity, or names that embody the aspirations of the seeker. They pick a name the evokes the qualities they wish to develop. Beyond the names of aspiration, there is a true name, a soul name, like Ra's secret name of mystery. Many witches discover this true name but, like Ra, are not apt to give it out to others, even covenmates. This name embodies their soul, and might be a name used between the gods and the witch. I know that's the case with my secret name. My mother and my husband know it, and know it only to be able to help me with healing spells. They both used it when I was very sick, and and having my true name made the recovery process go much more smoothly. The true name resonates with your soul as expressed in this lifetime, if not many lifetimes. It can give you clues not to what you aspire to, but who you are and what you are here to do.

• Some traditions, particularly those of the African diaspora, have other initiatory practices of "getting crowned." The initiates might be dedicated to a particular patron goddess, god, or spirit who is said to "rule" their head and guide their lives, offering certain gifts, blessings, and responsibilities, based on the nature of the entity. Others get merged with a totemic spirit of the tradition, linking all initiates and, again, conferring certain powers and possibilities. This "crowning" with the five gifts is the crowning of the higher self, your own divine essence, and it will not preclude work in these other traditions if you so choose. You might perceive your crown being given to you by a patron deity, and the process can forge a stronger relationship with that deity.

Appendix I: Witchcraft V Student Questionnaire

This is a copy of the application questions I ask all my Witchcraft V students to complete before starting the course. Answer these questions before you start Lesson One, and make sure that once you embark upon this course you have the wherewithal to complete it to the best of your ability.

The Witchcraft V application is designed to have you reflect on what you have learned, where you have been, and where you plan to go with your studies. Please answer the following questions as completely as possible. Answers can be very short, or very long, depending on the student. Longer is not necessarily better. The best answers are complete and to the point. Though the questions can seem deceptively easy, they are not. If you complete this application properly, you will be thinking about the bigger picture of your spiritual practice, and your purpose in taking this course. If you cannot answer these questions to your satisfaction, then wait until you can before formally embarking fully upon this course.

1. How do you define the words *witch* and *witchcraft*, both personally and historically?

2. How do you define the word *magick*?

3. Name at least five books that have highly influenced your development in witchcraft spirituality. They don't necessarily have to be specific pagan or witchcraft books, and this list should go beyond the four previous books of the Temple of Witchcraft series. How and why have they influenced you?

4. What cultures, traditions, mythologies, and systems of magick have influenced you and why?

5. Fully describe a profound ritual experience you have had where you have been the ritual leader or one of the ritual leaders. It can be a solitary ritual.

6. Describe a profound meditative experience you have had, guiding yourself through meditation.

7. Describe a divination experience you have had where you have done the divining for someone else.

8. What goddesses or gods do you feel an affinity to? Describe them.

9. Where do you feel the roots of witchcraft come from?

10. Where do you feel the modern Craft is going?

11. How balanced are the five elements, and your shadow self and higher self, within you? Is any one aspect in need of work or healing? What areas of your life are in greatest need of balance and healing? What are you doing now to bring them into balance?

12. Why are you taking the Witchcraft V: The Living Temple of Witchcraft course?

Appendix II: Integrating Meditation and Ritual into a Practice

When embarking upon the path of the high priest/ess, it can be quite difficult to create your own programs of practice if you have not already done so. Through these five levels of training, we learn a wide variety of techniques, meditations, and rituals, and it's hard to know when to use what, how to pace yourself, and when to change. The authority of a teacher, mentor, or even a book, laying out the path, is much easier. But now it is time to be your own teacher and authority.

Training yourself in anything requires a balance between discipline and gentleness. You have to find a middle point between knowing when to challenge yourself and when to be gentle with yourself, not pushing yourself too far too fast. You cannot coddle weakness because you will never grow, yet you cannot be so disciplined that you no longer enjoy life. It's like exercise. You challenge yourself to develop and improve in your sport, but you don't do so much that you constantly injure yourself or lose enjoyment for the game. I like to exercise, lift weights, and do yoga, but I also like the occasional cookie and love ice cream. I don't want to be so disciplined that I live in a world with no ice cream, for I think ice cream is a delight put here by the Goddess and God, yet I know I won't be able to serve them at my best if I'm constantly having ice cream, and the ice cream loses its specialness. We must have moderation in all things, including magick and meditation. Some people lose themselves to magick and never develop healthy life skills.

I suggest a regular magickal practice much like a regular exercise practice. We seem to get benefit from exercise at least three times a week, and I think that is the bare minimum for a magickal practitioner. Honestly, I'm a little more hardcore, and I think it should be daily, or at least six times a week. I know some priestesses who meditate twice a day, morning and night. I sometimes take breaks from my disciplined schedule, but generally I try to meditate six times a week.

You might want to say that integrating magick and spirituality into your everyday life makes you exempt from a regular practice. I'd like to say that. But I've found that in life, the most proficient and wise witches have been those who keep a regular practice. We call it a practice because we develop the skills and learn to bring them into our daily life. If we are not well versed in them, we will not have the skills when we need them most. By all means, use magick and meditation skills throughout the day. Find the magick in your car, office, and kitchen, but if you want to be a high priest/ess, then keep a regular personal practice going.

There are often other daily practices that I must consider a part of my spiritual practice, but they are not a substitution for my witchcraft practices. Regular exercise, be it in the gym or on the yoga mat, was incredibly difficult for me until I framed it as a part of my spiritual practice. I am in a tradition that sees the body as sacred. Better start acting like it. But exercise is not a substitute for ritual and vision working for me.

To begin, note the rituals and exercises that have had the most benefit for you. Look over the previous books and your magickal journal detailing your experiences. This is why it's important to have such journals. What exercises seemed to have the most impact? Which ones still have a strong impact when you do them? Which ones, when done regularly, left you with an overall benefit in daily life, health, creativity, and stress levels? Which ones don't you like, and why? Are you afraid of them? Are they simply not effective for you?

By answering these questions, you will have a good idea of where to begin in building your practice. Don't feel like you have to do everything. And don't feel so locked into a practice that you can't have an open space to do whatever you feel is necessary in the moment. Balance structure and discipline with creativity and spontaneity.

Learn to integrate aspects from all four branches, or learn to focus on one branch at a time. Each of the four branches is associated with an element, and some resonate more with day or evening work. You can focus on a particular branch when that Moon or Sun is in the sign of the corresponding element, or base it on the day of the week. Here is a chart to think about how to orient the rituals from each level into your life.

ITOW	Mornings	Sun/Tues/Thur	Aries, Leo, Sagittarius	Summer
OTOW	Evenings	Fri/Sat	Taurus, Virgo, Capricorn	Winter
TOSW	Evenings	Mon	Cancer, Scorpio, Pisces	Fall
TOHW	Mornings	Wed/Fri	Gemini, Libra, Aquarius	Spring

On the next pages are guidelines for potential practice schedules to aid you in creating your own regular schedule. Focus on the material of each lesson in this nineteen-month course (Volumes One and Two), but try to keep a regular practice and integrate what you already know into the foundation for this course.

EXERCISE
Practice Schedule

Make your own magickal work/play schedule and try integrating it into your life. Find out what works and what doesn't. Are you being too ambitious? You will find out pretty quickly. Is it too easy? Challenge yourself.

Example One

	Monday	Tuesday	Wednesday	Thursday	Friday
Morning	Yoga	Altar Devotional (*OTOW*) LBRP (*TOHW*)	Yoga Body Talking (*TOSW*)	Altar Devotional (*OTOW*) LBRP (*TOHW*)	Yoga
	Bless and charge breakfast, vitamins, teas, and herbs.				
Midday	Bless lunch with banishing pentacle to remove harm, and invoking pentacle to bring healing				
Sunset	Magickal cooking at dinner time—bless the food as it's made. Devotional of thanks to the Goddess and God for food and home.				
Evening	Affirmations (*ITOW*) Earth and Sky Meditation (*ITOW*)	Affirmations (*ITOW*) Chakra or Aura Cleansing (*ITOW*)	OFF	Inner Temple/Guides (*ITOW*) Elemental Meditation (*OTOW*) or Shamanic Journey (*TOSW*) or Qabalistic Pathworking (*TOHW*)	OFF

Example Two

	Monday	Tuesday	Wednesday	Thursday	Friday
Morning	Consecrate Tea Affirmation in *Instant Magick* to Get Parking Space at Office (*ITOW*) Filling Office with Blue Light (*ITOW*)	Consecrate Tea Altar Devotional (*OTOW*)	Consecrate Tea Affirmation in Bathroom Mirror	Consecrate Tea	Talk to Plants When Watering Houseplants
Midday	Occasional afternoon five-minute meditation with colored light (*ITOW*)				
Evening	Altar Devotional (*OTOW*) Sending Light (*ITOW*) Earth and Sky Meditation (*ITOW*) Self-Tarot Reading	OFF	Altar Devotional (*OTOW*) Cleanse with Incense/ Herbs (*TOSW*) Chakra or Aura Cleansing (*ITOW*) Shamanic Journey (*TOSW*)	Altar Devotional (*OTOW*) Elemental Meditation (*OTOW*) Inner Temple/Guides (*ITOW*)	OFF

Example Three

	Monday	Tuesday	Wednesday	Thursday	Friday
Morning	Gym Altar Devotional (*OTOW*) Smudging (*TOSW*) LBRP (*TOHW*)	Gym Altar Devotional (*OTOW*) Smudging (*TOSW*) LBRP (*TOHW*)	Yoga LBRP (*TOHW*)	Gym Altar Devotional (*OTOW*) Smudging (*TOSW*) LBRP (*TOHW*)	Gym Altar Devotional (*OTOW*) Smudging (*TOSW*) OFF
Sunset	—		—		
Evening	Affirmations (*ITOW*) Earth and Sky (*ITOW*) Inner Temple/Guides (*ITOW*) Healing Work	Affirmations (*ITOW*) Earth and Sky (*ITOW*) Chakra/Aura Cleansing (*ITOW*) Sending Light	OFF	Affirmations (*ITOW*) Earth and Sky (*ITOW*) Chakra/Aura Cleansing (*ITOW*) Sending Light	Potential Magick Circle Ritual with Spellcraft, Shamanic Journey, or Freeform Meditation

Example Four

	Monday	Tuesday	Wednesday	Thursday	Friday
Morning	1st Adoration (*TOHW*) LBRP (*TOHW*) Middle Pillar (*TOHW*)	1st Adoration (*TOHW*) LBRP (*TOHW*)	1st Adoration (*TOHW*) LBRP (*TOHW*) Middle Pillar (*TOHW*)	1st Adoration (*TOHW*) LBRP (*TOHW*)	1st Adoration (*TOHW*) LBRP (*TOHW*) Middle Pillar (*TOHW*)
Midday	2nd Adoration (*TOHW*)	2nd Adoration (*TOHW*)	2nd Adoration (*TOHW*)	2nd Adoration (*TOHW*)	2nd Adoration (*TOHW*)
Sunset	3rd Adoration (*TOHW*)	3rd Adoration (*TOHW*)	3rd Adoration (*TOHW*)	3rd Adoration (*TOHW*)	3rd Adoration (*TOHW*)
Evening	Affirmations (*ITOW*) Inner Temple/Guides (*ITOW*) or Goddess/God (*OTOW*) 4th Adoration (*TOHW*)	Sending Light (*ITOW*) 4th Adoration (*TOHW*)	Affirmations (*ITOW*) Shamanic Journey (*TOSW*) or Elemental Meditation (*OTOW*) 4th Adoration (*TOHW*)	Affirmations (*ITOW*) Ritual/Spell Work 4th Adoration (*TOHW*)	Sending Light (*ITOW*) 4th Adoration (*TOHW*)

Appendix III: Teaching the Temple of Witchcraft

The following are my own syllabi for teaching the five levels of witchcraft classes. Though they are designed ideally for a year-and-a-day course of study, doing one lesson per month with appropriate preliminary reading and study, I've found that I'm not always able to teach them in a year format, and due to traveling, I teach them either as seven-week intensives or in a weekend-intensive format. Ideally the student has read the text beforehand and will continue to practice and explore each lesson after the intensive is complete to truly master the material.

WITCHCRAFT I SEVEN-WEEK CLASS SYLLABUS

Required Text: *The Inner Temple of Witchcraft* by Christopher Penczak (Llewellyn, 2002).

Reading: The reading listed in each lesson is for the chapters covered in the actual lesson. If you want to be familiar with the lesson material prior to the lesson, you can read ahead. Some of the chapters appear out of order in an effort to maximize time and topics in a seven-week time frame. Witchcraft I is an intensive consisting of a large amount of information and experiences. Read as much as you can from lesson to lesson, and know that you can use the textbook to refresh yourself on various topics and exercises, during and after the course.

Preliminary Reading: Introduction, Chapter One, Chapter Two

CLASS ONE
Part 1: Introduction and History
Part 2: Energy and Magick
    Exercise: Feeling Energy
    Exercise: Ball of Energy
    Exercise: Feeling the Aura
    Exercise: Pushing and Pulling Energy
Part 3: Meditation
    Exercise: Total Relaxation
    Exercise: Candle Meditation
    Exercise: Counting Down to a Meditative State
    Exercise: Basic Visualization
    Exercise: Affirmations
    Exercise: Programming Your Trigger

Reading: Chapter Three, Chapter Four, Chapter Five, Chapter Six
Homework:
- Practice counting into and out of your meditative state every day.
- Choose or write your affirmations and do daily affirmations, and do them while in a meditative state.

- Bring a natural object of metal, wood, or stone, or a living object like a plant or piece of fruit.
- Think of a place you have never visited, but can easily visit in the next few weeks. Do not visit it, but have a clear idea of the location in your mind.
- Start your Book of Shadows journal, including a traditional journal and a dream journal. Write three pages a day.
- Be aware of your psychic mind and pay attention to your intuition. Follow it. Record it in your journal.

CLASS TWO

Part 1: Magick Theory and Ethics of Magick

> **Exercise:** Mental Projection
>
> **Exercise:** Correspondences
>
> **Exercise:** Vibrational Statements
>
> **Exercise:** Polarity of the Earth and Sky
>
> **Exercise:** Heartbeat Control
>
> **Exercise:** Sun and Moon
>
> **Exercise:** Tree Meditation

Part 2: Psychic Travel

> **Exercise:** Psychic Travel

Reading: Chapter Seven, Chapter Eight, Chapter Twelve

Homework:

- Visit your "target" of psychic travel and evaluate your psychic survey. Look for hits where sections or parts are similar. Don't expect it to be perfect.
- Practice the meditations you have experienced so far, including the affirmations.
- Continue journaling three pages a day. Keep a record of your dreams and meditations.
- Continue to follow your intuition.
- Start the habit of neutralizing harmful, unwanted thoughts and intentions.

CLASS THREE

Part 1: Protection Magick

> **Exercise:** Protection Shield

Part 2: The Power of Light

    Exercise: Showers of Light

    Exercise: Sending Light

Part 3: The Aura

    Exercise: Aura Gazing

Reading: Chapter Nine, Chapter Ten, Chapter Eleven

Homework:

- Check in with the person to whom you sent pink light, and the place where you sent blue light. Are there changes?
- Practice your meditations. A good session would include the earth and sky meditation, reaffirming your protection shield and sending light to yourself and others. Don't forget your affirmations. Continue to cleanse the aura every few days/weeks as needed.
- Place a protection shield around your home and your vehicle.
- Continue journaling three pages a day. Keep a record of your dreams and meditations.
- Continue to follow your intuition.

CLASS FOUR

Part 1: Spirit Guides and Indirect Contact: Muscle Testing, Pendulum, Automatic Writing

    Exercise: Pendulum

    Exercise: Muscle Testing

Part 2: The Inner Temple and Direct Spirit Contact

    Exercise: Visiting the Inner Temple

Reading: Chapter Thirteen, Chapter Fourteen

Homework:

- Bring the name, age, and city of residence of three people you know who are medically diagnosed with an illness. Fill out the sheet describing their illnesses. Be as complete as possible. Do not share this information with the class.
- Practice your meditations. Involve working with your spirit guides and visiting your inner temple. Try to visit your inner temple at least once a week.

- Continue journaling three pages a day. Keep a record of your dreams and meditations.
- Continue to follow your intuition.

CLASS FIVE
Part 1: The Chakras and Energy Healing
> **Exercise:** Aura Clearing
> **Exercise:** Chakra Opening and Balancing

Part 2: Psychic Healing and Diagnosis
> **Exercise:** Psychic Scanning
> **Exercise:** Healing Case

Reading: Chapter Fifteen, review Chapter Eleven
Homework:

- Get feedback on your health cases.
- Practice your meditations. Add the chakras to your earth and sky meditation. Continue to work with affirmations, sending light and a protection shield. If there are meditations you are having difficulty with, focus on them. If certain meditations work effectively for you, focus on them as well.
- Continue journaling three pages a day. Keep a record of your dreams and meditations.
- Continue to follow your intuition.
- Bring a small quartz crystal to be used as a past-life recording crystal (optional).

CLASS SIX
Part 1: Past Lives and Karma
Part 2: Exploration
> **Exercise:** Past-Life Exploration

Reading: Chapter Sixteen
Homework:

- Complete the self-test. Bring any questions you have not had answered.
- Meditate on a witch name.

- Bring your intention statement from the first class.
- Bring a small token or offering for the ritual, such as a flower, stone, candle, small piece of cake, chocolate, honey, a small amount of an herb, incense, or a piece of paper with your intention on it.
- Dress in black for the next class. Dress warmly as we might go outside, weather permitting.
- Bring a blindfold to be used for the shamanic journey.
- Practice your meditations. Visit your inner temple at least once a week. Ask your guides if you have any past-life connection with them.
- Continue journaling three pages a day. Keep a record of your dreams and meditations.
- Continue to follow your intuition.

CLASS SEVEN

Part 1: Shamanic Witchcraft

Part 2: Initiation Closing Ritual

Part 3: Discussion, Questions, the Broom Closet, and Maintaining a Practice

Reading: Chapter Seventeen, review Chapter Twelve

WITCHCRAFT I WEEKEND INTENSIVE CLASS SYLLABUS

Time	Day One	Day Two
10 AM	Introductions to the Craft Definitions, History, Intention	The Inner Temple **Ex:** Visiting the Inner Temple
11 AM	Altered Consciousness and Meditation **Ex:** Candle Meditation **Ex:** Counting Down to a Meditative State **Ex:** Basic Visualization **Ex:** Affirmations **Ex:** Programming Your Trigger **Ex:** Orange (Conjuring on Mental Screen)	
12 PM	Magick Theory, Holograms, and Hermetics **Ex:** Polarity of the Earth and Sky **Ex:** Mental Projection **Ex:** Sun and Moon	Past-Life Regression
1 PM	LUNCH	LUNCH
2 PM	Energy Work, Auras **Ex:** Aura Gazing **Ex:** Sending Light	Healing and Chakras **Ex:** Aura Clearing **Ex:** Chakra Opening and Balancing
3 PM		
3:30 PM	Protection Magick and Shielding	Health Cases
4 PM		
4:30 PM	Soul Travel and Projection	
5 PM		Shamanic Witchcraft **Ex:** Initiation Closing Ritual
5:30 PM	Spirit Guide Introduction	

Homework: Visit your travel target, bring in health cases

WITCHCRAFT II SEVEN-WEEK CLASS SYLLABUS

Required Text: The Outer Temple of Witchcraft by Christopher Penczak (Llewellyn, 2004).

Reading: The reading listed in each lesson is for the chapters covered in the actual lesson. If you want to be familiar with the lesson material prior to the lesson, you can read ahead. Some of the chapters appear out of order in an effort to maximize time and topics in a seven-week time frame. Witchcraft II is an intensive consisting of a large amount of information and experiences. Read as much as you can from lesson to lesson, and know that you can use the textbook to refresh yourself on various topics and exercises, during and after the course.

Preliminary Reading: Introduction, Chapter One, Chapter Two, Chapter Three

CLASS ONE
Part 1: Priestess/Priest, Divinity, and Magick
> **Exercise**: The Circle of Protection

Part 2: God and Goddess of the Witches
> **Exercise**: Meditation with the Goddess and God

Part 3: Introduction to the Elements
> **Exercise**: Elemental Cleansing Meditation

Reading: Chapter Four, Chapter Five, Chapter Six
Homework:

- Pick a mythic culture to study, such as Celtic, Greek, Roman, Norse, or Egyptian. Learn about the various goddesses and gods from that culture. Look into that culture's creation story. If you met a specific goddess or god in your meditation, focus on that direction. You can repeat that meditation and request a specific god or goddess you have read about.

- Practice skills from Witchcraft I, and experiment with the energies of the four elements. Later, learn how to not only invoke the four elements in your own body, but to invoke them into others for healing and balance.

- Start thinking about wands and other ritual tools. You can skip ahead to Lesson Three for ideas.

CLASS TWO

Part 1 & 2: The Four Elements

> **Exercise:** Journey to the Realm of Fire
>
> **Exercise:** Journeying to the Realm of Air
>
> **Exercise:** Journeying to the Realm of Water
>
> **Exercise:** Journeying to the Realm of Earth

Part 3: Spirit: The Fifth Element

> **Exercise:** Spirit Meditation

Reading: Chapter Seven, Chapter Eight

Homework:

- Bring an object that has some history to it, family history or otherwise, for the psychometry lesson.
- Bring a list of questions about your personal life that you would like answered for the divination lesson.
- If you have a favorite divination tool that you are proficient in using, such as tarot, feel free to bring it.
- Elemental checklist. In your Book of Shadows, answer these questions regarding the balance of elements in your life.

  > **Earth:** How are your physical health, exercise, and eating habits? How do you feel about your home environment? Does it grant you harmony? What is your relationship with money? Do you have enough resources, or do you need or want more? Why? What isn't being fulfilled?
  >
  > **Air:** How is your mental clarity, focus, memory, and sense of peace?
  >
  > **Water:** How is your emotional health? Are you in touch with all your emotions? When was the last time you cried openly, and why?
  >
  > **Fire:** What is your energy level like? Do you have enough? What is your passion?
  >
  > **Spirit:** How is your spiritual health and balance?

- Get "in tune" with the four elements physically. Pick one element per week, and spend time with the physical manifestation, as discussed in the lesson. Spend time on the ground, in the woods, or with stones and crystals for earth. Spend time in or

near lakes, streams, rivers, or the ocean for water. Spend time outside in the wind or around incense for air. Spend time before a campfire or several candles for fire.
- Practice traveling to the four elemental realms and deepening your experience with the elemental beings.
- Continue to study a cultural mythology.

CLASS THREE
Part 1: Ritual Tools
Part 2: Elemental Gateways
      Exercise: Opening Elemental Gateways
Part 3: Divination
      Exercise: Divination

Reading: Chapter Nine, Chapter Ten
Homework:
- Read Lesson Four.
- Cleanse and bless your home using the cleansing techniques.
- Write an altar devotional and try to practice it daily.
- Pick a divination tool, such as tarot or runes, and make it a part of your altar devotional.
- Write four quarter calls, and practice opening and closing elemental gateways.
- Continue your elemental attunements with your second element.
- Start gathering your altar tools. Most importantly, obtain or craft a wand before the last class and bring it to class.
- Continue to study a cultural mythology.

CLASS FOUR
Part 1: Sacred Space and the Magick Circle
Part 2: Writing Spells and Magickal Timing
Part 3: Casting the Magick Circle and Spell Work

Reading: Chapter Eleven, Chapter Twelve
Homework:
- Record your first spell in your Book of Shadows.
- Write your own magick circle ritual, using your previously written quarter calls.

- Continue to gather your altar tools and build your altar. If you have not brought your wand to class to be charged, bring it before the course is over.
- Bring a small bottle to contain some protection potion. If you don't have one, one will be provided.
- Get an astrological calendar and look it over. See if you can determine the phases and signs of the Moon and any other astrological information that will be helpful for your spells.
- Start to memorize the basic meaning of the planets and signs. Start notating the Moon sign in your journal, and notice how the energy affects you personally.
- Continue your elemental attunements with your third element.
- Continue to study a cultural mythology.

CLASS FIVE

Part 1: Natural Magick and Candle Magick
Part 2: Herbal Magick and Potions
Part 3: Ritual and Spell Work

Reading: Chapter Thirteen
Homework:

- Record your candle spell in your Book of Shadows.
- Pick five magickal herbs. Get to know them. Research them. Meditate with them. Learn the botanical, medical, and folk information on them. Record your findings in your Book of Shadows.
- Create your own formula for a potion.
- Continue to gather your altar tools and build your altar. If you have not brought your wand to class to be charged, bring it before the course is over.
- Continue your elemental attunements with your fourth element.
- Continue to study a cultural mythology.

CLASS SIX

Part 1: Symbol Magick
Part 2: Charm and Crystal Magick
Part 3: Ritual and Spell Work

Reading: Reread Chapter Thirteen
Homework:

- Record your charm spell or symbol in your Book of Shadows.
- Complete the self-test at the end, and come with any questions you need answered.
- *Write out*, to turn in, a complete magick circle ritual, and be prepared to discuss it in class. If possible, perform the circle before class, and record your experiences in your Book of Shadows.
- Pick five crystals or minerals. Get to know them. Research them. Meditate with them. Learn the folklore and history, as well as the geological information. Record your findings in your Book of Shadows.
- Like the elemental attunements, learn to attune to the Sun and Moon, simply focusing your attention and awareness on each.
- Continue to study a cultural mythology.

CLASS SEVEN

Part 1: Wheel of the Year Rituals and Being Your Own Priestess or Priest
Part 2: Questions and Self-Test
Part 3: Closing Ritual and Initiation into Becoming Your Own Priestess/Priest

Reading: Chapter Fourteen, Chapter Fifteen, Chapter Sixteen, Chapter Seventeen
Further Study:

- Be fluent and comfortable with circle magick.
- Celebrate each Moon with a magick circle.
- Celebrate the Wheel of the Year holidays.
- Write at least one Wheel of the Year ritual and perform it, alone or in a group.
- Create your own spells and magickal formulas, and keep track of your successes and mistakes.
- Continue to study a cultural mythology. Perhaps a particular goddess or god has struck you as personally important to your path, or stuck out as a potential patron deity. Work with that deity in your meditations and rituals.
- Continue mastering a divination tool or skill. Use divination prior to casting spells and when you seek guidance in your life.

WITCHCRAFT II WEEKEND INTENSIVE CLASS SYLLABUS

Time	Day One	Day Two
10 AM	Priestess, Priest, Divinity, and Magick **Ex:** The Circle of Protection	Sacred Space and the Magick Circle Creating Elemental Gateways
11 AM	God and Goddess of the Witches **Ex:** Meditation with the Goddess and God	
12 PM	Introduction to the Elements **Ex:** Elemental Cleansing Meditation	
1 PM	LUNCH	LUNCH
2 PM	The Four Elements **Ex:** Journey to the Realm of Fire **Ex:** Journeying to the Realm of Air **Ex:** Journeying to the Realm of Water **Ex:** Journeying to the Realm of Earth	Spellcraft Petitions and Candles Natural Magick Charms Symbols
3 PM		Divination **Ex:** Divination
4 PM		The Wheel of the Year
5 PM	Ritual Tools and the Altar	Closing Ritual and Initiation

WITCHCRAFT III SEVEN-WEEK CLASS SYLLABUS

Required Text: *The Temple of Shamanic Witchcraft* by Christopher Penczak (Llewellyn, 2005).

Reading: The reading listed in each lesson is for the chapters covered in the actual lesson. If you want to be familiar with the lesson material prior to the lesson, you can read ahead. Some of the chapters appear out of order in an effort to maximize time and topics in a seven-week time frame. Witchcraft III is an intensive consisting of a large amount of information and experiences. Read as much as you can from lesson to lesson, and know that you can use the textbook to refresh yourself on various topics and exercises, during and after the course. Lessons in parentheses ( ) indicate a chapter that can be reviewed for the current class.

Preliminary Reading: Introduction, Chapter One, Chapter Two, Chapter Three

CLASS ONE
Part 1: Witchcraft, Shamanism, and the Shadow
    Exercise: Tree Breathing
    Exercise: Meditation on the Dark
    Exercise: Distilling the Shadow
    Exercise: Emotional Body Training
Part 2: Dream Magick
Part 3: Middle World Earth Connection
    Exercise: Earth Mother Journey

Reading: Chapter Four, Chapter Five, Chapter Ten, Chapter Six, Chapter Fifteen
Homework:
- Distilling the shadow—every day.
- Keep a dream journal, and look for parallels in dreams with shamanic journeys.
- Practice tree breathing.
- Practice basic meditation skills from Witchcraft I.
- Go on a quest in a wooded area or park, to look for your own World Tree. Using your intuition, find a tree that calls to you, and meditate with it, either hugging it, or sitting with your back against the trunk.

- Start researching a second pantheon of mythic deities. Choose a culture whose shamanic traditions call to you. Pick a god or goddess from that culture, and write a 500–1,000 word paper discussing and describing that deity by the last class of Witchcraft III.
- Specifically, research earth and fertility goddesses from your chosen pantheon.
- Bring a blindfold to all the remaining classes if that aids your shamanic journey work.

CLASS TWO

Part 1: Tools of Shamanism
      Exercise: Building Your Own Witch Bag
Part 2: Power Songs and Sacred Sound
      Exercise: Sacred Sound
Part 3: Journeying Basics and Spirit Allies
      Exercise: Speaking to Another's Spirit Guides
      Exercise: Lower World Journey to Meet a Power Animal

Reading: (Chapter Six), Chapter Seven, Chapter Nine
Homework:
- Distilling the shadow—every day.
- Keep a dream journal, and look for parallels in dreams with shamanic journeys.
- Practice tree breathing.
- Start building your shamanic pouch and tools.
- Journey to find a power word or song for yourself.
- Research your power animal and meditate or journey with it. Look for material about the animal in your chosen pantheon's myths. Learn to send it out into the waking world.
- Research sky gods and goddesses from your chosen pantheon.
- Start your elemental journeys at home. Choose the element that is easiest or hardest for you to master, and journey to that realm, similar to Witchcraft II, but using shamanic techniques.

CLASS THREE

Part 1: Higher Self Connection
      Exercise: Upper World Journey
      Exercise: Higher-Self Connection

Part 2: Shapeshifting
    Exercise: Shapeshifting Journey
Part 3: Advanced Shapeshifting
    Exercise: Upper World Energy

Reading: Chapter Eight
Homework:

- Read Lesson Four. Research a God or Goddess you would choose to work with during the invocation exercise.
- Distilling the shadow—every day.
- Keep a dream journal, and look for parallels in dreams with shamanic journeys.
- Make a list of all the people you have unresolved issues with, both living and dead. Pick one, and do an act of dream magick, or lucid dreaming, writing out a question regarding how you can resolve your issues with this person. Keep the written question under your pillow and use the dream techniques (Lesson One) to receive your answer. Perhaps the dream itself will be the resolution.
- Practice tree breathing.
- Practice shapeshifting, both through meditation/journey—and in the quiet moments of your waking life.
- Start building an active relationship with your higher self. Check in when you need guidance, both through everyday experiences and deep meditation. Listen closely and follow the voice of your own soul.

CLASS FOUR

Part 1: Invocation
    Exercise: Invocation
Part 2: Past-Life Healing
    Exercise: Ritual to Revoke Past-Life Contracts
    Exercise: Healing Past-Life Regression

Reading: (Chapter Nine), Chapter Fourteen
Homework:

- Distilling the shadow—every day.
- Keep a dream journal, and look for parallels in dreams with shamanic journeys.

- Practice tree breathing.
- Research and meditate with several plant and animal spirits to understand their medicine. Seek out allies in the other worlds to be your "team."
- Complete your second elemental journey.

CLASS FIVE
Part 1: Shamanic Healing, Surgery, and Energy Work
    Exercise: Hands-on Healing
Part 2: Shamanic Healing and Spirit Medicine
    Exercise: Spirit Body Journey
    Exercise: Animal Spirit Medicine Retrieval Journey *or* Plant Spirit Medicine Retrieval Journey *or* Stone Spirit Medicine Retrieval Journey (partnered exercises)

Reading: Chapter Twelve, Chapter Thirteen, (Chapter Fifteen)
Homework:
- Distilling the shadow—every day.
- Keep a dream journal, and look for parallels in dreams with shamanic journeys.
- Practice tree breathing.
- Make a list of all the major illness and injuries you have had in life, and all recurring illnesses. Meditate on the sickness spirit of each, and try to find an unbalanced physical, emotional, mental, or spiritual pattern at the root. Journey to speak with sickness spirits and learn their teachings.
- Research the dark gods and goddesses in your chosen pantheon.
- Complete your third elemental journey.
- If you desire, create a healing chamber and work with your team of healing guides.

CLASS SIX
Exercise: Animal, Plant, or Stone Spirit Medicine Retrieval Journey (if necessary)
Part 1: Middle World Healing Journeys (Distant Shamanic Healing)
    Exercise: Distant Spirit Medicine Retrieval
    Exercise: Cosmic River and Witch Star Journey
Part 2: Meeting the Underworld Goddess
    Exercise: Journey to the Dark Goddess/God

Part 3: Soul Sickness
    Exercise: Soul Retrieval

Reading: (Chapter Fifteen), Chapter Sixteen
Homework:
- Distilling the shadow—every day. Bring in all your pages and notes to the last class.
- Keep a dream journal, and look for parallels in dreams with shamanic journeys.
- Try an act of dream magick if you have not done so already.
- Reflect on the role of the dark goddess and shadow in your life.
- Reflect on the meaning or event surrounding your soul loss.
- Complete your fourth elemental journey.
- Your god/goddess paper is due next class.

CLASS SEVEN
Part 1: The Gift of Shadow
    Exercise: Shadow Initiation
Part 2: Questions and Discussion

Reading: Chapter Seventeen, Chapter Eleven

WITCHCRAFT III WEEKEND INTENSIVE CLASS SYLLABUS

Time	Day One	Day Two
10 AM	Witchcraft and Shamanism Shamanic Cosmology	Shamanic Healing **Ex:** Speaking to Another's Guide **Ex:** Spirit Body Journey
11 AM	The Three Souls **Ex:** Tree Breathing	Medicine Allies—Animal, Plant, Stone **Ex:** Animal, Plant, or Stone Spirit Medicine Retrieval Journey (partnered exercise)
12 PM	Journeying Basics and Spirit Allies **Ex:** Lower World Journey to Meet a Power Animal	Tools of Shamanism **Ex:** Building Your Own Witch Bag
1 PM	LUNCH	LUNCH
2 PM	The Middle World **Ex:** Earth Mother Journey **Ex:** Invocation	Shapeshifting and Invocation **Ex:** Shapeshifting Journey
3 PM	The Underworld **Ex:** Lower World Journey	Soul Sickness **Ex:** Soul Retrieval
4 PM	The Upper World	The Gift of Shadow **Ex:** Distilling the Shadow (explain) **Ex:** Emotional Body Training
5 PM	Dream Magick	Underworld Goddess Ritual **Ex:** Journey to the Dark Goddess/God

The Witchcraft III Weekend Intensive is followed by an optional apprenticeship period for guidance and support in the process of distilling and facing the shadow.

WITCHCRAFT IV SEVEN-WEEK CLASS SYLLABUS

Required Text: *The Temple of High Witchcraft* by Christopher Penczak (Llewellyn, 2007).

Reading: The reading listed in each lesson is for the chapters covered in the actual lesson. If you want to be familiar with the lesson material prior to the lesson, you can read ahead. Some of the chapters appear out of order in an effort to maximize time and topics in a seven-week time frame. Witchcraft IV is an intensive consisting of a large amount of information and experiences. Read as much as you can from lesson to lesson, and know that you can use the textbook to refresh yourself on various topics and exercises, during and after the course. Lessons in parentheses ( ) indicate a chapter that can be reviewed for the current class.

Preliminary Reading: Introduction, Chapter One, Chapter Two, Chapter Three, Chapter Four

CLASS ONE
Part 1: Witchcraft and Ceremonial Magick
>   Witchcraft as High Magick
>   Magician—Air—Thought and Creativity

Part 2: Reality Maps and the Qabalah
>   Reality Maps
>   The Qabalah: The Tree of Life and the Four Worlds
>   Creating Your Own Reality Map
>   Sephira: Malkuth
>   Tarot Paths

Part 3: Earth
>   Elemental Rulers and Gifts
>   First World: Earth
>   Earth: Sovereignty and Protection
>>   Elemental Breathing—Earth Breath
>>   The Elemental Gifts: The Stone / Shield / Coin

Exercise: Malkuth Pathworking

Exercise: Elemental Earth Journey Seeking the Stone of Sovereignty

Reading:

Chapter Five, Chapter Six

Homework:

- Reflect on your views of reality and your magickal experiences. Think about what correspondences, symbols, and cultures are important to your magick.
- Notice your breathing patterns, and try to correct any uncomfortable or unhealthy breathing patterns.
- Do something to reflect your greater mastery over the earth element.

CLASS TWO

Part 1: Air and Hod

    Second World: Air

    Air: The Mind, Communication, Creation, and Understanding

        Breathing Exercises

        Elemental Breathing—Air Breath

        The Elemental Gifts: The Sword

    Sephira: Hod

    Exercise: Hod Pathworking

    Exercise: Elemental Air Journey Seeking the Sword of Truth

Part 2: Magickal Song and Story, Part 1

Part 3: Deconstructing the LBRP

    Lesser Banishing Ritual of the Pentagram (LBRP)

    Exercise: Lesser Banishing Ritual of the Pentagram (LBRP)

Reading:

Chapter Eight, (Chapter Four, Chapter Six)

Homework:

- Practice the earth and air breaths.

- Create and practice your own version of the LBRP, or learn and practice a traditional form. If creating your own, write it out and have a copy to turn in by the end of the course.
- Write or prepare a magickal story/song/poem/chant to share with class next week. You can create something completely new, or learn and retell an existing myth in your own words. In either case, it should have a mythic theme or be spiritually focused. Use your magick, your sense of energy, ritual, drama and spirit to make it a magickal experience for yourself and your audience.
- Do something to prove your greater mastery over the element of air and the Sword of Truth. Conjure a wind on a calm day. Give a speech in public. Be honest and truthful with a loved one. Find what seems most difficult for you, and do it.

CLASS THREE

Part 1: Water and Yesod

    Third World: Water

    Water: Compassion, Love, and Emotion

        Elemental Breathing—Water Breath

        The Elemental Gifts: The Chalice/Grail/Cauldron

    Sephira: Yesod

    Exercise: Yesod Pathworking

    Exercise: Elemental Water Journey Seeking the Cup of Compassion

Part 2: Magickal Storytelling, Part 2

Part 3: Qabalah and the Middle Pillar

    The Middle Pillar

    Exercise: Middle Pillar

Reading:

Chapter Seven

Homework:

- Create your own Middle Pillar–style ceremony and practice it, or learn one of the examples given in the lesson and practice it. Write it out and have a copy to turn in.
- Do something to prove your greater mastery over the water element.

- Practice the earth, air, and water breaths.
- Continue to practice your banishing ritual.
- Start thinking about your reality map. Meditate upon the symbols and information that are important to you. Ask for divine help and guidance.

CLASS FOUR

Finish Magickal Stories If Needed

Part 1: Fire

    Fourth World: Fire

    Fire: Will and Passion

        Elemental Breathing—Fire Breath

        The Elemental Gifts: The Wand/Staff/Spear

    Sephira: Netzach

    Exercise: Netzach Pathworking

    Exercise: Elemental Fire Journey Seeking the Spear of Victory

Part 2: Tiphereth, Divine Alchemy, and the Higher Self

    Sephira: Tiphereth

    Divine Alchemy

    Exercise: Tiphereth Pathworking

Part 3: Qabalah and the Light Body

    Circulation of the Body of Light

    Exercise: Circulation of the Body of Light

Reading:

Chapter Nine, Chapter Ten

Homework:

- Practice the earth, water, air, and fire breaths.
- Do something to prove your greater mastery over the fire element.
- Practice the Circulation of the Body of Light exercise.
- Continue practicing your banishing and Middle Pillar–style rituals.
- If you have not done so already, start organizing your thoughts and ideas to create your own reality map. Make lists of various correspondences, such as archetypes, animals, planets, and elements, and begin to arrange and organize them in a way

that is helpful to you. **Do not expect your reality map to be as complicated or complex as the Qabalah.**

CLASS FIVE
Complete Any Magickal Storytelling
Part 1: Spirit

> Beyond the Veil: Spirit
>
> Spirit
>
> > Elemental Breathing—All

Part 2: Geburah and the Reverse of the Tree of Life

> Sephira: Geburah
>
> The Reverse of the Tree of Life
>
> **Exercise:** Geburah Pathworking

Part 3: Four Adorations

> **Exercise:** Four Adorations

Reading:
Chapter Eleven, Chapter Thirteen

Homework:

• Practice all five elemental breaths in the order of earth, water, fire, air, and spirit.

• Continue working on your reality map. Ask for help if you are stuck. Consult with peers to see what they are doing. Tap into your inner creativity. Don't leave it all for the last week!

• Create your own Four Adorations ritual and practice it. Note how you feel in your magickal journal as your practice develops. Do the rituals change your affinity for the cycles of the day?

• Continue practicing your banishing, Middle Pillar, and Circulation of the Body of Light–style rituals.

CLASS SIX
Part 1: The Qabalah: Chesed

> Sephira: Chesed
>
> **Exercise:** Chesed Pathworking

Part 2: Creating Sacred Space and Qabalistic Magick

    Creating Sacred Space

    Qabalistic Magick

    Servitor Spirits and Constructs

Part 3: Discussion and Questions about Other Reality Maps

Reading:

Chapter Twelve

Homework:

- Complete your reality map and be prepared to present the basics of it for class. Have a copy to hand in.
- Continue practicing your banishing, Middle Pillar, Body of Light, and Four Adorations–style rituals.

CLASS SEVEN

Part 1: The Supernal Triangle and Knowledge and Conversation of the Holy Guardian Angel

    Supernal Triangle

    Sephira: Binah

    Sephira: Chokmah

    Sephira: Kether

    How to Do Pathworkings for Transformation

    Exercise: Binah Pathworking

    Exercise: Chokmah Pathworking

    Exercise: Kether Pathworking

Part 2: Presentation of Reality Maps

Reading: Chapter Fourteen, Chapter Fifteen, Chapter Sixteen, Chapter Seventeen

WITCHCRAFT IV WEEKEND INTENSIVE CLASS SYLLABUS

Time	Day One	Day Two
10 AM	Witchcraft and Ceremonial Magick High Magick vs. Low Magick Magician—Air—Thought and Creativity	Sephira: Hod Air: Communication and Truth The Elemental Gifts: The Sword **Ex:** Hod Pathworking **Ex:** Elemental Air Journey Seeking the Sword of Truth
11 AM	Reality Maps and the Qabalah The Tree of Life and Four Worlds Planetary Spheres and Tarot Paths	Sephira: Netzach Fire: Will and Passion The Elemental Gifts: The Spear **Ex:** Netzach Pathworking **Ex:** Elemental Fire Journey Seeking the Spear of Victory
12 PM	Sephira: Malkuth Elemental Rulers and Gifts Earth: Sovereignty and Protection The Elemental Gifts: The Stone **Ex:** Malkuth Pathworking **Ex:** Elemental Earth Journey Seeking the Stone of Sovereignty	Sephira: Tiphereth Spirit: Knowledge and Conversation with Your HGA **Ex:** Tiphereth Pathworking
1 PM	LUNCH	LUNCH
2 PM	Sephira: Yesod Water: Love and Emotion The Elemental Gifts: The Chalice **Ex:** Yesod Pathworking **Ex:** Elemental Water Journey Seeking the Cup of Compassion	Qabalistic Magick Servitor Spirits Fluid Condensers

3 PM		Ethical Triangle Sephiroth: Tiphereth, Geburah, and Chesed
4 PM	LBRP and Deconstructing the LBRP **Ex:** Lesser Banishing Ritual of the Pentagram How to do Pathworkings	Supernal Triangle Sephiroth: Binah, Chokmah, and Kether
5 PM	The Middle Pillar and Deconstruction **Ex:** Middle Pillar Circulation of the Body of Light **Ex:** Circulation of the Body of Light	Climbing the Tree of Life **Ex:** Climbing the Tree of Life Pathworking Ritual

The Witchcraft IV Weekend Intensive is followed by an optional apprenticeship period for guidance and support in the process of Deconstructing the Ritual of Ceremonial Magick and Making Your Reality Map.

WITCHCRAFT V SEVEN-WEEK, PLUS THIRTEEN MONTHLY CLASSES, SYLLABUS

Required Text: The Living Temple of Witchcraft, Volumes One and Two, by Christopher Penczak (Llewellyn, 2008 and 2009).

Reading: The reading listed in each lesson is for the chapters covered in the actual lesson. If you want to be familiar with the lesson material prior to the lesson, you can read ahead. Witchcraft V is an intensive consisting of a large amount of information and experiences. Read as much as you can from lesson to lesson, and know that you can use the textbook to refresh yourself on various topics and exercises, during and after the course.

Preliminary Reading: Introduction, The Seven Gates of the Goddess

CLASS ONE
Part 1: Introduction to the Temples of Initiation

    High Priest/Priestess

        What Does It Mean to Be a High Priestess or High Priest?

        What Does It Mean to Live a Magickal Life?

    Witchcraft as a Mystery School

    Common Points of the Mystery School

        Purification, Altered State, True Nature of the Universe, Higher Will

    The Places of Initiation Are Within

    The Seven Chakras as Seven Temples of Initiation

Part 2: Temple of the Root Chakra—Survival and Origin

    Exercise: Contemplation on the Temple of the Root

    Physical Origin

    Exercise: Inner Temple as a Mystery School Meditation

    Exercise: Skeleton Meditation

    Spiritual Origin

    Great Ages and the New Age

    Root Races and Soul Families

The Ancient Ones
The Story of the Great Ages
Exercise: Exploring Your Spiritual Origin in the Great Ages
Entering the New Age
Integrating Meditation and Ritual into a Practice

Reading: Lesson One

Homework:

- **Exercise:** Create a ritual that you can do daily to center yourself in your magickal life. Use tools from Witchcraft I, II, III, and IV. You can use material from your altar devotionals; basic meditation skills; shamanic breathing, centering, and smudging; the LBRP; and the Four Adorations. Practice it daily. Be prepared to share the basic idea with the class.
- Reflect on the role of a High Priestess/High Priest.
- Reflect on the Great Ages and Root Races. How do they frame the journey of your soul?

CLASS TWO

Part 1: Temple of the Belly Chakra—Society and Relationships
    Exercise: Contemplation on the Temple of the Belly
    Exercise: Seven-Body Healing
Part 2: Master-Teachers
    Exercise: Finding Your Master-Teacher
Part 3: Genetic Past-Life Memory
    Exercise: Ancestral Womb

Reading: Lesson Two

Homework:

- Daily grounding and centering meditation.
- Speak with your Master-Teacher regularly. Build a relationship.
- Reflect on your fears. Make a list of all your fears, resolved and unresolved.

CLASS THREE

Part 1: Temple of the Solar Plexus Chakra—Power and Fear

Self-Image—Astral Body

Exercise: Contemplation of the Solar Plexus

Exercise: Going Beyond Limits

Part 2: True Power and True Reality. What Are Your Limits?

List of Common Magickal/Shamanic/Power Experiences Pointing the Way to True Reality

Part 3: Shamanic Death and Initiation

Exercise: Facing Your Death

Reading: Lesson Three

Homework:

• Daily grounding and centering meditation.

• Speak with your Master-Teacher regularly. Build a relationship.

• If possible, physically confront the fears faced in your shamanic death initiation.

• When did you first realize that magick and mysticism were "real?" Describe your experience and write about it.

CLASS FOUR

Part 1: Temple of the Heart Chakra—Love and Balance

Exercise: Contemplation of the Heart Chakra

Balancing the Elements: The Inner Selves

Exercise: The Balanced Heart

Part 2: Healing Others

Exercise: Overshadowing with Your Healing Guide

Part 3: Peace through Perfect Love and Perfect Trust

Exercise: Gateway of Perfect Love

Reading: Lesson Four

Homework:

• Daily grounding and centering meditation.

• Speak with your Master-Teacher regularly. Build a relationship.

- Contemplate peace through Perfect Love and Perfect Trust. Do you have a sense of peace in your life? Do you live through Perfect Love and Perfect Trust? If not, why not?
- Write out a healing experience you have had helping another—formally or informally. If you have not done healing work with another, seek out someone and describe that experience.

CLASS FIVE
Part 1: Temple of the Throat Chakra—Expression and Listening
    Exercise: Contemplation of the Throat Chakra
    Teaching Witchcraft, Magick, and Healing
    Exercise: Class with Your Master-Teacher
Part 2: Self-Communication
    Exercise: Time of Silence

Reading: Lesson Five
Homework:
- Daily grounding and centering meditation.
- Speak with your Master-Teacher regularly. Build a relationship. Ask your Master-Teacher what lessons you need to learn, and ask to be taught them.
- Design a Basic Teaching Outline. If someone came to you and said, "Teach me witchcraft," what would you do? Where would you start? What would you prepare? Prepare notes for at least three meetings.

CLASS SIX
Part 1: Temple of the Third-Eye Chakra—Seeing and Knowing
    Psychic Vision
    Exercise: Contemplation of the Brow Chakra
    Exercise: Initiation of the Third Eye
    Exercise: Reading the Akashic Records
Part 2: Karma, Dharma, and Purpose
    Exercise: Gateway of Purpose

Reading: Lesson Six

Homework:
- Bring a blindfold.
- Reflect on your spiritual truth.
- Reflect on experiences in your current life or past lives that you consider traumatic, such as abuses, anger, abandonment, injury, fear, and shock.
- Daily grounding and centering meditation.
- Speak with your Master-Teacher regularly. Build a relationship.
- Make a list of all the aspects of psychic work that a high priestess or high priest should be familiar with. Are you familiar with these things? If not, rank them in order of importance and become familiar with them. Have you experienced any of them? Reflect.
- Bring all assignments due.
    Description of when you knew magick and mysticism were real.
    Description of healing experience.
    Basic teaching outline for at least three classes.
    List of all aspects of psychic work for a high priestess or high priest.

CLASS SEVEN

Part 1: Temple of the Crown Chakra—Union with Spirit
    Exercise: Contemplation of the Crown Chakra
    Spiritual Laws
    Exercise: What Are Your Own Spiritual Laws?
    The Diamond of Divinity
    Exercise: Create a modern pantheon of gods and goddesses.
Part 2: Soul Retrieval
    Spiritual Anatomy: Parts of the Soul
    Exercise: Soul Retrieval
Part 3: Initiation and the Year-and-a-Day Quest
    Initiation
    Year-and-a-Day Quest
    Make Your Goals
    Master Spell

Reading: Lesson Seven

Homework:

- Make your **modern pantheon list**, and begin to actively work with these gods and goddesses through meditation, prayer, and ritual. Bring this list to turn in at the next class.
- Make your **year-and-a-day quest** list, and be ready to turn it in at the next class.
- Daily grounding and centering meditation. Integrate magick, meditation, and ritual into your life.
- Speak with your Master-Teacher regularly. Build a relationship.
- Start your **master spell** for personal transformation. This spell will be done over five to thirteen Moons, and the objective is to create a personal transformation to fulfill your own spiritual awareness and growth, based upon the life lessons you feel you are experiencing in this Earthwalk.
- Seek out a student and teach at least one class. It can be formal or informal. It can be historical and educational, personal, or practical. If the student desires to learn more than the one class, continue as far as you feel comfortable. Not everyone is meant to be a teacher, but everyone should have some practical experience if it is needed at a later date.
- Seek out healing experiences, formally or informally. Work with others through education and philosophy, energy work, or ritual. You don't have to take a formal client, but look for opportunities to heal both yourself and others. Not everyone is meant to be a healer, but everyone should have some practical experience if it is needed at a later date.
- Prepare your presentations for the year-and-a-day study.

    1) **Magick circle**: You will be required to lead a magick circle ritual of no more than thirty minutes in length. You must make sure you have all ritual tools you need for it. The ritual can have any theme, mythology, magick, or meditations you desire. You may do it completely alone, or ask members of the class to take roles in it. You may memorize it or read it from your notes. The only requirements are that it must be some form of the traditional witch's magick circle and you must be completely responsible for its execution.

    2) **Religious survey**: Present one religious tradition or spiritual path that will be chosen for you in a five-to-fifteen-minute presentation. Create a one- to three-

page fact sheet on the tradition, including a short list of names, dates, beliefs, or texts that are important in that faith. Have copies for everyone in the class.

3) **Mythological survey**: Present one myth of the gods or goddesses, from one of a list of preapproved cultures, and tell that story to the class is a two- to ten-minute presentation. You should pick deities from your working pantheon.

4) **Biography**: Present to the class a short biography on a major figure in the modern witchcraft movement. Mention this figure's history, tradition, and contributions to the Craft.

Research for steps 2–4 must come from classical sources and printed books. The Internet can be used to supplement your research, but it cannot be your sole source of information.

- **Final project:** Create a final project to be completed by the end of the year study group. Your final project can be any major task associated with the Craft. It is based upon your goals and interests, and limited only by the bounds of your own creativity. It can be a written research paper, artwork, music, a new ritual design, seeing a healing client on a regular basis, teaching on a regular basis, certification in a healing art, or learning an in-depth tool such as tarot. Follow your own calling.

WITCHCRAFT V YEAR-AND-A-DAY STUDY

Attend monthly three-hour meetings for twelve months. In each meeting, we will spend the first hour in discussion on the spiritual themes and lessons of the zodiac sign the Sun currently occupies, as outlined in the text, including the labors of Hercules, Gifts of the Witch, and other topics as presented by the group. In the second hour, three different students will give presentations. One will present on a mythology of a goddess or god. One will give an overview of a world religion in relationship to how its theology and practice are different from or similar to witchcraft. One will present a short biography on a figure in the history of modern witchcraft. The last hour of the meeting will be devoted to a magick circle ritual written and led by another student. Duties of the students will rotate in a manner that is fair and equitable, depending on the size of the class.

The thirteenth and final meeting will consist of a short presentation of the final projects of each student, and after a short break, it will be followed by the final group initiation ritual descending through the seven gates and the thirteen zodiac lessons.

WITCHCRAFT V WEEKEND INTENSIVE CLASS SYLLABUS

Time	Day One	Day Two
10 AM	The Temples of Initiation High Priest/Priestess Witchcraft as a Mystery School The Places of Initiation Are Within The Chakras as Temples of Initiation	Temple of the Heart Chakra Love and Balance Balancing the Inner Elements **Ex:** The Balanced Heart **Ex:** Overshadowing with Your Healing Guide
11 AM	Temple of the Root Chakra Survival and Origin **Ex:** Inner Temple as a Mystery School **Ex:** Skeleton Meditation	Temple of the Throat Chakra Expression and Listening Teaching Witchcraft, Magick, and Healing **Ex:** Class with Your Master-Teacher
12 PM	Spiritual Origin Great Ages and the New Age Root Races and Soul Families **Ex:** Exploring Your Spiritual Origin in the Great Ages	Temple of the Third-Eye Chakra Seeing and Knowing Psychic Vision **Ex:** Initiation of the Third Eye **Ex:** Reading the Akashic Records
1 PM	LUNCH	
2 PM	Temple of the Belly Chakra Society and Relationships **Ex:** Seven-Body Healing	LUNCH
3 PM	Master-Teachers **Ex:** Finding Your Master-Teacher Genetic Past-Life Memory **Ex:** Ancestral Womb	Karma, Dharma, Wyrd, and Purpose **Ex:** Opening the Gateway of Purpose
4 PM	Temple of the Solar Plexus Chakra Power and Fear Self-Image—Astral Body **Ex:** Going Beyond Limits	Temple of the Crown Chakra Union with Spirit

5 PM   Shamanic Death and Initiation   Soul Anatomy
            Ex: Facing Your Death   **Ex:** Soul Retrieval

The Witchcraft V Weekend Intensive will be followed by a year-long apprenticeship where the student will be responsible for Lessons Eight through Eighteen in Volume Two, including twelve different rituals, biographies, religious studies, and mythology studies. The thirteenth lesson will be completed solitary or in a group ritual, and it will include a review of the final project and the final group initiation ritual descending through the seven gates and the thirteen zodiac lessons.

Appendix IV: The Old Laws

Here is a version of the "Old Laws" or Ardanes of Wicca, as proposed by Gerald Gardner in the 1950s as traditional material. In their original form, they were fairly difficult to read, and have been divided into 161 "laws" for better comprehension, though some of the "laws" appear fragmentary or are not really laws, but statements. A frequent criticism was the general familiarity with the Ten Commandments and a need to form the laws into something more easily recognizable. The 161 Rules of the Witch were popularized by Lady Sheba. Though she claimed them from her grandmother, most believe they were plagiarized from a Gardnerian or Alexandrian Book of Shadows.

They are included for educational and historical purposes only. I do not endorse these laws, personally follow them, or encourage my own students, covenmates, or tradition-mates to follow them. I only believe that they are important to know in a historic context for modern Wicca, and as points to inspire our own ethical and moral codes and group rules.

1. The Law was made and ordained of old.

2. The Law was made for the Wicca, to advise and help in their troubles.

3. The Wicca should give due worship to the gods and obey their will, which they ordain, for it was made for the good of Wicca as the worship of the Wicca is good for the gods. For the gods love the brethren of Wicca.

4. As a man loveth a woman by mastering her,

5. So should the Wicca love the gods by being mastered by them.

6. And it is necessary that the Circle which is the temple of the gods, should be truly cast and purified. And that it may be a fit place for the gods to enter.

7. And the Wicca shall be properly prepared and purified to enter into the presence of the gods.

8. With love and worship in their hearts, they shall raise power from their bodies to give power to the gods.

9. As has been taught of old.

10. For in this way only may men have communion with the gods, for the gods cannot help man without the help of man.

High Priestess and High Priest

11. And the High Priestess shall rule her coven as the representative of the Goddess.

12. And the High Priest shall support her as the representative of the God.

13. And the High Priestess shall choose whom she will, be he of sufficient rank, to be her High Priest.

14. For, as the God Himself kissed Her feet in the five-fold salute, laying His power at the feet of the Goddess because of Her youth and beauty, Her sweetness and kindness, Her wisdom and justice, Her humility and generosity,

15. So He resigned all His power to Her.

16. But the High Priestess should ever mind that the power comes from Him.

17. It is only lent, to be used wisely and justly.

18. And the greatest virtue of a High Priestess be that she recognize that youth is necessary to the representative of the Goddess.

19. So she will gracefully retire in favor of a younger woman should the Coven so decide in council.

20. For a true High Priestess realizes that gracefully surrendering pride of place is one of the greatest virtues.

21. And that thereby she will return to that pride of place in another life, with greater power and beauty.

Security

22. In the old days, when witchdom extended far, we were free and worshipped in all the greater temples.

23. But in these unhappy times we must celebrate our sacred mysteries in secret.

24. So be it ordained that none but the Wicca may see our mysteries, for our enemies are many and torture loosens the tongue of man.

25. So be it ordained that no Coven shall know where the next Coven bide.

26. Or who its members be, save only the Priest and Priestess and messenger.

27. And there shall be no communication between them, save by the messenger of the gods, or the summoner.

28. And only if it be safe may the Covens meet in some safe place for the great festivals.

29. And while there, none shall say whence they came nor give their true names.

30. To this end, that if any be tortured, in their agony, they may not tell if they do not know.

31. So be it ordained that no one shall tell anyone not of the craft who be of the Wicca, nor give any names or where they bide, or in any way tell anything which can betray any of us to our foes.

32. Nor may he tell where the Covendom be.

33. Or the Covenstead.

34. Or where the meetings be.

35. And if any break these Laws, even under torture, THE CURSE OF THE GODDESS SHALL BE UPON THEM, so they may never be reborn on earth and may remain where they belong, in the hell of the Christians.

DISPUTES

36. Let each High Priestess govern her Coven with justice and love, with the help and advice of the High Priest and the Elders, always heeding the advice of the Messenger of the Gods if he cometh.

37. She will heed all complaints of all Brothers and strive to settle all differences among them.

38. But it must be recognized that there will always be people who will ever strive to force others to do as they will.

39. These are not necessarily evil.

40. And they oft have good ideas and such ideas should be talked over in council.

41. But if they will not agree with their Brothers, or if they say,

42. "I will not work under this High Priestess,"

43. It hath ever been the Old Law to be convenient to the Brethren and to avoid disputes.

NEW COVENS

44. Any of the third may claim to found a new Coven because they live over a league away from the Covenstead or are about to do so.

45. Anyone living within the Covendom and wishing to form a new Coven shall tell the Elders of their intention, and on the instant avoid their dwelling and remove to the new Covendom.

46. Members of the old Coven may join the new one when it is formed. But if they do, they must utterly avoid the old Coven.

47. The Elders of the new and old Covens should meet in peace and brotherly love to decide the new boundaries.

48. Those of the craft who dwell outside both Covendoms may join either but not both.

49. Though all may, if the Elders agree, meet for the great festivals if it be truly in peace and brotherly love,

50. But splitting the Coven often means strife, so for this reason these Laws were made of old and may the CURSE OF THE GODDESS BE ON ANY WHO DISREGARD THEM. So be it ordained.

GRIMOIRE

51. If you would keep a book, let it be in your own hand of write. Let brothers and sisters copy what they will, but never let the book out of your hands, and never keep the writings of another.

52. For if it be found in their hand of write, they may be taken and arraigned.

53. Let each guard his own writings and destroy them whenever danger threatens.

54. Learn as much as you may by heart and, when danger is past, rewrite your book, an it be safe.

55. For this reason, if any die, destroy their book an they have not been able to.

56. For, an it be found, 'tis clear proof against them.

57. And our oppressors know well "Ye may not be a witch alone."

58. So all their kin and friends be in danger of torture,

59. So destroy everything not necessary.

60. If your book be found on you, 'tis clear proof against you alone, you may be arraigned.

Persecutions

61. Keep all thoughts of the craft from your mind.

62. If the torture be too great to bear, say "I will confess. I cannot bear this torture. What do you want me to say?"

63. If they try to make you speak of the Brotherhood, do not.

64. But if they try to make you speak of impossibilities such as flying through the air, consorting with a Christian devil or sacrificing children, or eating men's flesh,

65. To obtain relief from torture say "I had an evil dream, I was beside myself, I was crazed."

66. Not all magistrates are bad, if there be an excuse, they may show mercy.

67. If you have confessed aught, deny it afterwards, say you babbled under torture, say you knew not what you said.

68. If you are condemned, fear not.

69. The Brotherhood is powerful and will help you to escape if you stand steadfast, but if you betray aught there is no hope for you in this life or in that to come.

70. Be sure, if steadfast you go to the pyre, drugs will reach you, you will feel naught. You go to death and what lies beyond, the ecstasy of the goddess.

Tools

71. To avoid discovery, let the working tools be as ordinary things that any may have in their houses.

72. Let the pentacles be of wax so that they may be broken at once or melted.

73. Have no sword unless your rank allows it.

74. Have no names or signs on anything.

75. Write the names and signs on them in ink before consecrating them and wash it off immediately afterwards.

76. Let the colours of the hilts tell which is which.

77. Do not engrave them lest they cause discovery.

Conduct

78. Ever remember ye are the hidden children of the Goddess so never do anything to disgrace them or Her.

79. Never boast, never threaten, never say you would wish ill of anyone.

80. If any person not in the Circle, speak of the craft, say, "Speak not to me of such, it frightens me, 'tis evil luck to speak of it."

81. For this reason, the Christians have their spies everywhere. These speak as if they were well affected to us, as if they would come to our meetings, saying, "My mother used to worship the Old Ones. I would I could go myself."

82. To such as these, ever deny all knowledge.

83. But to others, ever say, "'Tis foolish men talk of witches flying through the air. To do so they must be as light as thistledown. And men say that witches all be blear-eyed old crones, so what pleasure can there be at a witch meeting such as folks talk on?"

84. And say, "Many wise men now say there be no such creatures."

85. Ever make it jest, and in some future time perhaps, the persecution may die and we may worship our gods in safety again.

86. Let us all pray for that happy day.

87. May the blessings of the Goddess and God be on all who keep these Laws which are ordained.

VALUABLES

88. If the craft hath any appanage, let all guard it and help to keep it clear and good for the craft.

89. And let all justly guard all monies of the craft.

90. And if any Brother truly wrought it, 'tis right they have their pay, an it be just. An this be not taking money for the art, but for good and honest work.

91. And even the Christians say, "The labourer is worthy of his hire," but if any Brother work willingly for the good of the craft without pay, 'tis but to their greater honour. So be it ordained.

QUARRELS

92. If there be any dispute or quarrel among the Brethren, the High Priestess shall straightly convene the Elders and inquire into the matter, and they shall hear both sides, first alone and then together.

93. And they shall decide justly, not favouring one side or the other.

94. Ever recognising there be people who can never agree to work under others.

95. But at the same time, there be some people who cannot rule justly.

96. To those who must ever be chief, there is one answer.

97. "'Void the Coven or seek another one, or make a Coven of your own, taking with you those who will go."

98. To those who cannot rule justly, the answer be, "Those who cannot bear your rule will leave you."

99. For none may come to meetings with those with whom they are at variance.

100. So, an either cannot agree, get hence, for the craft must ever survive. So be it ordained.

CURSES

101. In the olden days when we had power, we could use the art against any who ill-treated the Brotherhood. But in these evil days we must not do so. For our enemies have devised a burning pit of everlasting fire into which

they say their god casteth all the people who worship him, except it be the very few who are released by their priest's spells and masses. And this be chiefly by giving monies and rich gifts to receive his favour for their great god is ever in need of money.

102. But as our gods need our aid to make fertility for man and crops, so is the god of the Christians ever in need of man's help to search out and destroy us. Their priests ever tell them that any who get our help are damned to this hell forever, so men be mad with the terror of it.

103. But they make men believe that they may escape this hell if they give victims to the tormentors. So for this reason all be forever spying, thinking, "An I can catch but one of these Wicca, I will escape from this fiery pit."

104. So for this reason we have our hidels, and men searching long and not finding, say, "There be none, or if there be, they be in a far country."

105. But when one of our oppressors die, or even be sick, ever is the cry, "This be witches' malice," and the hunt is up again. And though they slay ten of their own to one of ours, still they care not. They have countless thousands.

106. While we are few indeed. So be it ordained.

107. That none shall use the art in any way to do ill to any.

108. However much they may injure us, harm none. And nowtimes many believe we exist not.

109. That this Law shall ever continue to help us in our plight, no one, however great an injury or injustice they receive, may use the art in any way to do ill, or harm any. But they may, after great consultations with all, use the art to restrain Christians from harming us Brothers, but only to constrain them and never to punish.

110. To this end men will say, "Such a one is a mighty searcher out, and a persecutor of old women whom they deemeth to be witches, and none hath

done him harm, so it be proof that they cannot or more truly there be none."

111. For all know full well that so many folk have died because someone had a grudge against them, or were persecuted because they had money or goods to seize, or because they had none to bribe the searchers. And many have died because they were scolding old women. So much that men now say that only old women are witches.

112. And this be to our advantage and turns suspicion away from us.

113. In England and Scotland 'tis now many a year since a witch hath died the death. But any misuse of the power might raise the persecution again.

114. So never break this Law, however much you are tempted, and never consent to its being broken in the least.

115. If you know it is being broken, you must work strongly against it.

116. And any High Priestess or High Priest who consents to its breach must immediately be deposed for 'tis the blood of the Brethren they endanger.

117. Do good, an it be safe, and only if it be safe.

118. And keep strictly to the Old Law.

PAYMENT

119. Never accept money for the use of the art, for money ever smeareth the taker. 'Tis sorcerers and conjurers and the priests of the Christians who ever accept money for the use of their arts. And they sell pardons to let men escape from their sins.

120. Be not as these. If you accept no money, you will be free from temptation to use the art for evil causes.

121. All may use the art for their own advantage or for the advantage of the craft only if you are sure you harm none.

122. But ever let the Coven debate this at length. Only if all are satisfied that none may be harmed, may the art be used.

123. If it is not possible to achieve your ends one way, perchance the aim may be achieved by acting in a different way so as to harm none. MAY THE CURSE OF THE GODDESS BE ON ANY WHO BREAKETH THIS LAW. So be it ordained.

124. 'Tis judged lawful if ever any of the craft need a house or land and none will sell, to incline the owner's mind so as to be willing to sell, provided it harmeth him not in any way and the full price is paid without haggling.

125. Never bargain or cheapen anything whilst you buy by the art. So be it ordained.

LAW OF THE LAND

126. 'Tis the Old Law and the most important of all laws, that no one may do anything which will endanger any of the craft, or bring them into contact with the law of the land or any persecutors.

127. In any dispute between Brethren, no one may invoke any laws but those of the craft.

128. Or any tribunal but that of the Priestess, Priest and Elders.

DISCUSSION OF WITCHCRAFT

129. It is not forbidden to say as Christians do, "There be witchcraft in the land," because our oppressors of old make it a heresy not to believe in witchcraft and so a crime to deny it which thereby puts you under suspicion.

130. But ever say, "I know not of it here, perchance there may be but afar off, I know not where."

131. But ever speak of them as old crones, consorting with the devil and riding through the air.

132. And ever say, "But how may many ride the air if they be not as light as thistledown."

133. But the curse of the Goddess be on any who cast suspicion on any of the Brotherhood.

134. Or who speak of any real meeting-place or where they bide.

Wortcunning

135. Let the craft keep books with the names of all herbs which are good, and all cures so all may learn.

136. But keep another book with all the Bales and Apies and let only the Elders and other trustworthy people have this knowledge. So be it ordained.

137. And may the blessings of the gods be on all who keep these Laws, and the curses of both the God and the Goddess be on all who break them.

Use of the Art

138. Remember the art is the secret of the gods and may only be used in earnest and never for show or vainglory.

139. Magicians and Christians may taunt us saying, "You have no power, show us your power. Do magic before our eyes, then only will we believe," seeking to cause us to betray the art before them.

140. Heed them not, for the art is holy and may only be used in need, and the curse of the gods be on any who break this Law.

RESIGNATIONS

141. It ever be the way with women and with men also, that they ever seek new love.

142. Nor should we reprove them for this.

143. But it may be found a disadvantage to the craft.

144. And so many a time it has happened that a High Priest or a High Priestess, impelled by love, hath departed with their love. That is, they left the Coven.

145. Now if the High Priestess wishes to resign, she may do so in full Coven.

146. And this resignation is valid.

147. But if they should run off without resigning, who may know if they may not return in a few months?

148. So the Law is, if a High Priestess leaves her Coven, she be taken back and all be as before.

149. Meanwhile, if she has a deputy, that deputy shall act as High Priestess for as long as the High Priestess is away.

150. If she returns not at the end of a year and a day, then shall the Coven elect a new High Priestess,

151. Unless there is a good reason to the contrary.

152. The person who has done the work should reap the benefit of the reward. If somebody else is elected, the deputy is made maiden and deputy of the High Priestess.

TRAINING

153. It has been found that practicing the art doth cause a fondness between aspirant and tutor, and it is the cause of better results if this be so.

154. And if for any reason this be undesirable, it can easily be avoided by both persons from the outset firmly resolving in their minds to be as brother and sister or parent and child.

155. And it is for this reason that a man may be taught only by a woman and a woman by a man, and women and women should not attempt these practices together. So be it ordained.

PUNISHMENT

156. Order and discipline must be kept.

157. A High Priestess or a High Priest may, and should, punish all faults.

158. To this end all the craft must receive correction willingly.

159. All properly prepared, the culprit kneeling should be told his fault and his sentence pronounced.

160. Punishment should be followed by something amusing.

161. The culprit must acknowledge the justice of the punishment by kissing the hand on receiving sentence and again thanking for punishment received. So be it ordained.

Author Rhiannon Ryall, in her book *Weaving A Web of Magic*, quotes from a fragmentary book known as *MacGregors of Appin Book of Wisdom*. The family owners of this book claim ancient lineage, but it has now been lost or mislain, and such claims have not been substantiated. If true, perhaps this is the source of both the Ardanes and much of the ethics of British Traditional Wicca as cited by Gardnerians and Alexandrians. I certainly have my doubts about anything claiming such a history, and even Ryall, who presents it, is uncertain if it is a "genuine fragment of the past" or not. Even if the document is fairly old, its roots may still be drawn from the Christian, not a pre-Christian era. In either case, they provide some interesting insights and an opportunity to think about your own moral structure and personal "laws." At the very least, they are a whole lot simpler than the previous 161, and they sum up much of the ideas found within the longer version.

The Laws

Here be the Laws: The Law was ordained of Old:

1. Treat others as you desire to be treated. Speak them fair. Kind words are as Pearls. Evil words are Swords.

2. Should another do you wickedness, do not seek revenge or return evil for evil. That which you do wrong destroys Spirit. If others do you wrong, they will pay the price. For...

3. The Evil you do another rebounds upon you threefold.

4. Never use your knowledge selfishly—for material gain, sex or to harm another. Use it for the help and good of all.

5. If by an action of yours, another is seriously harmed—beware—if you are not repaid for your crime in this life, it will be thrice in the next.

6. Never accept money for using your Art. Money often smears the character. You are but "human." You may be weak, and become corrupt and take more than you can give.

7. Never threaten. Never say you will ill of anyone.

8. Animals and birds are our brothers. Do not abuse them: even plants are living things. Kill only for food or in self-defense: not for "sport."

9. Should you receive many unexpected gifts, money or great crops or other good things; share with another, for the law saeth, "Give that ye may receive." Should you become selfish or grasping, you will find your ability to "receive" will become less.

10. If another should use the Craft to do you harm, it is lawful to "reverse the flow," this and this only. Do not seek further (extra) revenge from spite. Nor is it lawful to cast a curse.

11. You "own" nothing: All you have is "lent." Knowledge is your only true possession. Use it wisely and justly. It is all you take with you from life to life. The material possessions become the property of another. Your physical body eventually becomes nothing.

12. Do not try to impress others with your knowledge. Most are not ready. They will think you boast or are mad. You know what you know. You can do what you can do. Why need tell another? Discussion between trusted friends is permissible.

13. Do nothing you know to be wrong; others may consider you wise and good. If you know yourself to be weak and evil (though none other may know) you will grow to hate and despise yourself.

Another lesser-known book, called *The Devil's Prayerbook*, by A. Witch, is believed to be one of the first publications of "secret" Gardnerian material, has the Words of the Mighty Ones. These guidelines resonate with me far more than the more commonly known Ardanes.

The Words of the Mighty Ones

Keep your silence amidst the noise of the world, for there is my peace in that silence.

Keep peace between yourself and other beings and listen to all men. Even the ignorant among mankind may perceive a truth you do not see. Surrender not your spirit to any other, yet seek not battle but rather seek to avoid those people who trouble your spirit and spread vexation about them.

Seek not ambition too closely, for the most humble work must also be done and properly done, this pleases the Lord and Lady.

Those of the Craft are as your brothers.

Speak not of the Craft to the outsider for the world is plagued with misunderstanding. But remember that the world also has its virtues and ideals, and its people have their right also to seek for Deity.

Strive to be gentle and understanding with your fellow men and be tolerant of their motions, even if you do not understand them.

Regard the passing of the years without despair. Surrender the things of youth without sorrow, for age shall bring you deeper wisdom and greater understanding. Study, then, the secret way and cultivate the spiritual strength to shield you in unexpected misfortune.

Seek not to harm your own body, nor the body of any man or woman or child or animal, for all bodies are made of the substance of the earth and you shall not harm the earth mother. Therefore be gentle with yourself, for you are a child of the God and the Goddess. Therefore care for your body, keeping it clean and healthy.

Disgrace not the Craft before your fellow men and bring not disrepute upon its followers.

Remember that you have walked this world before and shall walk it again in time. You may fill this world with broken dreams and sadness and these shall stay with you for many lives. Yet this world is beautiful, though you are blind to its beauty.

Therefore be careful. Seek and be happy. Blessed be.

Appendix V: The Principles of Wiccan Belief

Established by the Council of American Witches.

Introduction: In seeking to be inclusive, we do not wish to open ourselves to the destruction of our group by those on self-serving power trips, or to philosophies and practices contradictory to those principles. In seeking to exclude those whose ways are contradictory to ours, we do not want to deny participation with us to any who are sincerely interested in our knowledge and beliefs, regardless of race, color, sex, age, national or cultural origins, or sexual preference.

Principles of the Wiccan Belief:

1. We practice rites to attune ourselves with the natural rhythm of life forces marked by the phases of the Moon and the seasonal Quarters and Cross Quarters.

2. We recognize that our intelligence gives us a unique responsibility towards our environment. We seek to live in harmony with Nature, in ecological

balance offering fulfillment to life and consciousness within an evolutionary concept.

3. We acknowledge a depth of power far greater than that apparent to the average person. Because it is far greater than ordinary it is sometimes called *"supernatural,"* but we see it as lying within that which is naturally potential to all.

4. We conceive of the Creative Power in the universe as manifesting through polarity—as masculine and feminine—and that this same Creative Power lies in all people, and functions through the interaction of the masculine and feminine. We value neither above the other, knowing each to be supportive of the other. We value sex as pleasure, as the symbol and embodiment of life, and as one of the sources of energies used in magickal practice and religious worship.

5. We recognize both outer and inner, or psychological, worlds—sometimes known as the Spiritual World, the Collective Unconscious, Inner Planes, etc.—and we see in the interaction of these two dimensions the basis for paranormal phenomena and magickal exercises. We neglect neither dimension for the other, seeing both as necessary for our fulfillment.

6. We do not recognize any authoritarian hierarchy, but do honor those who teach, respect those who share their greater knowledge and wisdom, and acknowledge those who have courageously given of themselves in leadership.

7. We see religion, magick and wisdom-in-living as being united in the way one views the world and lives within it—a world view and philosophy of life which we identify as *Witchcraft, the Wiccan Way.*

8. Calling oneself "Witch" does not make a Witch—but neither does heredity itself, nor the collecting of titles, degrees and initiations. A Witch seeks to control the forces within her/himself that make life possible in order to live wisely and well without harm to others and in harmony with Nature.

9. We believe in the affirmation and fulfillment of life in a continuation of evolution and development of consciousness, that gives meaning to the Universe we know, and our personal role within it.

10. Our only animosity toward Christianity, or toward any other religion or philosophy of life, is to the extent that its institutions have claimed to be "the only way," and have sought to deny freedom to others and to suppress other ways of religious practice and belief.

11. As American Witches, we are not threatened by debates on the history of the Craft, the origins of various terms, the origins of various aspects of different traditions. We are concerned with our present and our future.

12. We do not accept the concept of absolute evil, nor do we worship any entity known as "Satan" or "the Devil," as defined by Christian tradition. We do not seek power through the suffering of others, nor do we accept that personal benefit can be derived only by denial to another.

13. We believe that we should seek within Nature that which is contributory to our health and well-being.

Appendix VI: Self-Evaluation

Next to each skill or quality, rate your proficiency in the subject as good, fair, or difficult.

	Good	Fair	Difficult
Meditation	☐	☐	☐
Journeying	☐	☐	☐
Spirit Work	☐	☐	☐
Daily Practice	☐	☐	☐
Personal Development	☐	☐	☐
Personal Understanding and Mastery	☐	☐	☐
Living with Integrity	☐	☐	☐
Healing	☐	☐	☐
Psychic Ability	☐	☐	☐
Divination	☐	☐	☐

	Good	Fair	Difficult
Ritual Skills	☐	☐	☐
Spells and Manifestation	☐	☐	☐
Natural Craft—Herbs and Crystals	☐	☐	☐
Wheel of the Year Celebrations	☐	☐	☐
History and Written Knowledge	☐	☐	☐
Working Alone	☐	☐	☐
Working with Others	☐	☐	☐

What must you do to expand those skills and qualities labeled as difficult?

Review the five elemental levels of training.

	Good	Fair	Difficult
ITOW—Witchcraft I—Fire—Personal Power	☐	☐	☐
OTOW—Witchcraft II—Earth—Sacred Space / Manifestation	☐	☐	☐
TOSW—Witchcraft III—Water—Emotional Healing	☐	☐	☐
TOHW—Witchcraft IV—Air—Knowledge	☐	☐	☐
LTOW—Witchcraft V—Spirit—Initiation	☐	☐	☐

What chakra temples are your weak areas?	Good	Fair	Difficult
I—Root Chakra: Survival and Origin	☐	☐	☐
II—Belly Chakra: Purification and Relationship	☐	☐	☐
III—Solar Plexus Chakra: Power and Fear	☐	☐	☐
IV—Heart Chakra: Love and Balance	☐	☐	☐
V—Throat Chakra: Communication and Teaching	☐	☐	☐
VI—Brow Chakra: Vision and Knowing	☐	☐	☐
VII—Crown Chakra: Union with Spirit	☐	☐	☐

Have you completed the goals of Witchcraft V, as a mystery school?	YES	NO
1) Are you able to induce a trance state easily in yourself?	☐	☐
2) Are you able to purify the body, mind, emotions, and spirit?	☐	☐
3) Do you understand the true nature of the universe better?	☐	☐
4) Are you able to contact your higher will / higher self?	☐	☐

Do you live a magickal life? If not, why not?

What do you feel is left unfinished for you to do to consider yourself a high priestess or high priest?

Appendix VII: Wiccan Wisdom Teachings

In several versions of the British Traditional Wiccan Book of Shadows, there is a section known as "Wisdom Teachings" or "Various Aphorisms." This is a collection of folk sayings. Some seem to fit quite well with traditional Wiccan teachings, while others are less clear. Over the years, many witches have added to and subtracted from the teachings, but these are some of the ones most popularly handed down. For those looking for commentary and study on these sayings, I suggest *The Witch's Guide to Life* by Kala Trobe.

For witches this be Law,
Where ye enter in, from there withdraw.

An ye will secure the spell,
Cast some silver in the well.

Enhance thy trance,
With drug and dance.

Vervain and dill lend aid to will.

Trefoil, vervain, St.-John's-wort, dill,
Hinder witches of their will!

Upon the clock, dependeth not.

Success pursueth the persistent.

Guilt flees when none pursueth.

Power shared is power lost.

Seek thine enemy in secret.

Thoughts are things: as a man thinkest, so he is.

No one person can accomplish all.

Danger is never overcome without danger.

The past is fixed, yet the future may be bent.

Where communication fails, confusion follows.

Some things cannot be understood by mortal man. Many such must simply be accepted.

Rush in where angels fear to tread: the Gods are with you.

As a man thinketh, so is he. If you think small, you become small.

Remember the Passwords: Perfect Love and Perfect Trust, so trust the Universe and be at Home everywhere.

If you imagine and fear "I will get trapped," of course you will get trapped. Fear not, and you won't.

You are never less alone than when you think you are alone.

Fear not, for fear is failure and the forerunner of failure.

Pray to the Moon when she is round,
Luck with you shall then abound,
What you seek for shall be found,
In sea or sky or solid ground.

Bibliography

Agnese, Giorgio, and Maurizio Re. *Ancient Egypt: Art and Archaeology of the Land of the Pharaohs*. New York: Barnes and Noble, 2001.

Andrews, Shirley. *Atlantis: Insights from a Lost Civilization*. St. Paul, MN: Llewellyn Publications, 1997.

———. *Lemuria and Atlantis: Studying the Past to Survive the Future*. St. Paul, MN: Llewellyn Publications, 2004.

Bach, Eleanor. *Astrology from A to Z: An Illustrated Source Book*. New York: M. Evans and Company, Inc., 1990.

Bailey, Alice A. *Esoteric Astrology, Vol. 3*. New York: Lucis, 1976.

Bartlett, Robert Allen. *Real Alchemy: A Primer of Practical Alchemy*. N.p.: Quinquangle Press, 2006.

Bromwich, Rachel, ed. *Trioedd Ynys Prydein*. Rev. ed. Cardiff, Wales, UK: University of Wales Press, 1991.

Bruyere, Rosalyn L. *Wheels of Light: Chakras, Auras, and the Healing Energy of the Body.* New York: Fireside Publishing, 1989.

Budapest, Zsuzsanna E. *Summoning the Fates: A Guide to Destiny and Sacred Transformation.* Woodbury, MN: Llewellyn Publications, 2007.

Cabot, Laurie, with Tom Cowan. *Power of the Witch: The Earth, the Moon, and the Magical Path to Enlightenment.* New York: Dell Publishing, 1989.

Chumbley, Andrew D. *The Azoëtia: A Grimoire of Sabbatic Craft: The Sethos Edition.* Hercules, CA: Xoanon Publishing, 2002.

Clow, Barbara Hand. *Nine Initiations on the Nile with Barbara Hand Clow.* VHS. San Geronimo, CA: Infinite Eye Productions, 1996.

Cochrane, Robert, and Evan John Jones. *The Robert Cochrane Letters: An Insight into Modern Traditional Witchcraft.* Milverton, Somerset, UK: Capall Bann, 2003.

Conner, Randy P. *Blossom of Bone: Reclaiming the Connections between Homoeroticism and the Sacred.* San Francisco: HarperSanFrancisco, 1993.

Crowley, Aleister. *Liber LI: The Lost Continent.* San Francisco, CA: Stellar Visions, 1986.

Cunningham, Scott. *Living Wicca: A Further Guide for the Solitary Practitioner.* St. Paul, MN: Llewellyn Publications, 1993.

———. *Wicca: A Guide for the Solitary Practitioner.* St. Paul, MN: Llewellyn Publications, 1988.

Currot, Phyllis. *Witch Crafting: A Spiritual Guide to Making Magic.* New York: Broadway Books, 2002.

Donner-Grau, Florinda. *The Witch's Dream: A Healer's Way of Knowledge.* New York: Pocket Books, 1986.

DuQuette, Lon Milo. *Angels, Demons & Gods of the New Millennium.* York Beach, ME: Weiser Books, 1997.

Faerywolf, Storm, ed. *By Witch Eye: Selections from the Feri Uprising, Volume I.* Antioch, CA: Faerywolf/Carnivalia, 2005.

Farrar, Janet, and Gavin Bone. *Progressive Witchcraft.* Franklin Lakes, NJ: New Page Books/Career Press, 2004.

Ferguson, Marilyn. *Aquarius Now: Radical Common Sense and Reclaiming Our Personal Sovereignty*. Boston, MA: Weiser Books, 2005.

Fortune, Dion. *The Sea Priestess*. York Beach, ME: Samuel Weiser, 1972.

Flowers, Stephen E. *Lords of the Left-Hand Path*. Smithville, TX: Runa-Raven Press, 1997.

Freed, Rita E., Yvonne J. Markowitz, and Sue H. D'Auria, eds. *Pharaohs of the Sun: Akhenaten; Nefertiti; Tutankhamen*. New York: Bulfinch Press, 1999.

Gover, Robert. *Voodoo Contra*. York Beach, ME: Samuel Weiser, 1985.

Grimassi, Raven. *The Encyclopedia of Wicca & Witchcraft*. St. Paul, MN: Llewellyn Publications, 2000.

———. *Witchcraft: A Mystery Tradition*. St. Paul, MN: Llewellyn Publications, 2004.

Guiley, Rosemary Ellen. *The Encyclopedia of Witches and Witchcraft*. New York: Checkmark Books, 1999.

Gwyn. *Light from the Shadows: A Mythos of Modern Traditional Witchcraft*. Milverton, Somerset, UK: Capall Bann, 1999.

Harris, Mike. *Awen: The Quest of the Celtic Mysteries*. Oceanside, CA: Sun Chalice Books, 1999.

Heaven, Ross, and Howard G. Charing. *Plant Spirit Shamanism: Traditional Techniques for Healing the Soul*. Rochester, VT: Destiny Books, 2006.

Heaven, Ross. *Vodou Shaman: The Haitian Way of Healing and Power*. Rochester, VT: Destiny Books, 2003.

King, Serge Kahili. *Urban Shaman: A Handbook for Personal and Planetary Transformation Based on the Hawaiian Way of the Adventurer*. New York: Fireside Books, 1990.

Lamond, Frederic. *Fifty Years of Wicca*. Somerset, UK: Green Magic, 2005.

Liberman, Jacob. *Take Off Your Glasses and See: A Mind/Body Approach to Expanding Your Eyesight and Insight*. New York: Three Rivers Press, 1995.

MacLaine, Shirley. *The Camino: A Journey of the Spirit*. New York: Atria Books, 2001.

Margold, Harlan. *The Alchemist's Almanach: Reweaving the Tapestry of Time*. Santa Fe, NM: Bear & Company, 1991.

Matthews, Caitlín. *Mabon and the Guardians of Celtic Britain*. Rochester, VT: Inner Traditions, 2002.

———. *Singing the Soul Back Home: Shamanism in Daily Life*. Rockport, MA: Element, 1995.

Murray, Margaret Alice. *The Osireion at Abydos*. London: B. Quaritch, 1904.

Oakes, Lorna, and Lucia Gahlin. *Ancient Egypt: An Illustrated Reference to the Myths, Religions, Pyramids and Temples of the Land of the Pharaohs*. London: Hermes House, 2006.

Pennick, Nigel. *Practical Magic in the Northern Tradition*. Wellingborough, Northamptonshire, UK: Aquarius Press, 1989.

———. *Secrets of East Anglian Magic: New 2nd Edition*. Somerset, UK: Capall Bann, 2004.

Pepper, Elizabeth. *Witches All: A Treasury from Past Editions of the Witches' Almanac*. Tiverton, RI: The Witches' Almanac, 2003.

Red Star, Nancy. *Legends of the Star Ancestors*. Rochester, VT: Bear & Company, 2002.

———. *Star Ancestors*. Rochester, VT: Destiny Books, 2000.

Ryall, Rhiannon. *Weaving a Web of Magic*. Chieveley, Berkshire, UK: Capall Bann, 1996.

Sanders, Alex. *The Alex Sanders Lectures*. New York: Magickal Childe, 1989.

Sarangerel. *Chosen by the Spirits: Following Your Shamanic Calling*. Rochester, VT: Destiny Books, 2001.

Saunders, Kevin. *Advanced Wiccan Spirituality*. Sutton Mallet, UK: Green Magic, 2003.

Starhawk. *The Spiral Dance: A Rebirth of the Ancient Religion of the Great Goddess*. New York: HarperSanFrancisco, 1989.

Stevens, Jose, and Lena S. Stevens. *Secrets of Shamanism: Tapping the Spirit Power Within You*. New York: Avon Books, 1988.

Thoreau, Henry David. Walden: An Annotated Edition. Foreword and notes by Walter Harding. Boston, MA: Houghton Mifflin, 1995.

Thorsson, Edred. *The Book of Ogham: The Celtic Tree Oracle*. St. Paul, MN: Llewellyn, 1992.

———. *The Nine Doors of Midgard: A Complete Curriculum of Rune Magic*. St. Paul, MN: Llewellyn, 1991.

Trobe, Kala. *The Witch's Guide to Life*. St. Paul, MN: Llewellyn Publications, 2003.

Valiente, Doreen. *An ABC of Witchcraft Past and Present*. New York: St. Martin's Press, 1973.

Webb, Don. *Uncle Setnakt's Essential Guide to the Left Hand Path*. Smithville, TX: Runa-Raven Press, 1999.

Whitcomb, Bill. *The Magician's Companion*. St. Paul, MN: Llewellyn Publications, 1993.

Wilcox, Joan Parisi. *Keepers of the Ancient Knowledge: The Mystical World of the Q'ero Indians of Peru*. London: Vega, 2001.

Williams, David, and Kate West. *Born in Albion: The Rebirth of the Craft*. Thame, UK:- Mandrake Press, 2002.

Wolkstein, Diane, and Samuel Noah Kramer. *Inanna: Queen of Heaven and Earth: Her Stories and Hymns from Sumer*. New York: Harper & Row, 1983.

Online Resources

Adderley, Mark. "'Pa Gur' and 'The Spoils of Annwn." *Arthuriana: Arthur Complete*. http://faculty.smu.edu/arthuriana/teaching/lecture_welsh-lit_adderley.html.

Alogos. "Cultus Sabbati: Provenance, Dream and Magistry." *Xoanon Publishing, Ltd*. http://www.xoanon.co.uk/cultussabbati.htm:

Bible History Online. "Egypt." http://www.bible-history.com/subcat.php?id=24.

Branin, Mary. "The Celts & The Sea: History, Myth, and Cosmology." *Keltria: Journal of Druidism and Celtic Magick*. http://www.keltria.org/journal/d-bran-c.htm.

Budge, E. A. Wallis. "Discovery of the Amarna Tablets." http://members.tripod.com/~ib205/budge.html.

Catholic Encyclopedia. "Egypt." http://www.newadvent.org/cathen/05329b.htm.

Cooper, Diane M. "Exploring the Chakra System of the Nile with Famed Egyptologist Ahmed Fayed." *The Spirit of Ma'at*. http://www.spiritofmaat.com/archive/nov2/fayed.htm.

Encyclopedia Britannica. "Abydos." http://www.britannica.com/search?query=Abydos &ct=.

Pengwerin, Gareth. "A Taxonomy of the Major Keltic Deities and Their Interface with the Human Organism." http://www.geocities.com/tyghet/taxonomy.htm.

Smith, William, ed. "Heliopolis Syriae." *Dictionary of Greek and Roman Geography,* 1854.
http://www.perseus.tufts.edu/cgi-bin/ptext?doc=Perseus%3Atext%3A1999.04 .0064%3Aid%3Dheliopolis-aegypti.

Smith, William, ed. "Syênê (Aswan) and Elephantine Egypt." *Dictionary of Greek and Roman Geography,* 1854. http://www.perseus.tufts.edu/cgi-bin/ptext?doc=Perseus %3Atext%3A1999.04.0006%3Aid%3Dsyene.

Theban Mapping Project. http://www.thebanmappingproject.com.

Walker, Valerie. "Beginning a Daily Practice: A Practical Prescription for Those New to Feri, Part 1." *WitchWorlds: Feri Tradition.* http://www.wiggage.com/witch/daily practice1.html.

Westcott, W. Wynn. "Twelve, 12," in *Numbers: Their Occult Power and Mystic Virtues.* http://www.supertarot.co.uk/westcott/chap16.htm.

Index